To Rise in Darkness

TO RISE IN DARKNESS

Revolution, Repression,
and Memory in El Salvador,
1920–1932

Jeffrey L. Gould and Aldo Lauria-Santiago

Duke University Press
Durham and London
2008

© 2008 Duke University Press
All rights reserved.
Printed in the United States of America on acid-free paper ∞
Designed by Jennifer Hill
Typeset in Quadraat by Keystone Typesetting, Inc.

Library of Congress Cataloging-in-Publication Data appear
on the last printed page of this book.

To the memory of William Roseberry:
committed and
pioneering scholar,
extraordinary human being

Contents

Preface

When Reynaldo Patriz was a young child, his father took
him to a small finca at the edge of the cantón. Stretching his
hand over the barbed wire fence, he pointed down toward
some underbrush and said, "That's where your uncles are."
A few years went by before his father again spoke of his dead
brothers. He explained that the family had been "tricked by
ladinos" who had promised all kinds of things like land to
farm and new houses. Then the National Guard came in and
shot all the males over the age of twelve in all the cantones
of Nahuizalco. "The just were killed for the sinners."[1] These
were the same lines that Reynaldo's elderly neighbors used
on those rare occasions when they mentioned "el Comunismo." That's what they called the events of January 1932.

When the National Guard had beaten Reynaldo's cousin,
Juan Antonio, in a sugar mill at Izalco in 1978, his father,
normally impassive in the face of bad news, became visibly
upset. He took Reynaldo aside after dinner: "Look, don't
you ever get involved in any organization. I mean it. Never!
Remember what happened with el Comunismo!"

Juan Antonio later told him a different story about 1932. For Reynaldo's cousin, the peasants were getting screwed then just as they were now, and then everyone stood up to demand their rights. In response the National Guard murdered thousands of people. The time had come again to make a stand. This time it would be different, because people all over the country and all over Central America were rising up against the dictatorships and the rich. Adolescents and young adults like Reynaldo (then eighteen) looked up to Juan Antonio, but the older folks in el Carrizal gave him the cold shoulder.

These memories came rushing through his mind, as he peered through the brush at the edge of the ravine. It was shortly after dawn on 13 July 1980. He could make out a platoon of army troops advancing from the south toward the center of the village; led by an *encapuchado* (hooded man), the troops were dragging someone through the dirt. Reynaldo heard shots and screams from different points in the village. He waited until he saw yet another platoon march down a path from the north. Machine-gun bursts sounded from the south and then he heard a wailing sound. Harsh shouts, barked like orders, reached his ears, but he could not make out the words. He scurried down the ravine and inched his way along the stream bed at the bottom. Furtively glancing up to make sure he could not be seen, he advanced quickly until he came to a cave.

Patriz was stunned by the military occupation of El Carrizal, a *cantón* of Nahuizalco in western El Salvador.[2] He immediately connected the onslaught to the group of about twenty-five young folks led by his cousin who had been meeting, usually outside the village. He was on the fringes of the group that was connected to a national organization, called las Fuerzas Populares de Liberación. Thinking about how his father had warned him, Reynaldo thought that "maybe" they had been "asking for trouble." But this shooting was madness.

Another of his *compañeros* showed up within an hour, and that reassured Reynaldo. They agreed that they were best off staying put in the cave. After a few days of living on roots, plants, fruit from fincas, and the occasional iguana, Reynaldo headed back to El Carrizal. His uncle told him that the troops had killed over forty *muchachos*.

Reynaldo Patriz met one of the authors of this book in January 1998. At first he was an informant eager to make connections for Gould's oral history endeavor: interviewing the survivors of the massacres of 1932 throughout western El Salvador. After a very short time it became clear that he was more than a lucid informant with a sharp mind. Eventually he became a research assistant and production assistant on an ancillary documentary film project (see Afterword).

Patriz had been working for several years with the Pastoral Indígena, a lay church group that promoted community organizations in Indian communities. As a result, he had acquired a wide range of contacts throughout the cantones of Nahuizalco, and in other areas he demonstrated a marked capacity to communicate empathetically with strangers who shared his condition as a *pobre*.[3] He had also expanded his network through his work on the municipal electoral campaign with the Frente Farabundo Martí para la Liberación Nacional (FMLN). Its victories in the elections in Nahuizalco and many other western municipalities convinced most people that democracy and its associated freedoms had achieved a relatively firm footing, and therefore commentaries about the events of 1932 or 1980 would not result in persecution.

Patriz had his own agenda, notably a strong belief that the survivors of 1932 and 1980 needed to talk publicly for both therapeutic and political reasons about the massacres that had taken place in his village and region. His belief in the therapeutic value of doing so came from his own experience as a survivor of the massacre of 1980 and his observations of older neighbors and their burden of nightmarish, toxic memories. He also saw a political value in constructing a realistic narrative of the events of 1932—the preceding rural labor mobilization, the insurrection against the military regime, and the subsequent massacres—in light of the exceedingly fragmented memories of the period and the power of rightist discourse about both the 1930s and the 1980s (typified by the practice of the governing party ARENA to inaugurate every presidential campaign in Izalco with the slogan "Here we buried communism!").

The interviews often became three-way encounters. This trilateral space did not, however, resolve the problems inherent in the enterprise of oral history. Daniel James has underscored the oral historian's need to grapple with the issues of positionality, the tendency of the scholar to arrogate the representation of subaltern lives and consciousness. He also stresses the asymmetrical power relations between interviewer and informant that engender the potential for "symbolic violence."[4] These problems are not resolved in this book. Despite the trilateral nature of many of the conversations, the asymmetrical power relations between interviewer and informant were never fully redressed. Similarly, Reynaldo did not have the final interpretive word. This is a book produced in the North American academy about Central American subjects, with all the biases that this implies. To the extent that Reynaldo did participate in shaping the conversations and interpreting the testimonies, his presence posed a different problem of representation. Patriz did have a political agenda, as a militant of the FMLN and an indigenous activist. Although neither identity was fixed or necessarily congruent, his interpretations and contributions did involve "representing" subaltern subjects. Patriz's intervention nonetheless made a significant difference to this project precisely because of his agenda and his life experience, which allowed him to grasp the powerful afterlife of 1932. It shaped the existence of nearly everyone he knew, yet no one possessed more than a fragmentary understanding of what had occurred.

In García Márquez's famous fictional account of the massacre of striking banana workers in Macondo, a storm after the event swept away the town and all memory of the repression. As Greg Grandin has pointed out, "the novel can be read as an anticipatory truth commission, a revelation of terror to come."[5] The novelistic account of massacre and storm also had, however, a retrospective quality beyond the Magadalena valley of Colombia. In El Salvador a cyclone but two years after the massacres hit the west with particular fury, killing an estimated fifteen hundred people with nearly a thousand people unaccounted for, in effect "disappeared."[6] To survivors of the massacre, the cyclone "washed away the blood."[7] The storm also helped to enshrine the vastly unequal power relations in the region wrought by the massacres. One young man from Reynaldo's village recounted, "I remember my grandmother telling us that she had great necessities right after a great cyclone hit them. Everything was lost. They had nothing to eat; they were in great need. She went to don Manuel Borges and asked if he could be so kind as to give her some yuca for the sustenance of her children her family. He told her that he would be glad to give her the yuca, but in exchange of the legal papers of ownership of her land. And so for a few pieces of yuca her property passed to his hands."[8] Whether or not the testimony accurately described the loss of property, it graphically communicated how the community perceived the change in power relations, a change that in turn structured the limits of individual and collective memories.

Although García Marquez's fictional account inspired some research, the events of 1932 have generated even more scholarly interest than the

Colombian banana workers' strike and the repression of it.[9] Yet that research and analysis has been cut off from the survivors and their children, to the detriment of scholars and subjects alike. In this *diálogo de sordos* scholars and activists have offered a version of what the survivors and their families had done. The survivors have reacted with a blank stare: "We had nothing to do with that [the insurrection]."

Through his growing analytic skills (despite only an eighth-grade education), Reynaldo developed an ability to pose his own questions and analyze responses, both *in situ* and subsequently in conversation with Gould, during the long return trips on foot from remote cantones. Certain themes related to ethnicity and indigenous identities were best approached through Reynaldo's intervention. Indeed, probably the most interesting discussions about ethnicity occurred when Gould managed to keep quiet and let the conversation ensue between Patriz and the informant. On those all-too-rare occasions, when the scholar became less obtrusive if not invisible, a dialogue could develop, characterized by less guarded feelings and memories. Especially when Reynaldo and the informant knew people in common, the informant might comment, for example, that a certain indigenous family sent its children to school "like pure *ladinitos*," opening a window into a world of shame and resentment.

Reynaldo at times picked up on locally specific clues and codes suggesting that the informant had participated in the insurrection (or that an informant's father or brother had done so). A discussion would ensue about why the informant did not admit to his or her family's participation. This intuition about the problem of individual participation and memory led to a broader recognition that in the memories of Salvadoran indigenous people, their agency in the insurrection has been thoroughly suppressed. It was in the individual interviews that this suppression of indigenous agency became poignant, signaling the powerful role of the military in shaping memories.

This book confronts the tension between testimonial memories and historical interpretation while depending on those testimonies, however fragmented, to help formulate an analytical narrative. The enterprise avoids crossing the line over to *bad faith*, in part because of the shared commitment of the authors, Patriz, and others to at once respect the memories of *los ancianos* and to better understand the events of 1932 and their long-term political and cultural ramifications.

Ultimately the book attempts to weave into a coherent narrative individual memories, as described in over two hundred interviews, and a myriad of documentary sources from archives in El Salvador, Washington, London, and Moscow. Our hope is utilitarian, namely that the narrative provides greater understanding of the events of 1932 for a greater number of people than previous ones have been able to provide. Yet there are severe limitations to a narrative history written against the grain not only of counterinsurgent and insurgent documents but of memories recreated in a society that suppressed the events with particularly noxious forms of amnesia and distortion. We inevitably fall short of creating a definitive narrative of events.

This book intervenes on a terrain of conflicting narratives about events that have shaped the lives of people who simultaneously provide crucial material for its interpretation. They are, in Michel-Rolf Trouillot's terms, embodiments of these twin aspects of historicity: the ability to make or act in history and the ability to narrate the past.[10] This project's reliance on oral history to provide historiographic detail or even access to historical consciousness is also somewhat problematic. As James writes, "We might say that if oral testimony is indeed a window on the subjective in history—the cultural, social and ideological universe of historical actors—then the view it affords is not a transparent one that simply reflects thoughts and feelings as they really were. At the very least the image is bent, the glass of the window unclear."[11] These caveats are crucially important for the practice of oral history. However, when confronted by the paucity of documentary materials that would allow us to reconstruct ethnographically thick descriptions or to infer elements of consciousness, testimonies can be employed to approximate sociological and ethnographic realities in the past. That is, if certain codes of understanding are established (and here the role of Patriz was critical), it is possible to approximate ethnic and class ideologies and relations as they existed in the past. We employ a methodology based on a mutual interrogation of oral and written sources and a continuous cross-referencing between the two, moving from the micro and regional level to the national level of analysis.[12] This methodology permits us to make a contribution to the literature through the identification of the sociological and ethnic makeup of those involved in the mobilization and the insurrection.

The ethno-historical dimension of the book dialogues with the historical and ethnographic literature on mestizaje in Latin America. Since the early twentieth century mestizaje, understood as a nation-building myth of race mixture and a cultural process of "deindianization," has contributed substantially to Central American and Latin American nationalist ideologies and played a key role in shaping contemporary political culture. Gould has argued elsewhere that in El Salvador during the 1920s the development of mestizaje, as both discourse and process of cultural transformation, was not significantly different from parallel developments in Nicaragua or Honduras. In all three countries by the 1920s the emergence of mestizaje as a dominant national discourse interacted dialectically with the simultaneous disarticulation of the indigenous communities.[13] In all three countries state policies favoring ladino élites and the growth of agrarian capitalism led variously to cultural mestizaje, thicker identifications outside the communities, and a questioning of inherited traditional forms and markers of communal life. In western Honduras and western Nicaragua, for example, virtually all inhabitants had ceased to speak indigenous languages by the turn of the century. Similarly, by 1930 the majority of indigenous Salvadorans no longer spoke Nahuatl as their principal language.

Despite some similarities, the indigenous communities of western El Salvador were distinct from their Central American neighbors, primarily because of their geographical contiguity and their level of communal cohesion. Unlike in the other countries, where mestizaje formed a key element in a hegemonic project, in El Salvador the very intense and contradictory subaltern response, at least initially, thwarted the project.

The development of cultural processes of mestizaje placed severe strains on the indigenous communities and tended to isolate "traditionalists" from others. In El Salvador, unlike in Honduras or Nicaragua, some Indians responded to the ideology and practice of mestizaje with a discourse of ethnic militancy and revitalization. A contrary process developed in the Salvadoran departments of La Libertad, Santa Ana, and Ahuachapán. In those departments during the first decades of the twentieth century the advance of agrarian capitalism devastated the material basis of indigenous communities and contributed to a widespread rejection of the indigenous ethnic markers, such as language and dress. Yet thousands of rural workers and peasants who had no notion of indigenous identity participated in the mobilization from 1929 to 1931. It is this contradictory response to mestizaje that distinguished El Salvador from its neighbors, and the ability of the left to engage with both groups that guaranteed its stunning organizational success in the countryside.

The above discussion suggests that the use of the term "Indian" in the context of El Salvador during the 1920s and 1930s is quite problematic. Rather than a unitary category, we confront a continuum of indigenous identities and communal practices across the region. Typically these ranged from monolingual Nahuatl speakers in Santo Domingo de Guzmán to people ten miles away in Sónzacate who bore no identifiable ethnic markers yet were considered indígenas by their ladino neighbors. Those ethnic markers were of extraordinary importance, as Indians and ladinos of all political tendencies conflated them (and still do) with indigenous identity itself. As noted above, many people whose parents or grandparents would have identified as indigenous, especially in La Libertad and Ahuachapán, had no sense of indigenous identity. To the present-day observer this enormous variation complicates analysis; in the 1930s it greatly facilitated the advance of mestizaje as discourse and practice, holding an example of "civilization" both to more traditional indigenous populations and to ideologues of mestizaje and anthropologists.

Although it problematizes this wide variation of identities, this book employs the term "indigenous" to refer to people and communities who at the time referred to themselves as indígena or natural, as distinguished from ladinos (or non-Indians). In other words, by focusing on ethnic ideologies and relations as they were lived and understood at the time, this book questions the historiographical current that opposes "communists" to "Indians," without analyzing local forms of identity formation in their historical specificity.

El Salvador in Comparative Perspective

We explain why the Salvadoran élite and its religious and political allies had such a difficult time establishing minimal forms of hegemony or instituting significant social reforms that might have prevented the tragedy of 1932. Recent work in Latin American agrarian history and Lauria-Santiago's *An Agrarian Republic* have revised our understanding of the Salvadoran experience, situating it closer to the experience of the coffee regions of Venezuela,

Colombia, and Costa Rica.[14] In El Salvador land in coffee was only somewhat more concentrated than in the other countries, and labor was not based on a full-time proletarianized labor force or on coerced labor, unlike in Guatemala. As suggested by Jeffrey Paige, it was unique among Latin American coffee economies owing to the efficiency of its larger estates and the higher levels of concentration of its finance, export, and processing sectors.[15] The lack of state coercion in labor relations, the persistence of a landed peasantry, and the presence of an important layer of rural farmers and rich peasants challenge the traditional historiographical bipolar portrait of El Salvador. The recognition that the emergence of coffee growing did not result in the late-nineteenth-century dispossession of the peasantry has implications for this study.

The 1920s represented a period of intensive capital accumulation in the western part of the country that affected many rural people who experienced varying degrees of proletarianization and dispossession. This book dialogues in this sense with studies of agrarian revolt in Guatemala, Colombia, Mexico, Peru, Bolivia, and Cuba, which have all found that this complex middle ground of peasants resisting proletarianization can be the cauldron of rural rebellion.

Our study of the Salvadoran rural mobilization from 1929 to 1932 contributes to the historiography on twentieth-century revolutions. In broad strokes, it confirms the usefulness of Timothy Wickham-Crowley's multitiered analysis of social conditions as opposed to a strict structural analysis of revolutionary causes.[16] It traces the origins of two social groups, *colonos* (resident laborers) and "semi-proletarians" or "peasant laborers," and shows how they became open to radical organization. Scholars have rarely identified the colonos as a potential revolutionary subject. Our book suggests that to fruitfully study the radical or revolutionary potential of a particular group, we must root it and its relations in a historically specific context.[17] Rather than analyze the "revolutionary" potential of particular classes, we suggest that the struggles over their creation and their concomitant resistance to being proletarianized provide the key to understanding radical mobilization.

As suggested above, the contradictory responses to mestizaje in the context of struggles over class formation provide an analytical tool for understanding the success of the Salvadoran mobilization. This may well provide an interesting research path for analyses of other social movements. The successful Salvadoran mobilization of 1929–32 involved highly uneven cultural homogenizing processes in the context of a new phase of intense capital accumulation. In this sense the Cuban Revolution of 1933 offers the most promising terrain for such a culturally informed comparison. In Cuba communist union activists organized effectively among both field and mill workers in the sugar industry. They forged alliances between white and black Cuban workers, including many immigrants from other Caribbean islands.[18]

In both El Salvador and Cuba international politics played a role in the revolutionary movements. The strategic line of the Comintern pitted "class versus class," combated all forms of reformism as objectively aligned with fascism, and promoted an anti-imperialist agrarian revolution. Although the Comintern had little direct involvement in Cuba and virtually none in El Salvador, the acceptance of the line did limit the strategic and tactical options available while doing nothing to limit the revolutionary utopian dreams that circulated among the actors.[19]

The massacre of some ten thousand people that followed the revolt of January 1932 also lends itself to comparison. In the Dominican Republic (1937) and Cuba (1912), as in El Salvador, state repression had complex cultural and political motivations that went beyond the need to militarily suppress an insurgent movement.[20] Like the killings of thousands of Afro-Cubans in eastern Cuba in 1912 and the massacre of Haitians and Dominicans of Haitian descent by Trujillo's government in 1937, mass killings were pursued by the Salvadoran state for moral, political, and ideological purposes in specific geographical regions. In each case the targets of state repression were singled out in regionally specific ways; repressive forces spared other people of the same ethnic background in areas not affected by the insurgency.[21] In Cuba, Haiti, and El Salvador we would suggest, following Greg Grandin and the Comisión de Esclarecimiento Histórico of Guatemala, that the states did not have a strictly genocidal motive like Hitler, but did have the "intention" to liquidate blacks and Indians to accomplish their counterinsurgent goals (see chapter 7).

A Usable Past: Interpretations of Revolt and Massacre

During the past seventy years four themes have dominated interpretations of the revolt of 1932 and the massacre of some ten thousand people: political crisis, economic collapse, communist agency, and indigenous participation. Despite the richness of decades of discussion around these four axes, the question of how to characterize the revolt and its agents has remained unresolved.

Journalists, military officers, and professional anticommunists wrote the earliest accounts of the revolt. However tainted, writings by Joaquín Méndez and Jorge Schlesinger are still among the most important sources for study of the movement. Although the authors framed their narratives around the idea of the movement as a communist conspiracy which gained strength through the reformist opening created by President Arturo Araujo (March–December 1931), the empirical detail based on interviews and insurgent and counterinsurgent documents is of fundamental importance to any reconstruction of events.[22]

During the three decades following the massacres a singular, coherent mythology emerged that fomented commonsense notions about the danger of reformism and foreign communist manipulation of peasants.[23] By the 1960s a new generation of politically committed intellectuals began to question both the official anticommunist views and the largely dismissive interpretation by the Salvadoran Communist Party (PCS) that the revolt had been provoked by the regime and fatally flawed by the party's ideological deviations.[24] These writers, most notably Jorge Arias Gómez and Roque Dalton, sought to dialogue with the PCS and the distortions created by the official narrative of the revolt.[25] Although limited by their lack of sources and professional training, they did tap into collective memories and participants' stories, especially from within the PCS. Arias Gomez, who set out to produce an alternative history of the country's working classes, ended up more absorbed by his work as a political activist but did publish a biography of Farabundo Martí (1972).[26] Dalton, his political protégé, became the most important writer and poet to emerge from this period and contributed perhaps the most important piece: Miguel Mármol's narration of his life and participation in the revolt (compiled while he and Dalton were in exile and during a visit to Prague in 1966).[27] Published in 1972, *Miguel Mármol: Los sucesos de 1932 en El Salvador* quickly became a classic of Central American literature.[28] Recently Rafael Lara Martínez has criticized Dalton for consciously suppressing in Mármol's narrative the specifically indigenous role in the mobilization and insurrection. His critique is important in that it explains to some extent how the revolutionary left failed to understand the role of ethnic relations in the events of 1932. Yet like *I Rigoberta Menchú*, despite its constructedness and distortions, *Miguel Mármol* remains a fascinating and invaluable source for understanding the period.[29]

During the late 1960s El Salvador caught the attention of a number of foreign scholars who deepened the research on 1932 primarily through a study of national newspapers and interviews with military officers and members of the landowning class. The anticommunist commonsense of their informants to some extent framed their research questions. Moreover, these scholars explicitly investigated the social origins of the revolt despite their limited understanding of Salvadoran agrarian history.[30] Thomas Anderson's *Matanza* was the first serious monographic attempt to counter the official anticommunist hysteria and to provide a rich examination of the revolt and its social and political origins.[31] Anderson made a significant contribution by emphasizing both the class and ethnic dimensions of the movement, but his work remained limited by its narrow conceptual framework and lack of archival sources. Everett Wilson's dissertation was also an important contribution to the literature, providing an analytical framework for the failure of reformism during the 1920s.[32] It remains one of the most empirically sound and sophisticated interpretations of Salvadoran politics during this period.[33] Anderson and Wilson made critical contributions in their use of primary sources (short of archival work) and in their analytical integration of a broader socioeconomic narrative that saw in the economic crisis of 1929 the origins of the political crisis of 1932. But they were not able to fully flesh out the social origins, ideology, subjectivity, and practice of the rural movement.[34]

By the late 1970s a new generation of Salvadoran social scientists began to publish interpretations critical of extant works on the revolt.[35] The regime forced most of these scholars into exile, where they carried out more systematic research with secondary sources. None were able to carry out archival work or oral history work among the peasantry, with the notable exception of the Jesuit martyr Segundo Montes.[36] During the late 1970s and early 1980s the left relied on these analyses (and on Mármol) in their frequent reflections about 1932. As the regime relied ever more on the violent repression of dissent, the rapidly expanding left moved toward a revolutionary strategy. In that context left militants called on their followers to "retomar las banderas de '32,"[37] highlighting the depth of the alliance of the early 1930s between urban workers and campesino. To wit, Ferman Cienfuegos, a guerrilla leader, cited the incorporation of peasant smallholders into union leadership as an example of the left's creativity.[38] In somewhat paradoxical fashion, revolutionary leftists recognized the negative lessons from 1932. While recognizing the PCS's creativity in forging a multiclass alliance, they criticized their forebears for their petit-bourgeois ideological deviations and confusion, a consequence of the weak development of an industrial proletariat. And even while lauding the role of Farabundo Martí in pushing for a revolutionary strategy, the new left criticized the PCS for its failure to create a political and military vanguard and for its overreliance on Martí's.[39] The FMLN named guerrilla fronts after Feliciano Ama and Francisco Sánchez, the indigenous leaders, but in its narrative of 1932 it tended to subsume the ethnic dimension of the movement within a rigid class framework.

Although the revolutionary left made no scholarly contribution to the understanding of 1932, the newly heightened politics of memory eventually led to intensified research efforts. By the mid-1980s a new wave of publications by foreign scholars began to revisit the revolt, adding significant new sources and placing the revolt in the broader context of social revolution. Authors such as James Dunkerley, Héctor Pérez-Brignoli, and Jeffery Paige provided more complete and fluid conceptions of class, politics, and the state that eschewed singular ideological determinations. Leon Zamosc provided the first significant empirical additions to the narrative of 1932; he conceptualized rural Salvador as following a dependent capitalist path that involved "refeudalization" based on the growth of colonos.

The end of the civil war provided an opening for foreign scholars to bring a deeper level of archival research into discussions of the 1920s and 1930s. The identification and recovery of new regional archives and the reorganization of large portions of the AGN by Lauria Santiago during the late 1980s facilitated this work. Both Erik Ching and Patricia Alvarenga attempted sweeping research and interpretations of many aspects of Salvadoran politics from the nineteenth century to the 1930s. Their highly nuanced discussions of the revolt carefully consider municipal politics (especially indigenous politics), the previous political regimes, and the emergence of the left in the countryside. Alvarenga provided important insight into the popular politics of the 1920s, especially among people of indigenous descent, and into popular resistance to state power in general.

The incorporation of extensive archival and newspaper sources by these and other authors has opened new terrain for interpretive and empirical debates. In particular, new scholarship has emphasized the role of ethnic oppression and the participation of indigenous communities in the revolt. In an otherwise fine piece of scholarship, Pérez-Brignoli portrayed the revolt as resembling an Indian jacquerie, partially inspired by the urban ladino cadre of the PCS but cut off from it. Most recently Ching's work, building to some extent on that of Pérez-Brignoli, has repositioned the role of the PCS, arguing that the party was incapable of organizing the revolt and pointing toward the movement as an indigenous-peasant revolt without a clear communist ideological character.[40] Although Ching and Pérez-Brignoli have added significantly to the discussion, their work lends itself to interpretations that posit two noncommunicative spheres: one communist and the other Indian.[41] Taking that view beyond the authors' intentions, some commentators in effect revert to the classic anticommunist position that Marxist-Leninists manipulated innocent, aggrieved peasants.

As we will show, the portrait of a closed, separate Indian world in the Salvadoran west is partial and problematic; ethnic identity was neither rigid nor castelike. Most fundamentally, the perspective that posits a significant cultural gulf between communists and rural Indians and that stresses the autonomy of the rural Indian movement misses conversations across multiple, murky cultural divides. This book will narrate the remarkable story of how a united movement emerged out of so much cultural difference and conflict. It attempts to make sense of the mobilization and the insurrection by historicizing our analytical categories and recognizing the fluidity of the expressed and ascribed identities of the participants.

This historiographical current has prompted a broader discussion around a central question: "Was it communist?" A negative response implies communist manipulation, ineptitude, or irrelevance. But before even engaging this question, we need to confront an epistemological one: Where do revolutionary ideas and action come from? The classic Leninist response is that correct revolutionary ideas come from Marxist-Leninist science, which reflects and influences social practice but ultimately is the sole province of the Central Committee. Logically, revolutionary action can only derive from revolutionary strategy formulated by the proletarianized intellectuals of the Central Committee. Without accepting other aspects of the ideological tradition, those who ask "Was it communist?" tend to accept this classic Leninist epistemology. We emphatically reject this undialectical view of social consciousness and social action.

Methodologically, the assignment of grades of ideological purity to actors in the past seems at best an uninteresting pursuit. Rather, we reconceptualize the analytical separation between organizer and organized. What interests us is how this powerful movement derived from the active, mutually conditioning relationship between grassroots activists of varied identities and the different levels of leftist leadership. Rank-and-file activists were as "authentically" leftist as the PCS Central Committee and at least as important in shaping the development of the movement.

These historical agents did operate within a variety of organizations, and within them the PCS stood at the apex. Yet as we will argue, although the PCS considered itself the revolutionary vanguard, its self-definition did not necessarily shape reality. Rather, the Socorro Rojo Internacional (which the PCS had created as a front group) acquired an important degree of autonomy and a critical role in creating the emerging revolutionary discourse: a discourse that explained how growing numbers of rural people, Indians, and ladinos came to understand the world and their place in it. That the leaders of the SRI and the labor unions usually were also members of the PCS has intrinsic importance but does not allow us to reduce those movements to mere party appendages. Yet there is no denying that the pro-communist left as a whole was responsible for creating a field of vision in which the revolutionary seizure of power became an option for many subaltern actors.

The denial of a role to the communist left in the insurrection, regardless of scholarly intention, ultimately relegates the hundreds of local-level organizers of the movement to yet another mass grave, this one of historical oblivion. A cadre of ladino and indigenous leaders, with roots in the cantons, haciendas, towns, and workshops, propelled this movement forward. Often communist militants were themselves rural Indians, many of whom had been union activists on the coffee plantations for several years. Others merely shared the movement's goals: radical agrarian reform and overthrow of the regime and oligarchical rule.

This book shows that the revolt of 1932 derived from the transformation of a radicalized union movement that became revolutionary under the pressure of frustration among peasants and rural workers with the violent abrogation of democratic rights, combined with a rapid increase in rates of exploitation and dispossession. Before December 1931 only a minority of the left favored an insurrectionary strategy. As a result of the events delineated in chapter 5, we will show that the insurrection did result ultimately from the actions, choices, and direction of a coherent and self-conscious movement for social, economic, and political transformation. There is no doubt that the PCS leadership engaged in negotiations with the military regime, and that upon the failure of those negotiations they decided upon a date for the insurrection, eventually postponed to 22 January 1932, when they rose up. The discursive struggle to rescue indigenous agency from decades of trauma and neglect should not lead us to deny communist agency in all its dimensions, all its creative potential, and all of its flaws.

Chapter 1 of the book offers a detailed analysis of the structural transformation of Salvadoran rural society during the 1920s, marked by the consolidation of two important social groups, colonos (resident laborers) and semi-proletarians. With the multisided economic crisis of 1929, these two groups, "los occidentales," became the critical social subjects of the mobilization in central and western El Salvador. This chapter also focuses on the limitations of elite hegemony. Chapter 2 examines the emergence of reformist political currents that by the late 1920s challenged oligarchic rule and encouraged the partial democratization of the state. This chapter delineates how the frustration of political and social reform at the national and municipal levels directly contributed to the radicalization of the labor movement.

Chapters 3 and 4 probe the ethnic, political, and cultural dimensions of the rural mobilization. They show that virtually all subaltern and middle groups in central and western Salvador were represented on both sides of the conflict. Most significantly, these chapters attempt to elucidate the discursive expressions of ethnic militancy and populism. Chapter 4 concludes with a discussion of gender relations in the region.

Chapter 5 offers a detailed account and analysis of the highpoint of the mobilization during the latter part of 1931 and January 1932. Highlighting the relations between the grassroots and the national leadership, the chapter offers a portrait of the decision-making process that led to the insurrection. Chapter 6 presents a blow-by-blow account of the insurrection. Building on those produced in the 1930s and 1940s, it also incorporates material from the Comintern and Salvadoran archives. It departs from previous accounts primarily in its deployment of ethnographic and local detail, culled from oral testimonies.

The equally complex pattern of repression is the subject of chapter 7. It recounts the systematic massacres in Nahuizalco, Juayúa, Tacuba, and

Izalco of mostly male Indians. Yet the chapter tempers the view of 1932 as an anti-Indian massacre through its examination of non-Indian killings and the mild forms of repression employed in the heavily indigenous region south of San Salvador. Through an analysis of oral histories, chapter 8 probes the long-term cultural and political impact of the massacres on the region. Here the book shifts gears from an analytical narrative to an analysis of stories about the revolt and repression, as well as about the loss of two key ethnic emblems, indigenous female dress and the Nahuatl-Pipil language. This final chapter also describes the massacre in El Carrizal and another equally unknown massacre in the Department of Sonsonate in 1980. The silencing of the massacres and the brief mobilization that preceded them is due in part to the widespread myth of passivity of the western Salvadoran peasant, a direct consequence of 1932.

We address the larger problem of how local consciousness and national discourse are related. The gulf between them has both reflected and exacerbated the tragedies of modern Central American political cultures. It is our hope that our book will help to illuminate the hidden crevasses that dangerously lie beneath the political cultural landscape of contemporary Central America.

This book is the result of a collaborative effort between the two authors who have long been interested in the causes and consequences of the mobilization, insurrection, and massacre that devastated El Salvador in 1932. The book is also the result of a web of collaborations with Salvadorans and others.

Lauria-Santiago carried out extensive local and national archival research during the early 1990s, in close collaboration with the Archivo General de la Nación and numerous municipal governments throughout the country. Over the next decade, working with local and national scholars, archivists, and authorities, he helped organize and preserve a significant amount of archives that are now available to scholars and students. He worked especially closely with Eugenia López of the AGN. An Agrarian Republic, the first fruit of his work in the archives, provoked much dialogue in the Central American academy and challenged decades of received wisdom about the origins of the coffee economy and the class structure in the countryside from 1880 to 1920. Lauria-Santiago stimulated wide-ranging research projects on modern Salvadoran history and maintained a strong interest in the events of 1932 based on extensive archival research that carried into the 1930s.

Over the years the authors conversed about the events of 1932, recognizing the lacunae in their knowledge and the problems with extant analyses. Thus in 2001 they decided to combine their research efforts and expand their focus toward reinterpreting the mobilization that preceded the insurrection as well as the massacre itself and its political and cultural consequences. Gould obtained a John Simon Guggenheim fellowship in 2002 that permitted the drafting of chapters 3 through 8. Lauria-Santiago drafted chapters 1 and 2. A voluminous dialogue shaped the manuscript, involving numerous readings, commentaries, and discussions.

We are greatly appreciative of those collaborators mentioned above. In addition, we thank Rebecca Tolen for copy-editing assistance. Gould would also like to thank his colleagues at Indiana University, Daniel James, Peter Guardino, and Patrick Dove, for their careful readings and constructive criticisms of the manuscript. He also thanks Carmen García-Prieto for help with some translations, Luis Gonzalez, Mike Grove, Carol Glaze, and Dena Williams. He is also indebted to Alexander Rabinowitch for helping him to obtain a copy of the Comintern files pertaining to El Salvador. Gould presented papers based on parts of the manuscript and received helpful comments from the discussants, including Virginia Burnett and Claudio Lomnitz. We are grateful as well for Mauricio Alvarez's generosity in allowing us to use family manuscripts and photos. Gould also thanks his wife Ellie and his eldest daughter Gabriela for holding down the fort during his prolonged absence in 1998, and Ellie for her support and endurance of the difficulties of life in Sonsonate. A very hot and crowded school and the Salvadoran style of basketball and soccer posed unique challenges for Carlos and Mónica. He is appreciative that they met those challenges with grace and humor. Regrettably, Carlos, at seven, had to experience an armed holdup with a gun pointed at his father's head. He got over it quickly enough and eventually worked through the experience in several writing assignments that surely startled a few teachers in Bloomington.

We are grateful to Greg Grandin, Lowell Gudmundson, and an anonymous reader at Duke University Press for their perspicacious and sensitive readings of the manuscript. We would also like to thank Duke University Press for permission to use materials from our previous publications. Finally, we appreciate the editorial and technical assistance and encouragement we received from Valerie Millholland, Miriam Angress, and Fred Kameny.

Chapter One

Garden of Despair: The Political Economy of Class, Land, and Labor, 1920–1929

Outside the car windows . . . the wonderful panorama unfolds. Over and over
again we exclaim that all this is a perfect tropical garden. In places every inch of
land has yielded to human hands . . . It is a country worthy of a great people . . .[1]

Peering out of a railroad car during the mid-1920s, Wallace Thompson marveled at the Salvadoran countryside, and like others before him eagerly compared it to England and the United States. Foreign observers were thrilled with the image of tropical progress that they discovered in Salvador. Commenting on a trip from San Salvador to Santa Ana, Arthur Ruhl wrote, "The country was rich and carefully cultivated all the way, with cornfields that would make a Kansan gasp."[2] Similarly, an observer found the paved streets, handsome buildings, and cafés of the capital radiant and "dazzling."[3]

Agnes Rothery, a travel writer with an analytical bent, placed the smallholding peasant at the center of this portrait of peace and growing prosperity: "And as we continued our drive, up the seacoast to the capital, there is presented to us a complete picture of that agricultural structure on which the prosperity of this tiny republic so solidly rests. For about twenty years ago, the communal lands were distributed to the small landowners. At the same time all laws providing means of collecting money loaned or advanced to laborers were repealed. And every legal basis of peonage was wiped out. Thus was established a system of free labor—the foundation of any national prosperity. About seventy-five percent of the coffee is raised on property held by small landowners of the poor and the lower middle classes, and eighty-five percent of the national commerce is in their hands. So engrossed are these industrious and simple folk in their crops, on which their happiness and living depend, that they have no inclination for political agitation."[4]

Rothery and others underscored how the development of the Salvadoran peasantry coincided with the development of "free labor" and how the peasantry itself supplied the bulk of harvest labor for the coffee plantations. This depiction of a harmonious process, whereby a reasonably prosperous smallholding class emerged from the privatization of communal and ejidal lands, is substantiated to some degree by the historical record. Certainly the process that derived from the state privatization of ejidal and communal lands in 1881 did not directly lead to massive subaltern resistance, in large part because indigenous and ladino peasants were the immediate beneficiaries of much of the newly privatized land.

In this chapter we explore the contrast between this widely diffused image of progress and social harmony in the second and third decades of the century and the intense levels of social and political strife during the late 1920s and early 1930s. Did societal fault lines exist that had been invisible to the observers? What factors upset this social equilibrium? Scholars usually cite the impact of the world crisis on the coffee industry as the direct cause of the dramatic heightening of social conflict in Salvadoran society. However, other Latin American societies experienced similar economic collapses without such severe social and political effects.

Between 1900 and 1929 El Salvador experienced three intense cycles of rapid economic growth, each based on a doubling or tripling of the price of coffee followed by a period of decline. These booms helped to develop a dynamic economy, much of it oriented toward the commercial production of maize, sugar, and silver in addition to coffee. To observers during the teens and early 1920s, El Salvador seemed like a "progressive" republic on the verge of becoming modern, with a large and prosperous smallholding class and formidable wealth accumulated by an agro-financial oligarchy and a rural bourgeoisie.

Structurally the equilibrium between smallholders and the larger coffee planters did not hold, as the peasantry suffered an agonizing decomposition during the 1920s. One direct result of this new stage of primitive accumulation was that two new classes emerged. Peasant laborers, "semi-proletarians" with inadequate land to support their families, gradually increased their commitment to hacienda and plantation labor beyond seasonal coffee picking. The second group was formed by colonos, or resident laborers, whom landlords provided with plots of land in return for labor service and a portion of their crops. Not only did the number of colonos increase during the 1920s but they also found their relation to the landowners transformed substantively. At the same time that the socioeconomic equilibrium became unstable, the Salvadoran agro-export élite was unable to establish elementary forms of hegemonic domination over these new groups, in part because of its own recent formation.

Hegemony, despite the multitude of meanings ascribed to it, is still a useful analytical concept. We start with the most commonly accepted meaning, "the active consent" of dominated groups to forms of governance which they do not control. To achieve active consent, dominant groups must obtain legitimacy as economic and political leaders. That legitimacy can only be developed through the construction of institutions and practices, a process that usually takes generations.

As several critics have pointed out, hegemonic domination does not mean total acceptance or submission by subaltern groups. For Ranajit Guha hegemony implies a form of domination in which the element of persuasion outweighs coercion. Logically a state could also achieve dominance over society by having the coercion outweigh the persuasion. Guha thus defined the character of the colonial state as "dominance without hegemony."[5] That formulation allows him to explore how the colonial and postcolonial state in India could rule without recourse to constant violent repression yet without establishing long-term forms of hegemony. Given the conjunctural determinations of what Guha calls the organic composition of power, the connection between domination and subordination is inherently unstable. In that sense dominance without hegemony is a particularly unstable form of rule, and despite the vastly different circumstances between colonial or postcolonial India and El Salvador in the 1920s, this formulation seems apposite.

For the late William Roseberry, hegemony involves a fundamental acceptance of the "rules of the game." Those rules are more important than

El Salvador.

consent per se, for they establish an accepted discursive framework in which to express dissent.[6] It is in this sense that Roseberry proposed that we use the term "hegemony": "not to understand consent but to understand struggle, the ways in which the words, images, symbols, forms, organizations, institutions, and movements used by subordinate populations to talk about, understand, confront, accommodate themselves to, or resist their domination are shaped by the process of domination itself. What hegemony constructs, then, is not a shared ideology but a common material and meaningful framework for living through, talking about, and acting upon social orders characterized by domination."[7]

In order for élites to achieve the active consent of the dominated and not to rely largely upon fear and intimidation, they need to construct a linguistic code that can be shared and through which conflicts can be expressed and resolved. In Nicaragua, Somocismo established limited but effective forms of hegemony through a common language of liberalism and *obrerismo*.[8] Similarly, in a process that continued well into the second part of the twentieth century, a discourse of mestizaje also facilitated the eclipse of regional subcultures and the forging of a common identity and language between subalterns and dominant groups.[9] In Guatemala, despite a radically different ethnic composition and with virtually no effective nationalist ideology of mestizaje, the coffee élites established effective forms of domination, if not hegemonic forms, through what David McCreery defined as a colonial pact. Through this informal pact the state recognized the relative political and cultural autonomy of indigenous communities in return for loyalty to the state and a guaranteed supply of coffee labor. Until the revolution of 1944 that pact afforded some legitimacy to the state and to its élite allies.[10] As we shall see, Salvadoran élites tried to follow both the Nicaraguan and Guatemalan roads, but ran into powerful obstacles, often of their own creation.

Coffee Expansion and Élite Class Formation

At the start of the twentieth century El Salvador appeared to be among the most successful of the smaller Latin American republics. Its growing export economy and relatively stable intermingling of military and civilian political élites gave observers the sense of an unbounded potential for progress. Observers like Percy Falcke Martin, who visited in 1911, noted the country's high wages, lack of poverty, dynamic commercial élite, intensive use of land, and growing number of schools as indicators of successes similar to those of Porfirian Mexico.[11] For another observer, El Salvador was "credited with possessing the most stable government in the Isthmus, with the sole exception of that of Costa Rica. . . . Salvador can lay claim to being one of the most progressive States of South America."[12] The country's reformist experiments in government policy toward diversifying the economy and stabilizing state finances bolstered this impression. Some of these initiatives included promoting crops other than coffee, modernizing infrastructure, increasing taxes, and creating a national guard that would keep the military out of local governance.

El Salvador seemed poised to become a modern, civilian-run republic that enshrined the myth of Central America's most industrious population; but those expectations were not to be fulfilled. Instead, after the late teens a small agro-financial and banking oligarchy subordinated the state to its interests, introducing a rule typified by labor repressive policies and ending the experiments with reform and diversification. From 1913 to 1927 the Melendez-Quiñónez family dynasty (during which the presidency was occupied by three members of this extended family) controlled the governmental apparatus. During this period the country also experienced a significant opening to foreign investment and financing. The enhanced role of the state élite and increased monetary flows facilitated corruption. Worse yet, the country's capitalists demonstrated a persistent unwillingness to reinvest much of their wealth inside the country—indeed El Salvador's élite disinvested millions in profits, which it kept in banks and investments in the United States and Europe. The weakness of this model became visible during the export crisis of 1921, when coffee and silver prices and exports plummeted. The government's solution was to transfer a smaller state debt from British interests to banks in the United States, in a highly controversial loan that resulted in a bank-controlled customs receivership.[13] The ensuing spending bonanza financed by this loan marked the consolidation of an alliance between politicians associated with the dynasty and the agro-financial and finance élite built around sugar and coffee processing and export.

In El Salvador as in the rest of Latin America, the 1920s were years of dizzying change and fabulous wealth, "the dance of millions." By the mid-1920s El Salvador doubled its pre-war levels of coffee exports, eclipsing its much larger neighbor, Guatemala, as the leading coffee exporter in Central America. In 1926 El Salvador exported 1.1 million quintals of coffee (or 110 million pounds), whereas Guatemala exported 932,000 quintals and Costa Rica 402,000. The rise in coffee prices from 10.9 cents a pound in 1913 to a high of 24.6 cents a pound in 1926 not only conditioned the rise in exports but led directly to previously unimaginable incomes for large-scale owners and middle-level growers alike. A mid-sized grower producing 6,000 quintals during the mid-1920s realized profits of nearly $100,000. Large-scale growers typically netted profits of $500,000 annually. Over all, income from coffee production expanded from $3,320,000 in 1901 to $14,200,000 by 1920. Income would nearly double again by the late 1920s, nearly a fivefold increase in twenty-five years.[14]

Coffee production increased through the application of scientific techniques to cultivation, and as a result El Salvador achieved the highest productivity in the region. To cite a famous case, James Hill, an English immigrant, increased the productivity of his coffee trees by using fertilizers and carefully managing the shade and pruning. Hill's annual productivity on his Santa Ana plantation of four pounds a tree was among the highest in the world, and connoisseurs considered his coffee to be of the highest quality.[15]

Coffee production also increased through the incorporation of new lands into coffee cultivation. After a long period of slow expansion between the 1880s and about 1912, the amount of land dedicated to coffee increased from 61,000 hectares in 1916 to 100,000 in the early 1930s.[16] Most of the new coffee lands did not form part of large haciendas or plantations. In 1920 only the 350 largest of the 3,400 commercial coffee farms possessed between 75 and 300 manzanas (125–500 acres), accounting for 45 percent of national production.[17] The greatest expansion in production during the 1920s came from even smaller commercial producers with 10–50 manzanas of coffee, who produced about one-third of the country's crop. The slow but persistent growth of landholdings allowed some families to join the coffee élite despite relatively modest possessions at the turn of the century. The Guirolas, to cite an important example, acquired many new farms that had originally been ejidal plots.[18] In 1914 they owned three coffee farms in La Libertad; by 1929 they owned twenty.[19]

The story of the Guirolas was replicated throughout western Salvador, with negative consequences for the smallholding peasantry. By the end of the 1920s nearly all land suitable for coffee production had been planted or at least incorporated into existing farms. The expansion frenzy was so intense that large planters would "bid against each other in order to increase acreage or to be rid of undesirable neighbors."[20] The U.S. Agricultural Service estimated that land values per manzana ranged from $100 (in remote districts) to $500 (in good locations), at a time when wages were 50 cents a day.[21] But the potential profits from coffee production were not the only driving force behind the acquisition of land by commercial farmers. Land also became more valuable because it facilitated access to cheap labor from the growing ranks of the landless who sought subsistence plots within the farms.[22]

Increased concentration of processing, financing, and marketing accompanied the transformation of production. Few processors had the resources and networks necessary for managing the increased volume of coffee beans and the intensifying link between the financing of crops by farmers and the processing and marketing stages. Beneficio owners received the bulk of the profits, buying beans at 6–10 cents a pound and selling at 20–26 cents; much of the payment was to cover advances. This financing system allowed the wealthiest sectors to concentrate on the commercialization of the crop. The number of beneficios remained relatively small and concentrated—five highly modernized large-scale processing plants controlled 53 percent of production. These profits also became investment streams in other fields, including significant bank and investment holdings abroad, calculated at $25 million in 1920.[23]

The agro-financial élite also invested in other crops. High demand and high prices encouraged investors to transform former tenant-held land into export plantations. Cotton experienced a brief if dramatic boom during the 1920s, displacing many corn-producing tenants from low-lying coastal lands. Cotton production increased from 800 hectares in 1923 to 16,000 by 1924 and peaked in 1925 at 20,300 hectares distributed throughout six departments, producing 3,200 tons. In the eastern region, henequen expanded significantly during the 1920s. Exports increased from 255,000 kilograms in 1920 to 347,000 in 1922.[24] Most significantly, the agrarian élite invested in sugar, the country's second-most important commercial product. During the late nineteenth century, as the state enforced more successfully its monopoly on liquor production licenses and taxes, cane growing became an increasingly profitable activity. By 1923 cane plantings had increased to approximately 11,000 hectares compared to 80,000 for coffee.[25] As with coffee, sugar manufacturing became increasingly concentrated; the five largest mills controlled about 60 percent of total production.

Hard Work and a European Education:
The Contours of Élite Ideology

The upper echelons of the planter class and agro-export élite thus achieved astounding levels of wealth, only magnified by the contrast of the poverty that ringed their domains. One observer described their extravagance: "This moneyed class live in extreme luxury and style, in fashionable suburbs or on large country estates. Their thirty-room houses are splendid with the finest and most formal furnishings. They send—or more frequently take—their children to school in England, Switzerland, or France. And after the period of schooling is over, they make extensive trips abroad . . . While their estates are scattered throughout the Republic, Salvador is small enough for them to form a homogeneous set who dance in their own homes to music brought by radio from Chicago, keep up smart country clubs with golf courses and tennis-courts, and who aid progressive programs for public improvements of all sorts."[26] By various estimates the outer reaches of this élite constituted some one thousand families, many of them connected through social, business, and kinship ties—a tiny percentage of the country's approximately 300,000 families in 1930.[27]

The transnational status of the élite had a decisive impact on the consciousness of its members, fomenting highly salient images of progress and the desire to modernize Salvador at least in those aspects that directly affected them. Moreover, the European experience pushed them toward certain notions of political and social modernity. At the same time, a transnational existence in the 1920s limited their ability to fully participate in their modernizing mission and the development of politically hegemonic practices.

The Salvadoran élite resembled their Colombian counterparts of the upper Magdalena valley so brilliantly described by Michael Jimenez. Their cosmopolitan experience forged an image of modernity that excluded most other Colombians: "With the distinctions between the 'advanced' and 'backward' worlds gaining ground among members of a planter class educated and traveled abroad, they came to regard the Colombian people as an ever less apt vehicle by which to achieve modernity." Jimenez's fine-grained analysis of the limits of élite hegemony in Colombia is relevant to the Salvadoran case. Despite their cosmopolitan existence, neither élite conformed to a stereotypical view of an effete aristocracy. Their commitment to labor, even physical labor, was extraordinary, and might well have provided the basis for a common language with rural workers. Jimenez points out, however, that "the planters no longer regarded work as a common ground for Colombians. The hacendados celebrated their founding of the great estates during the second half of the nineteenth century in the upper Magdalena Valley. Having allegedly risked their fortunes, health, loved ones, and even their own lives in a titanic struggle to overcome nature in the tropics, these exemplar, 'workers of the hot country' congratulated themselves for having set the nation on a new course. But most other Colombians could barely measure up, in their view."[28]

A memoir of a coffee planting family in El Salvador suggests a similar ideological framework. The narrative of the Alvarez family history is built around an axis of hard work and a related myth of the self-made man, closer to the prevailing discourse in the United States and to some regional Mexican myths than to most other Latin American governing myths. Fresh out of medical school, Dr. Emilio Alvarez moved to El Salvador from Colombia to establish a practice in 1876. He went on to become a famed surgeon in San Salvador and invested in a small coffee finca, primarily for recreational purposes. A younger brother, Rafael, a Liberal militant in the Colombian civil wars of the 1880s, after military defeat welcomed brother Emilio's offer of a safe haven in El Salvador. He went on to become the manager of the coffee finca. From there, through the development of techniques to increase productivity and an intense work ethic, the family gradually acquired more holdings. Among its numerous achievements in the field of coffee production was the introduction of the highly resistant *izote* plant to combat soil erosion.

According to Carlos, one of Dr. Alvarez's nephews, "My father was untiring in his work, he'd go out on horseback very early to visit all the work sites and would not remember to return for lunch, returning home many times to have lunch at 3 or 4 p.m. and many times he would not eat until the evening; when he went to Santa Isabel he had to go through many fields as there were still no paths at the edges of the volcano." Carlos's father recognized the need to install a 200,000-gallon water tank on the finca, on the arid slopes of the San Salvador volcano. Carlos relayed the impact of this undertaking on his own consciousness: "I owe my love for work and the dedication that I was able to place on this sort of effort once I became an adult to my father's example who when I was 8 or 10 years old took me every day and into the evening, to the building site of the tank. I helped to insert the aluminum screws."[29] The narrative, passed down through the generations, reveals how the intense love of labor and applied intelligence allowed the family to fertilize and irrigate inaccessible, dry lands and led to the building of a water-powered beneficio to avoid the risks associated with selling to export firms. Most significantly, the notion of expanding landholdings through purchases at the market price, far from representing greed, involved applying science and hard work to previously unproductive land. The increase in the number of quintals produced justified this vision of expansion.

This organizing trope of labor and intelligence as irrigation and fecundity becomes central to the story of how the family transformed poor, even barren land into highly productive coffee plantations. Alvarez's project to turn "El Potosí" on the arid slopes of Volcán San Salvador into a coffee plantation elicited scorn from friends, other coffee growers, and even family members. Don Eugenio Araujo, owner of the famed hacienda "la Sunza" in Sonsonate, came to look at the land, possibly to buy it for his son Enrique. It was the dry season and the land looked desolate, the paths rocky and potholed. After riding all day, as the sun was setting, don Eugenio asked, "Where are you going to plant the coffee?" Rafael Alvarez responded that they would plant on all the land they had traversed. After a long silence,

Araujo commented that he would not purchase the land and that it would never be good for coffee. At the dinner table, when presented with the main dish, duck, Araujo responded that he didn't eat duck. The next day a neighbor overheard Eugenio comment to Arturo on the train that "don Rafael was going to lead his family into ruin." Don Rafael responded by calling the family to work harder and prove all the naysayers wrong. Years later Rafael's son Carlos (the author of the memoir) was riding on a train with Arturo Araujo, the future president of El Salvador, who asked him about El Potosí and whether it produced coffee. " 'Yes, sir,' I said, 'this year we just picked 15,000 quintals.' 'In cereza?,' he asked. 'No, sir, in gold [peeled],' I answered. 'No, it can't be,' he says. 'I'm sorry but it is true, and I invite you to visit us whenever you like.' A visit that never took place—the good man could not understand how it was possible that we were already producing 15,000 quintals when they had been working their Sunza for so long and producing less than 6,000 quintals."[30] That Araujo was eventually considered a traitor to his class—and utterly incompetent during his brief presidential administration—undoubtedly enriched a narrative destined for family consumption. It also suggests that élite divisions at times grew out of such competition, as noted by the U.S. agricultural expert. Yet the tale also evokes the basic tropes of Salvadoran producers: hard work, frugality (the ugly duckling for dinner), risk taking, courage, and manliness, measured in quintals produced.

Several years later, as coffee prices tumbled with the world crisis, Alvarez met with the banker Benjamin Bloom to pay him over $100,000 in interest. He offered Bloom one of his nationally produced cigarettes and Bloom scowled, asking him why he smoked that brand. Alvarez answered, "to be economical. . . . The good ones are very expensive."[31] This gesture, as $100,000 was passing through his hands and at a time when he was paying for his children's European education, suggests that a Yankee-like ethic of frugality and hard work was an engrained part of the family's values and practice (other members of the élite called themselves the "Yankees of Central America"). What might then have seemed like a blatant contradiction between such values and European educations nonetheless obeyed a coherent logic.

This ethos of labor and frugality might have carried over to labor relations, rewarding hard work. Indeed it seems that the Alvarez family was more humane in its treatment of its workers than others, providing cheese and *panela* to finca workers in addition to the traditional beans and tortillas. Notwithstanding this, throughout the memoir there is little recognition of those laborers who toiled alongside the *finqueros*.

A variant of the Alvarez experience and ethos of hard work is revealed by James Hill. The son of an industrialist in Manchester, Hill arrived in Salvador "penniless" and built up his coffee holding, until by the early 1930s he employed a small army of over three thousand people to pick coffee on his fifteen farms, two hundred workers in his mills, seven hundred women in the cleaning process, plus 250 in supervision, cleaning, cooking, and building. He earned a reputation as one of the most "modern" employers, willing to experiment with the organization of labor in an effort to increase productivity: "he treated both his trees and his workpeople more thoughtfully than was the custom in the neighborhood, yet it was plain that he knew how to drive: 'Won't have my people talking!,' said Mr. Hill emphatically. 'They can't talk and work, too. If they start gabbing, I put 'em on piece work. When a man hoes I want to see his hoe sink in like this, and he jabbed his stick in, vertically it mustn't just scrape. A work man, in a climate like this, ought to be sweating in half an hour. If I see a man with his coat on, I put him on piece work.' "[32] Hill's emphasis on others' work contrasts with the Alvarez narrative. Yet neither offers a vision in which the notion of "producers" would encompass the hard work of laborers, in a way analogous to a wide range of other ideological formulations.[33] In addition to this discursive lacuna with regard to labor, other ideological elements impeded the construction of hegemonic forms of rule. In particular, the European dimension of the élite's existence in all probability intensified the racial aspects of the ideology and in turn rationalized the treatment of the rural working class. In a statement of class and racial prejudice typical of the period post-1932, one cafetalero commented: "The lower class . . . has no civilization . . . is a primitive mass that instead of forming the basis for progress is a drag on it and a denial of it."[34] Racism not surprisingly influenced labor relations, as it provided planters with a justification for low wages and highly unequal land distribution. For élites, all dark-skinned rural workers were "indios."

The American journalist Arthur Ruhl conversed with the former president and large-scale planter Jorge Melendez about wages and labor: "Few of them did what could properly be called a good day's work, but their wants were so easily satisfied that when they had earned enough to exist they just stopped. When he tried to argue the matter, they just laughed at him, he said. As it was, they got their food and quarters and about 25 cents a day."[35] This notion that rural workers had no real use for higher wages formed part of the commonsense of the Central American planter class, and like racism it provided a coherent rationale for maintaining wages at subsistence levels. The attitude toward wages carried over to issues of land access. A report of the U.S. military attaché is instructive in this regard: "Their arguments usually come down to this; 'If we sell our land to these mozos we will have nobody to pick our coffee for us. The best thing for everybody is to keep things as they are. As a matter of fact we paid our mozos very high wages three years ago. What happened? Did they improve their living conditions? No. They simply stayed drunk two days a week longer than they do now. These mozos are not unhappy and as long as they do not know any better, why go out of our way to change matters.' "[36] Finally the church, a classic pillar of élite hegemony, had a relatively weak presence in the countryside. Although the church maintained good relations with the government, after the Liberal revolutions it had no explicit political role. In addition, it suffered from a relatively unfavorable economic situation that impeded any significant expansion into the countryside. In most communities that did have parish priests, they found themselves at once cut off from the official church and from popular forms of religiosity. According to the historian of religion Rodolfo Cardenal: "The Church authorities of San Salvador and their representatives in the towns [priests] played the role of carriers of a dominant ideology whose pretension was to annihilate the localism of the towns, their traditions, and their cultural codes. They sought to implant Catholicism, that is, uniformity of belief and cultural rituals, ruled by codes that were foreign to the reality of the people. The people rejected these pretensions."[37] This always latent conflict between official and popular forms of religion was usually more intense in indigenous communities. In short, rarely did indigenous or popular religious practices contribute to legitimizing élite rule.

There were, however, some points of intersection between élite and popular ideology and practices. Generally, where clientelism functioned well, especially in regard to land rental or credit, it was accompanied by deference to the patron. "It is well known that the children of the campesinos grew up attached to the home, to the father (tata) and the grandfather (tatita), to the father-in-law (whom they called mi señor) they offered appreciation and warmth."[38] Other evidence suggests that notions of deference to the patrono were in turn linked to a patriarchal ethos. Yet there are two caveats. First, as we shall see, the nature of such relations changed during the 1920s. In addition, those effective forms of clientelism tended to involve members of the provincial bourgeoisie more than the agro-export élite.

This sketch of ideological domination suggests a very weak articulation between the organizing elements. Within the élite broadly construed there did exist some articulation between the key elements of the discourse. First, consider the ideological ensemble *productivism, masculinity, patriarchy*. Notions of hard labor reinforced masculinity, which in turn legitimated patriarchy. The other ensemble, *progress, European imaginary, racial superiority*, highlighted progress and modernity spurred by European education and imaginaries, the province of the white race and European ancestry. If the articulation of these ideological elements did allow for a growing level of élite class cohesion, the ability to articulate with subaltern groups was more contingent on specific sociogeographical and conjunctural economic factors related to land, labor relations, and credit. The transformations of the 1920s created far greater stresses on both the internal and the external levels of articulations. In sum, the agro-export élite did not successfully cohere as a class for itself (to use the Marxian expression)—that is, as a group that could design policies and politics benefiting its own interests and at the same time elevating those interests as the will of society.

Not only did the oligarchy fail to create hegemonic forms of domination, but it had great difficulty in creating a corresponding institutional framework. The absence of foreign involvement and economic domination favored the development of a cohesive, nationally based agro-financial oligarchy. Nonetheless, it failed to establish effective political ties to the country's less affluent farmers, or even to those in what might be called a provincial bourgeoisie. When the agro-export élite formed organizations in the 1920s, they fostered predatory relations with subordinate factions. Officials in Washington characterized both the Asociación Agricola and the Asociación Cafetalera as narrow and dismissive of the needs and interests of smaller-scale producers.[39] The largest coffee exporters from the start had a controlling interest in the Asociación Cafetalera, allocating to themselves control of the organization's banking function.[40]

Everett Wilson first identified the relationship between the late geographical consolidation of the élite and its failure to cohere politically and institutionally: "before 1920 lingering political rivalries prevented the members of the administrative group from consolidating the support of any particular economic interest and further impeded the emergence of a clearly defined national elite."[41] With only a handful of exceptions, most of the country's wealthy families had stayed out of the national political arena, relying instead on local power-brokering, backroom deals, pressure, and negotiation, but rarely playing a prominent role in electoral or factional politics.

Unlike in Chile, Argentina, and Brazil, the élite did not organize a right-wing "conservative party." The ninetenth-century Salvadoran Conservatives had been soundly defeated during the Liberal revolutions. To the victors and to the immigrants who entered the early-twentieth-century oligarchy, a clerical-based party was unattractive. At the same time, the emerging oligarchy's economic power was not coincident with ownership of haciendas and control over a vast rural population. And there was no pressing need for the emerging oligarchy to organize politically. By the teens, when members of the oligarchy (roughly synonymous with the agro-financial élite) began to control processing, exports, and financing as well as amassing huge fortunes, they found it expedient to delegate power to an established political class made up of judges, lawyers, and businesspeople and backed by the military. It was only during the 1920s, as Wilson explains, that the élite began to organize itself: "By the end of the decade the previously fragmented wealthy groups formed alliances which were the bases of a new elite structure."[42]

Although they did not speak with one voice in the political arena, the oligarchs had an increasingly strong sense of their collective social and economic interests. They achieved their goals through two channels. First, they allied with local and national officials in the hope that they could control disputes over land, labor, and other resources. In addition, they worked with political bosses and others of the political class to gain favor, information, and concessions in their dealings with the state, especially in the provision of financing and services. They therefore tended to leave politics to a lesser alliance of rural bourgeois and petit-bourgeois sectors while maintaining certain veto and lobbying powers that they could exercise at critical junctures. Informal, personal networks characterized most of these political relationships. Their very fluidity meant that the Salvadoran state could not be a machine for the administration of oligarchic interests.

Rather, patronage-based networks held the state together, accounting for much of the corrupt and undemocratic character of political practices. Under these conditions neither the oligarchy nor the state created a strategy to cope with the social dislocations wrought by the boom and bust cycles of the 1920s.

The Agony of the Smallholding Peasantry

The land speculation boom and the growing power of the agro-financial oligarchy brought about a decomposition of the smallholding peasantry. The erosion of the smallholding class and the concomitant rise of new social groups in moments of severe economic crisis contributed to the rise of a massive labor mobilization for wage increases and land reform (see chapter 3).

Most contemporary descriptions of the rural economy around 1920 highlighted the symbiotic coexistence of smallholding peasants with larger commercial farms. Travelers mentioned the commercial connections between smallholders and larger landowners, united by the "energy and driving force that are nationally characteristic."[43] They noted that "plot after plot of coffee ground as large as village squares . . . each owned and worked by some peasant proprietor," and argued that the peasants and workers "had never suffered from the rapacity of large landholders."[44] These descriptions, while not entirely inaccurate for the preceding years, had become anachronistic by the end of the 1920s for a large and increasing number of rural Salvadorans. In particular, they failed to take into account the social transformations that were already under way in the countryside, particularly in the west, where the dramatic growth of the coffee industry increased friction between large commercial producers and the rural poor. They also failed to account for the layered nature of the agrarian landscape of the region. Colonial-era haciendas that had stepped up production and increased employment during the early twentieth century made up one layer. Even after some subdivision, these formidable and diversified properties often combined coffee, sugar, and grain production with cattle herding and logging. A significant smallholder and peasant sector, which had its origins in the process of privatizing community and municipal lands in the late nineteenth century, formed the second layer. Finally, the third layer encompassed rich peasants and entrepreneur-settlers who carved medium-sized commercial farms from municipal lands or previously uncultivated state-owned land. By the early twentieth century these three layers so blanketed the western countryside that no agrarian frontier remained.[45]

The expansion of the country's population during the early twentieth century compounded the effects of the closing rural frontier. The rate of demographic expansion had been increasing since the late nineteenth century, and by 1920 El Salvador had nearly two and a half times as many people as in 1880, when around half of the country's land was uncultivated.[46] Despite some emigration to Honduras and the Panama Canal Zone, the pressure on the land only increased during the 1920s as commercial use intensified.[47] In this situation peasant families had little choice but to partition their landholdings, seek wage work wherever they might find it, or attach themselves to the farms of larger landholders.

The rise in land values also spurred élite acquisition of peasant land, as did the precipitous drop of coffee prices in 1921 and the ensuing increase in loan defaults by smallholders.[48] In fact, some observers estimated that during the 1920s commercial landowners absorbed up to 30 percent of small properties.[49] The economy's vulnerability and lack of liquid capital meant that despite the heightened economic activity of the 1920s, the élite continued to rely on land investment and money lending as a long-term strategy, given the lack of liquid capital and the high cost of borrowing. To cite an important example, Emilio Redaelli, an Italian entrepreneur and mayor of Juayúa during the late 1920s, made loans and advances to the Indian peasants of the region and used these ties to mobilize labor on his farms.[50] Similarly, in Izalco the Barrientos family held mortgages on many small plots, controlled a myriad of small-scale transactions in coffee and other crops that enmeshed Indian and ladino peasants in ties of dependence and exploitation through mortgages, and bought crops in advance at far below market rates.[51]

The agony of the smallholding class—both loss of land and inadequate land to reproduce the family unit—directly pushed increasing numbers of rural Salvadorans into wage labor to provide for increasing portions of their subsistence. Estimates based on the level of sugar and coffee production indicate that the four departments of western El Salvador had a seasonal wage labor force of over 100,000 workers. The census category *jornalero* is imprecise, since it excludes women and includes urban day laborers as well as semi-proletarians. Nevertheless, the proportion of jornaleros to *agri-*

cultores does provide some insight into the advance of proletarianization in the countryside, since the great majority of jornaleros worked for wages on fincas and plantations. In Ahuachapán the proportion was 7:1, in La Libertad 13:1, in Sonsonate 15:1, and in Santa Ana 12:1.[52]

The birth of this new peasant laboring class (semi-proletarians) was largely unmentioned in public discourse. First one adult or child had to work more weeks on a hacienda; then another family member; and then another, until hacienda labor came to dominate their lives. The world of these peasant laborers took shape in the many rural settlements that were dispersed throughout the region. Many of those villagers found work during the planting, pruning, and harvest seasons on the coffee plantations.

During the boom years of the 1920s the increased availability of wage labor and small wage increases had partially compensated for the increased landlessness. The wage increase was due to the demand for labor occasioned by the expansion of cotton production in the east and public works projects. In some parts of the country coffee pickers could make two colones ($1) a day.[53] In 1929, however, the demand for public works employment began to decline just as the price of coffee tumbled, and as a direct result coffee workers' wages were slashed to 30 cents a day.[54]

Colonos also emerged from the smallholding peasantry. The 1938 coffee census underscores the importance of this group: 18 percent of the entire rural population of western El Salvador lived on commercial farms that produced coffee.[55] This represented about 55,000 people living on 3,000 farms, with the largest farms or haciendas employing a few hundred colonos each.[56] *Colonato* generally involved incorporating peasants into a farm or estate in exchange for access to any combination of meals, housing, land, wages, water, and firewood, perhaps with rent payments in labor, a share of the colono's crop, or cash payments.[57] In eastern El Salvador colonato usually entailed the payment of a fixed rent in kind, whereas in western El Salvador colonato also became important to farmers and hacendados as a way of securing cheap labor in addition to obtaining rent income or crop production.[58] Colono labor was cheaper, with lower cash transfers, and colonos could also generate additional income for the landowner through fees for land, housing, and the sale of goods in the hacienda store. In exchange for labor services at lower wages (at times no wages), estate owners usually provided their resident workers with access to small plots for food production. In 1929 an officer with the U.S. Agricultural Service described the world of the colonos: "Every finca operator makes an effort to have as many permanent laborers as possible. These workers known as 'colonos' are really one of the most important factors in the industry; they may be depended upon to work all-year-round and are trained in all the different operations, while the 'piece' worker is employed only during the picking season and his living conditions are, of course, not as satisfactory as the permanent worker who is provided with a small house, food and other necessities. Many of the larger plantations operate small commissaries, have their own chapels and are really small communities rather than farms."[59] Conditions on farms could vary significantly. Among the best-equipped were the Hill farms, described in these terms by Ruhl: "There was a common kitchen, where the women made tortillas and cooked beans and rice—the raw materials were included in their wages—and several barrack-like rooms, built round a court and fitted with double-tier bunks. They were dismal, flea-ridden caves, inappropriate enough, it seemed, to a climate where fresh air and space are the cheapest things, but security is security, and as long as the permanent laborers worked on the plantation they were sure of the use of a bit of land for a garden or a roof and enough to eat."[60]

When the decline in coffee prices began in late 1927, owners cut back on cash expenditures and eventually turned colonos into a captive labor force: under miserable living conditions, they were forced to work more for access to land, but without any of the customary benefits in terms of steady wages.[61] As Wilson pointed out, the terms of land tenancy changed in the 1920s. Landlords obliged all tenants to pay the terraje (rent) in advance, thus compelling them to assume all the risk. The social critic Alberto Masferrer condemned the new system, which involved both colonos and smallholders: "For a number of months this newspaper has reported the lamentable complaints of people who don't dare to cultivate someone else's land because the rental takes all the production and remains the same no matter what the yield."[62] Galindo Pohl recalled the situation in the department of Sonsonate. Before the 1920s, campesinos would engage in sharecropping with landlords to whom they would deliver one-quarter of the crop. They also provided several days of free labor and were available for paid labor. The situation then changed: "During the 1920s the [colono] obligation to work on the hacienda in exchange for wages had disappeared. Also in those years campesinos began to rent lands for cash payment, which the patronos saw with great pleasure."[63]

Throughout Latin America during the first half of the twentieth century, el colonato was the system of labor relations most conducive to social harmony.[64] Not only did the landlord or his administrator have close contact with the colono, but he typically had control over every aspect of life, fostering strongly dependent relations. As noted above, despite profound levels of élite racism and arrogance, hacendados often established patriarchal, dyadic relations with colono families, resorting to rewards and gestures of friendship more often than coercion to achieve their goals. Most significantly, the hacendado guaranteed access to land and offered a degree of protection from the calamities that beset rural life. Colonos often carried out the will of the landlord in the numerous quotidian conflicts with nearby villagers, involving land access, grazing, or water. In El Salvador as elsewhere, colonato was most successful on cattle haciendas, where land was abundant and labor requirements minimal in comparison with coffee farms and plantations.

Many western Salvadoran colonos maintained relations of loyalty and subservience to their patrón through the worst of the economic crisis and mass mobilization. Yet thousands of others broke their traditional dyadic links to the patrón and instead allied themselves with village laborers, whose relations with the colonos had often been antagonistic. The recent formation of large sectors of this class, combined with the rapid deterioration of wages and living conditions, were major factors in the anomalous political and social development of western Salvadoran colonos.

No Shelter from the Storm: The Planter Response to the Crisis

The world crisis struck El Salvador with particular ferocity. Coffee prices plummeted from 22.2 cents a pound in 1929 to 13 cents in 1930 to 8 cents in 1931. If living and working conditions had been poor before the crisis, by 1930 they had become intolerable. The planters responded to the precipitous drop in coffee prices with wage cuts that affected both semi-proletarians and colonos, By the end of 1931 wages in the rural areas had been cut further, to 15–25 cents for a day's work. Planters reduced wages to 50–60 percent of their 1927 levels.[65] In August 1931 the U.S. consul noted the effects of the steep decline: "It is evident that the purchasing power of the laboring classes, especially in the rural districts, has been distinctly curtailed. The ragged appearance of the workers is notable."[66]

The crisis squeezed western colonos in particular, from two directions: rent and other charges increased along with the workload, as wages decreased. A newspaper account graphically denounced the contemporary form of colonato: "Whoever has been one day alone in those so-called great haciendas will have noticed how the patronos treat their colonos: for one manzana of land that they rent for corn production they make them pay 15 or 20 in cash, or two fanegas of corn, and the poor colono also has to work the hacienda's crops for six or eight weeks for a miserable wage . . . The disgraced colono works only for the patron . . . There are patrones that for any reason deny part or all of their miserable wage to the jornalero [day laborer]."[67] In the eyes of semi-proletarians, conditions for colonos and other laborers deteriorated as a direct result of planters' responses to the crisis. By 1931 many farmers, including the wealthiest, were charging their workers for access to water and increasing prices in their company stores.[68] In an extensive report that year, the governor of San Salvador asserted that many patronos had been "abusing workers" by paying them in tokens. One plantation owner acknowledged to the governor that he was making more profits from his store than from his farm.[69] Similarly, plantation owners enforced their exclusive control over workers' earnings by excluding outside merchants from their farms to avoid competition.[70]

Wage cuts were one thing. Whether or not convincingly, planters could after all attribute them to the decline in coffee prices. Yet the extra-economic exploitation was so blatant that campesinos could not but question any claims by the landlords to paternalism and legitimacy. Other elements of campesino life on the farms similarly betrayed the élite's lack of concern for even the appearance of paternalistic obligations toward their workers. The same report by the governor of San Salvador castigated large-scale landowners for their failure to provide schooling of any sort for the families of thousands of colonos and workers[71] Another official report underscored the meager food rations, the miserable housing, and the lack of any medical attention to workers.[72] Somehow a decade's worth of savings, investments, and profits of 50–100 percent had left even the wealthiest landowners incapable of navigating the impending social crisis with offers of improved wages.

The planters' response to the crisis merely exacerbated the situation for the rural poor. In addition to the pressing problems of below-subsistence wages, abusive working conditions, and growing land loss, Salvadorans

Woman on country
road, 1939. Photo
by Carlos Alvarado,
courtesy of Mauricio
Alvarado.

Workers on
"El Potosí" Coffee
Plantation, 1939.
Photo by Carlos
Alvarado, courtesy
of Mauricio Alvarado.

Workers on
"El Potosí" Coffee
Plantation, 1939.
Photo by Carlos
Alvarado, courtesy of
Mauricio Alvarado.

Workers on
"El Potosí" Coffee
Plantation, 1939.
Photo by Carlos
Alvarado, courtesy
of Mauricio Alvarado.

also faced a food shortage. Throughout the late 1920s market forces, limited land for cultivation, and natural conditions made the country vulnerable to periodic food crises: while pushing many to the edge of starvation, these shortages also created opportunities for windfall enrichment for large-scale producers and merchants, especially the Meardi family.[73] Food shortages hit the western zone again in 1931.[74] This time the crisis was worse in the west, where an eruption of the Izalco volcano sent heavy ash, while rain damaged crops throughout Ahuachapán and Santa Ana, wiping out entire cornfields.[75] In May the interior minister complained to the departmental governors that many landlords only offered lands for corn cultivation with advanced cash payments: "We must urge the landowners to agree to rent them as is customary . . . reminding them that it is patriotic to help alleviate even in one small part the country's difficult situation."[76] This remarkable response by planters and hacendados revealed their utter incapacity to view the effects of the food or larger crisis in collective, strategic terms.

No Bridges Left Standing: The Limits of Élite Hegemony

By the end of 1931 a critical moment had been reached for the rural poor. Landowners, according to many, expected laborers to come to work only "for the food."[77] In the absence of systematic, effective practices of wage bargaining and given the state's failure to respond to the growing needs of the rural poor, many workers and peasants in western El Salvador turned to unions and eventually to revolutionary politics. Yet poverty, exploitation, and hunger alone cannot explain the successes of the Salvadoran left in building a revolutionary movement during 1930 and 1931. In chapter 3 we will examine the organizational practices of the left and the rural poor. Here we will touch on the consequences of the Salvadoran élite's incapacity to construct a discursive and institutional framework for communicating and negotiating with subaltern sectors. Élites throughout the Americas have always sought to maintain channels, bonds, and dependencies that divided workers and peasants, and tied them to a status quo.[78] Although individually the Salvadoran élites and especially the provincial bourgeoisie behaved in this fashion, ultimately they failed dismally. As we saw earlier, the élite's racialized view of the rural poor was an impediment to entering into serious negotiation with the workers and to entertaining a reformist strategy that might have allowed for a modicum of social improvement. Finally, as Carlos

Gregorio López has shown, nationalism was not at all the province of the élite. Rather, middle-class intellectuals propounded a version of nationalism that directly challenged the undemocratic character of the élite and the state.[79] Thus what was in other countries an important hegemonic form was largely unavailable to the élite.

During the decade preceding the crisis, the Salvadoran élites had remained socially distant from the rural poor and been unable to forge a common social or political project. This social gulf between élite and subaltern was not merely a function of the élite's transnational character. Rather, social distance was the product of a two-way perception, and the rural poor certainly formed perceptions of their own, in part through the relative autonomy of their traditions and ideologies. People who were children and youths during the late 1920s and early 1930s only recall two social groups, los ricos and los pobres. Regardless of political affiliation, that fundamental division structured all forms of discourse about politics and society, and the predominant use in testimonies of the plural category "los ricos" over the individual "patrón" is a significant index of its salience. This inchoate substratum of populist ideology both reflected and conditioned the social gulf that so sharply divided Salvadorans.

More than a decade before the crisis, observers noted a potentially dangerous distance between the owners and their workers. In 1916 Dana Munro, the noted scholar and diplomat, observed that "the lower classes have no more inborn respect for authority and love of peace than have those of Nicaragua and Honduras . . . If they are on the whole less prone to revolt, this is due to the fact that they are fairly contented under present conditions, and that they are held under control by a much stronger and better organized military power then in those countries. The government is maintained . . . not by popular respect for authority or by the will of the people, but by force."[80] Another observer of the social divide substantiated Munro's remarks during the 1920s: "The divisions among classes in Salvador . . . are so very hard and definite that the interests of no two of them coincide . . . These divisions are positive and acute in a way scarcely to be recognized in Europe outside of Prussia before the war. In Europe it is not absurd to suggest that, taken all around, the interests of all classes really coincide . . . In Central America it would be absurd to argue that the immediate interests of poorer classes are one with those who rule. Something of the Spanish conquest still remains."[81]

The élite's precariously low level of hegemony thus was apparent well before the advent of serious rural labor organizing. Yet another observer of pre-crisis Salvador stated that "the conditions to which its labor is subjected to (in order to keep down that one phase of production cost) are none too conducive to the nocturnal rest of a conscientious plantation owner."[82] More significantly, the planter James Hill commented in 1927, or two years before the dramatic increase in rural organizing, on the growing pressure among workers for land reform and the disdain they had for the property rights of the country's élite: "Bolshevism? Oh yes . . . Its drifting in. The work people hold meetings on Sundays and get very excited . . . Yes, there'll be trouble one of these days . . . They say: 'We dig the holes for the trees! We clean off the weeds! We prune the trees! We pick the coffee! Who earns the coffee then? . . . We do!' . . . Why, they've even picked out parcels that please them most, because they like the climate or think that the trees are in better condition and will produce more. Yes, there'll be trouble one of these days."[83] What is most remarkable about this testimony is the moment of its utterance, when there were no visible leftist organizations in the country-side. The language of class and the implied lack of legitimacy of a powerful oligarch like Hill stand out sharply in the reported dialogue. Although we do not know exactly how this radical language penetrated the countryside before the advent of union organizing in the late 1920s, it is likely that the language of obrerismo (see chapter 2) had a presence in the countryside through the work interactions between artisans and rural people. Regardless of its origins, the imagined division of the estate—even allowing for a dose of paranoia in Hill—strongly suggests a subaltern sense of the illegitimacy of the landed élite.

The testimony of the daughter of colonos on "San Isidro," one of the largest cane and coffee producing haciendas, echoed that of Hill: "I moved to El Guayabo with my parents when I was an adolescent. We were colonos here and so were all the families in the canton. [My father] worked as a caporal on the hacienda San Isidro. I picked coffee with my mother and we sold goods in the hacienda market. When I got married we got a plot of land as colonos. My parents were very active in the union, always going to meetings at night. They believed that they would break up San Isidro and give us the land."[84]

In indigenous communities a memory of land loss and of the time "when all the land was free" was even more powerful than among ladino (non-Indian) campesinos. In 1918, when the Melendez-Quiñónez regime organized the Ligas Rojas to combat the political opposition, it directly promoted the idea of returning the communal lands to the western indigenous communities.[85] Although it is doubtful that any land was returned, the Ligas Rojas legitimized the notion of returning the land to its rightful owners, and at the same time concretized an alliance between the regime and some indigenous communities in opposition to the local ladino élite. As we shall see in chapter 4, a significant ideological current circulated through those communities which defended indigenous land rights.

Although there were also conflicts within the subaltern classes between Indians and ladinos and between colonos and village-based semi-proletarians, the reconfiguring of productive relations and the expansion of salaried labor tended toward healing those rifts, while exacerbating the gulf between the élites and subalterns. Much coffee production took place on relatively small and mid-size farms, but the transformation of haciendas into large-scale coffee and sugar plantations, where hundreds of colonos and thousands of wage workers mobilized each year to pick coffee and cut sugarcane, did not at all lend itself to paternalistic relations between landowners and workers.[86]

Planters' arrogance and opulence ensured that the increasingly miserable wages symbolized in the phrases "to work for the tortillas" and "work just for the food" did not appear to rural laborers as the result of market forces. Although profit margins were not public knowledge, they must have appeared obscene to the workers. These trends increased the sense of moral outrage and political anger among many campesinos. Modesto Ramírez, for example, a peasant leader involved in the insurrection of 1932, recalled his politically formative experiences when interviewed after his arrest and just before his execution by the police:

I have been an honest worker. I lived in the haciendas that surround the Lago de Ilopango as a colono of some of the señores. The time came when they would not even offer work nor land, and if we got one of these it was under the worst circumstances and the most sterile of plots. Of the ten fanegas of corn that one manzana produces we had to return five or six as payment and for the right to live on the patron's land we had to pay fifteen monthly days of work without wage. Whoever did not fulfill this obligation was expelled from the hacienda, they'd burn the rancho [hut] we built with our own labor and at our own expense. I had to abandon my woman and children; the work was not enough to feed them and less to clothe and educate them. I do not know where they are. Misery separated us forever . . . And when have you seen that the authorities have sided with the poor against the rich? If we owe them they rule against us but when they owe us we can't find a court that will listen to us.[87]

Although Ramírez was a communist when he uttered these words, his story and its populist inflection were relevant to nonmilitants. This testimony condenses the forms of extra-economic coercion, class justice, and the pathos of poverty. While surely recounting an extreme form of élite domination, nonetheless the tale reflected aspects of colono experience that would have been credible to Ramírez's class brethren. In short, it provided a diaphanous vision of a social world of oppression bordering on slavery. Similarly, Alberto Shul, an adolescent from Nahuizalco, in the early 1930s traveled throughout the west looking for a decent job. He synthesized in one phrase his painful memory of his joyless adolescence and the underlying motive for rebellion: "We worked from six in the morning to six at night, for a useless wage"[88]

These and other testimonies of landlord abuse encouraged the notion among laborers and colonos that not only was the élite owning land illegitimately, but it really was a race apart, just as the oligarchy had suspected. Sidney Mintz insightfully made the distinction between "bad times" and "evil times" on the plantation: the difference resided in the perception of collective culpability by the landlords. Under some conditions, when subalterns recognized the landlords' or capitalists' culpability in their suffering, they come to "question the *legitimacy* of an existing allocation of power, rather than the terms of that allocation."[89] In western Salvador by the early 1930s, only a minority of the rural poor doubted that "evil times" reigned on the haciendas and plantations. Whether or not peasants and rural proletarians saw the evil as somehow otherworldly—the result of pacts with the devil, for example—there was no question to many that the wealthy landlords had become agents of these evil times.

There were, of course, campesinos in western Salvador who were deferential to the members of the élite and their claims. In particular, in towns and villages where Indians took part in the labor movement, ladino smallholders and workers were much less likely to join. In some towns smallholders survived without falling into the laboring ranks, in part because of their paternalistic ties to more prosperous farmers. Nonetheless, these patterns were not consistent from town to town. In western municipalities like Chalchuapa (Santa Ana) and the ladino cantones that straddled the border between Sonsonate and Santa Ana, where small and mid-size holders predominated, social relations were more harmonious and participation in the movement and revolt less visible.[90] Alastair White noted in discussing the insurrection of 1932 that "in places where the coffee-planters were not quite so cut off socially from the bulk of the rural population; where they did not own such large estates and generally resided in the local area rather than in a city; and above all where they cushioned their workers from the blow caused by the fall of coffee prices, the rebellion did not occur."[91]

Our research nonetheless has led to a paradoxical finding: despite the significant variations in the local, municipal-level histories of land and labor and their differentiated class and ethnic relations, an important convergence of popular sector experiences took place during the late 1920s, lending to the movement an element of strength despite the continued economic power of agrarian élites. Certain common memories also shaped the subaltern experience, in addition to the pervasive pattern of relatively rapid immiseration and a populistic sensibility. The memory and myth of easily available land during the nineteenth century, with a state-sanctioned practice of guaranteeing to communities sufficient land for their needs, persisted among the rural poor and contributed to views of latter-day élite landownership as illegitimate and ill-gotten.[92] These memories of land availability and land loss merged with a regional tradition of collective struggle in defense of communal rights, shaping a widespread ideological acceptance of radical agrarian reform. In addition, western Salvadoran workers and peasants were deeply rooted in the region and were not likely to "vacate," as occurred in other plantation zones in times of crisis but instead remained in the region and placed demands upon the state and élites.[93]

According to Galindo Pohl, a close observer of contemporary Sonsonate-can urban and rural society, although the memory of ejidal and communal land was present among indigenous and other campesinos, more significant was the issue of access to land to plant the milpa: "But while the campesinos, as colonos or residents of cantons and caserios where they possessed a plot, could plant corn, they could compensate for the ejidal plots they sold. They did not miss as much the ejido plot but the ability to plant corn . . . the campesinos began to complain that they could not control the planting of corn. In all the rural communities there had existed a relationship of dependence between campesinos and the land, but in that region there was also another important element, the association between campesinos and corn as body and soul of a legendary unity."[94] Galindo Pohl's argument is significant, if ultimately unverifiable. The indigenous campesinos of western Salvador had elaborate rituals surrounding la milpa, including collective labor, celebrations, and religious invocations.[95] Those rituals were not necessarily based on individual or collective ownership of land, yet they are hard to imagine as adaptable to land controlled by élites. Regardless, Galindo Pohl is correct to point out how the milpa was sacred to western campesinos. As the scourge of hunger infested the western countryside, the élite denial of access to land for the milpa became an act of profanity.

Two contrasting analytical models are both useful in understanding the massive and radical *prise de conscience* of the rural poor. First is James Scott's notion of "moral economy," whereby peasants are moved to revolt when the élite is no longer willing or able to provide what it had provided to the subaltern in the past as a means to obtain subsistence (usually land).[96] The vision offered by travelers and others of the harmonious rural society of the teens and early twenties was, if nothing else, that of a society in which élites and subalterns accepted certain moral economic notions of duty and obligation. During the crisis, there is little doubt that peasants, semi-proletarians, and colonos came to view that moral economy as bankrupt.

The complex process whereby communal and ejidal land was privatized during the late nineteenth century left memory traces that highlighted prior indigenous control over land and the access to open spaces for cultivation and pasture. Yet the process of removing peasants from their means of production and lands was too prolonged and variegated to create a sharp image of primitive accumulation. As the crisis of the late 1920s deepened, the experience of land loss combined with the degrading working conditions came to resemble a new stage of primitive accumulation. When landlords blocked peasants from access to land and those who had lost land became proletarians, then the memory of primitive accumulation, their collective expropriation, became a salient, meaningful image. This second stage of primitive accumulation in western Salvador and subaltern resistance then began to be "written in the annals of mankind in letters of blood and fire."[97]

The next chapter outlines the political landscape of the 1920s, revealing the tumultuous political currents that formed a wave of reformism and pushed aside the dictatorial Melendez-Quiñónez regimes and directly challenged the oligarchy. Reformist politicians, notably Arturo Araujo, drew support from an increasingly mobilized campesinado, yet their failure to deliver on the promise of rights for rural labor and agrarian reform would further radicalize the movement.

Chapter Two

A Bittersweet Transition:
Politics and Labor in the 1920s

During the 1920s El Salvador experienced a transition from authoritarian to democratic governance. In 1927 Pío Romero Bosque assumed the presidency and immediately broke with the Melendez-Quiñónez family, who had ruled the country for fifteen years. Supported by an incipient labor movement and by the urban middle classes, Romero Bosque used his political capital to institute fundamental reforms that democratized the electoral system at the national and local levels and further stimulated the growth of the urban labor movement and social democratic politics. Reformist political and intellectual currents sharply critiqued the hierarchical nature of society and supported the development of a labor movement that carried forth a mission of social transformation. Yet by 1931 the incipient coalition between the Partido Laborista, the key reformist political party, and the labor movement had fallen apart, and popular hopes in democratic social change had been dashed on the hard rocks of state repression. This chapter reviews the political development of the country during the 1920s in an attempt to understand the stillbirth of Salvadoran social democracy.

Urban Economic Growth

The rapid expansion of rural production and government spending during the teens and twenties also stimulated urban economic activities. The number of manufacturing and construction workers grew during these years, as the urban population expanded and San Salvador became a primary city, with a population of nearly 100,000. Although El Salvador had always had a large share of its population involved in artisanal and service work, census data show the rapid growth of relatively large nuclei of artisans in departmental capitals and some of the larger, well-located towns, such as Izalco and Tacuba. Many of these artisans were directly connected to the expanding agrarian economy: carpentry, metalwork, millwork, railroad work, and other occupations expanded along with the traditional agricultural crops. Haciendas always had many carpenters on their payroll; *ingenios* and coffee mills required electricians, mechanics, and masons. In a protected economy like El Salvador's, where high import taxes raised the price of imported consumer goods, cheap consumer goods were in high demand and provided opportunities for local manufacturing and repair workshops. Artisanal production increased significantly as more workers purchased basic consumer products. Cloth, shoes, clothes, soap, work tools, leather, matches, sugar, liquor, candies, furniture, cigarettes, bread, and metal products were common manufactured goods. Industrial and service occupations also expanded dramatically during the 1920s, including longshore work, rail work, mining, electrical and mechanical work, hauling and driving, textile work, and typesetting. Although most of these jobs were performed by men, women dominated the growing textile sector as well as the markets. By the late 1920s urban workers and artisans accounted for some fifty thousand people, 12 percent of the country's economically active population.[1]

By the early 1920s El Salvador had 4,600 civilian employees (the largest sector in Central America), 3,000 teachers, a large number of commercial and office employees, and a sizeable officer corps.[2] These middle sectors also began to organize themselves, as teachers, service, and sales and office workers formed associations that eventually gained collective bargaining and other rights from Romero Bosque's administration. This emerging middle class and urban work force would prove significant in the formation of a democratic opposition to the Melendez-Quiñónez regimes.

All in the Family: The Melendez-Quiñónez Years

The assassination of a reform president, Manuel Enrique Araujo, in 1913 signaled the beginning of a long period of authoritarian rule by the Melendez-Quiñónez family clan. Araujo approved measures that favored popular consumption and began to consider land reform. Although its circumstances were never clarified, it was widely assumed that the assassination was connected to Araujo's anti-oligarchic agenda. His vice-president, Doctor Carlos Melendez, assumed the presidency provisionally and for the following fourteen years controlled the state with his brother (Jorge Melendez) and his son-in-law (Alfonso Quiñónez Molina), who alternated in the presidency.

Initially the regime had roots in the personalistic but relatively competitive political (if not electorally democratic) system that allowed some openness among members of the country's professional class (doctors, lawyers, judges) and the agrarian bourgeoisie, with a power-sharing focus that precluded the continued hold of one faction on power. Although the highest levels of the oligarchy looked down on the Melendez and Quiñónez families as parvenus, during the late teens and early twenties the governing families were able to obtain support from élite as well as middle social sectors based on unprecedented export and internal tax revenues. The commitment of previous liberal regimes to the protection of small holders declined, as the governing clan fostered large-scale investments and subsidies for the development of rail, road, port, and communication infrastructure, along with notable increases in other areas, including urban schools and a modernized military.[3]

Through a combination of repression, electoral manipulation, cooptation, and patronage, the clan managed to garner support from local political bosses, provincial agrarian bourgeois, and urban entrepreneurs, including artisans, and thereby thwart the opposition from urban middle sectors and workers. Perhaps their greatest political feat was to neutralize threats from a fractious military that after initial resistance became more acquiescent and received an increasing share of resources in exchange. In the rural areas the regime initially relied on the Ligas Rojas, an organization which combined paramilitary, political, and patronage functions.

The Ligas represented an attempt by Alfonso Quiñónez Molina, whose campaign rhetoric underscored "the social question," to preempt and incorporate reformist organizing among workers and peasants. They were loosely structured mass organizations created and controlled by supporters of the Melendez-Quiñónez family and its official party, the Partido Nacional Democrático (PND). In many localities they offered a means for negotiating with local factions (especially indigenous leaders) and building patronage networks. The organization of the Ligas and the regime's drive to gain support among popular sectors had contradictory political effects. The Ligas certainly enshrined regime violence as an effective form of repression: their members would beat up and even kill opposition members. Yet to a limited degree, the regime necessarily allowed for the circulation of discourses about the "social question."[4]

The Ligas and the PND appealed to the indigenous people of Izalco as part of their drive to capture electoral support and organize las Ligas Rojas. The PND offered, in effect, to restore the communal lands to the indígenas of Izalco, who had lost them "in the name of civilization or due to a . . . loan shark."[5] Although it is doubtful that any land was actually returned to the Izalqueño Indians, the PND did cement an alliance with the leading indigenous cofradía in the town. That alliance simultaneously promoted the indigenous organization and supported it to a certain extent against the encroachment of ladino planters and farmers, particularly in disputes over water and transit rights.[6]

Despite the apparent stability of the the Melendez-Quiñónez regimes between 1913 and 1927, they experienced serious electoral challenges in 1918 and 1922. The first challenge to the governing clan came with preparations for the elections of January 1919. Tomás Palomo initially combined official backing with a promise of democratic reforms and built a significant base among middle-class and working-class groups. The family clan chose, however, to perpetuate itself in power by electing Jorge Melendez through electoral fraud and making ample use of the violent Ligas Rojas.[7]

In 1921 a protest of market women led to the regime's first full-scale use of violent repression. New currency policies based on a gold standard meant eliminating traditional forms of currency that circulated in markets. When mostly female vendors protested those policies in San Salvador, soldiers began to gun them down.[8] Led by the butchers, some market workers and vendors engaged in violent resistance, but to no avail. Simultaneously, shoe manufacturers and shop owners used the regime's backing of repression as an excuse for reneging on a settlement that had ended one of the first strikes in San Salvador. The crushing of these two popular initiatives alienated the nascent labor movement from the Melendez-Quiñónez regime. However, throughout its reign the regime refrained from frontal assaults against the labor movement, and the labor movement reciprocated.

The Melendez-Quiñónez regime had to respond to demands from increasingly heterogeneous rural and urban social groups while building a political system that would exclude all popular groups from electoral power. This contradictory policy became difficult to sustain, as both middle- and working-class groups became increasingly organized and vocal, in no small part because of the regime's pro-worker rhetoric.[9]

The regime became practiced at the art of producing desired electoral outcomes. An observer from the period noted how "managed elections keep [the opposition] from power. It must be admitted presidential continuance depends often enough on electoral fraud. There is no ballot; the bulk of the population is practically without letters in the crudest sense. They come to a table where there are armed officials. They give their names and vote, sometimes under stress. But the vote is registered as the man with the roll wills. Districts with a four thousand majority for change have a managed majority of two thousand for none. In the end, unless things get too bad to be borne, and even the President's friends at last grow discontented and desert him, most people of the educated classes satisfy themselves perforce with enforced order. They can at least trade and gamble and dance."[10]

On the rural front the Ligas and the PND provided only unstable vehicles for the regime. Their dilemma was that any attempt to mobilize rural workers and indigenous people in support of the more centralized political system yielded increased problems at the local level.[11] With heightened agrarian tensions in the countryside during this period a rural-based mass organization became too risky. In the end this risk, combined with outrage at the paramilitary use of the Liga, led to the demise of the organization in 1923.

Élite support for the Melendez-Quiñónez regime was more forthcoming, as "the backing . . . came from the coffee planter's aristocracy, which believed in order and economic progress but saw no reason to cater to the masses in either economic or governmental planning."[12] Even the regime's conflicts with the oligarchy were settled amid the economic boom of the mid-1920s, when sources in the United States noted how the "old animosity between President Quiñónez and the most important and richest families seems to have been settled" when the president danced with the wife of Miguel Dueñas, "by far the richest in all Salvador."[13] But ultimately the regime relied on a state of emergency and its concomitant use of state repression against the opposition.

An Embattled Opposition

The PND, fearing the growth of an autonomous labor movement, also attempted to promote an alliance with worker and artisans' organizations. Although the long-term impact of the regime's tolerance and even promotion of labor organization is unclear, there is little doubt that urban workers and especially artisans found themselves in a favorable conjuncture in which to organize and express themselves. And once the regime had accepted the legitimacy of unions, it was difficult to deny the basic rights of organization, when they proved not to be docile tools of the PND. Although statistics are hard to verify, according to the Pan American Federation of Labor there were some ten thousand organized workers in El Salvador by 1923, the largest number of any Central American country.

The nascent labor movement struggled for autonomy, and many of its militants supported the political opposition to the regime. Notwithstanding this, the populist discourse and tactics of the regime had salient effects on the development of the opposition movement. Although middle-class intellectuals played a vital role in the development of the labor movement throughout the 1920s, there remained latent class tensions within the opposition that thwarted its development. A judicial ruling that allowed Alfonso Quiñónez to run again for office despite having served as acting president ignited a protest movement led by students, artisans, and workers. That movement soon merged with the electoral campaign of Tomás Molina, gathering momentum in December 1922. To grasp the development of the opposition movement, we will examine two accounts of the opposition campaign of 1922 waged by Molina and the Christmas Day massacre that ended it. Manuel Hernandez Quijano was a writer and critic close to the opposition movement, Miguel Mármol a young shoemaker who became an activist in the campaign and later a communist union leader.

Hernandez Quijano's narrative focuses on three political demonstrations. The Quiñónez demonstration, according to the writer four-thousand strong, was to a "dispassionate" observer "shameful," because of its sociological makeup. "One only saw caites [a cheap sandal], palm sombreros, dirty shirts and calzones, since they had been recruited directly from their farm work or from bars."[14] The Ligas Rojas from various pueblos also participated. There is a subtle contradiction in his narrative in that the Ligas Rojas, even if coercion played some role in their organization, would not have come to the demonstration in such a completely disorganized manner. Rather, the class nature of the pro-Quiñónez supporters is simply repulsive to the writer: ignorant, dirty people who "obeyed" but could not "lead." Hernandez's repulsion both at the role of these regime supporters and at the marks of poverty on their bodies blurred his vision.

In sharp contradistinction, he portrayed the opposition demonstrators with rapturous strokes. The large number of demonstrators that gathered in support of the "blue candidate" (the party colors of Molina) on 17 December 1922 arrived voluntarily and almost spontaneously, as the result of a simple leaflet that had circulated around the capital a few days earlier. This was the largest demonstration in the country's history, with over twenty thousand participants. For Hernandez the quality of the demonstrators was as important as the number. All the "gremios" were represented, from the "academic" to the "servant" to the campesino. They were spatially organized by their group, "each guild with its own banner . . . and each man with his pennant . . . and his blue button in his lapel; since one has to realize that in the immense crowd you did not see even one palm sombrero nor one bare foot, a sign that there went the real, the conscious ones, those that form democracy."[15]

This remarkable portrait of the democratic opposition sheds light on a divide in Salvadoran political culture. For this middle-class critic, the opposition is truly democratic and representative of the nation precisely because of the way it respects and reproduces class hierarchy. Each group of society occupies its own place, without any effort to blur class lines. Indeed Hernandez's own class bias blurs his description, as it did in the description of the ragged pro-Quiñónez demonstrators. Immediately after mentioning that campesinos took part and that one could see neither a "sombrero de palma" nor a "pie descalzo," he describes the blue button in each man's lapel. Thus the narrator not only expunges the unwashed masses from citizenship but also excludes those male demonstrators who could not afford to wear jackets with lapels.

The regime cultivation of subaltern support and its use of the Ligas Rojas colored Hernandez's vision, such that he could not conceive of the poorest sectors of society as citizens. Conversely, the regime's use of populist language tended to legitimize the activity of urban and rural workers and campesinos.

On 25 December female supporters of Molina organized another demonstration several days after a pro-Quiñónez female rally had flopped. Hernandez writes, "At two in the afternoon, the women of the capital began to gather on the Avenida Independencia and just before four commenced the most beautiful parade that we had ever seen. That multitude of blue-clad women with huge banners of the same color was so imposing and beautiful . . . A group of girls led the march, followed by señoras and señoritas of the highest society, followed by the rest of the classes, until the market women and servants.[16] They shouted in unison, "Libertad, Libertad." The husbands, brothers, and fathers accompanied the women "to protect them," and "to help them home after the demonstration." But the peaceful demonstrators marched into a trap. The regime and its national guard had placed machine guns on the rooftops of buildings along the route of the marchers. At an agreed-upon moment the troops opened fire, first in the air and then at the demonstrators. The bloodshed continued on the streets as the Ligas Rojas, armed with machetes, attacked defenseless demonstrators. It is impossible to establish how many died on the afternoon of Christmas 1922, but various sources cite the figure of eighty. Hernandez identified fourteen dead (six women) and thirty-nine wounded (nineteen women). Artisans and shop employees accounted for most of the victims whose occupation could be identified.

The regime muzzled the press, and the official paper blamed the demonstrators, from whose ranks it said the shots were fired. According to Hernandez, the regime then sent its emissaries to the provinces to spread the official version of opposition culpability. A few years later Jorge Melendez offered this version to a journalist: "According to Don Jorge, those foolish people were pushing and shouting out there and a machine-gun was fired into the air to frighten them, and such panic ensued that they went stumbling over each other, several of their own weapons were discharged in the confusion, and eight or ten of them hurt."[17] At the same time, throughout the country authorities locked up dozens if not hundreds of "Blue" activists. With such a show of force and repression, no one dared wear the blue button of the Molinistas.

Miguel Mármol was not an eyewitness to the massacre because he was hiding out. Mármol had become an activist in the Constitutionalist (or "blue") party, after observing at close-hand the treatment of conscripted troops and the arbitrary and corrupt practices of the regime. Similarly, his labor activism pushed him alongside other artisan-workers into the democratic movement. Even after decades of communist militancy, Mármol continued to express admiration for the political work of "these bourgeois liberals."[18] In December Mármol was working as an electoral activist in his home town near the lake of Ilopango. The wave of repression that culminated in the Christmas Day massacre started days earlier with mass arrests of activists and continued for the next few weeks. Mármol's account of the massacre—presumably a distillation of what he heard at the time and how he analyzed it through a Marxist optic later—differs little from that of the intellectual Hernandez, except in two details: Mármol mentions neither the role of the high society ladies in the demonstration nor that of the Ligas Rojas. For Mármol the democratic opposition was primarily a popular movement led by middle-class liberals, and the enemy—the regime—represented the oligarchy. The discursive disjuncture is significant in that it points to a broader problem of communication within the opposition movement. Mármol and Hernandez shared a deep outrage at the face of the regime's brutal tactics. For Mármol, "A feeling of impotence fell over us Molinistas, and the most radical among us started to think that political activity like shouting 'Viva Molina!' and distributing leaflets was pure bull shit when the enemy had rifles and machine guns."[19] As the Molinista movement fell apart under the state of siege, Mármol gradually reinserted himself into the labor movement that the regime still tolerated.

An analysis of Hernandez's and Mármol's narratives suggests a division in political culture in the Salvadoran democratic opposition that was not clear at the time to its participants. Populist discourses that empowered the working and middle classes against the oligarchy circulated throughout society, promoted by the regime as well as by subalterns (see chapter 3 on populist discourse). Gould noted in *To Lead as Equals* how in Nicaragua the discursive and the political division between anti Somoza opposition and the popular movement formed a cornerstone of the architecture of the

Somoza regime.[20] Similar political cultural divisions across the continent had salient effects on democratic politics. The Argentine democratic movement of the 1940s notably found little common ground with the Peronist workers' movement.[21] In Costa Rica the workers' movement and social democratic activists found themselves on opposite sides of the barricades in 1948.[22] Our reading of the accounts of the demonstrations and massacre suggests that in El Salvador during the 1920s a similar division existed, but one that was neither visible nor acknowledged by either working-class militants or the middle-class and élite opponents of the regime. It would only become apparent toward the end of the decade when class divisions tore apart the social democratic Araujista coalition, with devastating political consequences.

Romero Bosque and Political Reform

Sometime in 1926 ex-President Jorge Melendez bragged to a British journalist about how he had selected his successor in 1923: " 'Well, you see,' he said, with one of his disarming smiles, 'you *externalize* your wishes, so to say. You let the notion get round that this or that man would be a good fellow for president. Then everybody begins to whisper to everybody else, 'Don Jorge wants So-and-So,' and they start forming clubs to support him. If the opposition wants to form a club, why you let them do so by all means—but one got the notion that when election day came round there were ways of managing things."[23]

His brother-in-law, President Alfonso Quiñónez, expected to be able to control the presidential succession after his own four-year term ended in 1927 in a similar manner. He expected not only to name his successor but to force him to quit so that he himself could assume another presidential term.[24] However, pressure for political reform had been building over the previous years across many domestic sectors as well as from the U.S. embassy. The Treaty of Peace and Amity (1923) committed the United States to recognizing only democratic governments; therefore the embassy opposed the efforts of President Quiñónez to perpetuate himself in power through a change in the constitution. By the mid-1920s urban workers, public employees, indigenous leaders, intellectuals, and liberal politicians all called for electoral reform. Melendez opted to give his backing to the minister of war, Pío Romero Bosque, who had a reputation as a reformer sympathetic to the labor movement, yet had faithfully served the interests of the Melendez-Quiñónez clan. Because of his reformist reputation and the authoritarian character of the regime, no opposition candidate emerged and Romero Bosque won the election unopposed.

Romero Bosque's *volte-face* remains enigmatic in that there was an undeniable personal factor in his decision to break with the previous regime and begin a process of democratic reform.[25] Yet as we have pointed out, the pressure for reform had been increasing, and Romero Bosque realized before and after his unopposed presidential election that he could command an important base of support for political change. In 1926, for example, artisans had organized the Subcomité Central de Obreros in early support of Pío Romero Bosque's nomination as the presidential candidate of the *oficialista* Partido Nacional Democrático. Artisans and workers also organized a large demonstration (fifteen thousand people according to the labor press) in support of Romero Bosque's candidacy.[26]

Once in power Romero Bosque quickly capitalized on that base among the urban popular and middle-class sectors. In June 1927 his newly formed Partido Civista's break with the powerful and well-established PND partially hinged upon its ability to recruit popular support in the cities. By August this new party claimed to have organized two hundred committees and enrolled 150,000 supporters.[27] In September a convention attended by five thousand supporters from throughout the country formally inaugurated the Partido Civista.[28]

Romero used his political capital to institute fundamental reforms that democratized the electoral system at national and local levels. The opening-up of the electoral system not surprisingly had powerful effects on local politics and culture. To cite one example, "obreros" (including small manufacturers), backed by a labor federation with some three thousand members, had previously controlled the local government of the city of San Vicente.[29] The liberalization of elections led to a local political insurgency, with a group of "rebel workers" renouncing the past, "when the worker was so happy because he could greet any Doctor or any riquito . . . ! What imbecilic times! We don't want an alcalde riquito . . . ; we want one who is a worker; but a conscious worker . . . not like the workers whom los señorones have selected in the past; we want a worker of character who will not let himself be handled by any señoron."[30] This statement, rich in populist vocabulary, in its local context suggests the limitations of what passed for "obrero" political control on the one hand, and the emerging cultural and political divisions within the "obrero" camp on the other.

Romero Bosque's first concrete step aimed to liberalize the municipal elections scheduled for December 1927. The central government pressured local officials to resolve political disputes by conciliating factions and attempting to reach a consensus (and single slates), while at the same time encouraging elections free of interference from public officials and "disorder."[31] This "conciliatory" style, which would also be used by Romero Bosque to manage the presidential elections of January 1931, reflected an attempt to overcome the intense factionalism and conflict that the clientelist system could no longer successfully negotiate. The policy opened the door to a great diversity of political challenges and conflicts involving a myriad combination of unsettled local issues and political factions. Generally Romero Bosque's interventions favored popular groups against the local version of the "oligarchy."[32] In Alegría, for example, the local oligarchy resorted to violent repression to ensure electoral triumphs.[33]

Romero Bosque's governmental reforms and the increasing marginalization of the networks associated with the PND led to a backlash. In the first days of December 1927 a military revolt broke out, mobilizing workers from the Melendez haciendas to support troops opposed to Romero Bosque.[34] The coup attempt failed, and the quick military trials and executions of its leaders in the army, National Guard, and police sent a clear signal that Romero Bosque would not compromise in his reform efforts.[35]

With Romero Bosque firmly in power, the old PND was in crisis at the national level, but its local supporters and clients attempted to keep supporters of the Partido Civista and Romero Bosque from office in the municipal elections of December 1927.[36] The results of those elections were ambiguous, as many PND militants joined the Romero Bosque forces in opportunistic fashion. In Santa Catarina Masahuat a dozen workers registered a complaint over the mayor's continued partisan activities just after Romero Bosque had ordered local officials to not intervene in the elections.[37] In La Unión a group of citizens complained to the interior minister that the mayor supported the election of General José Agustín Martinez, ordering them to vote for him and having the Guardia arrest those who would not.[38]

Between 1927 and 1930 some local factions sought accommodation with Romero's imperatives while trying to retain their hold over municipal

Municipalities of western El Salvador.

politics. The political opening at the same time encouraged political activism and contestation at the local level, and also opened the political door to labor and left organizing. Similarly, the liberalization of politics both responded to and further encouraged popular mobilization around new candidates.[39]

The Failure of Reformism in Juayúa

Emilio Redaelli, an Italian with Fascist sympathies, was deeply involved in the political and economic life of the coffee municipality of Juayúa, serving as mayor in the 1920s and 1931.[40] The owner of a coffee farm and manager of a major beneficio. in 1931 he became the president of the Asociación de Agricultores de Juayúa.[41] Redaelli was only the most visible player in a long-established network of élite-controlled municipal politics that the Romero reforms failed to dislodge from power.[42] Élite control over municipal politics in Juayúa was such that in the municipal elections of 1929 two allies, members of the élite, confronted each other: Maximo Rauda Salaverría and Emilio Redaelli. The overwhelmingly strong support for Araujo's candidacy in 1930 reflected a local effort to displace Redaelli's and Salaverría's stranglehold over town politics.[43] Yet the triumph of Araujo did nothing to overturn the local power élite.

Municipal Politics and Ethnic Conflict in Izalco

The opening-up of municipal politics had salient if contradictory effects throughout the country. Nowhere were the stakes higher than in those western towns where indigenous people competed with ladinos for control over resources such as land and irrigation rights, while also defending their cultural practices and political autonomy. Izalco, to cite a famous example, had a long history of social tensions and political conflicts between ladinos and Indians.[44] The collapse and disappearance of one of Izalco's two indigenous communities during the 1890s resulted in a complex process of mestizaje in what became known as Barrio Dolores.[45] Many ladinos settled in the town starting in the mid-nineteenth century, and by the early twentieth century a ladino élite had, according to an observer, "managed to dominate the indigenous masses; for some time the local authorities are ladinos and its flourishing progress is due to that fact."[46]

By the late 1920s ladinos outnumbered Indians, although the cultural dividing line between the two groups remained fluid and imprecise (see chapter 4). The surviving Indian community of the barrio of Asunción managed to navigate the difficult terrain of autonomy and subordination. The indigenous community leadership had long attempted to obtain state support in its disputes with ladinos. Under the Melendez-Quiñónez regime that relationship developed into an alliance between the alcalde municipal de indígenas and the PND, formalized from 1918 to 1923 in the formation and operations of the Ligas Rojas.[47]

During the 1920s ethnic conflicts over resources intensified.[48] Political reform at the national level thus increased the political stakes in Izalco. The principal ladino political boss was Tomas Sicilia, who since 1926 had helped to maintain ladino control over municipal politics.[49] Local people filed complaints against him in 1927 and 1928 for his attempts to keep his allies in power,[50] but like other PND leaders he became a reformer overnight, abandoning the sinking ship of the PND and joining the Partido Civista as a supporter of Romero Bosque.[51]

The municipal elections of December 1929 in Izalco involved two ethnically distinct factions both aligned with the Romero Bosque government. The "Indians" backed Salvador Cea, whom the local Ladino élite stigmatized as an "inexperienced illiterate." The "principales personas," allied with the departmental governor, backed Rafael C. Valdez, a ladino "obrero."[52] Cea's candidacy received support from a group that called itself "El Atlacatl" (in reference to the country's mythic Indian hero)—an alliance of Indians and some ladinos.[53] The ministry's investigation into the elections followed a complaint of 18 December 1929 by the Indian leaders José Feliciano Ama and Francisco Orozco that Tomas Sicilia had imposed Valdez as mayor. The Atlacatl faction claimed that Valdez's victory could only have been the result of electoral manipulation, since Indians formed a majority. The dispute focused on the control of the electoral Directorio, the body that oversaw the local elections and counted the votes. Control of the popularly elected Directorio had previously been tantamount to election. The Directorio had been formed from the ranks of the ladino middle class and artisans, and in his report to the ministry the governor claimed that "most people" backed Valdez and that the opposing party refrained from voting when they saw his support.[54]

The governor's investigation of the election considered Ama's accusation that Sicilia and the members of the Directorio had been drunk and had expressed their intention to veto a mixed-party Directorio and to use the police to keep supporters of Cea out of the voting hall. Many witnesses brought by Ama and Orozco testified that in fact the police had kept Cea supporters from voting. The governor ruled against the complainants and dismissed their request that he nullify the elections. But Ama and Orozco persisted, appealing directly to the Ministry of Interior. The ministry did not uncover "bribery," however, so the appeal was ultimately rejected.[55]

The electoral conflict of 1929 was significant in that it radicalized the discourse of municipal and ethnic politics. Feliciano Ama's protest is apposite: "[The fraud] opens the way to capitalist imposition which will be fatal for the people, when, from the public offices, the yoke of capital oppresses the employee, the worker, and the peasant."[56] The indigenous cacique's use of expressions such as "the yoke of capital" in his protest letter of 1929 is noteworthy, since it predates any significant left or labor presence, suggesting that labor organizers would find a receptive audience, already fluent in their language of class and populism.[57] At the same time, the description of obrerismo as synonymous with ladinos is remarkable for two reasons. Throughout Central America in the 1920s obrerismo was a reformist political expression of artisans. The opposition obrerista-indígena points to a political divide that would haunt Central American democratic and left movements. In Nicaragua during the 1920s, and in El Salvador and Guatemala in 1944, democratic obreristas and labor activists found indigenous campesinos on the authoritarian rightist side of the political spectrum. Ama's language of class pointed to a state of political flux into which the left was able to insert itself. Second, the identification of obrerismo with ladinos is important because it was an expression of racism, but also because it suppressed the significant presence of indigenous people among the artisan class. In this sense the statement tended to reinforce the social division in Izalco by conflating ethnicity with class. For Ama's faction in particular, the bitter legacy of the electoral process of 1929–30 was that Romero Bosque's democratic reforms had not reached their town, allowing the ladinos to continue to rule over them.

Nahuizalco: Four Disruptive Ladinos and the Indian Majority

Ethnic rivalries also dominated nearby Nahuizalco's politics. Since over 80 percent of the population identified as indigenous, the ladino middle class and élite politicians attempted to forge and dominate an alliance with an indigenous faction. As in Izalco, Nahuizalco's indigenous political leaders were embedded in a system of patronage, cooptation, and clientelism consolidated by the PND during the 1920s. In September 1923 a large group of Indians, referring to themselves as *criollos del pueblo*, wrote to the Interior Ministry requesting official support for their candidate, Gregorio Gutiérrez, and stating, "there is no way that we can accept that the mayor comes from the ladino party since the small number of ladinos who are trying to put in a mayor, do so in order to enrich themselves and to dominate the people in every way."[58]

Romero Bosque's policy of open elections brought heightened conflicts to Nahuizalco. For the elections of December 1927 the ladino faction led by Rodolfo Brito and Rafael Renderos faced the candidate of the "Partido de Indígenas," Pedro Mauricio, a former Liga Roja leader.[59] After Mauricio was elected, Brito and the ladinos successfully lobbied the governor to remove him because he was illiterate, causing a great deal of resentment among the Indian majority. The ladino group was not able to hold on to power in the elections of 1929. The military commander of Sonsonate advised the minister of war to consider the balance of power in Nahuizalco: "since for the supreme government it is better to have four thousand Indians content and not four ladinos for whom the municipality has served to swindle the poor people—when I have needed people in these barracks, none of these ladinos has ever presented himself; they spend their lives disturbing public order in that town. Hopefully, the Minister of Gobernación will take into account these arguments and not allow these individuals to make a mockery of the authorities."[60]

For the elections of December 1929 Rodolfo Brito again managed to gain control of the town, but "the Indians charged [him] with drunkenness and demanded that his victory be nullified." In response to the Indians' request the national government dispatched the deputy departmental governor, who was so busy with his own backlog of cases that he abandoned all hope of discovering whether Brito actually was a drunkard, and ruled in favor of the Indians simply because "they presented more witnesses than the opposition."[61] Yet as we shall see, politics continued to be a flashpoint for ethnic and class conflict in both Izalco and Nahuizalco over the next two years.

Reformism and Anti-imperialism

Ethnic conflict in western Salvador coincided with the growth of a discourse of mestizaje that primarily valorized an abstract and idealized version of the indigenous contribution to the country's history and culture. Mestizaje, promoted by the Mexican Revolution, circulated as a nation-building myth of gradual but inevitable race mixture and cultural "de-indianization," and reinforced a dominant view of society as increasingly and necessarily homogeneous ethnically. Throughout Latin America it allowed progressive intellectuals during the 1920s to take an active role in nation building by forging anti-imperial images, allowing for a greater inclusion of subaltern groups in a version of liberalism shorn of its most egregious racism and élitism.[62]

The Salvadoran writer Miguel Angel Espino expressed his understanding of the roots of nationalism in the following terms: "The dehispanicization of the continent . . . is one of those problems that in a hidden and latent way has been modifying the life of the continent. Because, it is proven that we are Indians. Of the five liters we have, one cup of Spanish blood courses through us; the rest is American fiber. From the crossing of the Spaniard and the American a new race resulted; to believe this race was Hispanicized was the error."[63] Reformist intellectuals cited Marxist and progressive thinkers like José Carlos Mariátegui as part of their campaign in favor of respect for Indians. Rochac, the governor of Sonsonate, wrote, "Central America, which has, in part, a considerable indigenous foundation has forgotten, has completely neglected the situation of its Indians." Although they tended to idealize a "pure" Indian culture, their views clashed sharply with traditional white and mestizo racism. According to Rochac, "Everything that is admirable in the Indian is his own; it is not owing to anyone, neither the priest, nor the teacher, nor the minister, nor the legislator, nor the magistrate. . . . The Indian is nothing less than a tender and sensitive man—no less than the white or the mestizo."[64]

These declarations, however paternalistic, stand in sharp contrast to élite racist discourse, which consistently portrayed Indians as inferior, backward beings who would squander any pay increase on alcohol and retreat into indolent barbarism if given any land. Some intellectuals went so far as to question the early returns of the Salvadoran census for underestimating the indigenous population.[65] By valorizing the indigenous contribution to society and offering solidarity with Indians, the ideologues of mestizaje helped to create the discursive conditions and political space for support of indigenous demands, and later for the cross-ethnic revolutionary movement that emerged between 1929 and 1931.

The discourse of mestizaje circulated in a vibrant ideological field. During the late 1920s political, military, and economic intervention in the region by the United States contributed significantly to the emergence of anti-imperialist organizations and discourses. Even before Sandino launched his armed resistance to the Marines in Nicaragua, in 1927, El Salvador had distinguished itself for its opposition to any form of intervention by Washington in the isthmus. Some of the Salvadoran élite even opposed the

Bryan-Chamoro treaty of 1916, which in effect created a protectorate in Nicaragua.[66] El Salvador's greater political autonomy from Washington went hand in hand with strong resistance by the country's middle sectors to foreign control of the country's economic resources, especially by the United States.[67] The loan and customs receivership of 1922 had produced great opposition, especially among students and artisans who thought that it undermined the country's sovereignty. Years later, resentment over the loan and receivership still generated significant popular opposition.[68] Throughout the decade intellectuals also continued to criticize the foreign-owned railroad monopoly of the International Railways of Central America.[69] During the latter part of the 1920s opposition to intervention in the isthmus by the United States increased, spurred on by the impact of the Mexican Revolution and the growth of unionist and nationalist currents. Gustavo Guerrero, Romero Bosque's foreign minister and head of the International Court, for example, played an important hemispheric role in resisting Washington's policies in the region.[70]

After 1927 the Sandinista resistance galvanized support in El Salvador: peasant and artisan committees raised funds for Sandino, protests were frequent, and dozens of Salvadoran male and female volunteers joined his forces, including most notably Farabundo Martí.[71] Anti-imperialist sentiment was widespread among artisans, students, and middle sectors. On 18 January 1927 artisans and students demonstrated in San Salvador against the government in Nicaragua, then allied with the United States.[72] Even Salvadoran farmers raised funds to send to Sandino.[73] Haya de la Torre, the founder of the Alianza Popular Revolucionaria Americana (APRA) and an outspoken critic of Washington's imperialism, visited El Salvador in 1928, giving public talks and publishing articles in the press.[74] This burgeoning anti-imperialist movement brought together urban middle sectors, workers, artisans, and university students, and led to vigorous debates in the press, with significant reformist and anti-imperialist editorializing. The anti-imperialist fervor was not limited to the capital. As Reynaldo Galindo Pohl wrote in his memoirs of provincial life: "In Sonsonate, it would have been hard to find a person who did not express anti-imperialist ideas."[75] Thousands of Salvadorans from diverse sectors attended anti-imperialist rallies. The anti-imperialist and nationalist themes became linked to other demands for reform, encouraging the transformation of the Federación Regional de Trabajadores Salvadoreños (FRTS) into something more than a labor organization. In one demonstration alone the FRTS mobilized ten thousand people in San Salvador, with speakers from the middle-class Liga Anti-imperialista alternating with workers. The speakers drew broad ideological connections, opposing the United States in conflicts ranging from its intervention in Nicaragua to its confrontation with President Calles of Mexico.[76] Radical nationalism and anti-imperialism became important components of the Salvadoran labor movement. A manifesto of the FRTS in 1926, for example, called for independence for Puerto Rico and the Philippines, internationalization of the Panama Canal, and nationalization of the railroads and other public services.[77]

The Universidad Popular emerged from this milieu, organizing lectures, classes, and presentations throughout the country with support from university students and radical labor leaders. In Ahuachapán in 1928 it sponsored a talk by Esteban Pavletich, a Peruvian APRISTA leader, Sandino volunteer, and anti-imperialist who helped organize the movement while in El Salvador.[78] Miguel Mármol underscored the transformative experiences for a working-class student at the Universidad Popular, which he likened to learning how to talk and "seeing the light at the end of a long, dark, and anguishing tunnel."[79]

The U.S. embassy became increasingly concerned over these displays of "anti-American sentiment," blaming Mexican and other foreign agitators while pressing Salvadoran authorities to expel foreign organizers and repress the anti-imperialist movement.[80] The most notorious case of repression against the movement took place on 24 November 1929, when the police arrested all the speakers at an anti-imperialist rally in Santa Tecla. Soldiers subsequently shot demonstrators who demanded the release of the prisoners.[81] These events contributed directly to the formation of a Salvadoran branch of the Socorro Rojo Internacional, a leftist organization that aided victims of political repression and would prove to play a decisive role in the mobilization of 1931 (see chapter 3).

During the 1920s persistent public critiques of the increasingly unequal distribution of wealth further challenged dominance by the élite. National newspapers such as Patria and Diario Latino routinely editorialized about the need for reforms in favor of peasants, rural workers, and indigenous people. The Heraldo de Sonsonate and other provincial newspapers also protested against forms of economic exploitation. One article decried how "the exploitative companies form a menacing plague that strangles justice and increases the percentage of the impoverished."[82] Exposés of rural labor condemned the large landowners: "Life on the fincas . . . is heavy, due to the monotony of the dailywork and the pitiful rations, which have been reduced to two large tortillas and beans mixed with chicken droppings, cooked without salt or onions; they sleep under the coffee trees."[83] Journalists attacked the concentration of land in the coffee economy and supported measures in favor of the dwindling group of small-scale producers.[84]

Proponents of the Minimum Vital ideology and the student movement also formed part of the reformist current. Alberto Masferrer promoted his program through his organization Unión Vitalista and his newspaper La Patria. The movement sought to "guarantee the basic necessities of life" for the country's working classes by promoting a harmonious balance between capital and labor and moderate land reform.[85] Reformist university students during the 1920s organized the Movimiento Renovacion and the National Association of Students (AGEUS). Their organizing efforts extended beyond the campus gates to include protests and mobilizations against foreign loans, high rents, trolley fees, electric rates, foreign monopolies, and militarism.[86]

Although the reformist and anti-imperial movements would ultimately fail, they did leave important legacies. The Salvadoran version of social democratic reformism, in particular, went further than other Latin American variants in promoting the rights of Indians.[87] Moreover, the movements of the late 1920s played vital roles in focusing public attention on the rights of labor and on the unjust economic structures prevalent in Salvadoran society.

The Radicalization of the Labor Movement, 1927–30

During the late 1920s there were worries at the U.S. embassy about the emergence of a leftist-controlled labor movement. The embassy repeatedly pressured Salvadoran authorities to censor mail and control communication between Salvadorans and Mexican and other Central American organizations. As early as 1927 sectors of the Salvadoran élite joined the U.S. embassy in expressing concern over the spread of what they saw as Mexican-supported "bolshevism." Although few Mexicans worked as organizers in El Salvador, officials and landlords feared the ideological influence of revolutionary-inspired land reforms in Mexico. Well before the birth of the rural labor movement, the chief justice of the Supreme Court, Arrieta Rossi, observed in 1927: "There is considerable unrest among the lower classes, especially in the outlying districts where bolshevist influence is evident."[88]

The concern of the U.S. embassy and the élites was premature but prescient. A radicalized urban working-class movement, now extending into the countryside, provided the foundation for the emergence of a revolutionary movement between 1930 and 1931. The transformations wrought by capitalist development favored the growth of the urban labor movement, in that both the introduction of machinery and the competition between manufacturing shops and larger enterprises caused significant discontent. The rapid growth of the urban labor movement hinged in part on artisanal resistance to full-scale proletarianization, combined with resentment toward the intensification of labor, without a commensurate increase in wages. Where union activists could not organize they nonetheless gained sympathizers, as an increasing number of the working poor deplored the conditions in factories and shops.

There was a great deal of fluidity in the relations between artisan shop owners and employees. A report by the FRTS in 1930 underscored this point: "Almost all of our workers have their own tools. Sometimes they do salaried work for a contractor; at times they work as artisans in their own houses, totally on their own. At times, this same worker is a contractor-boss, who exploits the labor of one or more workers."[89] Miguel Mármol himself exemplifies this same fluidity. After working in "factories" in San Salvador, he had acquired a level of skill and knowledge of styles that allowed him to earn high wages and "extra pay" in the provincial town of San Martín because customers specifically requested his shoes. Prompted by a desire for economic independence, he acquired small loans to set up his own shop, employing seven workers. In his memoir, shaped by arguments within the left, he justified this move as necessary for political reasons—a union activist would waste valuable time and resources struggling to survive economically in the face of a repressive employer: "[The shop] was an excellent cloak behind which to organize revolutionary activity."[90]

The FRTS report considered this petit bourgeois class position a flaw, like the concomitant sins of pride and shame a characteristic of "petit-bourgeois consciousness." Mármol retrospectively tried to defend the nascent labor movement from accusations of an artisanal or petit bourgeois mentality. His memoir does, however, reveal a joy in being one's own master and in possessing such skills as those of a shoemaker, allowing one to resist being transformed into a proletarian. That Mármol at once owned a shoemaker's shop, employing workers, and at the same time participated actively in union organizing drives was not at all an anomaly in early–twentieth-century Latin America, or for that matter nineteenth-century Europe. As E. P. Thompson wrote: "It is easy enough to say that this culture was backward-looking or conservative. True enough, one direction of the great agitations of the artisans and outworkers continued over 50 years, was to resist being turned into a proletariat. When they knew that this cause was lost, yet they reached out again . . . and sought to achieve new and only imagined forms of social control."[91] Similarly, throughout Central America urban artisans and manufacturing workers were in the forefront of struggles for the Central American union and of opposition to imperialism and intervention by the United States. They also worked for the right to organize unions and for land reform. As Gould noted in Nicaragua, during the 1920s "obrerismo" had become the dominant political idiom in towns and cities, a radical democratic ideology that stressed the opposition to the agrarian élite and to imperialism of "obreros" (primarily meaning manual workers, including shop owners). The growing differentiation of the manufacturing sector did not have immediate effects on this cross-class political ideology. "Because of their own membership in the class of wage earners, the lack of previous class conflicts in the crafts, and the objective need to standardize prices and wages among workshops, the obreristas demanded rights for the workers as a whole, including their own employees."[92]

Obrerismo formed part of the gelatinous ideological field of the artisan and manufacturing worker. That field is often assumed to have been exclusively anarchist, but the history is in fact more complicated. Laclau's distinction of popular democratic and class interpellations is apposite. By popular-democratic Laclau refers to an identity in opposition to élite rule, "united to institutions in which democracy is materialized" (see chapter 3).[93] In this sense artisans were bearers of this popular democratic tradition as literate subalterns under assault from transformed production relations, the arbitrariness of authoritarian rule, and the oligarchic cultural forms of the society. At the same time, both artisans and manufacturing workers resisted different forms of proletarianization. In the end, this resistance to full-scale proletarianization and its immediate effects was a key factor in the growth and radicalization of the urban movement.

In El Salvador the effect of the world crisis, combined with the growing introduction of machinery into the manufacturing sector, thrust an increasing number of small shop owners into the ranks of salaried labor or the unemployed. Both artisans and manufacturing workers experienced the impact of what FRTS militants called "capitalist rationalization." In a way reminiscent of early-nineteenth-century Europe, the introduction of machinery in El Salvador's manufacturing sector both displaced the smallest shops and tended to increase workers' productivity and energy expenditure within the shops and factories that survived.[94] Following established patterns, the greater prevalence of much machinery and the initial effects of the crisis led employers to hire more adolescents and children. A report by the FRTS on youth labor describes Dickensian conditions: young workers in factories and shops toiled from 5:30 in the morning until 10 in the evening for the equivalent of twenty-five cents, roughly half what was paid to adults. The report stated that youths made up 90 percent of tile, cigarette, brewery, and commercial workers. The situation of female youths in the factories was even worse: "They work until they become pregnant by the boss or his sons. They are thrown on the street for the pettiest reasons: for refusing to accept the gallantries of the boss, or for being seen with other men, outside of the factory." In a separate report on textile workers, a union activist noted that "in addition to the brutal treatment, they get searched when they leave and they don't get a break during the whole day. Many workers are victimized by bosses and foremen, who order a worker to stay after work and then they rape her and commit all kinds of shameful acts; the victims' complaints mean nothing to the authorities as they only favor the interests of the capitalists and bosses."[95] The denunciation of this treatment of young women and men did not lead to massive urban unionization. On the contrary, the FRTS made but weak organizational inroads among factory workers. By 1930 the only exception was in La Constancia brewery, which had a clandestine union of one hundred members. However, what the FRTS did gain was a growing moral authority against these inhuman working conditions in the shops and factories.

Political conditions also influenced the rapid development of the labor movement during the late 1920s. The urban labor movement had grown slowly during the Melendez-Quiñónez years, in response to varying degrees of tolerance of political unionism by the regime. Under Romero Bosque, the government actively promoted urban unions and sought to rationalize labor management relations. His government promulgated three important mea-

sures: full legalization of urban union activity; labor-management concil-
iation commissions; and an eight-hour workday for urban workers—the
most important measure both because employers' resistance to it provoked
labor mobilization and because the exclusion of the rural working class
provided an immediate entrée for the FRTS into the haciendas and fincas.[96]
Employers' resistance to the promulgation of the eight-hour day in July
1929 provoked a rash of protests and work stoppages in hotels, in bakeries,
and on construction sites.[97] On the docks of Acajutla, the country's most
important port, a general strike of longshoremen and laborers in demand
of the eight-hour day shut down operations. The government sent in the
National Guard to compel the workers to work, but the union continued to
protest.[98]

Early in 1930 the FRTS led one of the most important strikes in the
building trades, at the site where a construction company with financing
from the United States was building the "La Chacra" baths and a reservoir
(the Holland Water tanks). The company decreed a pay reduction from
$1.50 to $1.00 a day. In response, six militants organized a march of over
seven hundred workers to the FRTS headquarters, where an assembly laid
out strike demands. Although the Guardia arrived, when faced with this
spontaneous but rapidly organized movement the company rescinded its
wage cut. Notwithstanding the victory and the size of the workforce, the
union gained only twenty-five new members.[99]

The urban labor movement reached neither the size nor the importance
of its contemporaries in South America and Mexico, and classic forms of
working-class militancy did not characterize its development. Rather, the
FRTS educated working-class militants and prepared them to organize in
the countryside. The union federation could also reach a larger number of
supporters ready to protest on the streets against the government and the
élite.

The U.S. embassy estimated that the "agitators" numbered from several
hundred to two thousand. It complained that Romero Bosque's government could easily "eradicate" them by arresting the leftist leadership but
lacked the will to do so. Yet Romero Bosque refused to jail urban labor
leaders as long as they stayed away from the fincas and haciendas. In
November in Santa Tecla, however, government forces broke up a demonstration by the FRTS under pressure from local landowners, who called for
stronger measures against "outside agitators" and feared that the organiz-

ing would spread to their farm workers. As a result of union organizing around the eight-hour day and improved wages, one thousand "leading citizens" wrote a letter during mid-1929 to President Romero Bosque, complaining about his lack of energy in quelling strikes and labor demonstrations. In response, Romero Bosque tightened his policies, asking the military to put down any attempted strikes or demonstrations.

The élite concern was now well placed. A proto-communist left had indeed won control of the leadership of the FRTS. As elsewhere in Latin America, in El Salvador communists, anarcho-syndicalists, and reformists battled for control of the labor movement throughout the 1920s. The victory of those aligned with the communists had much to do with their organizing capacity, particularly in the countryside, and very little to do with either the class composition of the different groups or their strategy and tactics based on their political understandings.

Although the pro-communist left dominated the FRTS by May 1930, the movement that it controlled was far too diverse and ideologically eclectic to coerce into party discipline. The Partido Comunista Salvadoreño (PCS), founded in March 1930, followed the Comintern Third Phase line, which stated that in effect all non-communist political forces were objectively allied with fascism and imperialism. Comintern rhetoric against social democrats was especially venomous. The PCS counseled abstention in the presidential elections of January 1931. Yet the rank and file of the labor movement, especially the rural sector, became inspired by the electoral campaign of the Laborista Arturo Araujo, whom the FRTS/PCS leadership dismissed as a "social-fascist."

Don Arturo, Social Democracy, and the Presidential Election

The political climate of the 1920s, compounded by the post-1929 economic crisis, contributed to popular support for the presidential campaign of Arturo Araujo, a wealthy entrepreneur and reformist from Sonsonate. Araujo, one of El Salvador's largest sugar and coffee producers, was quick to respond to Romero Bosque's opening of the political system. Most of his properties were in the Izalco-Armenia region;[100] like many of the country's landlords, he resided in the city of Santa Tecla. In addition to other farms and investments, he owned the Hacienda El Sunza, Izalco's largest hacienda, which contained the country's second-largest coffee and sugar mills.[101]

Unlike most members of the country's economic élite who preferred to do their political work behind the scenes, Araujo was an active reformer.[102] Educated in Great Britain, where he became exposed to the Labor Party, in 1918 he gave financial support to and participated in a workers' congress.[103] He ran as an opposition candidate in the presidential elections of 1919, as the Melendez-Quiñónez clan began to establish its control over the country's political machinery. After the elections were allegedly stolen, the National Guard was sent to his farms to suppress efforts to organize a revolt,[104] but the two hundred guardsmen were only able to arrest his father, Eugenio Araujo.[105] After the official candidate was installed, Araujo and General Juan Amaya attempted a cross-border revolt that apparently had the support of the Honduran government, entering El Salvador with three hundred supporters. The Salvadoran army easily defeated the Araujistas, and they had to retreat into Honduras.[106] Araujo returned from exile in 1923, and throughout the 1920s he opposed the Melendez-Quiñónez group. During these years the "Araujistas" were identified as enemies of the National Guard because of its role as the arbiter of political control at the local level.[107] Araujo, himself active in local politics, took advantage of the political opening of 1927 to increase his role. In 1929 he supported a populist candidate in the municipal elections of Armenia, Emeterio Torres, against a candidate supported by the local élite, the *gente regularizada*.[108]

One critical contribution of the Araujista movement during 1930 and 1931 was that it helped to unite urban movements with rural demands for reform. A vivid image of the strength of Araujo's base was the massive parade of peasants who followed him into the city of Sonsonate as part of the presidential campaign of 1931: "Don Arturo, who was at the head of the parade, mounted a purebred mare, imported from England, and marched at a tight pace, with his hat in his hand, and saluted the crowd that had gathered on the sidewalks, doorways, and balconies. . . . Some three thousand men on horseback followed don Arturo, four abreast, with their hats pulled down tight and their mounts reined in. . . . Behind this impressive parade of riders and horses came an immense mass of people on foot, made up of peasants."[109]

Araujo's most visible allies were Masferrer and Felipe Recinos, former leader of the FRTS.[110] Araujismo sometimes shared and at other times vied with the left for the support of workers and campesinos. At the local level Araujo's multiclass alliance represented a challenge to the old patronage networks controlled by élites; nationally it led to a reformist political movement unparalleled in Salvadoran history until the 1970s. The alliance between urban professionals and workers had roots in the decades-old political culture of urban reformism, but its extension into mass rural support that did not rely on patronage networks was unprecedented.

Araujo's Laborismo, a Salvadoran version of social democracy inspired by his firsthand knowledge of the British Labour Party and the diverse ideological currents of Central American reformism, raised hopes of land reform among the rural poor and of political and economic reform among urban workers and artisans. One observer at the U.S. embassy noted "all kinds of election promises which led many farmers and laborers to think that the millennium was likely once Araujo was elected. There was rumored . . . that the big coffee estates would be divided and every family given its acre of ground . . . the unrest of the last few days may be laid partially to the rural population's somewhat hastily drawn conclusion that the president has turned his back on them."[111] Once elected, Araujo acknowledged the weight of these demands but was hard-pressed to fulfill them quickly, in what became one of the critical failures of his administration.

Historians have often interpreted the election promises of Araujo as a demagogic device of false promises by his organizers. Instead, we suggest that the expectation of land reform was a form of demand making by Araujo's supporters and the relatively autonomous factions and organizations that mobilized in his support. While at the local level agrarian reform was clearly a component of support for Araujo, at the national level (and mostly in San Salvador) Araujo was sending a different message. Whatever Araujismo meant at the local level, in San Salvador Araujo made it clear that he did not favor land reform, and he reduced his claims to one thing: work for all. In his first major public message in November 1930 he explained: "I must state that I am not nor could I be a communist . . . but yes, I am convinced that we must satisfy the needs of the people or at least alleviate their suffering . . . but we must do so from the point of view of the laborista doctrine, through an equitative distribution of work, NOT OF LAND, as some people have maliciously claimed that I have proposed, so that each person produces for his own sustenance. I know our laws that rule us and I could not therefore promise the abolition of private property. Laborismo affirms 'work for all' as the basic principle of all improvement of social conditions."[112]

Despite its contradictions between national and local discourses, or perhaps precisely because of its multilayered character, Araujismo formed the most dynamic element in the presidential campaign of 1930. Rallies, demonstrations, meetings, and committees were all part of the heightened incorporation of thousands of people into the country's electoral system. Araujo received significant shows of support from urban factory workers and artisans in San Salvador and San Vicente, as well as his home base of Sonsonate, where there were large demonstrations in November and December.[113] He was also the only candidate to campaign in the countryside.[114] Tacuba, Atiquisaya, Masahuat, Cuisnahuat, Armenia, Izalco, Juayúa, and Sonsonate, towns that would play a central role in the revolt of 1932, all had strong Araujista chapters.[115] In many of these places Araujo's supporters quickly came into conflict with local political élites, who used anticommunism against them.[116] The strength of Araujismo was evident to government officials, who kept close tabs on the number and affiliation of registered voters. By December 1930 Araujo was recognized as the clear leader in the race, with nearly 41,000 registered voters and the only strong party machine. The closest candidate was Alberto Gómez Zarate, with thirty thousand registered voters and the support of the traditional patronage oficialista networks.[117]

The complex role of the military officers was paradoxically heightened with the breakdown of the Melendez-Quiñónez regimes. A military intelligence analyst with the U.S. government thought that Araujo had enough popular support to get elected without bringing General Hernández Martínez into his campaign as his vice-presidential candidate, but that his government would not last without the military's approval.[118] In a meeting at the presidential palace, Romero Bosque brokered the agreement for Araujo to combine forces with Martínez.[119]

While allowing for free elections, Romero Bosque played an important role in attempting to position the candidates in relation to well-established power centers like the National Assembly, the U.S. embassy, the military, and the banks. Already in early 1930 a group of "prominent" citizens had lobbied Romero Bosque to select a single candidate for the upcoming presidential elections.[120] U.S. intelligence operatives reported that the president sought to divide the voting among many candidates to ensure that the winner would have to meet the approval of the National Assembly, which he controlled. Romero Bosque personally favored Enrique Córdova, who he thought would be easier to influence than Gómez Zarate. Sectors of the coffee élite also supported Córdova. Viewed as the "official candidate," Gómez Zarate was the favorite of the remnants of the Melendez-Quiñiónez faction and the PND.[121]

Élite groups were not happy with the electoral results and accused the government of fraud. To no avail, they asked the U.S. embassy to intervene in the election.[122] The results gave Araujo a wide victory, with 46 percent of the vote and much stronger majorities in the west:

Araujo 101,000

Gómez Zárate 64,000

Córdova 32,000

Gen. Claramount 16,000

Molina 4,000[123]

Araujo's sweeping victory was a testament to the power of the democratic opposition and labor movements that flourished during the 1920s. And yet the hope and promise that Araujismo embodied would be shattered shortly after he assumed office. The rank and file of the labor movement had provided his margin of victory because it was willing to disregard its sectarian leaders' vitriol against Araujo. Yet they had fought too hard and learned too much over the previous years to shrug their collective shoulders when the new president did not deliver tangible results.

Araujismo had to face expressions of anti-oligarchical popular anger which pushed hard against the pace and moderation of its reformist program. Events in San Miguel, eastern El Salvador, population 35,000, suggest the depths of that anger with which Araujo would have to contend. Popular grievances in the city were directed against a tiny group of landowner-merchants who also controlled local politics. The most notable member of the élite was Mauricio Meardi, probably the wealthiest man in the country. He was the owner of the Compañia Agrícola Migueleña, an unusual entrepreneur whose vast interests bridged coffee production, processing, marketing, retail sales, importing and exporting, construction, grain production, and finance. In 1934 his principal company was valued at $1.5 million.[124]

On 22 October 1930 a guilty verdict of stealing against José Soto, a commercial employee of a Meardi store, triggered a riot.[125] That day six hundred people, chanting "abajo el capital," marched to the courthouse to protest the verdict. The crowd then marched to the homes of the judge, the prosecutor, and prominent merchants. The next day the National Guard broke up a protest meeting, arresting two leaders, Antonio Mayorga and Heriberto Romero.

After the arrests protesters gathered in the plaza and called for a demonstration that evening. Suddenly the National Guard attacked the group and arrested six protesters, as the lieutenant colonel in charge of the military contingent shot into the crowd. That night three thousand people gathered and marched to the police garrison, demanding that Mayorga and Romero be freed. Later the crowd attacked several élite houses and Meardi stores, destroying and looting much of their property and stealing $10,000 from a safe as well as some weapons.[126]

On 24 October the government placed San Miguel under a state of siege and sent troop reinforcements. By the next day the local commander claimed that the city was pacified. Although both "Tato" Meardi, the primary target of the mobilization, and observers at the U.S. embassy believed that the movement was inspired by communists, in fact the left had no organizational role in the movement.[127] If Meardi and the U.S. State Department were off base about the origins of the movement, they were right that the violent protest was symptomatic of serious unrest and popular anger at the powerful merchant-planter élite and its continued control over institutions of government. That the left did not capitalize on this popular discontent in San Miguel revealed its geographical limitations. The dramatic expression of popular anger, however, and the language and iconography through which it was expressed—"abajo el Capital" and the specific attacks on élite symbols—announced to all concerned parties that throughout the country powerful forms of populist ideology lay just beneath the surface of social life.

Chapter Three

Fiestas of the Oppressed: The Social
Geography and Culture of Mobilization

Every night they had their comités. —Sotero Linares

They were real fiestas but they were also meetings. —Ramón Vargas

The confluence of popular anger against the élite, a large cadre of union organizers, and the strength of anti-oligarchical reformism created a propitious field for labor and the left. Indeed the rapid development of a revolutionary movement and the decisive role of rural subaltern groups in transforming the leftist agenda make El Salvador in 1929–31, along with Cuba in 1933, stand out in the history of the Latin American left. In this chapter we argue that a key to the success of the mobilization was the construction by the leftist militants, rural workers, and peasants of a new discursive, cultural, and political field as they struggled with employers and the state.

Between Town and Country

We have seen that in 1927 urban artisans in the nascent labor movement, operating under conditions of relative tolerance on the part of the administration of President Pío Romero Bosque, turned their attention to the countryside.

Beyond the relatively benign attitude of the government, the social and geographic accessibility of rural workers was the single most important factor favoring the union movement. Urban workers and artisans as well as indigenous and ladino campesinos opened new spaces of sociability that permitted communication of these new, revolutionary ideas. This interaction built upon and expanded existing cantonal and kin-based networks in the towns and countryside, and these networks expanded greatly as the growth of the coffee economy threw more rural folk into the labor market. The social distance between the urban artisans and rural workers was not insurmountable; there were numerous points of contact. Carpenters, for example, worked on haciendas, and campesinos sold their goods in urban markets. Urban youths and families participated in the coffee harvest.[1]

Jorge Fernández Anaya, a Mexican who played a crucial role in the FRTS and helped found the PCS, compared the favorable circumstances in El Salvador with the adverse ones in Guatemala: "It was undoubtedly very easy to get access to a hacienda [in El Salvador] and to get them to listen to you."[2] He observed: "In El Salvador, it was easier. Peons were Indians only in some places. Not all of the indígenas spoke Spanish but there were always people who could translate, and in any case it was easier to speak with Indians in El Salvador than with those of Guatemala. They had consciousness and this was important, because when we spoke to them about the interests of the working class, of the laborers, they grasped the problems. . . . There was a difference between the peon and the urban worker. But when you talked to the peons we understood each other, you could explain, and talk all you needed to."[3]

The artisans and workers were moved by a revolutionary ideal of equality, without themselves becoming engaged in direct class struggle. As noted in chapter 2, the level of social conflict in the cities was low in 1929 and 1930. Yet these literate workers were very receptive to the messages of equality that permeated all currents and stages of union activity, from reformists to anarcho-syndicalists to the FRTS, dominated by the PCS. Organizing among the campesinado deepened the meanings of that message. As in other times and places, urban workers and artisans became enamored of their new role as the carriers of revolutionary enlightenment, here rooted in El Salvador's radical liberalism of the late nineteenth century.[4]

Urban workers and artisans played a major role in the early stages of the rural labor mobilization. Artisans and artisanal workers (in small manufacturing shops) were critical in the origins of labor movements throughout Europe and the Americas, and thus in this sense El Salvador was not unique. Even in neighboring countries of Central America, artisans were pioneers of the labor movements. In Costa Rica artisans helped organize the powerful banana workers' union, which launched one of the largest strikes in the region's history. In Nicaragua during the 1940s shoemakers, printers, tailors, bakers, and other artisans journeyed to the countryside to organize workers. What made the Salvadoran case unique were the scope and success of the organizing drive, in part a function of the high level of sacrifice demanded by the FRTS, as revealed in a report by an ISR representative in March 1930: "During my stay in El Salvador, I would attend a different activity every night: elementary lessons on unionism, economic principles; these lessons are then put into practice on Saturday and Sunday. During the Thursday meeting, the organizers are elected and then they take propaganda material and instructions to various towns and haciendas; over the course of these weekly visits they help to organize and then support unions. Collections help to defray travel costs but if that is not possible, the organizer has to carry out the mission on foot. . . . on Monday, the compañeros listen to the organizers' reports. Then, they develop new orientations and demands based on the reports."[5]

Rotating organizers traveled between ten and fifty kilometers every weekend. Typically they carried union and political lessons in the form of graphics. Jorge Schlesinger's book, written as a cautionary tale for the Guatemalan labor movement (1946), reproduced leftist graphics to show the insidiousness of communist propaganda at work (see figure, page 66). To some extent the graphics reveal reductionist Marxist-Leninist analysis in pictures, especially the ones that describe the links between the imperial interests of the United States and Britain and the various presidential candidates in the elections of January 1931. Yet other graphics show an impressive degree of didactic skill in that they relate abstract ideas to aspects of contemporary reality. At the same time they offer a glimpse of the mentality of the revolutionary artisan or worker and his imagined point of intellectual contact with the rural masses. One graphic depicts the "Feudal Regime" and the French Revolution. The commentary then skips ahead some eighty years and betrays the still-strong revolutionary syndicalist influence by suggesting that with the Commune of 1871 the proletariat gained power but

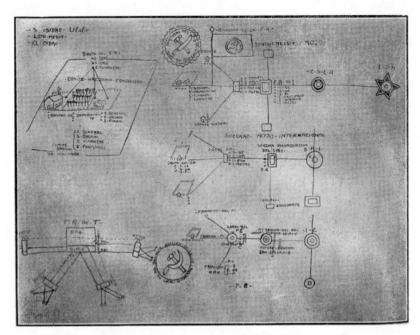

Agitprop outline of Salvadoran communist organization, from *Revolución Comunista*,
by Jorge Schlesinger, Guatemala 1946.

failed because there were no unions. Another graphic presents the "Capitalist Regime–Bourgeois Republic." Capital and capitalists are represented
separately at the top. Immediately below are the various types of "yellow"
unionists, followed by the military, "secretarios" (higher-level bureaucrats), and lawyers. A comment, "all of their titles are a gift of the bourgeoisie," applies to all three groups. A street labeled Clase Pobre divides the
image. The press is the only institution above the street with links to the
FRTS. Below the street are different kinds of taxes on the poor. Inexplicably,
the words "death factory" are included in the list. At the bottom of the page
are the unions and the *comités sindicales*.[6]

Although the messages were sectarian, there is little possibility that this
idiosyncratic graphic was copied from a Comintern manual, because its
explicit and implicit messages deviated from the official revolutionary ideology. The notion that military officials, bureaucrats, and lawyers are all
"awarded" their degrees and titles and status by the bourgeoisie, and that
the *colegio* sits squarely on the wealthy side of the street, is more revealing of

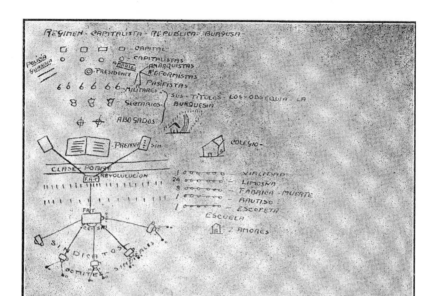

Agitprop outline of class structure of Salvadoran society, from *Revolución Comunista*, by Jorge Schlesinger.

the intellectual resentment and populism of the urban poor, most of whom had an elementary school education, than it is a reflection of a Marxist view. Moreover, the consistent message that the unions formed the key element of the revolutionary process and of the "dictatorship of the proletariat" was also far more akin to revolutionary syndicalism than to Marxism-Leninism. The rough ideological framework of the graphics reflects the ideological tumult of the "maximalist" period in Europe and South America (1919–23), in which militants gravitated from communism to a revolutionary syndicalist current and back again with little difficulty, given the collectively perceived imminence of the revolution.

The one schema that does give importance to the PCS and the Scorro Rojo Internacional (SRI) is curious in that it shows the coexistence of the SRI and the local union on the same hacienda, while at the departmental and national levels the SRI maintained no formal linkage with either the FRTS or the PCS (see figure, above). What probably struck both the activist who drew the picture and the campesino who looked at it was the connectedness of these movements that operated through space: from the hacienda to the pueblo to the department to the capital, and then beyond the borders,

closure No. 1
erican Legation   San Salvador

Despatch No 390
Nov. 10, 1930

MANIFIESTO

DE LA UNION SINDICAL DE PROLETARIOS DE SONSONATE

——ooooo——

A TODOS LOS TRABAJADORES Y TRABAJADORAS DE LA CIUDAD Y DEL CAMPO
ESTA REGION

——oo——

A TODOS LOS TRABAJADORES Y TRABAJADORAS DE LA CIUDAD Y DEL CAMPO DE
TODOS LOS PAISES

——oo——

CAMARADAS:

La Unión Sindical de Proletarios, una vez más, ha ocupado su puesto de combate y de lucha en los momentos en que se agudiza la crisis de toda la economía semi-feudal de este país, economía regulada, controlada y dirigida por los financistas de Wall Street y los estadistas de Washington.

En estos momentos, en que la economía nacional está abocada y a una bancarrota total, en que se advierte que la burguesía nacional parasitaria y semi-feudal de este país semi-colonial, trata de "justificar" la penetración del National City Bank, la explotación de nuestra clase se intensifica más y más. No puede ser de otro modo, porque el National City Bank, es el órgano financiero del imperialismo yanki que opera la concentración de la pequeña propiedad agraria en los países semi-coloniales de la América Latina en la que se encuentra como aliadas a las burguesías semi-feudales como se ve en este país y en las antillas: Cuba, Santo Domingo, Haití, Puerto Rico etc, etc.

La crisis cafetalera, que ha sido provocada por las maniobras financieras del imperialismo yanki, no tiene solución dentro del régimen actual puesto que éste la pretende resolver entregando las riquezas nacionales en manos de los imperialistas de Wall Street y echando sobre los hombros de nuestra clase laboriosa el peso de esa crisis, disminuyendo los salarios de por sí miserables, racionalizando la producción agrícola, para echar a la calle a millares de trabajadores, que están condenados al hambre, a la miseria y a la desnudez.

La Unión Sindical de Proletarios, que marcha, en su lucha implacable de clases, bajo las consignas de la Internacional Sindical Roja, directora de nuestra Confederación Sindical Latino Americana y de nuestra Federación Regional de Trabajadores de El Salvador, sólo encuentra, como único medio, para suprimir las miserias que nos impone el sistema capitalista, la organización de hierro de nuestra clase explotada para abatir a los explotadores y sostiene con toda energía revolucionaria las reivindicaciones económicas inmediatas de nuestra Federa-

ción: Supresión del fondo de vialidad, las ocho horas de trabajo, aumento de salario, trabajo y pan para los desocupados, que se encuentran en situación de hambre, de desnudez y de miseria pavorosas.

Sobre la base de esas reivindicaciones económicas inmediatas, la Unión Sindical de Proletarios, llevó a cabo una manifestación grandiosa el 30 de julio último culminando con la deportación, el encarcelamiento de algunos de nuestros compañeros; pero nuestra clase, fuerte en el espíritu de combatividad diaria, persistente, tenaz e implacable, no se amedrentó ante los atropellos policíacos de aquella fecha; y el 21 de septiembre recién pasado, acudió al mitin nacional que organizó la Sección Salvadoreña del Socorro Rojo Internacional para protestar, indignados, por los encarcelamientos de los compañeros de Santa Ana, Sta. Tecla, San Salvador, Tacuba, Jayaque, Zacatecoluca, Nuevo Cuscatlán, La Labor, Juayúa, Nahuizalco, Santiago Texacuangos, Los Planes de Renderos, etc., etc., y a quienes se les aplicaba, y aún aplica a algunos de ellos en estos momentos la más descarada JUSTICIA DE CLASE BURGUESA. No obstante que nuestra reunión se celebraba dentro de la mayor disciplina de clase, fué asaltada por la Policía y la Guardia Nacional nuestro edificio social, habiendo sido encarcelados 31 compañeros de los cuales fué flajelado, herido de la cabeza y roto de la dentadura, el compañero Luis S. Maraña; por el agente de policía PILAR HERNANDEZ y el cabo DONATILIO RAMIREZ, verdaderos perros asalariados de la burguesía semi-feudal y del imperialismo yanki.

El decreto fascista del 12 de agosto próximo pasado, con el cual se ha puesto en estado de sitio a la clase trabajadora, la represión gubernamental fascista llevada a cabo contra las organizaciones sindicales revolucionarias, y todos los otros hechos que nosotros denunciamos ante nuestra clase explotada, son los síntomas de la descomposición creciente del régimen capital ta del que será enterrador el proletariado junto con el campesinado de todos los países que en estos ...

:: Contra la Opresión Capitalista: EL FRENTE UNICO OBRERO y CAMPESINO !!
:: VIVA La Unión Sindical de Proletarios de Sonsonate !!
:: VIVA La Federación Regional de Trabajadores de El Salvador !!
:: VIVA La Confederación Sindical Latino Americana !!
:: VIVA La Internacional Sindical Roja !!

EL COMITE EJECUTIVO DE LA UNION SINDICAL DE P. DE S.

Sonsonate, Octubre de 1930.

Manifesto of FRTS, 1930, from U.S. National Archive.

especially to that land where the proletariat had seized power. After the union militants and campesinos talked about the meaning of the graphics, the campesinos would then discuss conditions on their finca or hacienda. Finally they would draw up a list of demands to be discussed at the Monday meetings in the urban center.

Beyond the effective use of graphics with a largely illiterate audience, other union practices specifically helped bridge the social distance between the urban organizers and the rural poor. The very act of traveling on foot to isolated cantons was impressive to the rural people. Similarly, word of the struggles and successes of the FRTS on behalf of the campesinos preceded the organizers. Mármol, for example, recalled that the fishermen's union he helped to organize in Ilopango went on to mobilize the workers of a nearby hacienda and won significant concessions, making them famous: "from Ilopango we went on foot to the Eastern and Western provinces, to Atiquizaya, to los Amates, to Zacetecoluca, to Chalatenango, etc. The delegates from Ilopango were heartily applauded by everyone at those meetings."[7]

In fact many unions were organized "spontaneously": labor organizers would often show up in a canton only to find it already organized. As a FRTS document reported, "continual pleas from the haciendas and villages to the Federation for organizers, and many times when they arrive on the scene they find organizations already in place, ready for action; the campesinos state: 'here change will rule.' "[8]

Both the spontaneous growth of the movement and the fluidity between town and countryside recall the Andalusian anarchist movement. Literate village craftsmen, known as obreros conscientes, played a vital role in educating their rural proletarian neighbors about libertarian communism and the abolition of the great estates on which they labored. Díaz del Moral painted a sketch of the rapidly expanding movement in the period after the First World War, which was led by "obreros conscientes" but rapidly developed a life of its own: "We who lived through that time in 1918–19 will never forget that amazing sight. In the fields, in the shelters and courts, wherever peasants met to talk, for whatever purpose, there was only one topic of conversation, always discussed seriously and fervently: the social question . . . In a few weeks the original nucleus of 10 or 12 adepts would be converted into the 100s; in a few months practically the entire working population, seized by ardent proselytism, propagated the flaming ideal frenziedly . . . once the village was converted, the agitation spread."[9]

The Anadalusian obreros conscientes, the literate artisans, had a role certainly akin to those of El Salvador. As Miguel Mármol pointed out, the hardest part of organizing was the initial effort to "crack the hard shell of tradition, fear and suspicion."[10] Commenting on earlier failed attempts to organize in the countryside, Mármol remarked that the militants had "created an impenetrable barrier between their 'enlightenment' and the 'backwardness' they ascribed to the people." Rather, Mármol and his compañeros started directly from the immediate expressions of need and interest by the fishermen and campesinos. Then, after they built up confidence and the campesinos and fishermen articulated their needs and feelings, the organization emerged, greeted like "the rains of May."

The elastic borders between town and country favored Mármol, himself of campesino stock, and in general aided the development of the rural labor movement throughout the country. Although there was a significant educational and cultural gulf between artisans and rural workers, the social geography that separated them was eased by the the tendency of many rural workers to actually reside in the same cities or towns, even if in more marginal areas. The fluidity of town and country was not unique to those two areas, and in varying ways, in Cuba and Nicaragua similar patterns of social geography also aided rural labor organization. In Cuba the massive expansion and the seasonal nature of the sugar industry contributed to relatively close links between industrial and rural labor, and a demographic circulation between town and country aided the development of the revolutionary movement of 1933.[11] In Nicaragua, even before the cotton boom, many rural workers and campesinos were neighbors in urban barrios in provincial towns like Chinandega. That proximity aided in the early development of the rural labor movement.[12] With the cotton boom and its attendant seasonal labor fluctuations, the divide between rural and urban declined even more. Some observers of the revolutionary insurrections of 1978–79 ascribe importance to the participation of seasonal cotton workers in the urban insurrection.

La Causa and La Presa

The labor movement suffered a major reversal in December 1929, but one that to some extent energized the movement and probably helped the left to consolidate its control. In a nationally famous case, on La Presa, a large plantation in Coatepeque, the National Guard evicted 345 colono families in the middle of a storm, claiming that the union had called for expropriation and subsequently distributing the land to the colonos. In reality the union had threatened a strike in demand of higher wages and an end to payments for water. But the élite family that owned the hacienda had the ear of the president of the Republic.

Guillermo Borbón, owner of La Presa, wrote to the president about the events of 3 March, offering a rare glimpse of élite attempts to remain in control of their workers: "For some days now, we have noticed that the Workers' Regional, with its base in Armenia, has intensified its campaign of subversive and Bolshevik propaganda among the hacienda colonos. They call on the colonos not to work on the hacienda and they hold unauthorized meetings; their speeches try to inculcate in the colonos the idea that the hacienda belongs to them and that they should sieze control of it . . . The (union) doesn't only spread this propaganda at la 'Presa,' but all over the country . . . it poses a serious danger for the Nation."[13] After Romero Bosque received Borbón's telegram he ordered the departmental governor to send a larger contingent to the hacienda, claiming that the workers had "violated the law." The local mayor reported, however, that the workers were only demanding a wage increase: "they acted so that they would get paid one more real."[14] In response to the arrests Miguel Martínez wrote to the interior minister, underscoring the contradiction between the democratic commitments of the government and workers' rights: "The Federal Executive Council demands the immediate liberty of the (imprisoned) compañeros . . . Even more, we believe that the actions hurt the freedom of organization, the most elementary rights that workers possess. Those measures are reactionary and strip the rights of the exploited to organize and push for economic improvement."[15]

Other letters from union leaders protested the arrests and highlighted the cycle of repression, outrage, and further action.[16] The FRTS turned the arrests of their four *compañeros* into a cause célèbre and mobilized mass demonstrations demanding their release. In short, they turned a defeat into a highly successful mobilizing issue.

Wage cuts, abysmal working conditions, and an absence of planter hegemony created optimal conditions for labor organizing throughout the coffee highlands. A phrase reportedly uttered by oligarchs—"Soon they will only come to work for the tortillas"—synthesizes the degree of élite arrogance and the severity of the crisis facing rural labor. Beyond this generalized breeding ground of discontent, we need to turn to case studies to better understand the mechanics of organization. Let us consider two relatively successful organizational drives, one on a hacienda and the other based in a town surrounded by coffee fincas. These cases highlight key characteristics of the FRTS organizing drive: the specifically cantonal form of organization, the festive form of urban meetings, and the exceptionally important role of lower-level *caporales* (foremen) in the rural unions. The form of cantonal union organization was particularly appropriate. Union members on each finca elected delegates who would then form the steering committee of the canton-based organization. At the most basic level, when labor organizers visited the canton they facilitated the organization and development of the union, most importantly keeping its activities out of view of the finca owners and managers. As police surveillance shut off the possibility of open urban meetings, the cantonal form of organization became increasingly important. The following description of union activity on the San Isidro hacienda provides us with some insight into how the labor movement could consolidate itself even though it did not follow a typical path of union organization: preliminary work, strikes, some bargaining success, and then more growth, reaching some level of strength before state intervention. Notwithstanding the growing control of the movement by the left and an intense rhetorical pitch of class struggle, there were fewer than ten strikes in the cities and countryside during the first period of rapid growth, from November 1929 to August 1931.[17]

San Isidro

Although strike activity per se was uncommon, rural workers and colonos engaged extensively in other forms of resistance that threatened élite political and economic domination. In January 1931 Gregorio Cortez Cordero organized meetings of a hundred workers in a ravine near Hacienda San Isidro, the region's largest coffee- and cane-producing hacienda, near Armenia. The size of the meetings revealed that the organizing drive had as yet only involved a small minority of the hacienda: a population of 2,400 people resided on San Isidro and an additional thousand laborers toiled at harvest time. Yet a newspaper article offered an overheated account of the activity: "They pass out communist leaflets and they urge workers to attack those who do not agree with those principles. Moreover, we have reports that the mayordomos and capataces are in dire straits as they are constantly threatened when they try to carry out the hacienda's orders."[18] Despite its alarmist tone, the article does highlight the union tactics at the point of production.

Social geography favored the union organizers at San Isidro. Much of the workforce resided in small and relatively proximate communities, at the centers of different fincas within the confines of the hacienda. Hundreds of other workers lived in autonomous cantons, primarily El Guayabo and Los

Mangos. Even though these families referred to themselves as colonos because they rented land and worked on the hacienda, they differed from traditional colonos in that they were not obliged to work and lived in their own dwellings. In their communities these peasant laborers formed strong ties of solidarity, confronting together their dependence on the hacienda for land and labor. El Guayabo and los Mangos were a short distance from the sugar fields and coffee groves of San Isidro but outside the direct control of management, and they became sites of intense and radical union activism. The hacienda also employed seasonal labor from the indigenous municipality of Nahuizalco and the bi-ethnic municipality of Izalco. Over seventeen hundred Nahuizalqueño rural laborers were already organized by mid-1930, and thus in all likelihood contributed significantly to labor organization at San Isidro.

Although labor organizers could take advantage of similar developments on other haciendas, at least one characteristic that favored labor was unique to San Isidro. Many *Volcaneños*, ladinos from villages on the slopes of the Volcán de Santa Ana, worked on the hacienda. Volcaneños had a long tradition of taking part in revolts and resisting state authority.[19] These people—ladinos—whose physical and cultural isolation conditioned the development of their own Spanish dialect had a reputation for violent behavior. Informants from San Isidro recall the important role of Felix Ascencio. Among other accomplishments, he reduced the number of machete fights among laborers. One informant recalls him addressing a worker, "Muchá, why are you fighting with a compañero de trabajo?" His charisma seemed to have carried the day. Ascencio, when organizing his compañeros, used class-rooted populist lines that remained etched in the collective memory of survivors from the epoch: "Un día San Isidro será de la majada" (One day San Isidro will belong to the crushed).[20]

The actions of both Felix Ascencio and another San Isidro union activist, Margarita Turcios's father, highlight the role of caporales in the labor movement. Nominally members of management, caporales typically received 50–75 percent more income than ordinary workers. But their higher salary scale did not necessarily alienate them from the rank and file. In their organizing they were able to make use of their greater grasp of the economics of the coffee industry, thanks in part to their literacy. Literacy not only enhanced their ability to understand the mechanisms of exploitation but made them the ideal locutors of the radical urban workers who visited

Margarita Turcios,
San Isidro. Courtesy
of the Museo de la
Palabra y la Imagen.

the fincas and haciendas. By and large, their job was not directly dependent on increasing the levels of productivity of the workforce (as opposed to ensuring the fulfillment of basic production goals), and therefore they were often viewed with respect by the jornaleros. Such was the case with Jesús Gúzman and Abrahám Gónzalez in Los Amates (a coffee canton west of Santa Tecla), coffee finca caporales who became the principal leaders of the coffee workers' union and later of Socorro Rojo. Gónzalez worked under the authority of a general foreman, and despite his union and later SRI militancy he worked harmoniously with the management of the finca. Gúzman, who worked on the other main coffee finca in the canton, was responsible for bringing the organization to the area, as he had befriended the FRTS organizer from Santa Tecla, Frutos Castillo. The two worked closely together and Castillo was a frequent visitor to Los Amates, accompanied by Gúzman.[21]

Miguel Velásquez was a caporal on the sugarcane, cattle, and coffee hacienda La Labor, in the Atiquizaya region. Originally a captain in the National Guard, he resigned for reasons that remain obscure and took the job on the hacienda. He became extremely well respected for his many talents in the field and his compassionate treatment of the field hands. This caudillo-like figure provided a powerful counterweight to the landlord, Onofre Durán, a man who the campesinos believed had made a pact with the devil.[22] When Velásquez started organizing the field hands, even those on La Labor who did not wish to join refused to turn him in. His reputation spread to neighboring fincas and haciendas. Similarly, one of the most important labor and left figures in the country, Modesto Ramírez, had worked as a caporal on a hacienda near Ilopango, east of San Salvador.

The organizing drive in Jayaque, a town surrounded by mid-sized commercial coffee fincas, twenty-eight kilometers southwest of Santa Tecla in the
department of La Libertad, shared some of the characteristics of the San
Isidro experience.[23] In particular, labor activists based in Armenia were
fundamental in the development of both unions. The Armenia branch of the
FRTS was important thanks both to its central location in the coffee zone
and to the activities of Gregorio ("Goyo") Cordero Cortéz. Known for carrying out his work on horseback, he is still widely remembered, perhaps more
than any other union activist in the West.[24] Cordero Cortéz was a founding
member of the Sindicato de Oficios Varios in Armenia, and he owned and
operated a small farm in the canton Las Tres Ceibas. At the FRTS congress in
May 1930, when the delegates from Guayabo questioned Fernandez Anaya's
sectarian stance against smallholders in the labor movement, they cited the
exemplary activities of Cortez Cordero. After the mass expulsion of the
colonos from La Presa, Goyo Cortéz became the key manager of their
defense, at the same time that he continued his organizational work.

In March 1930 a leaflet circulated that contained this text: "Invitation. La
Unión de Trabajadores de Jayaque issues a formal call to attend a meeting
on Sunday the 16th in the house of Manuel Murillo to discuss important
matters such as better salaries, the 8-hour day, better treatment; we are
exploited, poorer every day."[25] Murillo, an electrician, had recently arrived in
town from Las Cuchillas near Santa Ana, where state authorities had just
crushed the labor union on the hacienda in La Presa. He probably worked
with the *sindicalistas* in Armenia, who had come to the defense of the La
Presa colonos. The Murillos brought with them some resources. In addition
to his work as an electrician, he had a small finca and his wife set up a
business in town. The meetings at the Murillo household had the appearance of fiestas, with lots of *chelate* (a nonalcoholic, corn-based beverage)
and tamales. Although drinking was frowned upon, there was often music
and singing. The original small group of artisans quickly grew as rural
laborers started showing up for the Sunday meetings. Soon the house could
no longer hold the crowd and the union had to rent a small building in
town. Although somewhat less festive, the meetings in the rented building
were no less memorable. Once when Murillo was speaking to the assem-
bled members, two small campesino boys, dressed in rags, leaned against

the open windows. He gazed up at them and spoke to the crowd: "These hungry little kids break your heart. It's for them that we have to struggle." Murillo also punctuated his speeches with the phrase, "We can't go on just working for the tortillas!" The response was always thunderous applause, and the phrase "working only for the tortillas" was increasingly used as a rallying cry throughout the region. When fincas and haciendas stopped supplying their meager portions of rice and beans, workers needed to purchase the food at the company store, and sometimes workers received no pay once the value of their purchases was deducted from their wages.

From the small group at the end of 1929, the Jayaque union grew to 284 members by May 1930. Jayaque activists had also spurred the organization of another union composed of fifty coffee workers in the *caserío* of La Labor, four kilometers away.[26]

Fiestas and Meetings

Young boys who managed to attend the meetings remember the festive air above all else. These poor town boys witnessed the momentary transformation of the jornaleros into animated, friendly, and thoughtful people who became familiar with those such as Murillo and other town artisans who occupied a distinctly higher perch on the social hierarchy. Although they were too young to absorb many of the details, the basic thrust of the message was clear enough: *social equality*.[27] In a sense the meetings themselves foreshadowed a world where equality would prevail. Descriptions from the departments of Ahauchapán, Sonsonate, and La Libertad are remarkably similar in their emphasis on the atmosphere in the meetings. But there were differences between the relatively open meetings in the towns and cities and the usually clandestine ones in the countryside. After the anticommunist decree of August 1930 and the accompanying wave of arrests, most meetings were clandestine and held in the countryside. The movement baptized those meetings with the name *reuniones de barranca* (ravine meetings). One nonparticipant in the Izalco region recalls, "Every night they had their comités (meetings)." Rockets or conch shell horns announced the nocturnal meetings, typically attended by sixty to a hundred men and women. Testimonies suggest that the reuniones de barranca were emotionally charged and uplifting. Miguel Mármol described some of the meetings from 1929 and 1930 in the area around Lake Ilopango as well attended and exciting: "The nighttime meeting we called in a place known as Cujapa caused a sensation . . . I remember we went there from Ilopango as delegates from our Union . . . and when our arrival was announced the applause resounded all through the darkness. To get to these meetings we had to walk over many roads and paths . . . Everybody brought their own food and provision to these gatherings. It was moving to see peasant families arrive with all their kids, their bundles of tortillas, coffee, and sometimes even mats to sleep on when necessary. Whenever the union . . . had a chance to, a couple of steers or some pigs would be slaughtered beforehand to be shared amongst those attending."[28]

The open meetings in towns and cities exhibited an even more festive air that often disguised and perhaps even enhanced their serious purpose. In the cantons of Izalco, for example, union (and later SRI) meetings were fiestas, and chicha and tamales were served. In Atiquizaya one informant recalls that "they were real fiestas but they were also meetings where all the workers and campesinos took part."[29] Again, cooking and eating tamales were a high point of the festivities. In Los Gramales, in the hacienda district near San Julián, "the meetings turned into *parrandas* [parties characterized by drinking, music, and dance]. At most meetings, the participants sang revolutionary songs and rancheros."

The ubiquity of these lively meetings is intriguing.[30] It is hard to imagine that the festivities actually camouflaged the meetings, or that more than the occasional policeman was actually fooled. It is doubtful that dozens of rural folk streamed into a relatively small town to gather at the home of an artisan without raising suspicion. And it seems unlikely that more than a few campesinos would attend the meeting only for the social aspects. In other words, a purely functional explanation would not capture its meaning for the participants. Rather, these meetings suggest the emergence of a new form of cross-class sociability.[31]

The festive meetings recall Victor Turner's concepts of liminality and communitas. Turner defined liminality as "a state of being in between successive participations in social milieux dominated by social structural considerations."[32] This was a moment of tremendously creative social possibilities, prefiguring future social development and change. Although Turner's own studies in Africa focused on societies in which liminality formed part of a preordained ritual process, he also saw its spontaneous gestation in movements that emerged in response to radical structural change.[33] Liminal (or threshold) situations are propitious for the emergence of communitas, which is not a geographically based or kinship-based community: "the social bonds of communitas are anti-structural in the sense that they are undifferentiated, equalitarian, direct, extant, non rational, existential, I-Thou (in Feuerbach's and Buber's sense) relationships. Communitas is spontaneous, immediate, concrete—it is not shaped by norms, it is not institutionalized . . . Communitas does not merge identities; it liberates them from conformity to general norms, though this is a necessarily transient condition if society is to continue to operate in an orderly fashion."[34]

Here Turner followed the German theologian Martin Buber in drawing a distinction between I-Thou and I-It relationships. I-Thou relationships are unmediated by societal or ideological structures and engage the whole human being. I-It relationships are mediated by things. For Buber the I-thou relation is inherent in the notion of "we," which is in turn the basis of solidarity, the foundation of human communities and a new society: "a new culture, a new totality of spirit may come into being only if there will again be true community and togetherness, actual living together and with each other, a living immediacy between people."[35] Buber's constant refrain, "All real life is meeting," signals the usefulness of the concept of communitas in the Salvadoran context precisely because it forces us to focus our attention on the broader issue of how these new interpersonal relationships developed between people who previously had little to do with each other and whose cultural spheres were quite distinct. Let us further explore the fiesta form of meetings. First, militants extended a formal invitation to an individual. The invitation, whether to a fiesta or to a meeting, resembled a "gift" in that according to local codes it had to be reciprocated. This certainly created an obligation and occasionally an excuse to authorities: "I was invited [so therefore I attended]." Conversely, if one was not invited, then one would not participate in the movement—you could not, as it were, crash a meeting or fiesta. For the invitees, both campesino and artisans, the town festivals, as throughout the Americas, were always joyous occasions that mixed religiosity with iconoclastic behavior tending to momentarily challenge social hierarchies. Thus the fiesta or meeting was a readily acceptable social form available to the artisans and the campesinos. The content of these discussions is largely lost to us, but the form of communication and something of the meaning reside in the consciousness of those who remember them through oral testimony. We do know that the early union discussions in 1929 and early 1930 focused mainly on wages, working conditions, and social equality, and that later meetings of the Socorro Rojo emphasized above all else the struggle for land. They also probably stressed the Soviet example more frequently.

Most significantly, these meetings represented liminal moments in which new social modalities emerged involving artisans, urban workers, smallholders, and rural workers. Previously, urban and rural folks had interacted in a myriad of ways, but not as equals. These meeting-fiestas in constituting the unions began to create a new identity of "proletarians" who were socially equal. If two members passed each other on a path, road, or street they exchanged the greeting "Salud, camarada," and they used the term "camarada" constantly to consecrate their new identity as equals. Whatever negative connotations the history of communism has bestowed on this term, there is ample evidence in testimonies that campesinos used this term with a great deal of enthusiasm. Thus the meetings were important in creating a new sense of dignity and empowerment among the rural poor. They also provided an educational forum in which new grassroots leaders would emerge. Sotero Linares, who lived in a canton of Izalco, recalled, "They had their leader in Izalco where they took classes and received instruction and orders."[36]

The newly formed militants went to neighboring cantons and spread the message of rights and equality by placing the more abstract concepts into their lived experience, just as the artisans and workers had done when instructing them. In other words, the militants transmitted to new recruits hybrid understandings of what they had gleaned from graphics and discussions with the urban militants. Yet the messages were communicated along with new categories of understanding, including terms like bourgeois, capitalist, and proletarian.

Jorge Fernández Anaya, Marxism-Leninism, and Populism

Despite the stunning rapidity and extension of the union organizing drive, at the congress of May 1930 its principal leader, Jorge Fernández Anaya, delivered a devastating attack on the FRTS precisely because of the lack of ideological preparation of its militants. An indefatigable fighter who traveled on foot throughout the region, he was fully aware of the nature of the meetings and criticized what he considered the tendency to fetishize them:

"There exists in all of our compañeros a serious deficiency, and that is organizational passivity, and proof of that is that all of our compañeros share the belief that '*con solo reunir la gente*,' with that they acquire class consciousness."[37] Anaya linked the "ideological confusion" and lack of understanding of revolutionary theory with the petit bourgeois class origins of the leadership, who were primarily artisans and rural smallholders. In the countryside, "frequently the leaders are smallholders without any class consciousness. And they unconsciously detain the revolutionary march of union organization." He also complained that in the cities artisans and even "small industrialists" ran the unions. Anaya warned, "It is necessary to be aware that leaders who have special interests [intereses creados] in the moments in which the struggle acquires decisive characteristics, these are going to betray the revolutionary movement."[38]

Paradoxically, for Anaya the movement's rapid "spontaneous growth" was one of its fundamental weaknesses: "The masses have created the organization and have spontaneously come to the FRTS. It has been their desire for improvement, for raises, for better treatment, etc. that has brought the masses to the organization."[39] Anaya argued that in fact the FRTS was not engaged in real organizational efforts, but rather was content to allow for spontaneous mobilization. How can we understand this sharp discrepancy between Anaya's blistering criticism and the reality of the rapidly growing labor movement? Anaya had arrived in El Salvador in November 1929. Although he was the head of the Young Communists for the Caribbean region, he was highly aware of his own lack of theoretical and political sophistication. The classics of Marxism-Leninism had been unavailable to him in Mexico, and he had learned much of what he knew through conversations with the Cuban revolutionary Julio Antonio Mella during the six months preceding Mella's assassination in 1929. Mella, it should be noted, was a relative newcomer to Comintern discipline: he was suspected of ideological deviations, and some argue that the Comintern had him eliminated.[40] Regardless of the causes of the assassination, Mella's training certainly made Anaya insecure.

Anaya's correspondence with Comintern officials reveals his intense effort to think within the conceptual framework of Marxism-Leninism and his concern with his own ideological inadequacy—despite his high level of intelligence. At nearly every mention of the word "Salvadoran," for example, he begs forgiveness for his use of a "nationalist" vocabulary: "The deportation of Luis Villagrán and of all the foreign revolutionaries . . . I have to say that Villagrán was the only one, since all the rest are Salvadorans, excusing the use of the petit-bourgeois nationalist term."[41] This last sentence reveals a struggle within Anaya as he attempted to analyze, describe, and transform society within categories that were still strange to him. In this sense we can see that as Anaya and other actors and groups transformed the Third Phase Comintern version of Marxism-Leninism to apply to Salvadoran reality, he felt the immense responsibility to fix the meanings of the revolutionary ideology. His critique of the FRTS can be thus understood as an effort to push the political and cultural expressions of the movement into fixed categories. Anaya perhaps inferred the subversive potential of communitas, present in the meeting-fiestas: that is, the egalitarian, creative qualities that could not be contained within what Anaya imagined as a Marxist-Leninist party structure.[42]

Anaya's refusal to accept those subversive aspects of the meetings was also a rejection of what the Argentine theoretician Ernesto Laclau called "popular-democratic interpellations" within the ideology of the union members. As we have seen, to Laclau the popular-democratic identity was one opposed to élite rule, "united to institutions in which democracy is materialized."[43] Throughout modern history various groups of people outside the dominant power bloc have considered themselves (in his terms "been constituted as") "the people," in antagonistic relation to the prevailing dominant bloc. For Laclau people from diverse class backgrounds have historically suffered from various forms of political and ideological domination, and identify themselves in opposition to the power bloc as an "other," as an "underdog." This concept forms a key element of his theory of populism. He writes: "Our thesis is that populism consists in the presentation of popular-democratic interpellations as a synthetic-antagonistic complex with respect to the dominant ideologies . . . Populism begins where popular-democratic elements are presented as an antagonistic option against the ideology of the dominant bloc."[44] Laclau also argues that these "popular-democratic" elements need to be articulated to class ideologies, and that at the heart of any ideological struggle is a battle over these articulations—an effort to create a discourse in which one element condenses and expresses another. For example, in a right-wing populist discourse the nation expresses the people who express a race who express religiosity. In the most successful communist discourses, such as those of Mao, Tito, and the Italian Communist Party, the dominant symbols of the nation, the people, and the working classes all expressed each other in a way that suggested a "socialist populism."[45]

The on-the-ground ideological elements of the emerging, multiclass labor movement, and especially of the Socorro Rojo, were filled with populist-democratic interpellations in antagonistic relation to the dominant power bloc. Although the term "people" was rarely employed, laborers, artisans, peasants, and militants often identified themselves with comparable terms: *los pobres, la pobrería,* or *los oprimidos.* The most powerful and ubiquitous symbol within populist discourse was *los ricos,* which stood for the antagonistic bloc. Although as we shall see, Marxist class categories came to be used more frequently by rank-and-file militants, *los pobres* remained the dominant term in the popular idiom.

Laclau's analysis helps us recognize two fundamental reasons for the stunning growth of the Salvadoran left. First, he argues that populism emerges as part of a crisis of ideological domination, a consequence of a division of the power bloc, "in which a class or class fraction needs, in order to assert its hegemony, to appeal to 'the people' against established ideology as a whole; or a crisis in the ability of the system to neutralize the dominated sectors."[46] He adds that historical crises occur when both causes are present, as they certainly were in El Salvador. On the one hand, Araujismo represented just such a fracture in the dominant bloc. On the other, there were serious challenges to the old ideological system based on social differences and hierarchies, mediated by the church and local caudillos.

Another key factor in the explosive growth of the Salvadoran left may have been its "socialist populism," its ability to express a socialist program and goals in a populist idiom. Because of their youth, inexperience, and rigidity of thought (as well as the lack of a foreign adversary to strengthen the "national" element of populist discourse), Anaya and later Farabundo Martí could not grasp the populist dimension of the movement. Nevertheless, because of the organizational weakness of the vanguard—the PCS was only founded in March 1930 and may not have attained a membership of five hundred over the next two years—the leadership was never able to disarticulate the populist from the socialist ideological elements. Ironically, the failure to weaken the growing articulation between the two was crucial to the development of the movement. Of course, many militants understood the importance of the fusion and doubtless ignored entreaties to purify their base.

The power of Marxist discourse fused with existing populist mentality can be glimpsed in a peasant's account of some five decades later: "Socialism means that we are all equal, being on the side of the suffering, having medicine for everyone . . . We gotta to try to have a government of working folks . . . to administer the products of labor."[47] This passage illustrates how a campesino could appropriate the idea of socialism and make the concept appropriate to his or her reality. That kind of dynamic appropriation of political ideas is of course fundamental to the success of any subaltern protest movement and surely was in 1930. From an analytical standpoint, the discourse of the Marxist left is formed by such appropriations as well as its more formal enunciations. A rudimentary account of how theory relates to practice, and a window onto the forging of an interchange between formal expression and its appropriation, is provided by another informant regarding the encounter of the *iglesia popular* and campesinos in the 1970s: "Those that have an idea [of socialismo]. But those who do not struggle, understand nothing. If you never go near a meeting you are lost."[48]

Expansion and Limits of the Labor Movement

If Anaya did not capture the intrinsic importance of meetings, his analysis did point to certain salient characteristics of this rapidly expanding movement. In particular, his argument about the spontaneity of organization and recruitment was certainly valid, although his criticism of a consequent lack of interest in organizational work seems widely off the mark. The problem was not so much that the movement grew spontaneously but rather that its rapid expansion left the militants unable to meet the organizational needs of the unions or to prepare for government repression.

There is no way to measure this growth with any certainty. By mid-1930 the FRTS had at least fifteen thousand members, probably doubling its membership during the previous six months.[49] The map on page 84 shows how the labor movement progressed from December 1929 to May 1930 under Anaya's leadership. The organized sites of December 1929 were principally in the provincial cities and towns, with some bases in the nearby coffee areas. The expansion took place almost entirely in the coffee cantons near the cities and towns and on the larger haciendas. At times the FRTS expanded through the creation of new unions, as we saw in the organizational progression from Armenia to Jayaque to La Labor. Typically that

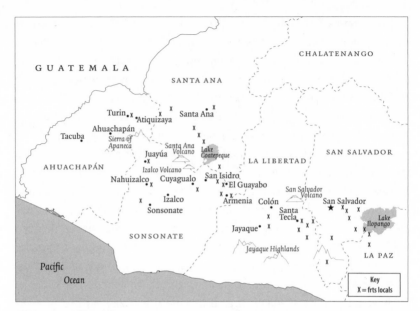

CHALATENANGO

GUATEMALA

SANTA ANA

Turin X · X Santa Ana · X
·X Atiquizaya
Ahuachapán X
Tacuba Sierra of X
· Apaneca
Juayúa Santa Ana Lake
·X Volcano Coatepeque
AHUACHAPÁN Izalco Volcano X LA LIBERTAD SAN SALVADOR
Nahuizalco Cuyagualo San Isidro
X · X ·X·El Guayabo
X X · X San Salvador
Izalco Armenia Colón Volcano San Salvador
Sonsonate · Santa ★ X X X
X Tecla X X X
SONSONATE Jayaque· X X Lake
X Ilopango
Jayaque Highlands X
Pacific X LA PAZ
Ocean
X

Key
X = frts locals

FRTS organizational bases, 1930.

progression moved along an urban-to-rural continuum. In other cases town-based unions became umbrella organizations as they expanded into the surrounding countryside. By mid-1930, for example, the Unión Sindical de Trabajadores de Jauyúa had six hundred members and the Sindicato Unión de Trabajadores de Nahuizalco over seventeen hundred. The unions held rallies and meetings in the towns, but they also had functioning branches in the cantons where workers, who returned from the haciendas every two weeks on Sunday, would meet.

Mapping the development of the union movement also reveals its limitations. Although the FRTS had a presence outside the coffee zones, it expanded mostly by organizing coffee workers and colonos on large estates.[50] The various non-coffee sites of organization around Lake Ilopango were an exception, owing in part to their relative proximity to San Salvador. There was also the fortuitous circumstance that the town of Ilopango and its surrounding cantons produced three outstanding and nationally prominent militants: Miguel Mármol, Ismael Hernández, and Modesto Ramirez. Their experience of organizing cattle ranch vaqueros, fishermen on the lake, and other rural workers outside the coffee industry was not replicated elsewhere. They achieved their most important success at the Hacienda Colombia, where the union organized laborers, colonos, and *terrajeros* (tenant farmers).[51] In February 1931 a strike broke out, reported upon by a journalist, whose voice of reason was anomalous within the Salvadoran fourth estate: "the movement was promoted by the peones, colonos and terrajeros of that hacienda; they were demanding a wage increase. Really, the mayors and some educated people have confused every act of protest with communism."[52]

The Birth of El Socorro Rojo Internacional

Shortly after his arrival in El Salvador in November 1929, Anaya suggested to FRTS militants that they organize a branch of Socorro Rojo Internacional (SRI), with the express aim of defending political prisoners. Anaya was a delegate of the Caribbean section of the SRI, and there is no reason to doubt that he expected to follow the model laid out in Moscow and New York. The SRI militants' primary tasks were to raise political consciousness among the proletariat about the relationship of the national bourgeoisie, imperialism, and repression and to mobilize public opinion against the incarceration of its militants. According to its statutes, the SRI was open to anyone who accepted the notion of class struggle. The SRI also "struggled against the racial oppression of workers who were black, Indian, Chinese or other oppressed nationalities."[53]

At the FRTS congress in May 1930, however, it was clear that most union members did not have much sense of what the SRI organization should look like, much less grasp its message of emancipation for minorities. Delegates discussed the relationship of the FRTS and the SRI; all assumed that the SRI would be founded by union militants. The delegate from "el Guayabo" offered the example of the indefatigable labor organizer Goyo Cortéz. At the same time that he was organizing and sustaining locals from San Isdiro to Jayaque, he was the head of the SRI local in Armenia, and in his capacity as SRI leader, he worked on behalf of the imprisoned union leaders of La Presa. The message seemed to be that individuals could and should belong to both organizations, but that the organizations had different objects of struggle and should act autonomously.

There was some discussion about the differences between the union and the SRI. The graphic of the FRTS leader Rafael Bondanza showed the participation in the SRI of "doctores" (probably meaning lawyers). As Anaya lectured about the SRI as an organization composed of "proletarians, farm

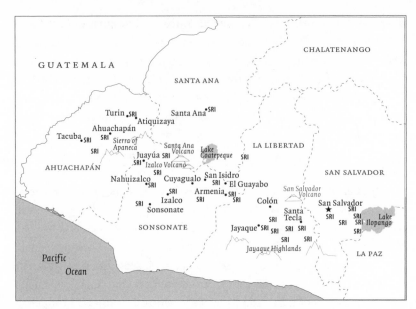

SRI organizational bases, 1931.

workers, and *colonos*," a rural delegate interrupted and referred back to Bondanza's graphic. Given the cult of the proletarian propounded by Anaya, this point was polemical. Anaya, who had called for the session of the FRTS to constitute the founding convention of the SRI, responded: "We can use these señores as SRI sympathizers, to aid victims of the reaction and imperialism, but we can't have the confidence in them to assign them leadership roles and we have to make sure that they don't get influence among the rank and file." Subsequently he clarified the point further: "We only use them as long as they are useful, but the minute they begin to work for ulterior or egotistical goals, then we have to expel them from our ranks."[54] This response certainly betrays the Stalinism of Anaya's proletarianization policy, rather than any SRI guidelines. Yet to the labor delegates there was an additional message, namely that this new organization had a wider mission than merely defense.

Repression and Radicalization, 1930

In June 1930 the government made its first serious moves against the left. Authorities arrested two progressive journalists and staged raids against union activists in Joya Grande and Shaltipe, near Santiago Texacuangos, a few miles east of the capital. In Ahuachapán the National Guard arrested fifty-five campesinos, whom the national authorities subsequently freed.[55] Police arrested workers and the unemployed in the city demonstrations as well.[56]

The pace of governmental action picked up dramatically in August. On the first of the month the authorities arrested ninety laborers in Nuevo Cuzcatlán and Nazareth, a few miles west of the capital, as they prepared to take part in a demonstration. A few days later the government announced that it had uncovered a communist conspiracy and arrested scores of militants charged with plotting an insurrection, supposedly scheduled for 6 August. Exiled to Guatemala, Anaya in an internal report scoffed at the charges of insurrection, "as if we were such imbeciles that we do things by decrees."[57]

On 12 August, using the insurrectionary threat cited by the departmental governors, the government issued a decree prohibiting any speeches, propaganda, meetings, or rallies "of a communist character" and ordering the arrest of all communist leaders. Whether or not the authorities actually believed that the FRTS activists were planning an insurrection, the press and government reports stirred up a hysteria that offered a pretext for further arrests. On 19 August the *comandante de puesto* in Jayaque denounced an attempted assault on the town. His troops arrested several people and confiscated fourteen machetes. On the same day Timoteo Flores, the comandante de puesto in nearby Sacacoyo, arrested eight union leaders, accused simply of being communists.[58] The mayor of Jayaque wrote to the minister of war two days later: "This city has been selected as a center of communist operations; they have met several times and they have had deomonstrations where speakers rail against the government and the established order. They appear to be union activists but their actions show them to be communists. Those actions have been prohibited by law. Since these people are unknown and come from various nearby villages . . . this city is fearful."[59]

Using the decree of 12 August as a pretext, the National Guard attacked labor demonstrations in ten towns and cities in western Salvador, carting off to jail hundreds of participants.[60] In September 1930 in Nahuizalco, an FRTS stronghold with over seventeen hundred organized seasonal laborers (including five hundred women), union members staged a protest. The National Guard arrested large numbers of demonstrators and hauled them off to Sonsonate.[61] Upon release they protested again, only to be arrested again.[62]

Although most rank-and-filers were eventually released after the wave of arrests, the persecution itself became the target of further demonstrations demanding freedom for the remaining jailed union militants. By late 1930 rural union members were so incensed at the state repression that ideas of insurrection began to circulate freely among the rank and file and local leadership.[63] Anaya considered the insurrectionary current serious, especially since Farabundo Martí was a proponent. Without directly accusing him of supporting this tendency, he wrote to Martí: "The idea, let's clearly call it the insurrectionary leftist tendency, is due to a lack of consciousness among some comrades. This is a negative tendency. It's not that we won't have to arrive at that point some time soon, but for the moment, this [position] is due to cowardice, lack of consciousness, and the panic caused by the alliance between national fascism and Yankee imperialism. To not consider our enormous responsibility to our class in these moments is to betray it. The daily struggle allows us to reeducate and perfect our leaders and militants."[64] Although in 1930 the national leftist leadership was able to exert its influence against any local initiatives toward armed rebellion, the dynamic of arrests leading to further organization and radicalization continued. In September 1930, shortly before his return to his native Mexico, Fernández Anaya wrote, with a tragic prescience: "Inevitably the revolution in El Salvador will be bloody. The ever-growing accumulation of concentrated hatred will give it a bloody character."[65]

The radicalizing impact of rifle butts, bullets, and prison cells conditioned the dialogue between the rank and file and the national leftist leadership. The rank and file pushed the leadership into more militant and radical ideological and tactical positions. This influence can be ascertained in the transformation of the Socorro Rojo Internacional. The largely peasant and rural worker movement transformed the SRI from an organization designed to defend the left and the labor movement against political persecution into a radical social movement. An internal PCS document from 1936 recounts the transformation of the SRI into the key revolutionary organization in the following terms: "Although Fernández Anaya had the intention of organizing the PCS legally, that year we only witnessed the formation of the SRI, into which the FRTS was almost entirely absorbed. Thus the economic base of the movement was converted into a combatative defensive organization. Martí was the abnegated leader of this process and the PCS began to form with the most battle-hardened and experienced elements."[66]

This account, covering the history of the revolutionary left from 1929 until 1935, collapses a yearlong process into the last two months of 1929. Beyond the lack of chronological precision, it fails to analyze why a union movement would be displaced by an organization designed to defend political prisoners. Despite this striking lacuna, the document does confirm the emergence of the SRI as the leading organization of the left, displacing the FRTS.

The expansion of the SRI during the latter part of 1930 and throughout 1931 (depicted in the map on page 86) was as dramatic as the growth of the FRTS over the previous year. The first SRI locals emerged in places where the FRTS had bases of support. Yet by the latter part of 1930 the SRI had established organizations in sites where the unions had not managed to set up locals, notably in Izalco and Tacuba.

Under the boot of police action, the SRI's commitment to fighting repression and aiding the families of political prisoners undoubtedly exerted a favorable impact on the mobilized rank and file. In addition to its role in resisting the first wave of government action, there were some less tangible reasons why the SRI became so popular. Some informants suggest that the name itself had great appeal for campesinos, combining the symbolic potency of the color red, the Christian associations of the notion of "aid" (socorro), and the promise of "external" (international) redemption. This latter theme was echoed by leaders of labor and the left from Juayúa, who warned the governor of Sonsonate that if the government did not release Farabundo Martí from prison, the "international working class" would "learn of the matter."[67] Similarly, socorro, in addition to its Christian inflection, also recalled the communitas of the festive meetings.

The SRI mobilized to gain freedom for the four union leaders, in jail for a year, who had led the movement in La Presa. In Santa Tecla an SRI demonstration on 27 November provoked enough anxiety at the U.S. embassy that officials there characterized it as a "threatened uprising." Seventy-five soldiers with machine guns blocked the demonstration. Troops captured Martí and three other organizers.[68]

Those arrests led to further mobilization against repression in general and more specifically in favor of the release from prison of SRI leaders, who declared a hunger strike on 17 December. The authorities responded by deporting Martí, which provoked two major protest demonstrations by the SRI in Sonsonate and Santa Tecla. On 21 December 1930 troops shot and killed several demonstrators in Santa Tecla and arrested approximately three hundred.[69] That shooting marked the virtual halt of leftist activity for the next three months. According to an internal SRI document, "During the period December 1930-March 1930, the section's work was almost entirely suspended due to the intense wave of terror."[70] The term "wave of terror" was perhaps hyperbole, but the killing of unarmed demonstrators was real enough, as were the mass arrests.

The dormancy of the revolutionary movement over the next months was also a result of the ascendancy of Arturo Araujo as a reformist presidential candidate. In the words of the PCS leader Max Cuenca, writing in 1932, "In spite of the fact that at the time the FRTS had sufficient influence, the working classes oriented themselves to the candidates who were sympathetic to the immediate demands of that particular period. The organizations of the working class were not faithful to the revolutionary spirit and most of them aligned themselves with the leading candidate of the bourgeoisie, Araujo . . . the masses were informed by the propaganda of the leaders of Araujo, that [after] the elections, the land would be distributed among [the workers]."[71]

The rise of Araujo's candidacy, which had a large base of support among the rural poor, combined with governmental intervention to set back the labor movement. This was especially true for the PCS, which pushed for an abstentionist line. Battered by repression, with its leaders in jail, exile, or underground, the PCS was at the nadir of its brief existence, and its call to abstain from the election was simply ignored by the rank and file of labor and the left.

The degree of organizational autonomy of the SRI is a matter of some dispute. Certainly the state authorities at the time considered it nothing more than a PCS organization. Scholars have not considered that relations between the PCS and the SRI merit serious attention. Despite what the Comintern and the government might have assumed, the Socorro Rojo in El Salvador did have a political and organizational life of its own. Max Cuenca referred to the SRI's autonomy as a problem when he reported that Farabundo Martí returned to El Salvador in February 1931, planning to reorganize the FRTS and the CP as well as to control "the independent forces of the SRI."[72] More significantly, its relative autonomy allowed the SRI to survive when the National Guard had beaten down the FRTS. Although communist militants led the SRI, it remained apolitical during the electoral campaign.

Unlike the small PCS group, the SRI did not campaign against Araujo, and unlike the FRTS it did not purge members who supported particular candidates. Thus in a special report on SRI activities in May 1931 in Izalco, General Tomás Calderón underscored that the militants had supported different candidates during the previous presidential electoral campaign. Of course this was in keeping with the official description of the SRI as an organization dedicated to the class struggle, open to all and tied to no political party.[73]

The SRI's flexibility also allowed it to become the leading organization promoting agrarian reform. Wedded to a strict interpretation of union activity, the FRTS failed to actively demand agrarian reform. The "tesis agraria" and the "Program for Agricultural Workers" approved at the FRTS congress in May 1930, to cite key examples, made no mention of land reform.[74] The SRI expanded primarily because it responded to the overwhelmingly popular demand for agrarian reform, intensified by the expectations raised by Araujo's campaign.[75] His election legitimized the demand for land reform without offering anything more than token efforts toward relieving the intense land hunger of the poor. The SRI thus became the vehicle of this newly awakened group.

Many informants throughout western and central El Salvador repeated the same words about the SRI: "Querían quitarles fincas a los ricos" (They wanted to take the fincas away from the rich).[76] As José Antonio Chachagua, a peasant from Ahuachapán, stated, "the rebels' slogan was that the colonos were going to be the owners."[77] In short, the growth and transformation of the SRI also coincided with the radicalization of the left's program. The campesinos of central and western Salvador took advantage of the unfixed, nonsectarian position of the SRI to recreate it in their own image.

Repression and Radicalization under Araujo, 1931

The promise and failures of Araujo's government contributed significantly to the radicalization of the social movements of 1931. Trapped between his ineptitude and the crushing economic crisis in the context of intense popular expectations, Araujo confronted enormous obstacles when he took office. Within a short period he faced an élite that would not pay taxes; a middle class that would not allow more foreign loans; foreign banks that would not loan money easily; a U.S. customs receivership; and an ineffective public service infrastructure with a long tradition of graft and corruption. A mobilized campesinado expected and demanded agrarian reform, but only a small amount of land was available for redistribution without confronting the oligarchy. To add to his woes, between March and July heavy rains and a volcanic eruption reduced the food supply in the west. Even the most able of reformist leaders would have cringed when facing these conditions.

Three weeks after Araujo's inauguration on 1 March, police arrested two SRI leaders in Sonsonate and brought them to the capital. Araujo called them into his office and offered them jobs in construction, warned them about the dangers of communism, and told them to "propagate Laborismo."[78] They politely responded that they would have to consult with their organization before accepting the jobs. From its inception Araujo's government also employed repression. In mid-March the police attacked a demonstration of two hundred unemployed workers in the capital. Before the end of Araujo's first month in office, the National Guard had arrested a dozen SRI activists in Sonsonate and in the cantons of Izalco and Nahuizalco.[79]

The SRI took advantage of the collapse of popular expectations for agrarian reform engendered by the campaign and shut off the limited space for negotiation or compromise. The government's actions against workers and campesinos made the left's vitriolic criticisms of the regime that much more credible. The SRI's most notable gains were in the cantons of Izalco, where the FRTS had made only a limited impact during 1930. During the organizing drive FRTS militants had some success in organizing indigenous workers in the canton of Cuyagualo, where many residents worked on coffee plantations during the planting, pruning, and harvest seasons. Other than that limited base, however, and unlike in nearly every other town in the coffee plantation areas, the FRTS had no organized locals in Izalco.[80] Thus the SRI's sudden growth in the indigenous and bi-ethnic cantons in early 1931 was significant. In those cantons, where semi-proletarians predominated, the organization rapidly recruited people who were eager for land reform and deeply offended by the repressive response of the government.

By 1931 over half the rural population of Izalco consisted of land-starved semi-proletarians, many of whom had become colonos in the region's larger commercial farms and haciendas. Leopoldo Barrientos, one of Izalco's wealthy ladino landowners, for example, had fifty-four adults as colonos and workers in his small Hacienda Comalapa and twenty-nine in his farm in Cantón Cerro Alto.[81] Many others worked on the huge haciendas in the eastern area of the municipality, in particular San Isidro and Los Lagartos. The town's social structure mimicked the vast differences in wealth so visible at the national level. In 1928 the town had thirty-eight men with capital worth more than ten thousand colones; at the bottom of the local hierarchy were thirteen hundred jornaleros.

Both ladinos and Indians participated in the SRI meetings, often held nocturnally in the cantons and on the haciendas. On 14 March 1931 the governor of Sonsonate reported an arrest of communist leaders after Farabundo Marti gave a "conferencia" in Piedras Pachas, a canton just east of Izalco.[82] On 7 April police commissioners again carried out raids in Piedras Pachas, arresting Alberto Masen.[83] The city was also the center of a major organizing drive for May Day, when the city awoke to flags and signs that read: "Viva the union of workers and peasants, down with social fascism, no to the loan, down with imperialism and its lackeys in this county, down with the Partido Laborista, creature of English imperialism, viva el Socorro Rojo Internacional, viva la Federación Regional de Trabajadores, down with the fascist decrees against the workers."[84]

This highly sectarian message was read by a sharply divided local polity. The indigenous people of Barrio de Asunción had generally been *gobiernistas* who supported the semiofficial candidacy of Zárate in the presidential elections of 1931. The ladino élite, led by Diaz Barrientos, also attempted to manipulate the elections in favor of Zarate.[85] Ladino artisans and workers formed the core of Araujista support. In the eastern cantons both Indians and ladinos also esteemed Araujo highly. His family's "Sunza" hacienda had the reputation of being a rural workers' paradise, such did the humane treatment afforded there to campesinos contrast with that on other haciendas and plantations. The SRI was most successful, it seems, when recruiting disaffected Araujistas who resided in the cantons, farmed small plots of land, and worked on the haciendas. Landlords aggravated the campesinos' desire for land by breaking with past practice, as many refused to rent out land except through cash payments.[86] Within months of the election, prompted by their friends, family, and co-workers from the cantons, the indigenous people of the barrio Asunción began to shift their allegiance from the bankrupt PND to the SRI.

The SRI in El Salvador adopted several other tactics that helped its organizing drive. First, as was done elsewhere (notably in the case of the "Scottsboro Boys" in Alabama), it deployed a rhetoric that personalized the targets of repression while also offering the promise of an organization capable of defending all its members. A typical statement of the SRI bulletin read: "Miguel Nájera, of Planes de Renderos, was brought to Police Head-quarters. This camarada has three helpless children; The SOCORRO ROJO INTERNACIONAL will help them and work so that compañero Nájera will be freed soon!"[87] The SRI delivered on material aid. When Alberto Másen's house in Piedras Pachas, Izalco, was burned under highly suspicious cir-cumstances three days before his release from prison, the organization committed its human and material resources to rebuilding it and turned the day of construction into a political meeting, attended by eighty people.[88] The SRI also organized soup kitchens at a time when they were not com-mon. One informant recalls that in the cantons of Izalco they would place soup bones over a fire in a large black pot labeled "SRI."[89] The group could also claim dramatic triumphs when the authorities released their prisoners: "They released all of the compañeros imprisoned in Sonsonate after 22 days; the commander of the Guardia told them: go see if you are still so eager to get involved! Everyone answered, 'That's exactly what we are going to do.' "[90]

Finally, the SRI developed the extraordinarily successful tactic of threat-ened and actual hunger strikes. The most famous was that of its leader, Farabundo Martí, who began his first on 6 May 1931. Ironically, he an-nounced the strike in protest of his treatment in prison, including his having been denied food since his arrest on 3 May. Thus the strike began as a way to publicize that treatment but rapidly turned into a means of denouncing the inhumanity of Araujo's government for "assassinating" Martí. Almost daily bulletins (written by workers, judging by the spell-ing) counted the hours of the strike: "Today, at 9:00 a.m. our compañero Agustín Farabundo Martí will have completed 14 days and six hours without eating absolutely anything . . . And while Martí is dying, assassinated, Araujo and his henchmen gaze on and smile like heartless criminals! Com-pañeros: ONLY WE, THE TRUE PROLETARIANS, see in this crime the clear and cold proof of what this burguesote Arturo Araujo is made of. We are called upon to save him from these vicious and heartless clutches."[91]

The SRI's denunciations followed a particular logic: the police arrested Martí without cause and treated him inhumanely. His hunger strike is there-fore the direct responsibility of the government and they are torturing him by not setting him free. "The assassin Araujo and his gang of henchmen contemplate impassively the slow death of our dearest camarada, knowing that the trial is a complete farce." The sheer drama and heroism of the hunger strike—more than two weeks without food or water—ennobled the figure of Martí. His character was such, the argument implicitly stated, that he had no alternative but to pursue the strike. By removing Martí's decision to begin a hunger strike from the argument, the SRI could blame the government for this "crime" of assassination.

Authorities hoped that the agricultural cycle would help them suppress the growth of the SRI. In May 1931 the governor of Sonsonate reported that "there is no news in this department; the communists appear to be inactive and the campesinos who had joined them, due to the rains that just started, are cultivating their fields."[92] The expectation that the planting season would slow support for the mobilizations proved to be mistaken. On 13 May the military commander of Sonsonate ordered soldiers to patrol the city streets at night, because the previous night "communist activity was noted in the Rafael Campo Park."[93] Authorities also noticed increased leafleting in the Izalqueño cantons of Cuyagualo and Piedras Pachas.[94]

17 May 1931: A Lesson Learned

The SRI called for demonstrations in favor of freedom for Martí and other political prisoners throughout its bases in central and western Salvador. The most significant of these demonstrations took place in Sonsonate on 17 May, in which from four to six hundred people, mostly campesinos, participated. Many came from the new base of SRI support in the cantons of Izalco. In keeping with the nonviolent symbolism of the hunger strike, the campesinos left their *corvos* (long machetes) at home. They proceeded rapidly and silently through Barrio Angel until they reached Rafael Campo Park. As Victor Angulo, an SRI leader from San Salvador, began his speech, police agents approached and informed him that the demonstration was illegal. Rather than contest the order based on the infamous decrees of 12 August and 30 October, the SRI leadership told the demonstrators to march back out of town.

After marching two blocks and now shouting slogans ("Viva el Socorro Rojo Internacional!," "Abajo el Gobierno Fascista de Araujo!," and "Abajo el Laborismo!"), the demonstrators reached the corner of Piedra Lisa, where soldiers stopped them. According to the police, the SRI leader Manuel Mojica wrestled a rifle from an officer and then shots rang out. Witnesses reported that the soldiers fired directly at the demonstrators. The shooting resulted in three dead demonstrators and over twenty wounded, while only one soldier was wounded. Police arrested over sixty people.

Not surprisingly, two radically different versions of events were propounded by the press and government on the one hand and the SRI on the other. The authorities attempted to portray the demonstrators as armed and aggressive, but they presented no evidence to suggest that any of them were armed. Reports also emphasized that the demonstrators carried signs saying "Respetad solo a los niños," implying that they were going to massacre all the adults. This slogan, combined with the participation of many Indians and campesinos, was presented as evidence that the troops had acted in self-defense, or at least in defense of the imperiled citizenry. Yet of the three pro-government witnesses who mentioned the SRI banners, not one recalled this slogan. Since there was no mention of the slogan in the initial hearing, which included official and other witnesses, there is little doubt that it was an ex post facto justification for the shooting.

Whether the SRI activists attempted to disarm soldiers or police cannot be determined. The SRI witnesses claimed that the police and soldiers blocked their advance and then opened fire as the marchers retreated down the same street. The SRI bulletin claimed that the soldiers attacked them, trying to yank away their banners. Those who were carrying the banners resisted. Many of the other demonstrators raised their arms in a sign of surrender. Then the soldiers opened fire, as did "burgueses" from their balconies. Another SRI bulletin reported that the "bourgeois," including Roberto Candel, were overheard gloating about their role: "I already screwed two of them who were running!"[95] Although this version is also impossible to verify, at least one demonstrator was shot in the back in front of Candel's establishment. The SRI and the rest of the left were absolutely convinced that the local élite, in complicity with local authorities, was responsible.

El Diario Latino offered one of the few relatively neutral accounts, observing that after the police's attempt to remove the crowd failed and troops were called in, the stones thrown by the protestors were answered with bullets.[96] Another impartial account of the incident, by Galindo Pohl, places all the blame for the shooting on the authorities.[97] Pohl, who was a middle-class adolescent at the time, recalls that most residents recognized the demonstrators to be unarmed and saw no justification for the troops's decision to open fire. The departmental governor fell back on the argument that the SRI had broken the law by holding the demonstration and that the authorities had to "teach them a lesson."[98]

The events of 17 May were significant for several reasons. First, Araujo's government aligned itself with the forces of repression. Several days after the event, Araujo denounced "vulgar agitators of violence" who "launched the masses into a struggle without glory, whose only results were corpses . . . and social disorder."[99] Other parts of his address did, however, suggest his desire for dialogue. He went to Izalco to speak directly to people and then offered an exculpatory explanation of the events that combined populism with the image of the "innocent" Indians. He claimed that the campesinos and workers were not "real" communists and that bourgeois elements in Sonsonate had paid people to start the violence.[100]

Araujo sent a political emissary to the region to engage in pro-government Laborista activities and ordered his ministro de gobernación, General Calderón, to provide a security assessment of the situation: The official investigation, led by General de Division Tomás Calderón, helps us understand how it was that military officials granted so little legitimacy to the social question during 1931. After questioning detainees and local officials, Calderón, who would later play a major role in the suppression of the 1932 revolt, concluded that "it is believed that this communist movement did not follow a preconceived plan against the government but rather, if allowed, would have amounted to plunder. It is class resentment whereby the impoverished are not satisfied with their lot and aspire to possess what does not belong to them. [Among] the leaders all tendencies of the last elections are represented. Among the captured communists there is no one party affiliation." At the same time, and in contradiction to his dismissal of the social origins of the movement, he noted that "Communism has extended itself a great deal; there are activities . . . throughout the department and municipal authorities have issued edicts against them but among these very authorities, mainly in [Sonsonate] there are some who share the framework of the same ideas."[101] Calderón echoed other discourses that reduced the movement to a childish explosion and denied its political character, a trope that would later become the core of how the 1932 revolt was remembered. This reflected other simplistic responses to the movement by government officials, who frequently construed leftist propaganda as a simple assault on private property, "to use force to appropriate what belongs to others."[102]

Araujo did waver in adopting a strictly repressive approach to the leftist threat. Yet his official endorsement of the anticommunist decrees of 12 August and 30 October, coupled with his tolerance of repeated actions by the Guardia and the police, suggest that whatever ambivalence he experienced, his strategy toward the left was predicated on an important role for the Guardia and the police. In light of his inability or unwillingness to carry out the land reform promises of his electoral campaign, there was little likelihood that he could coopt the growing base of the left.

For the demonstrators and their families, 17 May was a defining moment. The shooting represented a definitive rupture with Araujo's government, which many had supported. State violence also led many to the conviction that peaceful protest was not an option in their struggle for social justice. Both political consequences radicalized the SRI rank and file. In early June an indigenous widow of one of the martyrs informed an SRI leader: "Look, compañero. They killed my compañero but here are my sons and they will see the revolution."[103]

Addendum: Governor's Report on May 17 Events

At about 7:30 am on the 17th of May, a communist demonstration of roughly 300 individuals entered the city from the suburbs of "El Angel," led by the leaders Manual Mojica y Argripino Guevara, who shouted vivas for the Socorro Rojo and shouted for Martí's freedom; these demonstrators some of whom were captured are all from the cantons of Izalco and a few from this city of Sonsonate. When some police saw the demonstrators' signs and anti-government leaflets, they demanded that they disband the demonstration, but to no avail; they arrived at the Rafael Campo Park. When one of the leaders began to speak, then the police again ordered them to disperse and they did so. When an escort of the Eighth Regiment started to help the police, some communists rushed them and tried to take a rifle away from a soldier: there was no alternative but to open fire and thereby avoid anything more serious. They were chased and pursued until they were completely dispersed; the Mayor de Plaza Colonel Juan Ortíz and six communists were wounded in the affray. Two of them died, the leader Agripino Guevara and another who could not state his name because he was agonizing; the wounded are in the city hospital where they are being attended.[104]

Chapter Four

"Ese Trabajo Era Enteramente de los Naturales:" Ethnic Conflict and Mestizaje in Western Salvador, 1914–1931

Your explanation is very good tata padre, but you've got the wrong audience! . . . You should address those of your color. Before there were cheles in our pueblo we did not know the plague that you cursed.—Cited in Antonio Conte, *Treinta años en tierras salavdoreñas*, vol. 2, 97

The Indians were very conscious. Juan Hernández and the other compañeros of Cuyagualo went to San Julián to organize the laborers.—Fabián Mojica, Sonsonate, 1999

The events of 17 May at once revealed and concealed the deepening of an ethnic dimension to the mass mobilization. The majority of the demonstrators were Indians, yet both the left and the authorities tended to group rural Indians and ladinos into one "campesino" category. Over three-quarters of the demonstrators were adult jornaleros from the cantons of Izalco and the indigenous Barrio Asunción of Izalco.[1] But both the repressive forces and the SRI elided this ethnic dimension. The SRI denounced the hatred of "campesinos" by the bourgeoisie and repressive forces, while not singling out specific indigenous groups in Izalco: "Ferocious terror has been unleashed against all the campesinos; the jails are filled and there are many wounded inside their homes trying to heal themselves; those who are in the hospital are treated worse than dogs; the government has just sent more reinforcements to [Sonsonate]; they are

"Ese
Trabajo
Era
Enteramente
de los
Naturales"

on a war footing. HATRED AGAINST THE CAMPESINOS'IS HORRIFIC; TO DRESS LIKE A CAMPESINO IS ALMOST LIKE SIGNING A DEATH SENTENCE!"[2] Why did the SRI denounce hatred of "campesinos" rather than hatred of "Indians"? This sort of conflation was not by any means the special province of the Marxist Left. El Indio, a pro-Laborista bulletin, also made no distinction between the indigenous and ladino rural poor. For this social-democratic organ, indio was synonymous with the exploited and oppressed, those who started working at the age of seven "to earn their tortillas and a miserable salary to buy la manta which barely covers their burnt skin."[3] The reference here to a typically indigenous piece of clothing suggests that the mocito (a diminutive form of "peon") in question was an Indian, but the remainder of the text makes clear that it was meant to describe a nonindigenous campesino.

Although Marxist-Leninists tended to communicate in class as opposed to ethnic categories, this was not always so; the guidelines of the SRI did, as we have seen, emphasize the plight of blacks and Indians. In May 1929 the Comintern official Jules-Humbert Droz directly addressed the question of race to the founding convention of the communist-led Confederación Sindical Latinoamericana: "Many comrades have denied that there is a race problem in Latin America, affirming that blacks, Indians, and mestizos have equal rights and that nowhere does one find racial prejudice, similar to in the United States. It is true that there are no specifically racist laws but let us consider the facts. Who are the most exploited, miserable agricultural workers? Who are the campesinos whom the large landowners and the foreign companies expropriate? The Indians."[4] Droz then proceeded to analyze how indigenous struggles to recoup land appeared as luchas de razas and how transnational companies complicated the class struggle by introducing Afro-Caribbeans into the labor force on the continent: "Thus the racial factor penetrates and complicates the social question and we will carefully study these questions. . . . [Race] is also an element of instability in political and social relations."[5] Droz's analysis did not necessarily penetrate through all levels of the Comintern, but it does indicate that within the discursive limits of Marxism-Leninism, a recognition of the racial dimension of class struggle was possible. Thus, for example, a PCS document produced after the massacres refers to the campesino indígena sonsonteca as a social subject of the insurrection.[6] The revolutionary left, however, started out from a position heavily tinted with racist assumptions. In 1929 a Salvadoran leftist argued: "The revolution advances from the city to the country-side . . . It is necessary to make a concrete study of the Indian question. We must make the revolution in the city and then the Indian will come . . . It is the revolutionary minority that always triumphs. The indigenous layers ultimately will be dragged into the movement."[7] The Marxist-Leninists' fail-ure to distinguish between indigenous and ladino workers also reflected a degree of ladino racism, an assumption that the cultural practices and racist oppression of indigenous people were not worthy of special consideration.

Yet there was also a more emancipatory aspect to the left's use of the term "campesino," one that reflected the egalitarian ethos of the movement: workers and peasants were all equal within a revolutionary movement that fought to achieve a society where racial and class distinctions would be meaningless. Given the high level of local racism and ethnic animosity, the interchangeability of terms, by implying equality, probably helped to forge the difficult alliance between the ladino and indigenous poor.

In another sense, the class language of the SRI denunciation was accu-rate. For the provincial élite and military and police officials, the rebellious rural workers, who were dark-skinned and dressed in *pantalones de dril* and *sombreros de palma*, would all have been indios. The similarity of male dress and phenotype surely confused the provincial élite, and therefore the SRI would have been accurate to speak of a generalized hatred and discrimina-tion against "campesinos." Indeed the forces of repression, strongly influ-enced by the élite, did equate campesino with indigenous. According to Galindo Pohl, the comandante issued an order just to shoot at those with sombreros de palma, worn by all poor campesinos in the area.

Elsewhere Gould discussed the emergence of national-level discourses of mestizaje and their impact on local conflict in Central America.[8] He argued that Salvador before 1932 was not significantly different from Nicaragua or Honduras, where an emerging discourse of ethnic homogeneity supported ladino efforts to appropriate land and political power from indigenous minorities. All three countries of the middle isthmus underwent real or perceived processes of cultural mestizaje, defined here as a nation-building myth of racial mixture and a cultural process of de-Indianization that often accompanied the advance of agrarian capitalism. This process tended to divide indigenous communities in ways that aided ladino political and eco-nomic pursuits. In El Salvador, as in the other countries, indigenous people "looked" as if they were dropping their Indian identities. As one observer

102

"Ese
Trabajo
Era
Enteramente
de los
Naturales"

stated (however incorrectly), "The Indians have all been absorbed, and nearly everyone wears shoes and stockings."[9] Typically, national élites used the putative disappearance of "real" Indians as a way of undermining indigenous claims. This middle isthmian process was replicated in some respects in El Salvador, but with certain fundamental differences that provide a key to understanding the country's mobilization, rebellion, and repression. Unlike in the other countries, where mestizaje formed a key element in a hegemonic project, in El Salvador the very intense *and* contradictory subaltern response, tended to promote indigenous resistance. Those contradictory responses had a significant impact on rural mobilization.

Religion, Resistance, and Mestizaje

Antonio Conte, a Pauline missionary, participated in several evangelizing missions throughout western Salvador during the first three decades of the twentieth century. His reflections, published in 1934, allow us to glimpse the complexities of cultural mestizaje and in particular its relationship to religious practices.

For the early twentieth century Conte's understanding was quite sophisticated. At first glance he merely follows the discourse of the Jesuits in Central America in the 1870s, underscoring the relative purity and goodness of Indians in contrast to the corrupt, worldly ladinos.[10] He believed that cultural interaction with ladinos had disastrous effects on the Indians. For Conte the ladinos did not even "bring the benefits of civilized behavior" or thought to the Indian communities, because they were deeply steeped in European superstition in addition to having bad habits. In his words, "We do not affirm that baptized and evangelized Indians were saints . . . before mixing with ladinos, but no one can deny that this contact has been fatal for the Indians' simplicity, faith, fear of God, and obedience to the church . . . to the indigenous superstitions (with the lives of a cat) have been added the ladino ones originated overseas . . . the hope to die like a saint after a demonic life."[11] Conte singled out wealthy ladinos in particular for his scorn, and he returns to this theme repeatedly throughout his extensive ethnographic observations. Commenting on a mission to San Julián in 1927 and the lack of élite ladino religiosity, Conte wrote: "Here as everywhere, the wealthy are noticeably absent."[12] Conte's sympathy for Indians and hostility to the wealthy set him apart from most of the Salvadoran clergy and offered a vantage point to observe what he labeled as *ladinización*. He used that term (later adopted by anthropologists) to describe those forces that directly undermined indigenous markers and customs.

Conte astutely connected the process of ladinización to the economic transformations that accompanied the spread of coffee cultivation, thus adumbrating more materialist currents of anthropology.[13] In Tamanique, La Libertad, for example, Conte found that recent migrants from Chalatenango who had bought up land on which to plant coffee formed much of the town's population. In Jicilapa, a nearby village, Conte noted the presence of Indians but commented that "their customs and style of dress are 'ladinizando' rapidly" and opined that "this poor race deserves a better fate."[14] He also noted that ladinos from the northern Salvadoran towns of Tejutepeque, Suchitoto, and Tenancingo had taken over lands in Ishuatán, leaving the Indians "in a state of misery. . . . The Indians are now on the outskirts of town or along the beaches '*aculados*' as they say along the *esteros* . . . stricken by malaria and on the verge of extinction."[15]

For Conte ladinización was a material and cultural process involving the loss of indigenous ethnic emblems, shaped by a dramatic shift in power relations between Indians and ladinos. Although Conte's chronology is somewhat vague, the socio-geographic description is nonetheless significant: the ladinos' acquisition of recently privatized lands displaced Indians in certain highland communities. The municipalities of Comasagua, Sacacoyo, Tepecoyo, Jayaque, and San Julián in particular experienced this economic and cultural transformation, from indigenous peasants with access to communal lands to ladino coffee finca owners and de-Indianized workers.

This part of the country encompassed mountainous regions to the south and west of San Salvador. The relatively inaccessible mountain range along the coast and the neighboring coastal flatlands had remained largely uncultivated. In part because of this frontier aspect, La Libertad provided excellent conditions that secured it the fastest rate of growth of coffee production in the country during the 1890s and early twentieth century. Most significantly, its Indian communities were small, weak, and politically isolated. Unlike Izalco and Nahuizalco, the indigenous communities in La Libertad had rarely established alliances with outside political factions or participated in the conflicts of the postcolonial era. Further, the ejidal and communal land systems were never extensive.

These communities so poignantly described by Conte were easy prey to

104

"Ese
Trabajo
Era
Enteramente
de los
Naturales"

the advancing coffee economy and culture. In his words, "El grano de oro les ha atraido a muchos ladinos y ahuyentado a gran parte del elemento indígena" (the golden bean has attracted many ladinos and has driven off a large part of the indigenous element).[16] The loss of land, according to Conte, led to a physical marginalization that in turn had two salient effects. First, the poor land and living conditions afflicted the Indians physically and brought them to "the verge of extinction." Second, political and economic control by ladinos over the municipality and village life created pressures that led to the rapid decline of indigenous language and dress. Conte thus describes how in the highlands of Jayaque, the physical marginalization of some Indians corresponded with the cultural transformation of others. Although his chronology is not precise, the dates of his missions suggest that much of the transformation in the highlands of Jayaque occurred between 1912 and 1926. Commenting on the cultural transformation in one highland village, he reported: "Chiltiupán of 1926 does not resemble the town we knew 15 years ago."[17] A government investigation in 1913 had already highlighted significant indigenous land loss in the region, particularly in Ishuatán. It also pointed to the widespread adoption of nonindigenous dress in the highlands of Jayaque. One explanation for the chronological discrepancy concerning the process of ladinización could be that the missionary focused more of his attention on language as the key ethnic emblem.

Language was a crucial ethnic marker. Although it is impossible to estimate the number of Nauhatl-Pipil (locally called Nahuate) speakers with much accuracy, there is no doubt that the indigenous language of western Salvador was in decline by the end of the nineteenth century. In 1901 the Swedish ethnographer Carl Hartman wrote, based on his research in the late 1890s, that "the language is spoken by over one-quarter of the indigenous inhabitants [of western El Salvador], in other words, by between 20–30,000 individuals." In 1909 Walter Lehmann, the German linguist, estimated that approximately sixteen thousand people spoke Nahuate. According to Conte, the language entered a rapid decline in the Jayaque highlands between 1912 and 1930, years of expansion of the coffee industry. Thus although by 1930 the indigenous population, including the scattered communities of eastern Salvador, represented approximately 20 percent of the national population (or some 300,000 people), the number of native speakers, including bilinguals, probably did not surpass 25,000.[18]

Oral testimony substantiates the findings of Hartman and Lehmann and points to a fairly obvious pattern that emerged well before 1930: Nahuatl was weakest in those areas of greatest contact with ladinos and with primary schools. Public education in the town centers of Juayúa, Nahuizalco, and Izalco and in several cantons before 1932 had a pronounced negative effect on Nahuatl usage. Most Indians in town and in the immediate surroundings, born between 1890 and 1910, did not converse in Nahuatl with children or friends, using the language only on special religious occasions or with monolingual parents. In those regions where coffee plantations bordered or absorbed villages, Nahuatl was only spoken by the eldest generation (born before 1880), and the generation who were young adults in 1930 were not at all conversant in the language.[19]

Conte's brief description of ladinoization encapsulates a transformation as a result of which many poor highland residents by the mid-1920s would forget that their grandparents had spoken Nahuatl, dressed in indigenous dress, and belonged to relatively vibrant communities. In 1930 he visited Jicalapa and commented: "This indigenous population is 'ladinizing' right before our eyes. Only a dozen elderly men and women speak 'nahuate.' We were surprised and moved to see that children and young people have no interest in this language, so synthetic and full of imitative harmony."[20] Reflecting a common élite view, Conte described the modernization of the village, and in so doing implied that Indians could not maintain their ethnic markers and become "modern." Whether or not indigenous people involved in this transition shared his perspective, it is clear that the ethnic markers of dress and language were becoming the sine qua non of identity to many Indians and non-Indians alike. Several elderly informants who grew up in the highlands of Jayaque during the 1920s had no recollection of people whom they identified as indígenas in their communities.[21] All the informants reported that the only Indians with whom they had contact, apart from rare exceptions, were those of Izalco, although a few identified the more isolated cantons of Tepecoyo as indigenous.

One informant recalled how children mocked an elderly woman, the only Nahuate speaker in the area around Jayaque, calling her la Toña Muda (Toña, the deaf mute). That the woman stood out as different in the eyes of the children reveals just how powerful the ladinización process was in the highlands. The informants' definition of "indigenous" depended entirely on the ethnic markers of dress and language. Local registries re-

106

"Ese
Trabajo
Era
Enteramente
de los
Naturales"

produced the erasure of the indigenous population noted by informants and by Conte. To cite one example: in 1919 only one birth out of forty was listed as indigenous in the formerly indigenous municipality of Tepecoyo.[22]

In Gould's study of Nicaragua, he argued against an analysis that mechanically links mestizaje to proletarianization and the development of coffee capitalism.[23] Rather, he emphasized agrarian capital's multidimensional assault on indigenous land, labor, and political autonomy. Conte offers convincing evidence of what seems like a monocausal connection between the development of the coffee industry in the highlands of Jayaque and the loss of ethnic markers. At the same time, his description recalls a process that Gould described in Yúcul, Matagalpa. In this situation the Vita family, who were Italian immigrants, in effect expropriated an indigenous village and turned its residents into colonos on its coffee plantation: "Vita's proletarianization of the Yuculeños was accompanied by a process of ladinoization so thoroughgoing that the grandchildren of [an indigenous leader] do not recall that he was an Indian, much less a leader of the Comunidad Indígena. The Yuculeños between 1916–1950 lost contact with the Indian villages but ten miles away. Gradually they began to look upon the Indian women who came to pick Vita's coffee in the thirties and forties as people of a different ethnic group. The Yuculeños called them the 'mantiadas' for their dress, and those of 'lenguaje enredado' for their Spanish-based dialect. Thus, in one generation the Indians of Yúcul had lost their own ethnic identity."[24]

Despite the erasure of a specifically indigenous identity, the Yuculeños did maintain a separate, nonindigenous one, and in the 1960s they led a union drive that broke the back of the colonato system. To Die in This Way describes this cultural transformation as one of several strategic responses to the multipronged assault that accompanied proletarianization. The parallels with the highlands of Jayaque are striking. Both histories indicate that the rapid growth of coffee capitalism can dramatically affect indigenous cultural forms. At the same time, they suggest that the rapid movement of the subaltern group away from traditional ethnic markers did not translate into ideological submission. On the contrary, the highlands of Jayaque, like Yúcul, became a hotbed of a radical union movement. We can assume then that the loss of indigenous identity strictu sensu did not stifle a sense of opposition to the local élite. To orthodox Marxists such a proposition would have seemed almost tautological: social being determines social consciousness, hence proletarianization transforms corporative (or ethnic) consciousness into class consciousness. But a generation of cultural studies scholarship has definitively ruptured the assumption of a causal connection between material processes and consciousness in general, and more specifically that between proletarianization and class consciousness.

107

"Ese
Trabajo
Era
Enteramente
de los
Naturales"

Thus in interrogating the relationship between ladinoización and radicalization, To Die in This Way argued that communities such as Yúcul were politically and culturally open to dissident political forces precisely because of their unique history. In the highlands of Jayaque as well, previous forms of cultural distinctiveness and their memories of primitive accumulation distinguished these "mestizos" from others. The combination of memories of accumulation and fluency in national cultural codes facilitated communication with non-Indian leftist organizers in both Yúcul and Jayaque.

If this distinctive form of collective mestizaje was one response to agrarian capitalism in both countries, migration toward the agricultural frontier was another response of the indigenous people of the Nicaraguan highlands under the pressure of agrarian capitalism and the accompanying assault on their communities. In El Salvador in the 1920s many people, perhaps thousands, who might be described, however ambiguously, as "Indians," migrated to the Honduran coast to work on banana and sugar plantations.[25] A third strategic response was to retreat into more closed communities. Thus, for example, some highland Nicaraguan communities made conscious efforts to have contact with ladinos and governmental authorities only when absolutely necessary, such as for trading. In El Salvador some groups and communities made similar attempts to limit their contacts. The communities that maintained the sharpest lines of demarcation were those outside the coffee districts and those that had the greatest means of economic self-sufficiency. Nahuizalco, in particular, had an important handicraft industry, manufacturing petates for the army and baskets for the coffee industry. Although by the 1920s there were few indigenous families who avoided coffee labor altogether, the handicraft industry and smallholding in Nahuizalco, Izalco, and Santo Domingo still provided a material basis for many to avoid complete economic dependence on ladinos. Small individual and communal plots supported the handicraft economy, by providing access to the raw materials tule and carrizo.[26] Yet by 1930 a Protestant missionary in neighboring Juayúa reported, "[the Indians'] lands and property have dwindled away year by year."[27] The economic crisis also

108

"Ese
Trabajo
Era
Enteramente
de los
Naturales"

affected the handicraft industry and the vast regional commerce that sustained it.

Santo Domingo de Guzmán also was a handicraft center, specializing in pottery. It was a prototypical case of a community that maintained strict barriers against the encroachment of ladinos. The report of the departmental governor in 1913 underscored the Santo Domingo Indians' "hatred for ladinos."[28] Father Conte, who usually found "uncontaminated" Indian communities appealing, was less than thrilled with his encounter. Reporting on his mission of 1912, he lamented alcoholism and rampant illiteracy: "an Indian town where they speak Nahuat and express themselves in Spanish with difficulty . . . We have not found a more degenerate town, caused by chicha and la leche de tigra . . . If we require only one 'padre nuestro,' no one will get married in Santo Domingo. Several times people have told us that it is a conquest-era town; we are now convinced that . . . it is an unconquerable town."[29] Conte was frustrated at the inaccessibility of Santo Domingo to his teachings, which was primarily a result of its residents' weak command of Spanish, high level of illiteracy, and ignorance of the most fundamental precepts of contemporary Catholicism. His ethnographic details also suggest that this municipality had responded to the wave of ladinización sweeping the entire swath of the central and western parts of the country with strong communal defenses of political and cultural autonomy. Although Santo Domingo represented the epitome of a "closed" community in El Salvador, it was also quite exceptional, owing in large part to its relative physical isolation and, more importantly, its distance from coffee and cane lands. Cuisnahuat, to cite another relatively traditional community, lay outside the coffee zone but closer to its borders. Santo Domingueños survived through handicraft production and smallholding for basic grains production; like the Nahuizalqueños, they had significant trading contact with ladinos. However, unlike Cuisnahuat and in Nahuizalco, Santo Domingo had unattractive lands that helped to dissuade ladinos from settling there. Until 1932 this pueblo was unconquerable, because ladinos had little motivation to conquer it.

Sociogeographic explanations account for the Salvadoran Indians' unique response to the discourse and practice of mestizaje, which questioned the validity of indigenous identity and institutions in a putatively homogeneous, modernizing society. In both El Salvador and Nicaragua, and to a limited extent in Guatemala and Honduras, the cultural processes of mes-

tizaje placed severe strains on indigenous communities and tended to isolate "traditionalists" from others. However, unlike in Nicaragua and Honduras, the repertoire of indigenous responses in El Salvador included a
strain of ethnic militancy and revitalization.[30] That unique response probably derived from the relative economic importance, communal cohesion,
and geographic contiguity of indigenous groups. In Nicaragua, for example, the small indigenous communities of El Chile, Susulí, and Samulalí in
the department of Matagalpa were simply too small and too fragmented to
engage in any kind of autonomous movement. The other Nicaraguan indigenous communities were too widely dispersed geographically and too much
divided along political and generational lines. And throughout highland
and western Nicaragua and western Honduras, at the moment when cultural, political, and economic institutions came under severe assault by the
state and ladino planters at the turn of the century, the loss of ethnic
markers and the process of communal disintegration were already further
advanced than in El Salvador.[31]

Conte's account highlighted some communities in western El Salvador
that withstood the onslaught of ladinización. Underscoring the equivalence
of physical health, material well-being, and cultural vitality, he wrote, "The
truth is that you have [Indians] who are full of health and happiness and
own properties in Cuisnahuat, Teotepeque, y Jicalapa but . . . whites are
taking their land." In particular, he singled out Cuisnahuat as a municipality where Indians still maintained more of their cultural integrity and
control over land. He relates an anecdote from the mission of 1912 hinting
at a resurgence of ethnic pride that both coincided with the pressures
toward ladinoization and adumbrated future forms of cultural resistance.
In 1912 Father Carlos had just finished a sermon on *amancebamiento* (living
in sin). The indigenous mayor of Cuishnahut asked for permission to address the missionaries: "Your explanation is very good, tata padre, but
you've got the wrong audience! We shouldn't be the object of your criticism,
rather you should address those of your color. Before there were cheles
[whites] in our pueblo, we did not know the plague that you cursed. With all
due respect, I tell you this so that you blame the guilty and not their victims.
Good night and God bless you."[32] Conte also underscored other expressions of ethnic pride, pointing to the intimate relation between traditional
religious practices and cultural resistance. One incident occurred in the
Jayaque highlands in 1912. The missionaries considered a locally made

109

"Ese
Trabajo
Era
Enteramente
de los
Naturales"

110

"Ese
Trabajo
Era
Enteramente
de los
Naturales"

image of San Pedro to be a diabolic semi-human, semi-animal idol, "like those that their ancestors adored."[33] The parish priest "could no longer stand the image" and ordered a new one from a sculptor. The local Indians became furious: "He must be a mason, the Judas who stole our miraculous patron and replaced it with a 'chele sonso' who looks like a gringo."[34] When some residents reported seeing San Pedro in the forest crying and calling for justice, a large crowd seized the priest and carried him to the alcaldía to be imprisoned. An opportune telephone call brought the montada (mounted troops) from Santa Tecla to save him.

The missionaries learned that such behavior was not exceptional and that it was unwise to attack indigenous religious symbols. Conte recalled an incident among the indigenous people of Tacuba, who practiced highly festive wakes for "angels" (infants). The noise was so loud that the priests could not sleep. Father Eugenio went outside to demand that the mourners quiet down. He returned trembling with fear. The dueño del velorio had threatened him: "Look here curita, if you plan on living in peace with us, keep to your own things, and allow us to celebrate as we please, because the angels deserve everything!"[35]

The two anecdotes suggest the confluence of religious beliefs and ethnic solidarity. There is a marked contrast between the positive reception of the missionaries and other priests and the bitterness of the indigenous response to any perceived assault on their practices. The use of the term chele sonso (white fool) in the Teotepeque account ties religious imagery to racial pride. In much the same way, the use of the disdainful diminutive curita reflects a latent rage at any cultural or religious offense. And in 1913 the Sonsonate departmental governor's report stated that the indigenous people of Izalco were peaceful except when ladinos challenged their religious beliefs or practices.[36]

Throughout Mesoamerica during the first decades of the twentieth century, indigenous communities resisted efforts by the Catholic Church to reform their religious practices. According to the historian Rodolfo Cardenal, "The cofradía was the first cause of conflict. Concretely, the official religion impugned the free administration of the cofradía's goods and properties and their venerable customs and uses considered alien to all Catholic morality."[37] Cardenal's study emphasizes the enormous gulf between the church and popular religiosity, which the church found "incomprehensible and alien to true Catholicism, of which the Church was the only interpreter."[38]

Nahuizalco was the scene of bitter conflicts between official and popular forms of religiosity. Religious imagery was crucial to the reproduction of ethnic solidarity among the Nahuizalqueños. Hartman reported that at the end of the nineteenth century Nahuizalqueños worshiped ancient stone idols, including a man-sized one at the town's entrance known as *señor del camino*. The Nahuizalqueños forcefully opposed the efforts of the town priest to remove their idols. He went so far as to dynamite an idol that he claimed was used in human sacrifice. Yet older idols continued to form integral parts of the agricultural cycle. During the evenings at planting time, the Indians lit candles and incense near the idols. Once the rains arrived they moved the idols from the *milpas* (cornfields) and buried them in river-beds until the next planting time. Over a decade after the privatization of lands, the Nahuizalqueños still practiced elaborate communal rituals around corn planting: throughout the milpa, they dug holes into which they poured a small quantity of *chiliate* (white corn flour). Once the planting was done they placed sharpened shovels at the cardinal points of the milpas to protect them from hurricanes.

Two decades later Conte reported a similar distance between the Catholic Church and everyday religious practices in Nahuizalco: "They render absolute tribute to the cross. For them, the cross is a person of flesh and blood . . . he sees, hears, walks, has a sombrero and lives with other crosses."[39] As elsewhere in western Salvador, the Nahuizalqueños remained at odds with the local representatives of the Catholic Church. According to local informants, the struggle between indigenous religious practices and the local priests continued into the 1920s. For example, in 1929 Indians protested that a ladino had stolen their image of the *niño dios*, and threatened to use their machetes to retrieve it.[40] More significantly, *El Heraldo de Sonsonate* reported the following incident in Nahuizalco in April 1931: "The inditos also have their bitter moments. Yesterday someone told me that four ambitious ones have plotted to take away from the mayordomo of the Cofradía del Santo Entierro, el Señor and other images . . . and since the priest gets taken in by the sacristán . . . the four ambitious ones have decided to remove el Señor."[41] The mayor of Nahuizalco also supported the attempt to remove the imágen, alleging communist infiltration of the cofradías.[42] The alliance of "los cuatro ambiciosos" with the priest to appropriate the image was consistent with Church-Indian conflicts in the rest of Central America.[43] The intervention of the mayor, however, was a clear signal of increased blurring of the line between religious and political conflict.

112

"Ese
Trabajo
Era
Enteramente
de los
Naturales"

There was another religious dimension that contributed, at the very least indirectly, to a weakening of hegemonic structures. Since the early years of the twentieth century Protestant missionaries had penetrated throughout the country, and by the 1920s they had managed to attract a small group of faithful. In 1931 in San Salvador, for example, 150 children attended a Protestant Sunday school; in Nahuizalco and Juayúa, despite persecution, the Protestants were having limited but growing success. In 1930 forty-four Nahuizalqueños attended a ceremony celebrating the Baptist congregations' second year of existence.[44] There seem to have been two sources for the qualified Protestant success. First, as has been amply documented for the period a generation later in Guatemala, some indigenous people saw Protestant churches as a way to exit the cargo system and others saw it as a way of becoming "modern," among other things by rejecting fiestas and the drinking that accompanied them. Protestants also offered a kind of critique of wealth and power. For example, one Protestant missionary commented that in Juayúa and Santa Catarina Masahuat Indian landownership was less extensive, with the result that local campesinos were living "under the tutelage of wealthy planters."[45] The Reverend Roy MacNaught was attuned to the problem of ladino racism, at least after the massacre. Upon learning of the death of one of his converts and helpers in Nahuizalco, MacNaught commented: "As he was a faithful worker in the gospel, he had many enemies; as he was an Indian, he had other enemies among those who consider themselves superior to this race and cannot bear to see an Indian prosper."[46]

Father Conte recognized the subversive character of Protestants and paranoiacally lumped them together with Bolsheviks. For example, of his visit to the city of Ahuachapán in 1930, he wrote: "The Lutheran-Bolshevik propaganda has terribly ravaged Christ's flock."[47] Much of Conte's writing on Protestantism amounted to crude attacks, such as imagining that Protestants converted people who believed that "if faith alone saves us, then let's eat, drink, and have a great time."[48] Yet by equating the power of the Catholic Church with authority in the larger society, he did connect the small Protestant advance with social contestation: "the spirit of darkness is chipping away at the little remaining fear of God that kept the residents in line . . . it undermines the principle of authority and opens the door to all manner of disorder and misdeeds."[49]

Very few Protestants supported the labor movement, and their missionaries lambasted communism with as much fervor as any priest. Notwithstanding this, many testimonies linked Protestants to the mobilization. In particular, informants in various towns claimed that the leftist labor organizers disguised themselves as Protestant ministers. Those testimonies may have been influenced by the massacre of January 1932, when Protestant Indians were singled out for execution and accused of taking part in the uprising. There is thus little doubt that the growth of Protestantism, if not necessarily another form of religious protest by Indians, probably did contribute to the generalized sense that all things ideological were up for grabs.

Language and Resistance

Religion was the key arena, but not the only one, in which ethnic solidarity was reproduced and cultural mestizaje was resisted (though one might argue that indigenous religious practices were one of the highest expressions of cultural mestizaje). Language formed another field of contention, one absent from the struggles of Nicaraguan and Honduran Indians (except those of the Mosquito Coast), since their indigenous languages had become virtually extinct by the turn of the century.

According to Andrés Pérez, an informant whose father had been close to the pre-1932 political and cultural leaders of Nahuizalco, language preservation was the focus of popular mobilization. Referring to the late nineteenth century and the early twentieth, he related his father's teachings: "My dad would tell me that los abuelos claimed that they were too old to learn another language. According to the law, no Nahuizalqueño could speak publicly in Nahuatl. According to the governor, to speak Nahuatl made the people backward. They visited the mayor and told him that they couldn't accept another language. Then they treated them like an opposition group. My grandfather told the mayor, as an Indian he shouldn't be against his brothers. The mayor was close to the government and told him that those who did not accept the law were communists. The abuelos said: We can't accept the law. We were born in our language. They threatened to kill many people. The weakest began to teach Spanish."[50] There is no documentary evidence to substantiate Pérez's charge about the prohibition of Nahuatl. In fact in 1924 the national government financed a study of Nahuatl-Pipil in Nahuizalco. However, the development of primary school

114

"Ese
Trabajo
Era
Enteramente
de los
Naturales"

education for the children of townsfolk undoubtedly had a negative impact on language use and probably provoked opposition from traditional sectors of the municipality's indigenous population. According to the departmental governor's report, in 1913 the Indians in Nahuizalco did not send their children to school, so as to avoid mingling with ladinos.[51] A novelistic version of the introduction of schools to Salvadoran indigenous regions recounts the battle to push castellanización. In *Ola Roja*, by Machón Vilanova, a lawyer states, "When I was in the Sub-Secretaria de Estado, I did everything possible to improve the condition of the Indians, but, to a great extent, this did not happen due to their lack of cooperation. Almost resorting to violence, we managed to get the children to receive their classes in Spanish. They spoke our language in school, but outside they would go back to speaking Nahuat."[52]

Despite the resistance, by 1930 primary education had spread to some of the cantons of Nahuizalco and Izalco, and with it the stimulus to speak Spanish at the expense of the indigenous language.[53] Oral testimony suggests that the church strongly discouraged Nahuatl-Pipil before 1932, just as priests prohibited the use of Lenca in western Honduras during the late nineteenth century.[54] The contradictory attitude of the church toward indigenous language undoubtedly reflected its multiple ideological currents. Conte, for example, a Pauline, would have been furious with any priest who attempted to denigrate, let alone prohibit, the language he loved. Yet as a missionary he was constantly on the move, neither needing nor wanting to forge alliances with local ladinos. Paradoxically, as Gould noted in the Nicaraguan context, the most ardent defenders of Indians were in areas where they were least effective: national intellectuals who rhetorically and even politically valorized Indians had little local knowledge of their relations with ladinos.[55]

Apart from its dubious assertion about a prohibition of Nahuate, Pérez's testimony tells us about collective memory and perhaps indicates some facets of communal history before 1932. First, it suggests that the ladinos' scorn for Nahuate and its rejection by the younger generation were felt quite strongly, perhaps as painfully as if the language had been prohibited. It also suggests the political importance of the perceived assault on the language. Although much of the language transformation was subtle and largely unconscious, there was very possibly a conscious effort to resist it. For example, Conte mentioned the eager support among village elders in the highlands of Jayaque in 1930 for his effort to preserve a written version of their dialect of Nahuatl-Pipil.[56]

It is also highly plausible that an organization rooted in what had formerly been a civil-religious hierarchy, Los Abuelos, should have considered the attack on language vitally important. The growing loss of language may well have pushed many of the elders toward a multitiered resistance, as suggested by Pérez, including a defense of land and political control. Finally, some bilingual Nahuate speakers continued to speak their native language as a deliberate expression of pride and resistance against those who equated "speaking well" with the Spanish language.[57] Although most Nahuate-speaking parents either encouraged or accepted that their children answer them in Spanish, some Nahuizalqueño parents as late as 1930 scolded their children for not having pride in their language.

Racism, Resistance, and Mobilization

Language and religion were thus two key sites of indigenous cultural cohesion and resistance, which in turn sustained other forms of ethnic pride that affected Indians regardless of their mode of dress or expression. Certain communal practices, for example the use of voluntary, collective labor in agriculture and house construction, also fostered cohesion. The indigenous people in Cuisnahuat socialized their male adolescents in a manner that promoted group solidarity and cultural pride: they gathered all young, single men between 8:00 and 9:00 p.m. in a large, open house.[58] and after socializing for an hour they would sleep in this casa de solteros.

Ironically, the state fostered another form of youthful solidarity. The ethnographer Hartman in the late 1890s reported seeing a line of twenty Indians tied together with a rope, escorted by armed soldiers. When he asked if they were prisoners, a companion commented that they were "volunteers" from Nahuizalco who were marched from their home to the barracks in San Salvador. Later he found out that "when they are needed, El Salvador's barracks fill up with indígenas who have to fulfill their military service. They are often more reliable and more courageous than the ladinos."[59] In 1913 the departmental governor commented that Nahuizalqueños made the best troops because of their valor and discipline.[60] Rocío Tábora finds that the heavy recruitment of western Honduran Indians in the early twentieth century contributed to the process of cultural mestizaje; it

"Ese
Trabajo
Era
Enteramente
de los
Naturales"

is as yet unclear whether the military had a similar impact on Salvadoran Indians before 1932.[61] There is little doubt, however, that what appears to have been a segregated recruitment process both enhanced intragroup solidarity and further ennobled masculine values of physical force and courage.

Evidence of other forms of indigenous pride and associated practices is scattered through the written record, and somewhat elusive. One of the clearest statements of the discourse of ethnic revitalization can be found in the words of an inebriated Nahuizalqueño at a wedding attended by an Italian journalist: "When needed, El Salvador's barracks fill up with indígenas who have to fulfill their military service. They are often more reliable and more courageous than the ladino soldiers."[62] Foreign observers also noted signs of indigenous pride. Wallace Thompson, for example, wrote: "It is an amusing turn of the tables that much of the independent labor that works for extra high wages at picking time comes from the Indian communities where the aborigines have their own huts and their own bits of farm land. Thus, the 'civilized' Indians of Salvador holds himself at a higher value than his mixed-blood cousin."[63]

Expressions of respect and disrespect were at the core of indigenous pride and ladino racism. The quality of racism, not surprisingly, varied by class and intensified with the degree of political or economic conflict. Faced with the political control of Indians, for example, a group of ladinos of Cuisnahuat sent the following protest to the national government: "We, the true Indians, the Indian kings! The pure ones. . . we know what the white people do not. We await our time. We are the owners of the mountains, the valleys, the coffee plantations, the houses—everything you can see."[64] Referring to indigenous political control of the municipal government of Santa Catarina Masahuat, near Nahuizalco, a ladino resident commented: "the few semi thinkers that reside here wanted to put in a young white named Escobar, a poor, but honest man. The problem is that to get a white [elected] among all these indigestos is going to be difficult."[65] The use of the term indigesto, also employed in Boaco, Nicaragua, had the connotation that Indians were nauseating.[66]

Informal residential segregation contributed to racism in élite and popular sectors. In a pattern congruent with that of much of Mesoamerica, in predominantly Indian municipalities, ladinos occupied the town center surrounded by Indian barrios and villages (see figure, page 120). Poor ladinos often inhabited separate cantons or separate valles within the cantons. Such segregation probably contributed to the perpetuation of deep prejudices among ladino élites and campesinos. Many believed that Indians were *malos*, that is, practitioners of evil witchcraft. Some associated the indigenous *refajo* (a colorful one-piece cotton garment for women) with witchcraft. Others considered indigenous women "filthy," since they imagined quite erroneously that the women wore no undergarment beneath the refajo and did not wash it.[67]

117

"Ese
Trabajo
Era
Enteramente
de los
Naturales"

Middle-class and élite racism often revolved around the notion of Indians as impediments to progress. In another article on the political situation in Santa Catarina Masahuat, a reporter commented: "That town has always been governed by illiterate men; for them progress is unknown. Yet, through good fortune and the influence of a few powerful men during the years 1926 and 1927 the municipal government was formed by the capable, educated [capacitado] sector of the population, in other words, the ladinos and among their other accomplishments was the installation of drinking water. But during the last two years, the local government was in the hands of Indians and progress stagnated."[68] This idea that Indians were antithetical to progress was widespread throughout the continent; it was repeated even by the most ardent supporters of Indians, as we saw with Conte.[69] Even what middle-class admirers the Indians did have could not overcome their own racist stereotypes, invariably referring to the Indians with the patronizing term *inditos* (the diminutive form, insinuating the childlike character of Indians). Carlos Estrada of Nahuizalco, for example, wrote a column in *El Heraldo de Sonsonate* attacking the élite for their attitudes and practices, arguing that they mistreated the "inditos whose work helps them to earn the money with which they travel."[70]

One of the first middle-class reactions to the incorporation of Indians into the mobilization was to criticize their ignorance and gullibility. A Nahuizalco ladino, worried about the growing strength of the left among the Indians after the events of 17 May, referred to the "unwary poor people who . . . are stirred up by the ambitious who deceive them with chimerical promises that will lead them only to punishment."[71] The obvious implication of this typical piece of ladino discourse was that the Indians were incapable of reason and were easily manipulated. Ladino racism in western Salvador before 1932 was certainly no more venomous than elsewhere in Central America where analogous bi-ethnic communities existed, for exam-

"Ese
Trabajo
Era
Enteramente
de los
Naturales"

ple in the highlands of Matagalpa or in western Honduras.[72] The deep, es-sentialized beliefs about Indians impeded the development of cross-ethnic friendships and liaisons. Similarly, the younger generations of the former indigenous communities seem to have developed negative beliefs about the older generations of self-identified Indians.

In light of this level of racism, indigenous hostility toward ladinos, and the left's lack of cognitive tools to deal with cultural difference, it is re-markable that a cross-ethnic labor movement emerged so successfully. The rural mobilization preceding the events of May 1931 and leading up to the insurrection of January 1932, in addition to intensifying local forms of racism, involved rural workers and peasants who despite their variegated forms of identity responded positively to the class ideology promoted by leftist activists. Those class-rooted, populist messages and activities, as we have seen, appealed to a wide range of people: those who regarded Indians as a somewhat backward "other," those who identified strongly with indigenous political authority and culture, and those who simply did not care. The positive response to the radical movement involved dif-ferential social and political reactions to the discourse and practice of mestizaje.

In Nahuizalco and in the town of Izalco, traditionalists played an impor-tant role in the mobilization. Consider the testimony of Andrés Pérez about his father and grandfather, like him indigenous residents of the canton of Pushtan: "My grandfather had belonged to an organization commonly called Los Abuelos in Nahuizalco, dedicated to protecting indigenous cul-ture, political autonomy and land. My father, Juan Pérez was one of the few literate people in Pushtan. He worked as a colono on a cattle hacienda, on land that earlier had belonged to the community. When the Socorro Rojo started organizing in the area, my father became the organizational secre-tary. It was for him no different than Los Abuelos."[73] Although leftist mili-tants did not support specifically pro-Indian demands, their appeal lay in their nonracist forms of daily interaction and their broad, egalitarian, and emancipatory language, which Indians interpreted as support for their po-litical, economic, and cultural rights.[74] In Pérez's testimony we see that the mobilization of the late 1920s was a continuation of the struggles of Los Abuelos (a *consejo de ancianos*) against encroachments on land and restric-tions on religious and cultural expression.

119

"Ese
Trabajo
Era
Enteramente
de los
Naturales"

Throughout the nineteenth century civil-religious hierarchies effectively governed municipalities in the west. Rodolf Cardenal writes: "The integration between the religious and the civil followed the same structure of the towns which were organized by a political-religious cargo system. . . . The only people who could obtain political positions were those who had previously attained prestige, carrying out duties in the religious sphere . . . To serve the saint was to serve the people and vice versa."[75] During the first decades of the twentieth century political pressures challenged the cargo system throughout western El Salvador. In Izalco the Alcalde del Común was effectively excluded from direct political power over the municipal government. However, he did maintain a significant political presence as a representative of the indigenous population to the departmental and national governments, while holding a position at the apex of the religious cargoes. In Nahuizalco the situation was different, as the alcaldía municipal had by the 1920s become completely divorced from the religious cargo system, and no religious authority also had political authority. It seems likely that the overwhelming demographic dominance of the indigenous population in Nahuizalco (over 80 percent in the 1930s) did not make a separate polity (such as the "común') seem necessary. In Izalco, where by the 1920s the indigenous community, located primarily in one barrio, was equal or smaller than the ladino population, a separate alcaldía indígena was a useful institution.

In Nahuizalco, the transformation of Los Abuelos into a political organization responded to the breakup of the civil and religious hierarchy. Its ideological tilt to the left did have political costs, most notably in municipal politics. As noted in chapter 2 and by other historians, municipal politics were an important site of ethnic conflict during the 1920s and 1930s.[76] The bitter local political conflicts in Nahuizalco and Izalco spilled over into the mobilization. In Nahuizalco the former local indigenous political élite, made up primarily of urban artisans, merchants, and small-scale farmers, had engaged in decades-long conflicts (and occasional alliances) with local ladinos. For example, a dispute over the privatization of some remaining communal land sharply divided the indigenous political élite between those who allied themselves with wealthy ladinos and those traditionalists who began to look left for allies.[77]

"Ese
Trabajo
Era
Enteramente
de los
Naturales"

Late nineteenth-century view
of Nahuizalco. Photo by Carl
Hartman, courtesy of the Museo
de la Palabra y la Imagen.

Indian Women in Nahuizalco,
1898. Photo by Carl Hartman,
courtesy of the Museo de la
Palabra y la Imagen.

The leftward tilt of Los Abuelos further split the indigenous political élite. Thus a former municipal leader, Cupertino Galicia, rejected the repeated entreaties of his former political allies to join the movement.[78] Galicia was a prominent member of the cofradías and had suffered at the hands of the church-ladino alliance. In 1931, when he was *mayordomo* of a festival, people allied with the priest yanked the image of the Beatísima from him. He was also related to a prominent Nahuizalqueño union leader. Nevertheless, he rejected the movement.[79] As a "middle farmer," he employed farm laborers who joined the mobilization. Political and ethnic ties notwithstanding, Galicia and others like him watched the expansion of the Socorro Rojo with apprehension, and in 1932 feared for their lives.

In Izalco, a municipality divided roughly equally between ladinos and Indians, the indigenous cofradías played a significant role in the mobilization. As in Nahuizalco, control over the cofradías became a flashpoint for cultural conflict. In Izalco, though, as noted earlier, the battle for municipal control also included struggles over water and *acequias* (irrigation ditches).[80] The political and ethnic divide was far sharper and more complex in Izalco, as witnessed in the presidential elections of 1931, when ladino artisans and workers joined indigenous and ladino campesinos in support of Araujo against a coalition of indigenous people (in the barrio Asunción) and the ladino élite. It is therefore all the more striking that by 1931 ladino artisans and workers in Izalco joined indigenous campesinos in the mobilization. As early as August 1930, the National Guard had arrested ladino and indigenous carpenters.[81] In the critical elections of January 1932, a ladino carpenter, Eusebio Chávez, was the left-wing candidate for mayor, primarily but not exclusively supported by the Izalqueño Indian group.[82]

Thus far we have focused on the "traditionalist" response to the varied political, economic, and cultural pressures on the indigenous communities rooted in the towns of Izalco and Nahuizalco. However, even in those centers of ethnic militancy, the lines between assimilationists and traditionalists were extremely fluid. Throughout the rest of western Salvador the quality of ethnic relations was even more intricate, revealing other facets of the subaltern response to the processes of cultural mestizaje and ethnic conflict. In the cantons of Izalco, home of most who took part in the demonstrations of 17 May, many people considered "Indians" distanced themselves considerably from the people of the urban barrio of Asunción, who were often more closely identified with indigenous markers of dress

122

"Ese
Trabajo
Era
Enteramente
de los
Naturales"

and language.[83] Informants who were children in 1930 recall how their parents would use indigenous work clothes and then, when they approached the town limits, change into ladino clothes. Notwithstanding what appears to have been an accelerated pace of cultural mestizaje in the cantons (including more language loss than in the indigenous barrio of Izalco), there were still sharp distinctions between indigenous families in the villages and poor ladinos who had migrated to the area over the previous twenty or thirty years. These distinctions did not coincide with class distinctions: Indians and ladinos found themselves among the ranks of laborers, colonos, and smallholders in roughly similar proportions.[84] In the canton of Cuyagualo, however, ladino migrants had become smallholders and indigenous families were colonos on coffee fincas owned by wealthy Sonsontecos and Izalqueños.[85] Whatever their broad class similarities, Indian and ladino neighbors did not get along harmoniously. In the words of an indigenous resident of Ceiba del Charco, an ethnically mixed canton, "The ladinos didn't want to be with the Indians."[86] In bi-ethnic cantons or villages, those involved in labor and leftist organizations were indigenous. Sotero Linares, a ladino agricultural worker from the canton of Cuntan (Izalco), commented: "This work was done entirely by los naturales, by the most Indian (de los más inditos). And we who were of mixed blood knew nothing about it."[87] In the bi-ethnic cantons of Izalco, as we shall see, ethnic divisions were highly salient in the mobilization and insurrection.

In Los Arenales, a predominantly ladino canton that borders the coffee-producing zone of Nahuizalco, the rebellion and repression took the form of a civil war rooted in ethnic differences. In the eyes of many of the ladino campesinos (rural workers, semi-proletarians, and small proprietors), the mobilization had a definite ethnic character that excluded them. Despite the class rhetoric of the mobilization, Indian rebels were capable of killing their class brethren, especially ladinos opposed to the movement. Jesús Velasquez, a child in Los Arenales in 1932, recalls the fear and hatred of his family (ladino smallholders) toward the indigenous rebels. He witnessed, and his grandfather participated in, the massacre of hundreds of Indians in El Canelo. He recalled the words uttered by his grandfather: "Otherwise they would have killed us."[88]

Yet regardless of these deep ethnic antagonisms, indigenous militants were perfectly capable of transcending local ethnic boundaries when they organized rural workers on haciendas or in neighboring ladino villages. As

Fabián Mojica,
Sónzacate. Courtesy
of the Museo de la
Palabra y la Imagen.

"Ese
Trabajo
Era
Enteramente
de los
Naturales"

Fabián Mojica, a ladino carpenter and labor organizer, underscored in referring to his organizational work in Cuyagualo and Cuntan in 1930, "The
indígenas were very conscious. Juan Hernández and other compañeros of
Cuyagualo themselves went to San Julián to organize the laborers."[89] In
other words, militants of indigenous origin, who experienced sharp conflict
with their ladino neighbors, had no difficulty working politically with poor
ladinos of other locales, such as those who labored on the coffee plantations of San Julián.

Indians from Cuisnahuat, despite their aforementioned hostility toward
ladinos in the same municipality, worked in the labor movement with ladinos from the village of Los Gramales, five kilometers away.[90] Migrants from
Suchitoto and Ilobasco had populated that village over the previous generation. Some owned small farms and others worked on haciendas. The
workplace interaction of ladinos from Los Gramales and Cuisnahuat Indians enabled them to overcome their cultural differences and join the same
movement. Tacuba, a bi-ethnic coffee producing municipality north of
Ahuachapán, also became a hotbed of radical labor. According to Conte, in
1915 there were approximately seven thousand Indians and three thousand
ladinos in the municipality. Estimates around 1930 increased the ladino
proportion to 40 percent.[91] Ladinos occupied the town center, but they
shared the urban space with Nahuate-speaking Indians who lived in Chi-
lapa, a large, irregularly arranged barrio of ranchos. Although the town's
ethnic relations reflected class divisions, the surrounding countryside was
more complex, similar to that of Izalco. Various informants described the
inhabitants of some cantons, such as Los Arcos, as mostly ladino *pobretones*
or *poquiteros*. Rural Tacubeños, Indians and ladinos alike, worked on the

124

"Ese
Trabajo
Era
Enteramente
de los
Naturales"

coffee farms, yet according to Conte relations between them were poor during the teens and twenties. He wrote about the indigenous population of Tacuba in 1915: "Unlike their brothers in the rest of the Republic, the tacubeños hide from the priest . . . and are very shy around ladinos. It made us laugh to see the children hide behind the doors of their rancho or in some gully when we walked by."[92] Informants recall the sharp ethnic separation, symbolized by the Indians' epithets *mulatos* and *mulatillos*, used to describe all ladinos regardless of phenotype. Despite this deep hostility, the SRI, under the leadership of three ladino brothers, was able to recruit a mass following within both groups. The Cuenca family had become prosperous as cattle ranchers and coffee buyers. The sons were thus able to attend the university in San Salvador, where they became exposed to radical ideas. Their intimate knowledge of the local sociogeographic terrain probably aided them in their recruitment efforts. The eldest brother, Alfonso, became the PCS candidate for congressional deputy for the department of Ahuachapán, presumably based on his large bi-ethnic base of support in Tacuba.

Similarly, Julián Ortiz, an Indian jornalero from Nahuizalco, rose through the ranks of the SRI to become a key departmental leader. According to General José Tomás Calderón, special delegate of Araujo who traveled to Sonsonate to investigate the events of 17 May, some two hundred of the protesters spent the night at the hacienda where Ortiz worked: "This individual is indígena and one of the most active communists of that canton and to whom the other indígenas blindly obey."[93] Although Calderón was right that Ortiz was a leader and an Indian, he was wrong about the ethnic makeup of his followers in El Cacao, in a hacienda region whose workers were overwhelmingly non-Indian. Ortiz's case is significant. In Nahuizalco, where ethnic divisions were deep, he had become a highly successful organizer of ladino jornaleros and a respected leader of the SRI. The biography of another Indian, Francisco Sánchez, who became the principal SRI and FRTS leader in the Juayúa area, was quite similar in that he was an Indian who organized ladino and indigenous workers alike.

General Calderón likely shared the misconceptions of the British and U.S. embassy officials and others in the Salvadoran élite, who did not usually make any distinctions between Indians and other rural poor people in western Salvador. Notwithstanding their view that all the rural poor were "Indians," such analytical distinctions are important if we wish to understand the broad appeal of leftist organizations during the early 1930s.[94] If we have to cast aside the notion of an indigenous mobilization and rebellion *tout court*, what difference did these ethnic ideologies and conflicts make in the mobilization? In some places and at some times, they mattered a great deal. In particular, with the notable exception of Tacuba, in those areas where Indians and Ladinos lived side by side the mobilization often appeared to be an indigenous movement, and poor Ladinos, after the insurrection, became willing recruits for the forces of repression.

125

"Ese
Trabajo
Era
Enteramente
de los
Naturales"

In the department of La Libertad, the historical processes of land concentration and labor relations fostered by the coffee boom, and the unique forms of consciousness of ex-members of indigenous communities, created a predisposition toward alliances with leftist militants. As we mentioned above, the Nicaraguan highland communities that the coffee industry had transformed or absorbed became centers of the radical labor movement four decades later. It seems probable that in La Libertad, as in the Nicaraguan communities, the memory of primitive accumulation—ladino appropriation of former communal landholdings—and the shared cultural codes, especially language, facilitated the circulation and acceptance of leftist ideas.

The radicalization of the laboring classes in the department of Ahuachapán took place in a complex ethnic tapestry. In 1930 the department experienced ethnic conflict per se only in Tacuba. Ladinización had affected a large barrio in the city of Ahuachapán and nearby cantons during the previous decades. In 1892 in the city of Ahuachapán, 54 percent of births were listed as indígenas, yet by 1930 few if any people in the barrio or adjacent cantons identified themselves as Indians or possessed any ethnic markers.[95] The urban and rural workers who participated in the labor movement had only the remotest connections to an indigenous past, although it is possible that like their comrades in La Libertad they possessed memories of the loss of communal land.

In the eastern part of Ahuachapán there was virtually no indigenous presence.[96] Father Conte, for example, related a local legend that maroons who had escaped from Guatemala founded the city of Atiquizaya (population fifteen thousand in 1915). He added, "The truth is that the color of the skin, the hair, the mores and customs do tend to give credence to the legend."[97] Oral testimony from Juayúa and Nahuizalco suggests that the people from Turín and Atiquizaya were phenotypically mulatto. The other

126

"Ese
Trabajo
Era
Enteramente
de los
Naturales"

primary area of leftist recruitment, among the permanent residents of the coffee and sugar haciendas on the mountain slopes north of the city, leading up toward Juayúa and east across the Llano de Doña María, lacked both indigenous identity and ethnic identification in recent history.

The ethnic mosaic of Ahuachapán posed less of a challenge to the left, thanks in part to a religious phenomenon. Throughout the department, the cult of the Virgin of Adelanto melded together in spiritual unity many Indians from Tacuba and poor ladinos. They participated in a quasi-millenarian movement based across the border in eastern Guatemala. In the town of El Adelanto, Guatemala, a young virgin woman, Petrona Corado, claimed to have returned from the dead to perform miracles. During the late 1920s and early 1930s the cult of the Virgen del Adelanto attracted hundreds of Guatemalan and Salvadoran peasants to the town. The Virgin of Adelanto appeared throughout the area of Ahuachapán bordering Guatemala, particularly in Caña Brava, Agua Fria, and Hechadura. Informants recall that a white paper screen was set up in front of the devout. Some recall that only virgin girls could see the Virgin of Adelanto and hear her words. Evidence suggests that the Virgin preached a message of radical social change and thus became identified with the left. At least some grassroots leftist militants participated in pilgrimages, and several informants in the west strongly associate the cult with the radical movement. Some informants on the left and pro-Martínez commentators argued that militants manipulated the cult in order to gather crowds to whom they could proselytize without fear of government repression. Not surprisingly, landowners and local authorities felt much threatened by the peasants' and workers' passion for union meetings and for the Virgin of Adelanto.[98] By late 1931 authorities in both countries suppressed the cult; Salvadoran officials charged that Socorro Rojo used it as a cover for its activities.[99]

Patriarchy and Violence

The cult of the Virgin of Adelanto attracted a large following of women, some of whom also participated in the leftist movement. Indeed the participation of women in the movement challenged the rigid patriarchal norms and relations that characterized Salvadoran indigenous communities, and to a somewhat lesser extent ladino communities. Ironically, the patriarchal norms themselves, in particular those related to notions of masculinity, also indirectly aided the mobilization.

We are employing the term patriarchy in its most general sense, as a system of customary (and judicial) laws, symbols, ideas, and practices that support male domination over females and children. All of Salvadoran society was of course patriarchal—males had unquestioned control over women and children. There were, however, significant differences between élite and popular sectors in their child-rearing practices and between ladinos and Indians in their codification of male and female marital roles. To a significant extent, differences in male control over female sexuality formed part of the ethnic boundaries in rural Salvador.

Indigenous patriarchy was by no means unique to El Salvador; male elders ruled in most other indigenous societies (indeed in most societies of any kind).[100] In *To Die in This Way* Gould noted that in Central America, as elsewhere, strict limits on female sexuality enforced indigenous endogamy, and at the same time, "structures of indigenous patriarchy presented an extraordinarily powerful symbol to even sympathetic outsiders."[101] As in western Honduras, ladinos often claimed that some Indians practiced incest and in general ladinos considered Indians' sexual practices barbaric. Some indigenous practices in the early twentieth century were certainly different from those of other Salvadorans.[102]

Endogamous marriage practices like those of other Central American Indians were essential to maintaining indigenous patriarchy. Arranged marriages and patrilocal residence patterns, in particular, were customary among both Salvadoran and Nicaraguan Indians during this period.[103] As in other societies, endogamy and male control over women were central to preserving the indigenous community, or at least so it appeared to the village elders.[104] An official publication in 1916 underscored the uniqueness of indigenous patriarchy and its connection to community governance: "at times several generations live under one roof under the common guardianship of the elders, the supreme command of the house-hold is invested in the oldest man who constitutes, as it were, the court of last appeal. These 'mayores' are called 'ahuales' and form the counselors of the community."[105]

Although Father Conte was generally sympathetic toward indigenous cultural practices, extreme forms of patriarchy repelled him. Commenting about Cuisnahuat in 1912, he wrote: "For the woman, the duties, for the husband, the rights. While she sweats, carrying goods like a pack mule up and down hills, he struts behind her, smoking or chewing cane . . . Inside the home, the situation is worse for the poor woman: she has to do everything, while the man growls and threatens her with a whip, which he uses

128

"Ese
Trabajo
Era
Enteramente
de los
Naturales"

on her to show his jurisdictional power! Instead of complaining, the unfortunate slave carries about her business as if nothing has happened and even is happy to know that these caresses of her master that her parents obliged her to marry are a sign of unequivocal love."[106] Although it is debatable whether indigenous patriarchy was more oppressive in El Salvador than in other parts of the Americas, marriage and sexual practices were highly codified.[107] In Panchimalco, an indigenous community south of San Salvador, the elderly informants of the anthropologist Alejandro Marroquín recounted that in the early twentieth century the community shared a belief that the eleventh day following the start of a new moon was propitious for procreating healthy, strong bodies, and that an earlier date in the lunar cycle would produce "cowardly men." Thus according to Marroquín's informants, on *once luna*, around nine o'clock, municipal authorities would walk the streets beating a drum and at intervals shouting, "Now is the time to conceive, gentlemen." From their homes people would then respond, "We're working on it." For the next eight days sexual relations were encouraged. After the eighth night, municipal authorities prohibited relations (an enforceable regulation, since the thatched roofs shook during the act).[108]

During the 1920s the growing number of indigenous women economically obliged to work on plantations and haciendas loosened the bonds of patriarchy. Arthur Ruhl's comments about James Hill's coffee plantation are apposite. He relates the owner's words: "They used to do nothing, just take care of their babies, cook for their husbands, and potter 'round their places. But I kept urging them to work and now I have plenty. . . . Why, lots of these women go round now with silk stockings on, while they're carrying armfuls of brush and dirt. Naturally, they tear 'em to pieces."[109] Hill implied that the women engaged in everyday resistance, which resulted in wage increases, allowing them to purchase luxury items such as silk stockings. We can speculate that some women workers, after such experience and presumably after acquiring new consumer tastes, would become active in the labor movement.

The increase in the number of indigenous women plantation workers also resulted in more voluntary and involuntary relations with ladinos of different classes.[110] Father Conte alluded to the sexual appetite and power of the landlords when he reported on the mores of the largely indigenous coffee town of Jujutla, Ahuachapán: " 'If the boss has three, four or more concubines, why can't we have ours?' say the *mozos* and *peones*."[111] Along the same lines, the FRTS denounced the patrons' abuse of the daughters of colonos: "In some *fincas* and haciendas the *patronos* or their sons exercise the privilege of the *pernada* and the young daughters of the *colonos* only can develop relationships with laborers after the boss or their sons abandon them. The girls then often become mothers of a *patrón's* child."[112] Abuse by landlords was directed at indígenas and ladinas, provoking anger among both groups. While the increase in élite power and the decrease in the pool of indigenous men after 1932 may have colored informants' memories of the previous period, there is little doubt that abuse of indigenous women by ladino landowners formed an especially salient image in indigenous eyes. Moreover, at least some of the movement activists were products of forced unions.[113]

The left was able to count on the support of women who pushed the limits of patriarchy by joining the movement in large numbers. One-third of the members of the FRTS in Nahuizalco were women, and informants who participated in union meetings in Ahuachapán and La Libertad recall a significant presence of women. Female participation in the labor movement was of great importance, because it signified a transformation of patriarchal relations, empowering women within the contours of indigenous and campesino communities. Remarkably, during the insurrection three of the most prominent political and military leaders were women (see chapter 6). It is possible that the work of the Pauline missionaries debilitated indigenous and campesino patriarchy, thus creating a precondition for female participation in the labor movement. Conte recalls how in the Jayaque region, "the semi-slave women still impose their rights, lashing out against the despotism of the fathers and husbands."[114]

Extreme forms of corporal punishment were common among Indian and poor ladino families, and perhaps contributed to a predisposition toward violence.[115] There is substantial evidence that child rearing practices in western El Salvador were quite severe. The Swedish ethnographer Hartman reported on a conversation with an elderly indigenous informant at the turn of the century: "A punishment of yore was to hang the child by his feet from the roof and the give him lashes with a chichicaste or light a stick under his head so that the smoke would produce massive itching. 'These were the ancient methods that never failed . . .' an elderly man told me."[116] Although these practices were no longer employed, Hartman commented, a whip always hung by the door of the rancho. It is probable that by 1930 indige-

130

"Ese
Trabajo
Era
Enteramente
de los
Naturales"

nous and poor ladino children grew up in an atmosphere colored by the violent assertion of paternal authority. Consider the following testimony of Salomé Torres, a child in the highlands of Jayaque during the 1920s. His mother died of illness when he was still a child, and the pain of that loss was still great when his father became ill: "As my father lay dying on his *petate*, he suddenly arose and hobbled over to a corner of the hut and reached down to pick up a stick. 'Salomé, come over here!' he said to me. I was scared, but I walked over to my father. He started striking me on my back and rear end with the stick. 'This way you will remember me so that you will always behave.' Then he died."[117]

There is no doubt that rural Salvadoran society was (and still is) violent. Journalistic accounts of the time emphasized that Indians were ready to use their machetes at the slightest provocation.[118] A Canadian ship captain relied upon common élite and middle-class knowledge when he reported that on Saturday nights, drinking often led to bloodshed in rural cantinas: "In the course of the evening it is quite common for a quarrel to break out, and often the participants . . . 'have it out' with their machetes. They stand up to one another with the utmost bravery, quite often until one of them is killed, and showing the utmost indifference to the most appalling wounds."[119] This report and others evoke an intensely violent rural culture, one that predisposed campesinos to resist violent repression as a means to demand respect.

Deep ethnic and gender cleavages tended to exacerbate the class tensions that pervaded western Salvador. Yet those cleavages did not affect the mobilization uniformly. Subalterns responded differently to the powerful homogenizing discourse of mestizaje, propelled by the thoroughgoing material transformations discussed in this and preceding chapters. In those communities where Indians had lost their land and political autonomy, especially La Libertad, the obliteration of ethnic markers proceeded at an accelerated pace with a profound effect on local identities. Yet even this "assimilationist" response was not one of complete submission to the ladino élite. Rather, subalterns remembered how the coffee growers' land was acquired and resisted the growers' treatment of their laborers. Traditionalists offered a multi-pronged resistance to the wave of mestizaje, perceived as an assault on their land, livelihoods, and culture. Their politics of ethnic resurgence were of decisive importance in Nahuizalco and Izalco.

Despite its ideological insensitivity to indigenous culture the left, as the events of 17 May revealed, was able to connect politically with indigenous people: with traditionalists, assimilationists, and those to whom indigenous identity was utterly irrelevant. As argued in chapter 3, the left could relate to these groups precisely because the groups to a significant degree organized themselves within a broad leftist discourse. The rank-and-file leadership thus straddled different worlds. A militant might form part of a tightly knit indigenous canton and simultaneously organize ladino rural workers and attend meetings with urban workers and artisans.

Similarly, without developing anything resembling a feminist agenda, the left benefited from contradictory responses to patriarchy. During the first decades of the century increasing female participation in the coffee economy as well as voluntary and involuntary relations between indigenous women and ladino men challenged the rigid prevailing forms of indigenous patriarchy. Rape (real or imagined) by coffee planters angered campesinos of all backgrounds, and the left mobilized that rage into its discursive attack on the oligarchy.

The left did not insert itself seamlessly into this mosaic of class, ethnic, and gender relations. Although it grew organically with the distinct groups (Indians, women, rural workers), the leftist leaders—from the canton to the central committee—did not possess a clear focus of the complex society in which it was immersed. Despite the presence of traditionalists among the rank-and-file leadership, the left (writ large) never understood the cultural stakes for them, nor did it grasp the depths of ladino racism in some smallholder communities. The failure of the left's ideology to catch up with its practice ultimately did damage to itself and to those people its militants fought so hard to emancipate.

Chapter Five

"To the Face of the Entire World": Repression and Radicalization, September 1931–January 1932

"Look compañero. They killed my compañero but here are my sons and they will see the revolution."—Indigenous widow to a PCS militant, June 1931

Like "el Norte," the wind that blows through cities, towns, and villages in December, the movement swept through the region in 1930 and 1931, shaking everything in its path, then subsiding, and then gathering force again. As in other times of revolutionary change, for the activists the possibilities were imminent and endless. Every protest, every meeting, every strike portended the "final battle" with the enemy. Time was telescoped for individuals and groups. One day a campesino was invited to a meeting. The next week he attended a demonstration where police roughed him up and arrested him. He emerged from jail ready to battle to his death with the bourgeoisie. Further repression only accelerated the radicalization process and the cries for revolutionary resistance. When "el Norte" came in December 1931, blowing away the last rains and bringing out the sun, the winds of social change had reached gale force.

Following the events of 17 May, Araujo's administration became increasingly committed to a repressive response to the left. In early June police arrested Martí and others while they were conducting a meeting of three hundred in Armenia.[1] Martí's arrest announced a period of intense government surveillance, which only intensified when on 13 July Araujo declared martial law.[2] In August the government called in the cavalry to break two municipal workers strikes in San Salvador.[3]

133

"To the
Face
of the
Entire
World"

Araujo's ability to meet the minimal needs of government employees, let alone launch any reforms, hinged on a loan from the United States. Congress turned down the loan in the wake of nationalist-inspired protests by workers and students.[4] It finally approved a smaller loan, insufficient to meet even a reduced government payroll.[5] The dispute revealed Araujo's political weakness, augmented by the divisions within his own party.[6]

The Partido Laborista began to crack under the stress of anti-popular repression and governmental inaction. A putatively pro-government demonstration in July revealed the depth of Laborista alienation from the government. Araujo brought between five and ten thousand rural workers to a rally in the capital. After marching to the Casa Presidencial, they joined a second demonstration of thousands calling for the resignation of all Araujo's ministers because of their inaction on land reform.[7]

Araujo and Labor Party leaders faced the delicate and difficult task of persuading their rank-and-file supporters to stay away from SRI activities and ensure that local authorities did not harass or arrest Laborista activists.[8] Araujo himself at times directly undermined the coherence of the Laborista party, especially as local élites appropriated party leadership. Consider the case of Juayúa, a flashpoint of leftist activity. In July four hundred unemployed workers petitioned Araujo for assistance. When the president visited the town in September he was greeted by Redaelli, the local boss, and wined and dined by the local élite. Araujo promised a band, one hundred barrels of concrete for the plaza, and a school with a basketball court—as soon as he could find the funds. For the landless and the unemployed, Araujo offered nothing.[9]

The suppression of a union meeting on a coffee plantation near Zaragosa in La Libertad marked another watershed in the government's relations with the left. Some two hundred workers attended the meeting, on 23 September. The local landlord called on the National Guard, who arrived on the scene. Apparently without violent provocation, the Guardia opened fire with submachine guns, killing fourteen campesinos and wounding twenty-four. The assault at Zaragosa was by far the most serious act of state violence up

134

"To the
Face
of the
Entire
World"

to that point, and it stands out in the record of action against the left and the labor movement over the previous two years. State violence over the previous year, although not severe by Latin American standards, had the effect of pushing the movement in a more militant direction, and the killings at Zaragosa did not intimidate but rather radicalized the campesinos. By November the Socorro Rojo reported having recruited five hundred new members in the Zaragosa area.[10] The strong push toward militancy was guided less by ideological interpretations of reality than by cultural repertoires of Indians and peasants—including, as we have pointed out, a sense of embattled dignity tinged with large doses of masculine pride—which found state repression, regardless of intensity, to be intolerable.

In the words of a leftist leader, "Our campesinos will not come to any demonstrations unless they are armed with [corvos], and you better believe it."[11] The government's use of force against the rural movement radicalized the struggle and placed the communist leadership in a position where they had to either accept a retreat into passivity on the part of their peasant and Indian militants or advance toward some form of armed struggle. For example, PCS leaders in Sonsonate related to the Central Committee the rank and file's desire to storm the city prison to free political prisoners rather than participate in any more unarmed demonstrations.

Rank-and-file rural laborers and peasants pushed the movement toward armed resistance. A report of the PCS in October 1931 stated, "to the next call we make, they will not respond without bringing along their arms (corvos or machetes), because it is unjust that unarmed persons get massacred . . . now, we arrive at the EPOCH in which we can no longer detain the REVOLUTIONARY WAVE that is rising everywhere, ready to conquer POWER through life or death."[12]

Marxist terminology, especially "bourgeois," "proletarian," and "class struggle," entered the language of the mobilization through the Third International and the PCS. As we discussed earlier, the use of camarada as a greeting became extremely popular among the rural militants. There is evidence that indigenous activists directly appropriated such Marxist language to describe their social world. Consider the following dialogue, recalled by Eugenio Díaz Barrientos, one of the key economic and political figures in Izalco. In an interview with Segundo Montes in 1976 he recalled a conversation with Feliciano Ama, an indigenous cacique, landowner, and former political ally. Ama was a driving force behind the political organization of the comunidad indígena of the Barrio de Asunción.[13] As we have seen, he had expressed himself in a language of class as early as December 1929. Yet he maintained traditional clientelistic ties through the election of January 1931 by supporting the candidacy of Zárate. He broke those ties during Araujo's administration. In response to Díaz Barrientos's entreaties to desist from his leftist political activities, Ama told him: "Look, patrón. What you say is true in that we have been and will always be friends. But you are a capitalisto on one side and we workers on the other, the proletariat; we are no longer the same, because you are capitalisto, but I will always treat you with respect and you will treat us with affection."[14]

We could look at this statement as an example of a superficial indigenous understanding of Marxism. The use of *capitalisto* (common among indigenous people) instead of the grammatically correct *capitalista* certainly could point to such a conclusion. In view of Ama's status as a landowner and seasonal employer of workers, we can see this usage as exemplifying an imposed language that directly subverted indigenous cultural categories such as *indígena* or *natural* and ladino. However, there is an alternative reading: class categories were useful if not necessary to break through the cultural and ideological constraints imposed by the traditional categories. The appellation *patrón* is then interesting because it refers in El Salvador at this time not to an economic relation but rather to a political and cultural relation of clientelism. Although during the previous decades the indigenous community had a significant degree of political autonomy, in the last analysis it was dependent on élite-controlled hierarchies, and its leaders recognized this subordinate status. For example, we have noted that the indigenous community of Izalco over the previous decades had delivered its votes to the officialist party. Thus to create a labor movement and contest local power relations it was necessary to break previously harmonious relations with patronos such as Díaz Barrientos. In this sense "we are no longer the same" signifies the transition from indigenous clients into a relatively autonomous social and political force of "proletarians." The linguistic transformation was important, for without the new forms of conceptualization and vocabulary it would have been difficult to express the notion that despite long-standing ties of friendship, Ama now considered Díaz Barrientos a political antagonist. Nothing had changed except Ama's way of understanding his position in the world, one that transcended the traditional ethnic and clientelistic categories and that by referring to class opposition staked a claim to independent political action.

Raymond Williams's categories of analysis are useful for understanding

136

"To the
Face
of the
Entire
World"

the changing cultural patterns of western Salvador. For Williams, "emergent" cultural forms are the "new meanings and values, new practices, new relationships and kinds of relationship [that are] continually being created. But it is exceptionally difficult to distinguish between those which are really elements of some new phase of dominant culture . . . and those which are substantially alternative or oppositional to it: emergent in the strict sense rather than merely novel."[15] Residual cultural forms are those that though formed in the past are "still active in the present."[16]

Western Salvadoran society in the early 1930s was experiencing a rupture in cultural forms. Traditional patrimonial cultural forms, in Williams's terms, were at once residual and dominant. Yet the challenge of radical, emergent cultural forms that eschewed deference to the élite momentarily broke the bonds between the residual and the dominant. In this sense, for indigenous people in particular, residual notions of friendship and respect remained meaningful although they were no longer tied to a political, economic, and cultural edifice but rather coexisted uneasily with emergent notions of equality.

In *The Last Colonial Massacre* Greg Grandin makes an important argument about the role of the left during the mid-twentieth century in shaping the emergence of different styles of modernity and modern forms of identity, what he calls "an insurgent individuality." Arguing against a view of the left as a totalitarian slayer of the individual, Grandin argues, "Rather than eliminating the boundaries between self and society, collective action distilled for many a more potent understanding of themselves as politically consequential individuals. Such insurgent individuality, I argue, was fundamentally necessary to the advancement of democracy, to the end of forced labor, and to the weakening of other forms of exploitation and domination. But this sense of agency was defined neither by radical autonomy nor by isolated freedom: rather, collective actions laid bare the social foundations of the self."[17] For Grandin "Latin America's old left . . . bridged the fault lines of modernity, linking nation and the world, community and state, and self and society."[18] This alternative form of modernity allowed the individual, who was torn away from traditional communal and familial relations, to begin to relate to the broader society not only as a self-interested "individual" but with a new collective identity, rooted in the traditional community but with new horizons that stretch beyond the milpa, village square, or plantation. Commander Brodeur, drawing on Salvadoran counterinsurgent discourse, glimpsed the emergence of this alternative identity: "It appears that up to a short time ago, this low class of labourer was content with its lot, or at least indifferent to the appalling conditions under which it worked . . . conditions in fact not far removed from slavery. But when here and there a few managed to better themselves, realization began to dawn upon these latter of the unhappy, indeed unjust lot of their class. It was to these few slightly superior types that the principles of Communism . . . appealed most strongly."[19] Regardless of the sociological accuracy of the observation—that is, regardless of the purported economic superiority of the local activists—the analysis does reveal how the activists acquired an important vantage point. This distance from communal relations allowed them to make connections between the state and economic exploitation, and to provide a link between their rapidly changing communities and the oppositional forces in society—in short, to become agents of this alternative modernity. This divergent form of modernity present in Ama's discourse, however incipient, suggests how the left was successful in attracting strong support among indigenous populations, despite an ideological orientation which was not particularly sensitive to ethnic forms of identity. The repression of 1932 cut short the flowering of this alternative modernity, as did the Guatemalan counterrevolution in 1954.

137

"To the
Face
of the
Entire
World"

Even as a Marxist vocabulary expressed these emergent forms of modernity and helped to transform subaltern understandings of their social and political world, the indigenous and campesino linguistic appropriation also had significant impacts on the Salvadoran left. On the one hand, the adoption of these class categories obfuscated relevant local histories and relationships, in effect contributing to the left's blind spot with regard to ethnic relations and the complex local histories of ethnic factionalism in municipal politics. On the other, it was clearly the rank and file that first placed armed rebellion on the leftist agenda as early as 1930, against the wishes and better judgment of most leaders. Despite the revolutionary "class versus class" rhetoric prevalent during the Comintern's "Third Phase," there is no evidence that the international movement in any way supported an insurrectionary strategy in El Salvador.

An incident in Ahuachapán in November 1931 revealed the growing acceptance of an insurrectionary solution among the popular sectors, particularly in the west. In response to efforts by the Communist Party to register their candidates for the upcoming congressional and municipal elections, the government arrested leftist leaders in Sonsonate, Ahuachapán, and Santa Ana. In Ahuachapán, according to an internal SRI report:

138

"To the
Face
of the
Entire
World"

"The day of compañero Hernández's capture more than 600 camaradas mobilized spontaneously, camping on the outskirts of the city, but when they found out that they were not going to attack the city, they left with some displeasure."[20]

Miguel Mármol, who was sent to stop the threatened attempt to free political prisoners, corroborated this report, underscoring the militancy of the Ahuachapán rank and file: "Our candidate for Mayor of Ahuachapán . . . told us that the barracks were under siege by a contingent of 900 campesinos who had decided to settle accounts for the arbitrary acts by the authorities . . . He said that the urgent pleas of the Commander of the Regiment, Colonel Escobar, hadn't done a thing and that the local leaders of the Communist Party requested a delegate from the Central Committee to come and quiet down the peasants and get them to go back to their homes before it turned into a slaughter.[the21] Later the PCS national leadership sent Mármol to Ahuachapán on a similar mission to persuade militant campesinos to avoid an armed confrontation with the National Guard. One of the Ahuachapanecos threatened, he reported, that the next time he would have to "face our machetes even before the class enemy."[22]

This incident could be used as proof of the distance between a rural movement and the Communist Party leadership. But that interpretation would miss a crucial point. Many campesinos—rural workers and smallholders— lived in or near the city of Ahuachapán.[23] They were prepared to assault the barracks to free local communist leaders, many of whom were urban artisans. This moment also reveals how the regional mass movements continued to push the national leadership into increasingly militant postures.

The arrest of the PCS candidates in Ahuachapán was part of a major national crackdown on the left during November 1931. Government authorities arrested hundreds of activists in the west and around San Salvador. The resort to massive repression during the middle of an election campaign revealed the inability of Araujo's government to deal with the left and the growing protest movements.

The Coup of 2 December

The radicalization of the western countryside certainly played a role in the military coup of 2 December that overthrew Araujo. Contemporary observers and historians have focused on the dissatisfaction of younger military officers with the administrative chaos, especially the failure for months to pay the troops. The involvement of Vice President Hernández Martínez in the coup has also formed a central part of this question. In June Martinez, serving as both vice president and minister of war, led a protest by the army against the so-called *código rojo*. This law had allowed Romero Bosque to try and execute the military coup conspirators of 1927 within forty-eight hours. Incredibly, Martínez and other officers demanded the reinstatement of the military right to "insurrection." Hernández Martínez himself called the código rojo unconstitutional.[24] Araujo refused to give in to this pressure. The tension between Araujo and Martínez intensified on 27 November, when officers rejected the ten days' back pay that Araujo offered the military. Martínez, having been placed in charge of the negotiation, agreed with the rejection, arguing that it was insufficient. On 1 December Araujo, perhaps suspecting that Martínez's loyalty was in doubt, removed him from his cabinet position of minister of war, placing his long-trusted ally and brother-in-law Salvador Lopez Rochac in the position. This move angered many army officers.[25]

U.S. military intelligence believed that an élite-led conspiracy involving higher-level officers had been in the works for at least a month, led by the oligarch Francisco Dueñas. The worker and peasant mobilizations and the possibility of leftist triumphs in the upcoming municipal and congressional elections played a role in prompting the conspiracy. This group did not work directly with the officers but after the coup pressured them into accepting Martínez as president.

Initially there was confusion about the military revolt and the status of resistance by Araujo supporters in the police and army.[26] By 4 December, however, the directorate was clearly in control of the state apparatus. The new military directorate quickly found itself supported by the country's financial élite, who offered new loans within a day of their seizure of power.[27] Despite the financial backing of the oligarchy, for the left a mixture of hope and confusion colored the first weeks of the military directorate regime. The leftist leadership had apparently been aware of the possibility of a coup but was unsure how to respond to it. In their first manifesto the PCS did not condemn the new regime, but rather called on it to revoke the emergency anticommunist laws and to expropriate land from the Melendez-Quiñónez oligarchic group. In a similar vein, on 12 December *La Estrella Roja*, a paper linked to the PCS, in its first issue offered its congratulations to the junta

140

"To the
Face
of the
Entire
World"

and then explained: "In reality, the clumsy mistakes of the Araujo administration imposed the moral obligation on the military to overthrow it, and to that we add the sacking of the national treasury by his cronies." The editorial suggested that the military junta could actually join forces with the oppressed and overthrow the capitalist class: "This is the moment for your sublime mission and if you fulfill it your heroic efforts will not be in vain."[28] The PCS was in a state of confusion about how to respond to the new regime, since it was possible that the government would opt for a progressive agenda. In a report in mid-1932 Max Cuenca stated the sense of the Central Committee that "if the Party came out against the directory it would make it impossible for the Party to participate in the municipal elections."[29]

It was indeed difficult to read the junta's political intentions through its actions, and its initial measures compounded the uncertainty reigning on the left. Although the new military government did not respond directly to the PCS, its first declaration indicated a measure of support for urban and rural workers. The junta gave public indications that it would eschew anti-labor violence, and the military regime even freed some 210 political prisoners.[30] Four days after the coup the regime allowed the Communist Party to open an office in San Salvador with an inauguration attended by some six hundred people. Three days later the police did shut down the headquarters and take party lists, but allowed it to reopen as an election headquarters—the municipal and congressional elections were postponed for two weeks. Although the authorities in the western departments were less tolerant of the PCS, they did allow offices to open and remain open.[31]

During the first weeks of December the PCS and Martínez's regime shared a sense of mutual wariness and ambivalence, but not hostility. In mid-December Martínez brought in local leftist leaders to engage in a dialogue with him. He met with Gregorio Cordero Cortéz, the renowned rural labor leader from Armenia and PCS congressional candidate. Cortéz reported that he was "well received" by Martínez, who claimed that he would obtain concessions from the plantation owners for the workers.[32] Throughout his political career Martínez consistently displayed a populist style. Such a style would not have been inconsistent with a strategy of cooptation to neutralize the left, while enhancing Martínez's stature with the laboring classes. The pressure from the United States, manifested by its public refusal to grant diplomatic recognition to the regime, likely prompted Martínez to keep his options open with regard to labor.

141

"To the
Face
of the
Entire
World"

Taking advantage of the political lull and uncertainty, on 9 December, at the peak of the coffee harvest, unionized rural workers in western Salvador began what rapidly became the first sustained wave of strikes in Salvadoran history. From 9 to 19 December strikes broke out in the departments of Santa Ana, La Libertad, and Ahuachapán in demand of higher wages and better working conditions. These were not "spontaneous" work stoppages in the sense of unorganized and unplanned actions. Rather, since March 1931 the left (first as the SRI and then as the reorganized FRTS) had begun to organize in preparation for strikes during the coffee harvest (October–February). Organizers and supporters traveled from farm to farm, spreading news of the strikes and helping to organize work stoppages in protest against cuts in the piece rates.

These were among the first full-fledged strikes in the Salvadoran countryside. Although there had been work stoppages in the countryside before, they had rarely lasted more than a day before they were ended by negotiations or repression. While the Comintern subsequently criticized the PCS for separating political from economic struggles during this critical period, there is evidence that these economic strikes did have a political dimension. At least some militants, such as Miguel Mármol, had conceived of the strikes as the prelude to a nationwide general strike. Further, the strikes had a political dimension in that they directly contested power relations. Mármol wrote about his experiences as an organizer in December 1931: "We communists were traveling through the rural zones of [Sonsonate and Ahuachapán] as if the plantations and haciendas were already the peoples,' such was the mass support we were getting."[33] Socorro Rojo militants wrote, "These strike struggles in the villages against wage cuts will lead to broader and greater strikes . . . the masses only follow the PCS."[34] Finally, for a variety of reasons ranging from bankruptcy to fear, some landowners abandoned their plantations, allowing de facto occupations by coffee workers.

Martínez's regime, thrown on the defensive, seemed eager to negotiate (or even ally with) the strike leaders in the west.[35] In his meetings with rural workers' leaders in San Salvador, Martínez "expressed a great desire to gain from the bosses concessions that will improve the material lot of the workers, as, for instance, the setting up of a school for workers on the plantations, giving them seeds."[36] Not surprisingly, Martínez's sympathetic approach to the local leftist leaders spurred grassroots activists on to further action, as they nurtured the belief that Martínez backed their struggle.

142

"To the
Face
of the
Entire
World"

Numerous informants, sympathetic or not to the left, share the belief that Martínez backed the labor movement and that activists pushed ahead with a sense that the regime would support them. Fabián Mojica, for example, recalls a conversation in which Esteban Morán, a ladino leftist leader of Izalco, told him that Martínez had urged him on with the phrase "Ese hueso tiene hormigas" (this bone has ants). Both Mojica and Morán had interpreted the phrase to mean that the system had to be overturned. Eusebio Chavez, PCS candidate for mayor of Izalco, reportedly received a message in December from Martínez, "Siga adelante."[37]

The apparent neutrality of the regime and the timid response of the landowners emboldened the rural labor movement. On 20 December some twelve hundred workers in the Santa Tecla region launched strikes on six plantations owned by the powerful Dueñas family.[38] The strike ended after two days when the local union won an increase from 20 cents to 30 cents per bag of coffee. Two days later 390 resident laborers on two other nearby haciendas owned by the De Sola family launched a strike in protest against *terraje* rates—rental payments traditionally made in crops but during the crisis made, at the landlords's insistence, in cash.[39]

The strike movement followed the overall rural labor pattern of telescoping historical time, leaping over the traditional developmental stages of labor movements. Although these were among the first rural strikes in Salvadoran history, they rapidly turned into a movement resembling a regional general strike. The strike wave was not limited to La Libertad: in the Santa Ana volcano region, nine hundred workers struck the Regalado plantation demanding greater water rations and an increase in piece rates. Strikes also broke out on coffee plantations in the departments of Ahuachapán and Sonsonate. A high level of prior organization accompanied by a broadening and deepening sense of solidarity among western campesinos offers one explanation for this rapid development of the movement, atypical of labor history in other parts of the Americas or Europe.

Although initial demands aimed to block piece rate cuts, the second week of strikes saw laborers demanding increases beyond the restoration of the cuts. In a strike on the Regalado plantation, the union demanded an increase from 15 to 22.5 cents per bag of coffee. Strikers seemed to have a precise target: the agricultural élite. All reported strikes took place on the largest plantations owned by the oligarchy, leaving smaller commercial farms unaffected. Although leadership of the left was undisputed, there was a significant degree of local autonomy, as evidenced by the negotiated solutions to the plantation strikes against the Dueñas and to another on a coffee and cane plantation of twelve hundred manzanas owned by the De Sola family.[40]

143

"To the
Face
of the
Entire
World"

Despite the scope and militancy of the movement, the National Guard adopted moderate tactics in response to the strikes. On the De Sola haciendas the guard offered sympathy for the strikers but opposed using coercion against strikebreakers. Guard members also made friendly suggestions about negotiation tactics: for example, that only a small number of delegates should participate. As late as the last week in December, in response to a request from a *cafetalero*, President Martínez intervened directly in a strike in La Libertad so as to resolve the conflict peacefully. At least some coffee planters favored a moderate policy of negotiation with the strikers and the Left.[41] One coffee grower in La Libertad recounted that workers on a friend's plantation organized a union and then went out on strike to support demands for better food, higher wages, the eight-hour day for adults, and the six-hour day for minors. Recognizing that this was but one case of a much broader movement, he wrote, "It is worth asking: what are the employers going to do? Are they going to ask the government to send the armed forces to shoot up the bands of unarmed indios? The patrono who has that point of view would be stupid. The longer it takes to realize that violent measures cannot resolve the problem, the worse it will be for him . . . We have to say to all the patronos that if they do not all come together to face the problem, they will allow El Salvador to suffer a social chaos which will victimize them."[42]

By late December such an enlightened view was becoming a rarity. The more repressive sectors of the agrarian élite attempted to regain the offensive. As early as September they had started raising money for a rural guard. Shortly before the coup the Ahuachapán branch of the Asociación Cafetalera de El Salvador had passed a resolution calling on the government to enforce "greater and more efficient property guarantees against Bolsheviks and communists who have here become a serious threat against the tranquility and productive activities."[43] The association forwarded the resolution to the new government on 8 December. By early January the regional agrarian élite was raising thousands of dollars a day for the National Guard. In a budgetary crisis, such gifts were surely appreciated by Martínez's regime.

The refusal of the U.S. State Department to recognize the de facto regime also forced it into a tighter alliance with the cafetaleros, who generally got

144

"To the
Face
of the
Entire
World"

along well with the legations from the United States and Britain. This combination of State Department opposition to Martínez and élite pressure offers the best explanation of the volte face of the regime, from a populist overture to the left toward violent suppression of the movement.[44] Martínez knew that he was fighting to stay in power. He indicated as much on 16 December, in a conversation with a railroad manager. Martínez confessed that unless the United States promptly recognized his regime, he would face "troubles which he felt certain he could not suppress."[45]

Although the transition from negotiation to repression was not linear, by the end of the second week of strikes the regime seems to have changed its course. One incident highlighted this reversal. In response to pleas from the Regalado family, the government sent troops with orders to shoot strikers on their large plantation on the slopes of the Volcán de Santa Ana. Despite the orders the strikers were able to establish communication with the troops and avert bloodshed. Although the strike was resolved peacefully, the dawn of the new year was greeted throughout the west with the expectation of violence.

Municipal Elections

A political rally in El Refugio, a relatively unimportant cane and coffee municipality in eastern Ahuachapán with fewer than two thousand inhabitants, revealed the spread and depth of PCS electoral support. In late December militants from Atiquizaya traveled the short distance to El Refugio to support the formation of the electoral slate of the Partido de los Trabajadores. A smallholder was their candidate for mayor, and laborers on the cane and coffee fincas were the candidates for *regidores*. The municipal secretary reported no violence at the demonstration, which according to her "lasted a long time."[46] However Benjamín Cárcamo, a landowner and candidate for mayor on the Independent ticket, described the same events in alarming tones: "grave events . . . by the communists, stirred up and supported by those of Atiquizaya." He therefore officially withdrew from the race, "in order to avoid fatal events."[47] Although the details are sketchy, it seems clear that the show of support for the candidate of the left was strong enough to drive away the only other candidate in the election, thus ensuring a left victory in El Refugio. Martínez's regime viewed this and other instances of the left's growing electoral strength in the west and prepared to thwart its electoral victory by any means necessary.

On 31 December *El Diario de El Salvador* reported, "Armed forces have been sent by different routes to small towns in the departments of Sonsonate and La Libertad. Reliable sources allow us to inform the public that the troops' objective will be to guarantee order during the elections. Various local commanders have requested these troops since recently they have noted strike activity on the part of workers, and especially those who, not having work, spend their free time spreading subversive propaganda, taking advantage of the liberties granted by the government."[48] The article both reports the facts of the troop movement and editorializes in favor of repression. The regime foreshadowed its electoral strategy several days before it dispatched its troops to the west. On Sunday 27 December the Ahuachapán branch of the PCS was holding a meeting at its headquarters to choose its representatives to the electoral board. Three hundred townspeople waited outside for the results. According to the Cuenca report, "The police broke into the convention and carried off the lists of those workers who registered and who had decided thereby, to vote for the communist candidates . . . The [police] threatened to shoot if the workers did not retire. The government [forces] dissolved the convention right there . . . The [PCS] candidate for Mayor was persecuted, along with other candidates on the list."[49]

Despite the PCS protest, local and national governmental authorities refused to acknowledge, let alone redress, the interference with the campaign. Nevertheless leftist organizations proceeded to prepare for the elections, fully aware of the strong possibility that the authorities would impede their municipal and congressional victories. A report in late December to the international secretariat of the SRI stated: "The Party is mobilizing itself and will go into the elections of deputies. In the municipalities of the Occident and the Center triumph is assured, the enthusiasm is large, still larger in the departments of Ahuachapán, Sonsonate, and La Libertad. The feelings are very excited."[50] By the party's own estimates, it would win 40–45 percent of the national vote.[51] Since the left was relatively lacking in support in the eastern part of the country, this estimate was high. Yet the assessment that the party would win the mayoral and congressional races in most of the western municipalities and in the capital was eminently reasonable.[52] Through its organic ties to the unions and to the Socorro Rojo, the PCS was able to galvanize the support of large numbers of urban and rural workers and others, despite its recent emergence from a semi-clandestine existence.

146

"To the
Face
of the
Entire
World"

During the first few days of January, in response to the threat of fraud and intimidation, the left developed a two-pronged strategy.[53] First, the FRTS "suspended" the rural strikes. It withdrew the pickets so that the workers could travel to the towns and cities to vote. The PCS and its allied organizations instructed their rank and file to line up regardless of whether they received permission to vote, to demonstrate party strength. The PCS also prepared to continue the strikes immediately after the elections and to expand the movement to other plantations. The post-election strike movement would combine trade union demands and political protest. Anticipating an antidemocratic response by the regime, the left attempted to prepare its rank and file for this eventuality, counseling pacific protest whenever possible, but armed resistance when faced with state violence.

The left's national leadership correctly assessed the regime's sharp rightward turn and also grasped the rank and file's simultaneous commitment to an electoral option and armed resistance against violent repression. We get a sense of these apparently contradictory commitments in the person of Marcial Contreras, a carpenter and PCS candidate for mayor of Ahuachapán. According to Mármol, "in Ahuachapán the townspeople had already prepared a plan—that if victory was denied them by fraud, they would attack the barracks and impose the popular will by armed force."[54] Mármol implied that Contreras supported this plan. Even so, a letter of 1 January 1932 from Contreras to the departmental governor reveals how seriously local leaders and the rank and file took the elections, suggesting their confidence in victory and their moderate hope for free elections: "The Communist Party has the honest desire to act with decorum and to demonstrate to the face of the entire world that it has the discipline and is not just a band of robbers, that communism pursues legitimate goals and is not synonymous with pillage. The Party will present itself properly [during the elections], and has prohibited any shouting of vivas and mueras; we only hope that the authorities will prevent the other parties from addressing inflammatory or hurtful words at our muchachos, which we know perfectly they seek to do . . . so that confronted with our victory, they could nullify it due to violence."[55]

This letter allows us to glimpse the importance of concepts of honor and dignity in local leftist discourse. In fact the resolve of the campesinos to abstain from participating in unarmed demonstrations also had something to do with honor, dignity, and a fear of further physical abuse. In indigenous areas the daily lack of respect shown by ladinos to Indians was an additional source of accumulating ressentiment, which fueled the Indians' militancy. Sheila Fitzpatrick builds on the standard definition of *ressentiment*: "a state of hostility maintained by the memory of an offense which it aspires to avenge . . . ressentiment (like vengeance) must always be present in the mix of emotions that lead people to support revolutions and commit acts of revolutionary violence."[56] Testimonies that offer a distant echo of these emotions include statements like "ladinos didn't want to be with Indians," and "God is not ladino."[57] Yet it would be a mistake to assume that intense commitment, propelled by ressentiment and a sense of dignity, was separable from more ideological goals: the Indian and ladino campesinos consciously struggled for land claimed by the élite, local political power, and decent wages and working conditions.

The PCS platform for the municipal elections articulated some of these goals but in general betrayed an urban bias. Several planks addressed child labor, prohibiting the employment of *niños* (presumably children under twelve) and calling for a six-hour day for those under eighteen. The platform also demanded an eight-hour day for men with no corresponding salary cuts, a seven-hour day with equal pay for women, maternity care, and paid leave. As for the unemployed, it called for direct financial and food aid as well as for the creation of labor banks. Several demands related directly to the urban poor, including 50 percent reductions in taxes in the market and in rent (with free rent for the unemployed and those who lived in *mesones*), reductions in public transportation costs, and water and electricity for the mesones and poor barrios. Another plank provocatively attacked military training in the schools and the "militaristic plans of the *patronos* and the regime."

Although some of the labor planks were applicable to the countryside, only one sentence specifically addressed rural labor: "Reasonable wages, protection, and defense of the *colonos* and their right to food and lodging even when they are not given work." In light of the left's overwhelming support in the countryside, it is striking that the immensely popular issue of land reform was omitted.[58] In all probability this omission reflected the urban slant of the document; PCS militants probably considered land reform to be outside the purview of municipal governments.

The preamble, however, surely resonated with the rural poor. After describing a recent past in which *terratenientes* used worker candidates to push

148

"To the
Face
of the
Entire
World"

their own interests, the party announced: "From now on, this farce has to stop, and the working class and peasantry must elect municipal governments composed of workers and peasants who respond to the interests of their class party, the Partido Comunista, whose immediate program is to remove the capitalist class from control of those organisms that it has always manipulated to impose onerous taxes on the immense masses of consumers."[59] This was a straightforward appeal to class power at the municipal level, based on an identification of the PCS, through its links to the FRTS and the SRI, as a legitimate class representative. This appeal would have been received differently in indigenous and non-indigenous communities: the issues of local political power weighed somewhat more among the indigenous, since traditionally local authorities had significant control over resources, especially irrigation and land. Thus, for example, Antonio Calvo, capitán mayor of the National Guard in Izalco, wrote to the departmental commander that according to his informants the Communist candidate for mayor, the candidates for *regidores*, and their followers were going to "impose their mayor without waiting for elections" on 20 December. In Nahuizalco, before the coup, the indigenous candidate Pablo Cruz emerged from a split along ethnic lines in the Araujista Labor Party. In early November 1931 Francisco Brito, a ladino *destazador* working with a group of "last-minute *Araujistas*" had displaced Cruz as the candidate of the Labor Party. Subsequently Cruz and his Comité Laborista de Indígenas allied themselves with the Left.[60] Although the exact nature of the shift in party allegiance is unclear, there is little doubt that the existing strength of the rural unions and the SRI were important factors. Francisco Brito, along with the anti-PCS candidates in Juayúa and Izalco, would become the object of rebel rage during the insurrection. And in Cuisnahuat a slate described by authorities as Laborista/Comunista gained much support among the majority indigenous population, only to have its electoral participation blocked.

Although the level of political conflict at the municipal level was more intense in indigenous municipalities, Contreras's letter and Mármol's report about Ahuachapán underscore the importance of local political stakes to non-Indians and the reach of the populist dimension of leftist discourse. The testimony of a schoolteacher in Santa Tecla reveals something of the impact of the campaign for local power on a non-Indian population: "Yesterday, for the first time, I saw simple campesinos come together, unarmed and in perfect order, without malicious leaders or academic swindlers. This inspired me and it struck me as a school teacher, to publicly give my support and guidance towards a new democracy . . . I understand that as a member of an oppressed class, we all suffer from misery and all have the same goal: 'the greatest good for the greatest number of people.' "[61]

149

"To the
Face
of the
Entire
World"

This curious mixture of the language of Lockean liberalism and radical populism points to the broader appeal of the movement, in turn related to the profound divisions in Salvadoran society, where, as in Mexico, school-teachers could consider themselves members of and voices for the op-pressed classes against a ruling oligarchy. The letter also underscores the sense of order and decorum that permeated public demonstrations on the left, a behavior that would be attested to during the elections even by un-sympathetic observers. It is echoed in Contreras's letter: "to demonstrate to the face of the entire world that we are not a band of robbers."

The words of the PCS candidate were tragically ironic: in the collective memory of the survivors of the massacres, the PCS and its supporters would be remembered as *una horda de salteadores*. But the words were also prescient: three days after Contreras wrote them, the regime blocked PCS voters from voting in Ahuachapán, and elsewhere the elections were canceled or marred by fraud. According to the British consul, "the suspension of the elections in the West was due to growing unrest of plantation laborers produced by the activities of agitators and the depressed conditions of coffee and sugar industries."[62] A lieutenant in the National Guard and others emphasized that Martínez used the elections to gauge the level and makeup of Commu-nist support.[63] The regime may also have blocked an electoral victory by the PCS in an attempt to curry favor with the United States. There is no doubt that it solidified its alliance with the agrarian élite.

The regime may have decided to thwart the PCS victories, but its officials and local authorities did not follow uniform tactics. They allowed elections to proceed in Ahuachapán, where the National Guard blocked PCS support-ers from voting, but postponed elections in many PCS strongholds such as Tacuba and the ladino municipalities of Turín and Colón. Perhaps they feared overwhelming losses in less populated municipalities such as El Refugio, where there seemed to be little opposition to the PCS. The regime did not want to spread its limited coercive apparatus too thinly by interven-ing in every western municipality, and therefore the tactic of postponement was appropriate.

The Ministry of Gobernación's order to postpone the elections through-

150

"To the
Face
of the
Entire
World"

out the department of Sonsonate went unheeded.[64] In Juayúa the government carried out elections but prohibited the left's participation. In Izalco the officialist candidate Miguel Call won the election by a margin of 758 to 1. According to official tabulations, in Nahuizalco Francisco Brito beat the indigenous candidate Pablo Cruz by the somewhat less lopsided margin of 918 to 371.[65] Given the correlation of political forces in town—in 1930 FRTS already had over seventeen hundred members in Nahuizalco and the municipality was over 80 percent indigenous—these figures are highly dubious. Local informants recall that the "Communists won the elections and it was stolen from them."[66] The regime also perpetrated fraud in the city of Sonsonate. Reynaldo Galindo Pohl, the former minister of foreign relations, wrote in his memoir about Sonsonate: "According to authorized sources, including some semi-official ones connected to the local hierarchy, like the director of Police, the Communist Party candidates were ahead in the municipal elections of Sonsonate. But the result had been predetermined by the authorities . . . 48 hours before the election the result was known . . . 'Those in charge rule' was the justification."[67]

In San Salvador Miguel Mármol noted that election day had a festive air. "It was our speakers and our choruses with the little daughters of workers and peasants singing revolutionary songs like Red Flag and the International that created a happy, enthusiastic atmosphere."[68] The British consul similarly reported that "the queue of communist voters were quite orderly and they did not appear to be furnished with the same inducements to vote as were offered to their opponents."[69] Other parties had significant followings in San Salvador, and the authorities there apparently denied the PCS a plurality by closing the voting booths before its voters had a chance to vote. The electoral authorities called upon the "bourgeois" parties to vote first. At the same time, the PCS made the mistake of ordering its peasant voters (from the city's outskirts) to vote before its city supporters did. This tactic played into government hands, as the authorities challenged and nullified many of the rural votes. They also blocked many rural voters within the municipal boundaries from entering the city. When PCS leaders realized that they might lose because of these machinations, they ordered their supporters to merge into the lines of a rival party. That party protested, and in response the authorities terminated the voting, despite a substantial number of voters, PCS and others, who had not yet voted. Notwithstanding what by many accounts seems to have been a concerted effort to block its victory in the capital, the PCS fell only sixty-three votes shy of winning the election.[70]

It was in Ahuachapán that the regime's efforts to block a PCS victory were most blatant. According to party reports, "there was such a large majority [on the PCS line] that they mobilized the armed forces to prevent the workers from reaching the voting tables. By 4:30 these workers demanded the right to vote and rushed to the tables but police prevented them from voting . . . we had about 5000 [on line] . . . the candidate was elected with 90 votes [total votes cast] . . . Delegates then instructed them to go back to their organizations "and back the plantations and fincas."[71]

Miguel Mármol, the PCS leader who had originally opposed an electoral strategy precisely because he could predict the regime's response, summarized the elections: "There was great enthusiasm during the elections. However, their triumph in almost all of the western part of the country was nullified. The result was tremendous and the fraud led to even more violence and more discontent."[72]

"Alli Comenzó El Comunismo": Violence in the West

"Don't pick for less than 50 cents per arroba!" Antonio Valiente, a former union member from Turín, recalls how hundreds of workers streamed into the canton of Santa Rita on January 4, the day after the election, calling on workers to join the strike. For Valiente and other nonleftist workers and their managers, the movement surely appeared to be an "invasion." In addition, the strikers employed "pressing" tactics to ensure unanimity in front of the bosses and the army. Although not unusual in the annals of strikes and rebellion, the Salvadoran labor movement previously had avoided coercive tactics. The violent tone in which the strikers ordered work to stop was a reflection of both the anger and the seriousness of the militants. Valiente slipped away and went home to Turín to wait out what he correctly foresaw as a coming storm of violence.

El Tránsito was a mid-sized coffee finca owned by the Arriaza family; Rogelio Arriaza, forty years old and resident in Ahuachapán, was its owner and manager. Before the coup he had belonged to a faction of the Partido Laborista and been a candidate for regidor in the city.[73] Situated in the canton of Santa Rita on the northern slopes of the Sierra de Apaneca, El Tránsito was one of some fifty similar fincas within the municipal bounda-

152

"To the
Face
of the
Entire
World"

ries of Atiquizaya. Colonos who cultivated basic grains for consumption and limited sale on the market resided on the fincas and formed the permanent labor force.

According to contemporary leftist accounts, corroborated by local testimonies, the strike developed peacefully during the morning, and the small detachment of guardsmen fraternized with the approximately four hundred strikers. A PCS broadside explained what happened next: "The capitalists Rogelio Arriaza and Rafael Herrera Morán got the Guardia drunk so that they would assassinate the striking comrades."[74] Other accounts add that the owners gave the Guardia "a good lunch" before the soldiers killed several strikers. According to Cuenca's report to the Comintern six months later, "They began to attack the pickets, smashing, breaking heads, and in this way dispersed the pickets. Then they went to their houses and later they came back with machetes and killed every one of the soldiers."[75] Local testimonies support the newspaper accounts that the strikers killed two of the six guardia: Miguel Angel Zelaya and Indalecio Ramírez.

Within hours the regime sent "truckloads of troops" from Santa Ana to subdue the rebellious strikers. Antolín López recalls that from his hut in la Montañita he looked across the slopes of coffee plantations and saw what seemed like a huge "blue ant hill," as blue-clad army troops swept through the area. For López, "Allí comenzó el comunismo." The strike and troop movement represented the beginning of "communism," the multi-vocal word that would encompass all the bloody events of January. For three days the troops combed the hillside fincas and haciendas searching for strikers, leaving behind burned huts and dead campesinos, including residents who had remained neutral during the strike.[76] The Guatemalan consul in Santa Ana reported on 13 January that a cuadrilla of Guatemalans picking coffee in the Atiquizaya region was attacked by the National Guard, "who confused them with the communists." Four of the Guatemalan coffee pickers were killed.[77] Armed with the weapons taken from the small detachment of Guardia, some of the strikers engaged in sporadic resistance against the troops. According to one newspaper account: "Yesterday [5 January] there was bloodshed in Turín, Ahuachapán. The communists . . . attacked the armed forces with firearms. The authorities responded with firearms to repel the attack. The first and second Comandantes were killed and several Guardia were injured."[78] Violence not only further enraged the rebels; it also terrified antagonists and observers alike. One informant recalls how elders counseled young adults tempted to join the strike movement, "Don't get involved! It's nasty out there!"[79]

But it was precisely those subaltern bystanders whom the strikers urgently tried to reach, with methods ranging from persuasion to intimidation. Although most of the Santa Rita strikers were among those who had attempted to vote for the PCS in Ahuachapán and Atiquizaya, few informants recall any links between the Santa Rita strike and the elections. Today, seven decades later, they live and work in the same villages. There are several possible explanations for why the elections do not stand out in testimonies. That most informants were children or adolescents in 1932 undoubtedly helps to explain why they forget the political dimension, just as they tend to forget the demand for a reduction of *terraje* (they do, however, remember the names of the dead guardia and the local union leaders). Another important reason is that in subsequent official discourse the events surrounding the elections were largely suppressed, especially any links between the elections, the strikes, and the insurrection. Beyond the ravages of official memory and the inadequacy of personal memory, it is also very likely that the strike leaders intentionally downplayed the explicitly political dimension of the movement to reach the apolitical workers.

The aggressive post-electoral strike movement was a mass movement, but it probably did not actively involve the majority of rural workers and semi-proletarians. In the departments of Ahuachapán, La Libertad, and Sonsonate there were between eighty and ninety thousand coffee pickers during the harvest in the early 1930s.[80] Although it is impossible to measure with precision, the number of rural workers involved in unions and the SRI most likely did not surpass 25,000 to 30,000 in those departments.[81] Thus for the local leftist leadership there were two organizational goals: to maintain the cohesion of the grassroots movement and to convince the neutral workers through a combination of intimidation, cajoling, and education. The growing sense of urgency and crisis pushed the movement toward "pressing" tactics, yet always complemented by a strategic consideration: political education would come from the confrontation of strikers organized around immediate economic demands and the state. This two-tiered form of organization and struggle—an economic struggle for the uncommitted combined with a political and economic struggle for the committed —was not particularly clear to either subaltern or élite observers at the time.

D. J. Rogers, British consul and coffee planter, writing on 7 January, attempted to offer a broader view of the conflict:

> To the onlooker, it appears that many of the planters have only themselves to blame for this state of things. They have lived extravagantly; they have wasted profits on expensive holidays abroad; they have borrowed heavily. With few exceptions they have done nothing to improve the condition of their laborers, who live in miserable huts, roofed with palm leaves which in many cases they have to pay rent to the planters . . . Further, some planters adopt an arrogant and insulting demeanor towards their employees and commit various offences against them and their families. It is in the districts where the most unpopular planters have their estates that there is most unrest . . . Within the last week or two labor unrest has been aggravated . . . Ahuachapán and Sonsonate are especially bad. Serious affrays have taken place between the strikers and the National Guard, in one, which I am informed on good authority sixty strikers were killed. It is difficult to know accurately what is going on in the west for the newspapers, although not subject to censorship omit or minimize these matters. I learned, however, that a body of well-armed men estimated at 1500 moves about from one plantation to another intimidating workers and preventing them from picking coffee much of which is being lost. These men claim to be adherents of President Araujo.[82]

Rogers distanced himself from his own role as a coffee planter, but his reading of the situation was undoubtedly based on conversations with British and Salvadoran planters and high-level regime officials. He emphasizes two factors: the economic conditions of the plantation workers caused by abusive, wasteful native planters, and the role of "outside agitators." This is a classic formulation of counterinsurgent discourse that tells us more about the worldview of its formulators than about a complex social and political reality. The report echoes the previously cited testimony that suggests the existence of a minority, moderate position within the coffee élite, which may have previously been aligned with Araujismo. In Ahuachapán, for example, the Partido Laborista was divided even before the coup, with one group aligning itself closely to planters' interests.[83] It is a safe assumption that Rogers reflected the views of at least some other planters. We can therefore hypothesize that there were still members of the élite during the first weeks of January who believed in the possibility of a negotiated solution to the conflict and recognized the necessity of reform.[84]

At the same time, it is instructive to recognize the limitations of this perspective. Although in an earlier report Rogers had cited labor unrest as a cause for suspending elections in some western towns, neither he nor the press made any connection between electoral fraud and post-electoral violence in the countryside. Newspapers and official reports (including those of the U.S. State Department) omitted entirely any mention of the municipal elections in relation to the strikes.

By not recognizing the legitimacy of the strikers' implicit demand that the electoral travesty be rectified, Rogers and others helped create a discursive field which demonized communist agitators: according to the consul, they inflamed the masses with a program "which is the slaughter of the landowners and the appropriation of their lands."[85] Once the political, democratic dimension was stripped from the movement, the discourse could portray strikers as a lawless, violent, and uncontrollable mob. The regime drew on this perspective when it refused to negotiate with the PCS, describing the events in Ahuachapán as "the work of simple rioters who do not obey the concrete orders of the central committee of the Communist Party."[86]

The image of a roving band of agitators and strikers was not pure fear and fancy: bands of rebellious strikers did indeed push the PCS toward insurrection and at the same time formed the nucleus of the revolutionary forces. Let us examine these *simples amotinados*, this "large body of armed strikers" that moved from plantation to plantation. These bands emerged in Ahuachapán after the elections and regrouped on 5 January, after the first full-scale confrontation with troops who opened fire with machine guns. There is no way to verify Rogers's estimate of fifteen hundred roving strikers with any degree of accuracy, but over the next few days government troops killed anywhere between thirty and four hundred people in the department of Ahuachapán, including armed and unarmed strikers and uncommitted campesinos. Notwithstanding the terror, there is strong evidence that the bands regrouped and appeared as far west as Tacuba and as far east as La Libertad during the following week.

Newspaper and official reports alternately described these bands as "Communist," "Araujista," and unemployed.[87] What meanings lurk behind those descriptions? In what sense were the strikers communist? By assembling numerous, albeit partial, testimonies and other documentary evidence, we can put together a portrait of these rebellious strikers. On the

156

"To the
Face
of the
Entire
World"

most obvious level, the mobile and militant strikers had either campaigned for or tried to vote for the Communist Party candidates in Ahuachapán, Atiquizaya, Turín, and Tacuba. Since they lacked patronage ties with the party, we can assume that there was a significant degree of conscious backing for the PCS. That support may have derived from respect for the honesty and militancy of working-class candidates, such as the carpenter Marcial Contreras. Likewise, it may have derived from support for the PCS municipal platform and the Socorro Rojo's well-circulated demand for land reform. That support was also a logical outgrowth of the labor-organizing efforts by leftist militants since early 1924 in the city of Ahuachapán, and starting in 1928 in the surrounding countryside. Most recently, PCS strike leadership had solidified that political support in the December wave of labor unrest. Finally, there is strong circumstantial evidence that the strikers directly followed the guidelines of the regional PCS leadership. To wit, they followed PCS directives when they left their pickets on the fincas and plantations in order to vote and then again when they went on strike immediately after the elections. Thus it was not unreasonable for frightened and hostile observers to refer to the strikers as "Communists" even though according to internal party documents there were only seventy members of the PCS in the entire department of Ahuachapán.[88]

What then of the accusation that these strikers were Araujistas? The same British consul wrote in the following week that there had been "serious affrays between the national forces and the Communists, and the loss of life on both sides has been considerable." After repeatedly identifying the "armed strikers" as "Communists," he wrote: "These men are armed with revolvers which points to the existence of funds coming from outside, as otherwise they would carry machetes. They appear to be an organized body of men and under the leadership of foreigners. They claim to be supporters of ex-President Araujo. The district in which they operate is that in which Señor Araujo was most popular. The Communists in La Libertad Department do not appear to be particularly in his favor . . . the labourers themselves have no doubts about their programme, which consists of the slaughter of the landowners and the appropriation of their lands."[89]

Although the notion that foreigners were in control of the movement (along with the image of hundreds of strikers armed with revolvers) appears to be almost a reflex of counterinsurgent prose, the rest of the analysis is intriguing, and apparently based on contact with knowledgeable people. In particular, the description of the strikers in Ahuachapán as both Araujistas and Communists, in contrast with the strikers of La Libertad, has some credibility, in part because of its specificity in differentiating levels of support in the two departments. There is other evidence to support the claims of collaboration between Araujistas and the left, and of Araujista support for insurgent action in the region across the Guatemalan border. There is no doubt that Araujo had exceptional support in Ahuachapán, where in the elections of January 1931 he won two-thirds of the vote; he received less than 50 percent nationwide.[90] In a statement in January 1932 Mario Zapata, a leading PCS student and intellectual, wrote, "Ingeniero Araujo still has supporters among the campesinos; many still adore the fetish who could not respond to them, but with the propaganda about him being the defender of the needy, he still has altars in the hearts of some campesinos."[91]

Unlike the consul, Zapata saw Araujista support as a potential problem for the PCS. Yet he also recognized that Araujistas were involved in many of the popular struggles and that the insurrectionary strategy was predicated on "taking advantage of the . . . Araujista agitation."[92] However, this does not invalidate the notion that many of the strikers supported the former president, who may well have been looking for a strategy to return to power. Not only did campesinos and workers ignore past sectarian animosity between the pro-communist left and Araujismo, but so did political militants. In several western municipalities such as Cuisnahuat, Laborista candidates for municipal office became PCS candidates after the coup of 2 December. Government reports from December 1931 also refer to "Laborista/Communist agitators." Moreover, the PCS candidate for congressional deputy in Sonsonate was the Laborista Tomás Mojica, brother of the imprisoned SRI leader Manuel Mojica.

Considering that the PCS and the left had been denouncing Araujo's government with sectarian invective such as "Abajo la dictadura fascista de Araujo!" from early in his administration, it is striking that activists could hold two such antagonistic allegiances. Nevertheless, the annals of subaltern protest history are replete with examples of support for antagonistic political tendencies. During the conflicts between communists and anarcho-syndicalists that raged in Argentina, Brazil, and Mexico in the late teens and early twenties, numerous rank-and-filers acted as if the differences were irrelevant and maintained twin loyalties. Many German workers after the First World War had no trouble working together despite nominally belonging to warring communist parties (the KPD and the KAPD).[93]

158

"To the
Face
of the
Entire
World"

The notion that these bands were made up of unemployed field hands also deserves attention. One newspaper account referred to "those unemployed who devote their leisure hours to disseminating subversive propaganda."[94] Other reports similarly link unemployment with rebelliousness. At the same time, coffee growers complained to the government that they needed coffee pickers. The growers mentioned that workers from Honduras and Guatemala had not arrived as they usually did, but neither had those from other departments.[95] More alarmingly, in early January coffee planters alleged that they were losing the harvest because of a labor shortage and actively recruited more workers from Comapa, Guatemala.[96] At that time strikes were breaking out all over the west. In short, the strikers were unemployed either because they were on strike or because, in a less combative manner, they merely refused to work for the newly reduced wages.

It is notable that ethnicity was not a significant factor in these groups. Although some indigenous coffee pickers undoubtedly took part in the strikes, informants consistently refer to the strikers as "ladinos" or state that they were non-Indians. Informants identified them as "campesinos," yet they did not all live in the countryside. Rather, townspeople from Ahuachapán, Turín, and Atiquizaya often picked coffee, and many worked as full-time farm laborers. There is little doubt that many of these "urban" campesinos participated in the radical movement."[97] A woman from Ahuachapán, twenty years old at the time, stated that the strikers were "from the *cantones* but also from the pueblo . . . they were all ladinos." She also remembers that female militants in town organized other women but does not recall women involved in the strikes or insurrection.[98]

Our sources do not permit a complete portrait of this pre-insurrectionary movement—newspapers were censored and archival records are silent. We can summarize its primary sociological characteristics: the bands comprised mainly male, non-Indian campesinos, including farm laborers, colonos, and semi-proletarian seasonal pickers, who lived in towns and in the countryside. Their tactics in demand of higher wages and decent working and living conditions ranged from using roving pickets who drove off nonstriking laborers to occupying haciendas. The strikers both followed and influenced local PCS leaders, despite some allegiance to former President Araujo.

Grassroots influence on the PCS became critical on 4 January, when party militants and sympathizers in Ahuachapán met with the delegate of the Central Committee and "insisted that he demand from the Central Committee that in view of the fact that the Party had gained a tremendous majority during the election campaign, they should be given orientations in order to prepare a movement by which they could secure by force what they had previously failed to secure."[99] At this critical juncture the Ahuachapanecos, while resisting violent repression, were clamoring for what was in effect a regional insurrection to install their municipal authorities. Acting autonomously from the Central Committee, on 7 January the local leadership made a direct appeal to soldiers: "The government of the rich has sent troops to crush the workers. Comrade soldiers: you belong to our exploited class and must not fire one single shot against the workers. Workers, peasants and soldiers should form workers,' peasants' and soldiers' councils in order to establish a workers' and peasants' government. You must disobey your officers and commanders because they are against the workers. Name your delegates to coordinate with us. Let's finish off the officers and commanders and forge a red army composed of soldiers and commanders picked from the soldiers' ranks."[100] Although this dramatic call to mutiny and rebellion probably had little effect on the government troops, it may well have had a powerful effect on the PCS leadership in San Salvador, who by 5 January had become aware of the government's use of force against the movement. At the very least, the Ahuachapanecos placed the entire left in the line of government fire at the same time that the leadership in San Salvador was still looking for ways to forestall an insurrection.

At the very moment when PCS militants in Ahuachapán were issuing insurrectionary manifestos, the national leadership was considering the viability of the electoral road to power. Legislative elections were scheduled for Sunday 10 January. Notwithstanding the extreme unlikelihood that the regime would allow PCS victories in the legislative elections, the PCS Electoral Commission continued to proceed as if the elections were a real option. Consider the letter from the Central Committee to its comrades in Santa Ana on 8 January. After laying out detailed instructions for PCS electoral activities over the next few days, the letter stated: "We must combat the idea that we won't be able to elect congressional deputies. It is an error to argue that because we did not triumph in the municipal elections due to the machinations of the bourgeoisie, we should not participate in the congressional elections."[101] The letter went on to urge the Santa Ana leadership to organize strikes, in part to elevate political consciousness and in part so that "the government does not concentrate all of its forces in Ahuachapán."[102]

The two documents reveal a sharp contradiction between the strategy of

160

"To the
Face
of the
Entire
World"

the local leaders and grassroots militants of Ahuachapán, who had essentially declared an insurrection to insure, at a minimum, local leftist rule, and at least some members of the national leadership, who still maintained hopes of an electoral solution to the political crisis. Part of that hope depended upon negotiations with the regime. On the same day that the Central Committee laid out its electoral and strike strategy, it named a five-member committee, including a congressional candidate from Ahuachapán, to negotiate with the Martínez regime.

The next day, 8 January, members of the PCS delegation arrived at the Casa Presidencial to negotiate with Martínez, who declined to meet with them, claiming that he had a bad toothache. Instead they had a brief meeting with the minister of war, Colonel Joaquín Valdéz. According to the report of the delegation, the meeting started off on a bad note, as Valdéz disclaimed knowledge of the events in Ahuachapán, which he said were the domain of the Ministry of Gobernación. The PCS delegation then proposed that to avoid further bloodshed the government should call off its troops; in return the party would ensure that the strikes were peaceful and only dealt with economic issues. Valdéz rejected any compromise, saying that he could not accept a pact with the PCS since it was "a clandestine organization."[103] A newspaper account is at odds with the details but not the substance of the delegation's report: according to the paper, "a functionary stated that the Communist Party wanted a pact," but the talks failed because the government asserted, as noted above, that the events of Ahuachapán were due to "rioters" whom the Communist Party could not control.[104] In other words, the PCS leadership was in no position to negotiate because it was not directing the strikers in Ahuachapán. This view contradicts the report of the PCS that underscored Valdéz's ignorance (feigned or not) about the strikes in Ahuachapán.[105] Regardless of his motives, when Valdéz abruptly left the room the message was clear: the regime was going to continue to clamp down violently on all protest and was unconcerned about the prospect of further bloodshed.

A Flawed Vision, a Fatal Decision

On 10 January the Central Committee of the PCS convened a plenum to discuss the issue of insurrection.[106] The leadership was convinced—and the day's events would bear them out—that the legislative elections would be a farce and that the regime would not waver in its repressive strategy. The fifty delegates to the plenum were under intense pressure from departmental branches in the west to move toward an insurrectionary strategy. In addition to the actions and proclamation of the Ahuachapenecos, strikes and violence were spreading to other areas in the west: on 7 and 8 January troops crushed strikes and broke up meetings in the departments of La Libertad and Sonsonate. According to Cuenca and Mármol, PCS and SRI leaders in both departments also began to clamor for armed insurrection.

161

"To the
Face
of the
Entire
World"

Although analytically it is possible to separate the national leadership of the PCS and the SRI from those in the west who pushed for insurrection, the historical reality was much blurrier. We argue against the notion that Higinio Pérez or Saturnino Pérez, grassroots leaders in the cantones of Nahuizalco, and Francisco Sánchez, the indigenous leader in Juayúa, were not bona fide leftists or that they were somehow operating in noncommunicative spheres, isolated from the "true communists" of the capital. On the contrary, one of the central arguments of this book is that the labor and leftist movements succeeded precisely because they subverted the sharp boundaries between city and country, educated and illiterate, ladino and indígena. That said, after the elections and the anti-strike repression the great majority of the "westerners" saw no alternative to insurrection, whereas some members of the national leadership only reluctantly joined an insurrection that they believed was doomed.

A few PCS leaders opposed the insurrection: Mario Zapata, the student leader and member of the commission who met with Colonel Valdéz; Max Cuenca, a chemist and one of the few intellectuals in the leadership; and Ismael Hernández, the secretary general of the SRI.[107] Both publicly and privately, they were convinced that the insurrection would fail because of the superior military force and preparedness of the government forces and the left's weakness in the eastern regions. Yet the great majority of those present at the plenum backed the insurrectionary option. For the purposes of analysis, it is useful to break down the decision-making process into two components. The Ahuachapanecos' proclamation to the troops to eliminate their officers and fight for a government of workers, peasants, and soldiers indicated that they had already decided to launch an insurrection or convert a proto-insurrectionary movement into a full-fledged one. As we have seen, the movement had its own dynamic, rooted primarily in class conflict in the fields, political outrage about the municipal elections, and to a lesser ex-

162

"To the
Face
of the
Entire
World"

tent anger at the overthrow of Araujo. Large groups of rebellious strikers throughout the west were either engaged in or prepared for violent conflicts with the troops. They had some arms and continued to inflict limited casualties on the troops. Many had survived the initial repressive wave and regrouped in the mountains north of Santa Rita. Indeed, on 11 January one report stated that nearly a thousand rebels had massed outside Tacuba, ready to attack. In short, when the communist militants met in San Salvador, they were faced with the choice of either supporting what amounted to the start of an insurrectionary movement or attempting to pacify it.

The plenum approved a plan that depended in large part upon support from within the military. Its principal objective was the assault on the military barracks of the major cities in the west and the capital. The takeovers would be of three types: internal use of troops loyal to the revolution, external storming of the barracks, and a combination of internal and external forces. In preparing for the insurrection, the PCS called for a nationwide general strike. A handwritten document drawn up two years after the insurrection sheds some light on the distinction and interconnection between los *occidentales* and the national leadership: "The armed forces blocked the strikes in the western zone and the general strike was not carried out, the [central committee] sent a commission to President Martínez in order to negotiate but those who met them stated that the government claimed that the campesinos only had machetes: since it had machine guns it would not accept an agreement: when los occidentales realized this, they launched a battle to the end; this is what provoked the insurrection."[108] As with almost all documents post-January 1932 (PCS or otherwise) the chronology is somewhat fuzzy, but the thrust of the argument is clear enough. This summary, substantiated by other documents, suggests that the post-election strike wave, a continuation of the December movements, formed part of a de facto PCS strategy to wrest concessions from the government. The document also echoes other leftist accounts that argue, whether as part of a conscious design or not, that the intransigence of Martínez's government directly provoked the insurrection and deprived the movement of all other acceptable options. But most significantly, the author, a survivor of the repression of 1932, uses a category, los occidentales, which refers to the western movement as a whole: the rank-and-file ladino and indigenous workers, colonos, peasants, and the local leadership. That social subject had emerged and grown over the previous two years. In January 1932 the occidentales took the historical stage briefly before the military and its élite allies smashed them into oblivion.

Although it is unclear how many of the fifty delegates were from the west, their demand for a general insurrection was heard. For the other delegates fear of violent, lethal repression against the western rank and file weighed heavily in the decision to launch an insurrection. Yet in another sense, the decision was the fruition of the ideological struggles of the pro-insurrectionary current within the PCS. In September 1930 the Mexican militant Fernández Anaya wrote about the principal problems of the newly founded PCS: "The other tendency is . . . for immediate insurrection . . . who cannot stand the persecution or the struggle against national-fascism, or the need to keep on organizing the masses . . . I should be clear. Martí shares this tendency."[109] Throughout the previous eighteen months those who shared this (informal) tendency had argued that grassroots support for armed violence as a response to the violent repression provided the rationale and the potential means for revolution. For this minority group and for Martí, the decision to call for a general insurrection was the fulfillment of a long-standing strategic objective. Since November Miguel Mármol had argued in favor of a general strike strategy as opposed to an insurrection. Faced with the brewing civil war in the west, he became a proponent of the insurrectionary option. Ironically, he then had to convince Martí that the moment was ripe: "The discussion was intense and heated. Farabundo Martí [interim PCS secretary] finally agreed with my proposal, accepting that the duty of the party was to take its place as the vanguard of the masses, in order to avoid the greater, imminent danger and disgrace for us of an insurrection that was out of control, spontaneous or provoked by the actions of the government in which the masses would go alone and without leadership onto the battlefield."[110] Those present believed that the violence on the election lines and in the fields had already provoked the beginning of a revolutionary movement that would be ruthlessly crushed by the military. For them it was a matter of "honor" that they lead the insurrection. This justifiable and palpable fear of elimination of their comrades in the west, a sense of "revolutionary honor," combined with more strictly ideological factors.

Although the Comintern had nothing directly to do with the decision of 10 January, the pro-insurrectionary position found ideological support in the fundamental postulates of the Comintern's "Third Phase," notably the

164

"To the
Face
of the
Entire
World"

"class versus class" strategy. Based on an assumption that the collapse of the world capitalist system was imminent, this strategy had some internal coherence in the European context, however flawed and tragically divorced from political realities. Yet it was never clearly translated to the "colonial" and "semicolonial" world. Rather than present a road map to socialism, to Latin America, the Comintern exported only extreme sectarianism. Its insistence on combating all reformist alternatives (rooted in the notion that social democrats were social fascists) had devastating implications in El Salvador. Most significantly, the PCS and its allies could not conceive of any kind of support or negotiation with Araujo's government. Whether Araujo would have been at all interested in any sort of political truce is unanswerable, but he certainly was open to some kind of dialogue with the individual leaders of the left, including Farabundo Martí. By the same token, accepting the Comintern "third phase" line foreclosed any possibility of a formal alliance with the Araujistas after the coup, despite some, even significant, enthusiasm of the rank and file for their own variant of Laborismo and their positive image of the deposed president.[111]

The example of the Soviet Revolution and its putative support of course helped the Salvadoran left to mobilize peasants and workers. But since the coup, there had been virtually no contact between the PCS or SRI and the Comintern. The PCS decision-making process was endogenous, as Comintern letters and reports made agonizingly clear. According to a Comintern official, "the Salvadoran comrades made it virtually impossible for us to give them practical, concrete guidance," because of what he referred to as their "self isolationism."[112] To PCS leaders, their pleas for assistance fell on deaf ears.

In January 1932 most of the PCS leadership feared losing the adherence of its political base, and at the same time believed that with the support of elements in the military the "agrarian, anti-imperialist revolution" could triumph. Thus an ideological commitment to insurrection and fear of losing the base strongly conditioned the perceived need to lead what would have otherwise been a "spontaneous" revolution. Rank-and-file and regional leaders in the west were determined to meet repressive force with popular violent resistance. But again we should recall that the decision to fight went beyond self-preservation, vengeance, and honor: political ideology, especially the right to land controlled by the élite and to local political control, also conditioned decisions among the indigenous, peasants, and workers in favor of armed resistance.

How can we assess the PCS reading that a "spontaneous" revolution was inevitable, with its concomitant probability of extremely violent repression? There is no doubt that by early January well over a thousand people in Ahuachapán were committed to violent resistance against the state. In the department of Sonsonate, grassroots militants were pushing for an armed assault on the prison to free their imprisoned comrades. Finally, in La Libertad the strike movement was beginning to resemble that of Ahuachapán. It is worth noting, however, that as late as 15 January the strike movement on San Isidro (in Sonsonate, near the border with La Libertad), involving fifteen hundred workers, came to a negotiated settlement.[113] Notwithstanding leftist leadership of the rebellious movements in the three departments, a party call for a national insurrection would have been necessary to convert these thinly articulated political and social forces into an armed revolutionary movement.

The explosion of strikes and protests also skewed the vision of both the PCS national leadership and the western rank-and-file leaders. In particular, both groups failed to appreciate that their support in the west and in San Salvador was uneven. An urban artisan or worker, for example, might have been ready to vote for the PCS but not necessarily to participate in an armed insurrection. The different levels of support would become significant during the insurrection and in its recreation in memory. Not only did the PCS leadership fail to distinguish the quality of its support, it proved unable to grasp the degree of hostility present in virtually all sectors of society. The campesinos who consciously ducked the revolutionary wave, like those cited above, also posed objective limits to recruitment. The need for "pressing" tactics during the strike mobilizations indicated that even among their most solid base of support in the coffee sector, many workers remained on the sidelines out of fear, apathy, or antagonism. The tremendous growth of the labor movement obscured the existence of this uncommitted group, who at the very least would limit the number of committed revolutionary troops. The movement also had its non-élite antagonists. Ladino smallholders in some indigenous areas often bitterly opposed the left. Many in the urban middle class, such as professionals and shop owners, were fearful and resentful of the growing pride and assertiveness of the rural and urban poor.[114] This serious underestimation of the degree of "anti-revolutionary" sentiment would have severe consequences, especially during the counter-revolution. In short, the PCS leadership's reading of reality was partially, but significantly, flawed. As Elizabeth Wood reminds us, other radical move-

166

"To the
Face
of the
Entire
World"

ments, such as the South African general strike of the 1980s, triumphed or made great progress with similar or lower levels of popular support.[115] Yet despite what would have been a strategic minority in a strike or an electoral contest, or even a civil war, the insurrection had virtually no chance of success in the absence of effective support from within the military.

The left did have a significant, if poorly organized, presence within the regular army. The PCS started to actively organize in the military in mid-December. It also infiltrated volunteers into the military who were stationed in San Salvador (el Zapote), as well as in Ahuachapán and Sonsonate,[116] and managed to heavily infiltrate and organize the Sixth Machine Gun Regiment. Clandestine groups also operated within at least two barracks of the regular army in San Salvador.[117] A secret police report suggested that 50–60 percent of the regular army and 30 percent of the National Guard were leftist sympathizers.[118] Yet regardless of the high level of sympathy for the left among the troops, the officer corps remained almost uniformly loyal to the regime.

By 16 January the military had already discovered and eliminated most of the revolutionary conspirators in its ranks.[119] Following leads from the captured soldiers, police arrested the PCS leaders Farabundo Martí, Mario Zapata, and Alfonso Luna and captured the military plans for the insurrection and other documents. In another arrest they found seventy-five bombs. On the 19th, according to the British consul, "a large gathering of communists took place in Atlacatl park about a mile and a half north of San Salvador, the object of which was to be an attack on the Cavalry Barracks. National Guardsmen were hurried to the spot and scattered the communists."[120] As a result of a prior accord, the revolutionaries were expecting soldiers in the barracks to surrender and join the insurrection. Officers were tipped off, however, and disarmed the company that was preparing to join the revolutionary forces. Many were arrested, tortured, and killed.[121] The guardsmen then opened fire on the insurgents outside the barracks. Why the insurgents in San Salvador initiated the insurrection early remains a mystery, explicable only by their recognition that the military was already prepared to execute the revolutionary soldiers in the First Cavalry Regiment.

On the morning of 20 January, after the arrests and the regime's declaration of a state of siege, the PCS Central Committee convened to discuss its options. The failure to organize the military effectively blocked the possibility of arming the insurrection with automatic weapons and other firearms. With a state of emergency having been imposed by the military, communication with the provincial centers became extremely difficult. A minority of three on the Central Committee pushed to postpone the insur-rection, arguing that it could not succeed because of the disarticulation of the army network and the lack of weapons, and because the police and the National Guard had captured the plans. If the insurrection were called off, the government would lack justification for perpetrating a massacre. The majority of six on the committee claimed that the government was already preparing a massacre and that the only option was to fight in defense of the rank and file and their imprisoned comrades. In the words of the minority leader, the majority argued against postponing the insurrection "because so many of our comrades were in jail . . . more arrests were being made and it was clear that all comrades were to be shot and they thought it would be better that all of us should have the same destiny. None of them showed any logic or clear analysis of the situation and none of them could logically explain why the action was justified."[122]

167

"To the
Face
of the
Entire
World"

There is no doubt that adherence by the PCS to Marxism-Leninism, although interpreted differently by the rank and file and by the leadership, created an ideological field in which revolutionary violence was acceptable to both. Yet the resistance in the west and the decision of the Central Committee were also contingent, emotional responses to the repressive measures of the state and the outrage that violence caused among its vic-tims, their friends, and their comrades. The call to arms issued on 20 Janu-ary 1932 evoked this sense of outrage and the continued affronts to the dignity of communists and their supporters. The manifesto underscores the causal relation between the elections and the armed resistance to repres-sion, but most significantly it offers a glimpse of the mentality of the communist leaders:

> We the workers, they call us thieves . . . and steal our wage, paying us a miserable wage and condemning us to live in filthy tenements or in stinking barracks, or working day and night in the fields under rain and sun. We are labeled thieves for demanding the wages that they owe us, a reduction in the workday, and a reduc-tion in the rents that we pay to the rich who take almost all our harvest, stealing our work from us. To the insults are added killings, beatings, jailings . . . we have seen the massacres of workers, men and women and even children and elderly, workers from Santa Tecla, Sonsonate, Zaragoza, and right now in Ahuachapán. According to the wealthy, we do not have a right to anything, and we shouldn't

168

"To the
Face
of the
Entire
World"

open our mouths. . . . In Ahuachapán, after the National Guard didn't let our comrades vote by order of the rich folks, they beat them. . . . Our compañeros from Ahuachapán are valiantly defending themselves with their weapons in their hands.[123]

This manifesto reveals something of the social and cultural elasticity of the movement and the openness of communication between its constituent parts. Although written by PCS leaders, it is surprisingly devoid of jargon and clearly related to the experiences of its intended audience. It speaks in a populist idiom about *ricos* and basic citizenship rights. Moreover, the themes of honor and respect—"they call us thieves"—resonate with and sharply recall the PCS mayoral candidate's protestations of decorum. The manifesto also calls on campesinos to seize the land of the wealthy and "to defend your revolutionary conquests, with no pity for the rich." It urges workers to arm themselves to "defend the proletarian revolution," and to form a government of workers,' peasants,' and soldiers' councils. The ending—a direct call to the soldiers: "Kill your officers!"—is curiously discordant and somewhat disassociated from the rest of the text. It reads as if its authors had immersed themselves in the daily struggles of the coffee workers, only to realize at the end that the soldiers would have to execute their officers to "win" this proletarian revolution.

Another manifesto, supposedly issued on 16 January, called on communists to use "terror without mercy" against the bourgeoisie. Miguel Mármol, with apparent justification, claimed that the government had prepared and circulated this document.[124] A close reading, in conjunction with an analysis of references to the manifesto by the Comintern and PCS exiles, suggests that at a minimum the regime added key articles to the manifesto. The explicit calls for using "terror" and executing individual members of the bourgeoisie are odd formulations for Marxist-Leninists, however rudimentarily instructed. The phrase recalls the placard supposedly carried by the demonstrators in Sonsonate on 17 May that threatened "Respetad Solo a los Niños"; the government used this undocumented threat as justification for violent repression. The instruction to turn over the best cars to the "Red commanders" also seems contrived.[125] Whether or not falsified, the document was successfully circulated by the government and newspapers. It certainly conveyed a message of terror to the middle class and wealthy and seems also to have alienated urban workers.

Miguel Mármol recalled the day of the insurrection. For years he had dreamed about the day of liberation of the Salvadoran proletariat. Yet when he awoke that day he recognized the dawn of a nightmare: "The 22nd, the date fixed for the insurrection I was going around coordinating cells in San Salvador . . . on foot, without even a penknife in my pocket. And what hurts the most is that the revolutionary spirit of the masses was incredibly high . . . Already by that awful 22nd of January, the enemy had seized the initiative from us: instead of a party that was on the point of initiating a big insurrection, at least that's how all the cadre in San Salvador talked about it, we had the appearance of desperate, persecuted, and harassed revolutionaries. From one moment to the next, the work was in practice abandoned and everyone tried to save themselves from the unrestrained repression."[126]

Chapter Six

Red Ribbons and Machetes:
The Insurrection of January 1932

Pero un día en tu quebranto
Rompiendo el yugo te alzaste
Quisiste que fuera todo
De todos como en el cristo
Al primer soviet de américa
Lo hicieron mierda a balazos—Pedro Geoffroy Rivas, "Un Romance de Enero" (1935)

It was as dark as night during the daytime on 22 January; the ash from volcanoes in Guatemala covered western Salvador. The falling ash resembled a "snowstorm in Canada," wrote a Protestant minister in Juayúa. Peasants were startled to see birds collide with one another in confusion. As the darkness of the day turned to the darkness of night, the haunting whistles of conch shells echoed throughout the mountain valleys. On the outskirts of Ahuachapán, Sonsonate, Izalco, and Santa Tecla rocket flares shot up into the thick, smoky sky. People interpreted the volcanic signs with dread or hope, but most understood that the conch shells, whistles, and rocket flares announced the beginning of the insurrection. That night and before dawn on the 23rd, between five and seven thousand insurgents assaulted the military barracks in the departmental capitals of Ahuachapán, Santa Tecla, and La Libertad and took over several municipal seats in central and western Salvador.[1]

Who were the revolutionary fighters? Cultural details about the rebels have historiographical importance because of the notable imprecision in previous accounts, a deficiency that has had significant political ramifications. Indians, ladinos, and others with indeterminate and fluid ethnic and class identities participated side by side in the insurrection. The great majority had experience working on the region's coffee farms and haciendas: the mobile strike force of coffee workers discussed in chapter 5 made up most of the insurgent troops in Ahuachapán and a minority of the forces in Juayúa and Nahuizalco. Many informants in the Nahuizalco area claimed that those who occupied their town came from Turín and Atiquizaya and were distinguishable as "mulattoes" (in both senses, as ladinos and as people with phenotypically mulatto features). In addition to those from the region around Atiquizaya and Turín, the insurgent forces included many ladinos from the Ahuachapán region whose cultural identity differentiated them from Indians far more than their physical appearance did.

Indians from the barrio of Asunción in Izalco and campesinos of more fluid identities from its outlying cantons participated in the failed attack on the Sonsonate barracks on the night of 22 January. Similarly, many indigenous peasants from the cantons of Nahuizalco and indigenous and ladino peasants from the cantons of Juayúa joined the forces that occupied their towns. Indigenous and ladino peasants in the Tacuba area defeated the military garrison there and occupied the town for several days. Coffee workers from the Cumbre de Jayaque staged the failed attack on Santa Tecla barracks (eight miles west of San Salvador). Many of their parents and grandparents had possessed indigenous identities. but the vast majority neither wore indigenous dress nor spoke indigenous languages. Finally, indigenous peasants from the Panchimalco region to the south of San Salvador and nonindigenous peasants and workers from the rural areas to the east staged minor attacks in the area of the capital.[2]

La Libertad: The Attack on Santa Tecla

Two insurgent forces planned to attack the army barracks at Santa Tecla. On the night of the 22nd the first group of campesinos entered the small town of Colón, eight kilometers northwest of Santa Tecla. The British consul reported: "The communists attacked Colón on the night of 22nd January and killed the town Clerk and the Commandant and wounded the

Principal insurrectionary sites.

telegraphist and some women. The attacking force was composed of about 400 men led by an Indian belonging to the town called Lino Argueta aged 78 who had been very active in the communist cause. The inhabitants of the town hurriedly organized their defense and in the fight which resulted, the Indian Argueta, although he had received three gunshot wounds in the body and severe machete gashes in the face, still managed to encourage his men until he collapsed dead."[3]

There appear to be two reasons for the revolutionary force's attack on Colón. First, the regime had suspended the municipal elections, which the PCS had expected to win. Second, during the campaign the local comandante had confiscated ninety-six corvos from the rural activists, which they wanted to reclaim. After that confrontation the insurgent forces retreated into the surrounding hills, where they regrouped and set out on a march toward Santa Tecla. The force that attacked Colón came from nearby towns and cantons in the coffee region, including Talnique, Sacacoyo, Agua Fria, El Tránsito, and Las Moras, and it reflected the same heterogeneous mixture that characterized the region as a whole.[4]

As one column advanced on Colón, another large column formed in Los Amates, a coffee-rich canton ten kilometers west of Santa Tecla. Doroteo

López, then an eighteen-year-old *apuntador*, recalls how some five hundred campesinos had come down from the Cumbre de Jayaque and the villages of Comasagua and Jayaque and gathered in the plaza of Los Amates. A couple of hours before dawn, they set out toward Santa Tecla. At dawn the two columns merged in the coffee groves on the outskirts of Santa Tecla. As they started to leave the coffee finca at Las Delicias, they were met with bullets. An army unit, reinforced by the National Guard, sprayed the revolutionaries with machine-gun fire for an hour until the nearly one thousand insurgents dispersed. A large group retreated down the Carretera Panamericana. Upon reaching Colón it engaged in a battle with a hastily organized civic guard. After a brief skirmish the insurgents, already weakened by the encounter in Santa Tecla, set off for the forested hills. The column from la Cumbre retreated up the road. Doroteo López recalls, "At 6:30 those who survived started their retreat. At 8 the last of the defeated passed by."[5] Their retreat was not entirely chaotic: rather, some insurgent troops set up blockades along the road to protect the retreat of the others into the coffee-covered highlands of Jayaque.

The disastrous attack on Santa Tecla did not end the insurrection in La Libertad. After their defeat at Las Delicias in the early morning of the 23rd, many of the retreating rebels formed guerrilla bands that attacked various towns and occupied plantations. A military report dated 24 January reads: "In the hacienda Zapotitlán there were 300 Communists gathered . . . We were also informed that in the Hacienda Chanmico . . . there were 250 Communists who were heading towards the railroad line . . . at three in the morning . . . the comandante of San Julián reported that the troops had left . . . and that the Communists were assassinating people in San Julián and that they were marching towards los Lagartos. Then, the stationmaster at Bebedero informed us that in Los Lagartos there were about 250 Communists and that from . . . Ishuatán there were about 400 Communists heading there in groups of 45."[6]

Izalco and Sonsonate

On the evening of 22 January insurgents marched toward Sonsonate city from various towns and plantations to the west and north of the provincial capital. The insurgent force numbered over one thousand, including Indians, mainly from Izalco and its cantons, and many ladino campesinos from other towns and villages. Armed mostly with corvos, the rebel force included some one hundred ladino campesinos from Los Gramales, a lowland village near the San Julián coffee plantation district. They joined forces with a similar contingent from the more isolated indigenous town of Cuisnahuat.[7]

Margarita Turcios recalls how the campesinos of Los Mangos, a canton east of the vast San Isidro hacienda, passed through her canton, Los Guayabos, on the evening of 22 January. Bastions of union activism on the San Isidro Hacienda since early in 1930, the neighboring ladino cantons both supplied recruits for the assault on Sonsonate. Turcios recalls that most of the insurgents came from Los Mangos. Despite their leftist sympathies and their labor activism, her father and other neighbors in Los Guayabos apparently did not join in the attack.[8]

Throughout the day on 22 January large groups of Indians filed out of Barrio Abajo in the direction of the Volcán de Izalco. Early in the evening, on the slopes of the volcano in the canton of Cuyagualo, indigenous men gathered and filed down the path through the *cafetales* down to Cúntun, where they were greeted with shouts of "Viva el Socorro Rojo Internacional!" by hundreds of indigenous people from the Izalqueño cantons of Ceiba del Charco and Piedras Pachas. Together this group of several hundred men marched toward Izalco, where they met up with those from Barrio Abajo and a smaller group of ladinos, mostly artisans and jornaleros, from Barrio Dolores.

At nine o'clock the insurrectionists, some six hundred strong, with red bandanas hanging from their corvo sheaths, entered Izalco shouting, "Viva El Socorro Rojo!" The British consul reported, "The inhabitants were wakened by revolver shots in the center of the town followed by blows on the doors, upon which the communists were beating with their axes, machetes, and clubs. Other communists ran up and down the streets beating on their knives with stones. The leaders cried out to their friends to join them, promising them immunity."[9] The recently imposed mayor, Miguel Call, and Rafael Castro, a cafetalero friend from Chalchuapa, exited a cantina and shot their revolvers at a group gathering on a street corner. The rebels raced after them. Some shouted "Viva el comunismo hijo de puta!" When Call ran out of bullets, the crowd hacked him with corvos. Severely wounded, Castro managed to find refuge, only to die from the wounds a few days later.

The revolutionary forces captured the town hall, where they installed as mayor Eusebio Chavez, a ladino carpenter and recent PCS mayoral

Looted store Izalco. Photo by Commander Victor Brodeur, National Archives of Canada, negative no. PA125138.

candidate. Other insurgents captured the local *cuartel*, which had been abandoned by the few soldiers and their commander. As in Colón, a woman led a group under the command of José Pashaca; the insurgents brought fourteen wealthy ladinos to the cuartel, where they imprisoned them. Other groups looted houses, shops, and a pharmacy.

Alfonso Díaz Barrientos, a wealthy landowner, fired on one group of rebels from the rooftop of a neighbor's house and killed several of them. Díaz Barrientos knew he was a marked man, given his political and economic prominence and his former close patronage ties to the Indians and the leftist movement, notably its leader José Feliciano Ama. Rather than storm his house, the insurgents ignored him as they prepared to move on Sonsonate.

Hundreds of revolutionary troops marched toward the city of Sonsonate from Izalco. Other columns joined them on the road through Sónzacate; at eleven o'clock that night over eight hundred rebels entered Barrio El Angel from Sónzacate. Shouting revolutionary slogans, they marched through the streets to the strategic center of the city that housed the Eighth Infantry Regiment, the National Guard post, the railroad station, and the Customs House. Approximately one hundred rebels approached the city center, where they confronted a group of about fifty soldiers preparing to board trucks and cars in order to move on Izalco. Colonel Bará prudently ordered the retreat of his soldiers back into the barracks. He also ordered that the vehicles be lined up in front of the barracks. But seventeen rebels managed to climb on board the backs of the trucks and then stormed inside the barracks gate, which was still open. Once inside they engaged in hand-to-hand combat, managing to avoid the gunshots of the army officers. The soldiers of the Eighth Regiment, mainly recent rural recruits from the area, did not fire on the insurgents, revealing their wavering loyalty and lack of military discipline. But one officer, armed with a "Solotur" submachine gun, sprayed the insurgents with bullets and killed them all.

Insurgents overran the customs building, where they killed four of the eleven guards and then sacked the building, destroying furniture and documents. They also managed to capture weapons. Another rebel group unsuccessfully attacked the National Guard headquarters. Driven back by machine-gun fire, they suffered quite a few casualties while killing five Guardia.[10] At 7:00 in the morning on 23 January the rebels retreated toward neighboring Sónzacate, a mile and a half east of the city on the road to Izalco. It is not at all clear why the insurgents retreated, since they had not suffered large losses in Sonsonate and had acquired some armaments. In any case Sónzacate, a bastion of leftist support, was an obvious place to regroup.

There the insurgents received reinforcements from villages in the area. Late in the morning, Colonel Bará led a mixed battalion of National Guard and regular troops to attack the insurgents. Although most of the rebels were still only armed with corvos they had an overwhelming numerical advantage. Julia Mojica ("Red Julia"), sister of the imprisoned communist leader and carpenter Manuel Mojica, led some fifteen hundred to two thousand rebels against the troops.[11] Her forces were able to drive back the government troops. According to Tito Calvo, an officer and native of Izalco, "Those courageous Indians almost made it to the machine guns, one grabbed the foot of the machine gun."[12] After an officer and several soldiers fell dead, the government troops retreated to Sonsonate.

This was the only significant insurgent military victory during the insurrection. Rather than pursue the government troops back to Sonsonate, this large battalion of what they called the "Red Army" broke up, most returning to the Izalco region and others to Nahuizalco and Juayúa. Many of those who returned to Izalco continued into the countryside to recruit for the Red Army.

Ten minutes before midnight on 22 January an estimated six hundred campesinos from the Atiquizaya region and from the cantons of Juayúa occupied the town with little resistance.[13] A group of eighty men marched to
the telegraph office and destroyed it. Another group attacked the cabildo
and killed one of its defenders while the others escaped. In the municipal
building they destroyed much of the archive. Benjamín Herrera, one of the
leaders, scrawled his initials on the wall: "BH, Enero 23 Juayúa 1932."[14]

A group of over one hundred insurgents then marched toward the house
of the former mayor, an Italian with fascist sympathies and a long history
of conflict with the local labor movement: "many townsfolk also joined
them . . . so, you see, they burned down the house of don Emilio Redaelli,
who had been mayor, they burned his house, burned his business . . . they
killed him . . . but most of the people were from town, resentful ones,
right?"[15] The assassination of Redaelli—shop owner, coffee exporter, and
general manager of a coffee beneficio—came to symbolize the barbarity of
the insurrection for opponents and bystanders throughout the country.
Campesinos still recall the corridos sung about his execution. In one account, a crowd gathered outside his house. He emerged on the balcony
with a gun in his hand, asking, "What do you want?" The crowd shouted,
"Money!" Redaelli responded, "Wait, I'll bring it." Upon his return, and
before he could dispense the money, people in the crowd started shouting,
"We want the heads of the rich! We want the bosses' lives!" A hailstorm of
rocks knocked Redaelli down. The crowd surged toward him. According to
one version, someone urinated in his mouth when he begged for water;
according to another, people stomped on his face in response to the same
request.[16]

With more insistence and more success than in Izalco, the insurgents
called on the population to join them, using various forms of threats and
less coercive forms of persuasion. They obliged residents to wear red ribbons symbolizing solidarity with the movement. They also expected people
to address each other as *camarada* and to shout "Viva el Socorro Rojo!" A
man named Soriano, informants recall, refused to shout the slogan. According to one version he was a shop owner and anti-communist, and
according to another he supported the insurrection but refused to shout
because he was too tired. One rebel threatened him: "Shout Viva el Socorro

Rojo Internacional!" He responded, "If I knew this 'Socorro,' I would, but I don't know it."

"Shout Viva el Socorro Rojo, hijo de puta!"
"You've got the wrong mother; I don't shout."
"This is over!" the insurgent shouted, and his comrades killed Soriano.[17]

Without a doubt, a strong threat was associated with the revolutionary pleas for solidarity. Yet there are also versions that ascribe to the townsfolk a considerable degree of voluntary support for the movement: "since they entered town triumphantly and took it over, many people joined them, thinking that they were going to rule in the future."[18] Many townsfolk who did not form part of the initial mobilization joined in looting stores (and may have had primary responsibility for the killing and probable torture of Emilio Redaelli). A sixteen-year-old colono who came to town recalls the strange scene: "I asked a guy on the street what was going on. He replied, 'Be quiet! Today we are on top. Today we are doing well because we are running the show.' "[19]

The rebels appropriated seven trucks from the wealthy, and early on the morning of the 23rd they set out to reinforce the rebel troops in Sónzacate. Another small group of rebels took vehicles to Izalco to establish contact with the movement there. That same morning the Reverend Roy Mac-Naught peered out of his house: "I saw the red flag flying from the town hall; we were under communistic rule for the first time."[20] Who were the leaders of this "communist" government? Indian and ladino jornaleros and artisans, all with backgrounds in the labor movement, formed the local leadership. Francisco Sánchez, an Indian jornalero who had lived in town and had been active in the labor movement for several years, was their most renowned leader. Benjamín Herrera, "a green-eyed, white" jornalero, twenty-nine years old, who resided on the outskirts of town, was the other main leader. Others in the leadership group included Juan Antonio Mirón, a ladino jornalero, and Narciso Molina, a ladino tailor.[21]

According to the PCS leader Max Cuenca, "Our comrades who were on the list of candidates took charge of the administration of those places, proclaiming Soviets and raising on the public buildings the red flag, with hammer and sickle . . . The Soviets had as an immediate task the resistance against government troops and, therefore, no immediate attention was paid to the plantations. But these local Soviets in charge of administration immediately disposed of grain deposits and warehouses and proceeded with the distribution of these."²² Despite their memorialization in Geoffroy Rivas's poem (see the epigraph at the beginning of this chapter), there is no hard evidence to back up Cuenca's assertion that the insurgents proclaimed "soviets." In Juayúa the PCS had not been allowed to field its candidates in the election, and perhaps for that reason the insurgents did not install the PCS candidate as in Izalco. Narciso Molino, who would have been their candidate, did participate in the leadership, but the principal leader was Francisco Sánchez, who had established a strong following thanks to his record of labor activism and his ability to relate to town and country workers, both ladinos and Indians. Moreover, the prison terms that the regime had imposed on him for his militancy earned him the esteem of the rank-and-file SRI militants. According to various informants, although he was from the canton of El Zapote, he had resided in Juayúa for some time and even in the town, "el tenía pueblo."²³ He was the obvious choice to head the local revolutionary government.

Sánchez gave a speech denouncing the January elections, after which a high school student, Arturo Carvajal, shouted out, "Cabildo abierto!," thus giving a colonial-era format to the local revolutionary takeover. After the meeting, at which Sánchez was acclaimed the new mayor, Carvajal read the new *bando* (official proclamation) in the four corners of the city. The insurgents performed this revolutionary proclamation in venerable colonial garb, with a festive air. A band played after each reading, and rockets were set off.²⁴ Once Carvajal finished reading the bando, the musicians returned to the plaza in front of the Cabildo. According to several accounts, whenever they stopped playing for very long, Sánchez ordered them to start up again in his indigenous-based dialectal Spanish, "Que toque el banda, maishtra!"²⁵

Juayúa under revolutionary rule was deeply intimidating to the area's élite, but quite festive to the occupying campesinos and many of the poorer townsfolk. Sánchez and the other leaders combined music, speech making, and collective shouting of slogans as markers of the insurrection. According to one newspaper report, well into the night of the 23rd the crowds shouted, "Vivas" to Araujo, the SRI, the Ejercito Rojo, and communism as well as "Death to Martínez, Death to Capitalism!"²⁶

Counterinsurgent documents suggest that Sánchez and his followers pursued their goals with logic and purpose. As the British consul reported,

"On the whole, the behavior of the communists in Juayúa was more methodical than might have been expected. This was due to the authority of Francisco Sánchez. One of his first orders was that all the liquor in the bars should be poured out on the ground."[27] He also provided food for his troops by compelling fifteen townswomen, dressed in red, to prepare tortillas from a quintal of corn apiece. According to Raúl Sigüenza, "On the 23rd they began to break into stores. They broke into the houses of Mateo Roldán, Manuel Aguirre, and of the Chinaman who sold gasoline when they used to sell it in cardboard boxes . . . they used it to burn down the house of Emilio Redaelli."[28]

The occupying forces and their town supporters engaged in systematic looting: all the goods were brought to the town hall, where the "red" government set up a distribution center. The Reverend Roy MacNaught saw a political motive in the looting, as did informants who reflected on a similar situation in Nahuizalco: "The 'reds' distributed the spoils with a lavish hand; in fact, they wanted all those, who were not otherwise lined up with them, to share in their ill-gotten gains in order that they might be thus identified with their cause . . . men clothed in rags carrying off fine clothes, bright colored, woolen blankets, hats, implements; women bearing proudly on their heads sheets of corrugated iron, measures of corn, bolts of cloth; children with their pockets full of candies, handkerchiefs and toys . . . Thus was the town of Juayúa sacked."[29]

Whether or not the insurgents organized looting and distribution for recruitment purposes, Sánchez also seemed to be concerned with more long-range redistributive goals. In other towns the revolutionaries had destroyed the municipal buildings in part to eliminate the property records and create a de facto basis for land distribution. Sánchez made a more systematic move: "He caused all the title deeds of landed property and houses to be delivered to him and then drew up a plan of division among his own men."[30] Such measures responded to the level of class mobilization and resentment in the countryside. According to one plantation owner, "On Saturday night, the 23rd, a big mob of them came through here, on the way to attack Nahuizalco. They had no time to cut me up since they were in a rush to get there so they made do with just shouting blasphemies at me and threatening that I would be one of the first to fall into their hands. In this mob, this immense, chaotic multitude, there were like 200 of my mozos and those of my brothers and neighbors. Those whom we thought were humble and honorable, to whom we had given lands for their harvests without charge and to whom we had paid their salaries punctually."[31]

Nahuizalco

Early on 23 January, when an insurgent group from Juayúa passed through Nahuizalco, its members shouted to townsfolk to prepare to join the insurrection when they returned that night. During the course of the day many ladinos (who made up some 10 percent of the population) attempted to escape or hide. Indigenous insurgents blocked most of the exits from the town, but several families managed to leave and others, as in Juayúa, attempted to hide in the homes of the poor. Unlike in Juayúa, most of Nahuizalco's urban poor were Indians and generally sympathetic to the revolutionary movement, which they interpreted at least partially in ethnic terms. There are various reports that Indians shouted, "Viva los indios de Nahuizalco," interspersed with other explicitly leftist slogans. One ladino recalled that as a child he hid in an Indian hut. An indigenous child who lived there danced around, exclaiming joyfully "Today we have the ladinos."[32]

The insurgents returned earlier than expected. A ladino resident recalled the events that unfolded at 3:00 in the afternoon: "We realized that they had raised the red flag on the pole over the Guardia headquarters and the plaza was filled with about 800 Communists, listening to one of their leaders reading a speech. They constantly shouted vivas to Communism. Meanwhile the people, in their houses, awaited their final moment."[33] Alberto Shul, ill in bed, recalled his grandmother exclaiming: " 'A lot of people on horse back with red badges have taken over the alcaldía . . . It looks like they are from Turín y Atiquizaya.' " Shul added: "And they looted the town."[34]

All the informants in Nahuizalqueño, like some of those in Juayúa, remembered the horseback-riding revolutionaries as ladinos from Turín and Atiquizaya. These insurgents were in all likelihood the same people who had started fighting the Guardia in the roving strike movement that erupted during the first week of January. There is no way of reconstructing their role in Nahuizalco or in Juayúa beyond the likelihood that they gave military support to the movement.

There was no uniformity of action in the two occupied towns. In Nahuizalco the rebels burned the archives of the alcaldía and with it all land records, rather than gather the titles to institute a more formal land reform. In contrast to what took place in Juayúa, the insurgent troops broke the locks of the shops in town for immediate, as opposed to formal, redistribution. Ramón Esquina, a young boy in the canton of Tajcuilulaj, a few miles northwest of town, recalls the night of 23 January: "My god! My god they're going to kill us . . . and we heard the sounds of the locks and chains being smashed. The next day all of the stores had their doors wide open and the people went in and took what they found: rice, coffee, sugar and then went off."[35] Whether, as so many informants claimed, the communist leaders broke open the shops to tempt the Indians into a *robo* is somewhat doubtful, as hundreds of Nahuizalqueños were involved in the takeover.[36] In any event, the open store doors tempted some less committed, impoverished residents of the town.

As in Juayúa, the insurgents commanded townswomen to prepare tortillas for their troops. Despite threats of bloodshed the rebels killed only one ladino civilian, and that happened in unclear circumstances. In a manner reminiscent of the attempts to establish revolutionary legitimacy in the other occupied towns, the mostly indigenous rebels marched through the streets of Nahuizalco shouting, "We want the head of Chico Brito!," a reference to the ladino mayor of the municipality.[37] The insurgents had captured Cipriano Brito, son of the mayor, and forced him to shout, along with the rest of the crowd, for his father's head. But the mayor escaped harm, as he managed to hide and wait out the storm.

Ahuachapán

On the night of 22 January Luis Alfonso Castillo joined with his campesino comrades in the SRI from the Llanos de María region and began to march toward the cuartel on the eastern side of Ahuachapán. This group of several hundred campesinos joined a much larger and better-armed group that had been engaged in sporadic armed conflict with the Guardia over the previous two weeks. From the canton of Achapuco, a few miles west of the city, several hundred insurgents gathered and marched toward the city center. Some shooting broke out near the barracks at ten o'clock, but most of the Ejercito Rojo waited on the outskirts of the town until rockets announced their first charges at around 1:00 in the morning. From one to two thousand revolutionaries armed with corvos, picks, pistols, some mausers, and shotguns attacked the barracks in Ahuachapán, while a smaller group attacked the center of town, occupying and then destroying the municipal building.[38]

The insurgent leaders ("Red Commanders") sent small groups to break down the massive gates of the barracks with iron pick hammers. From inside the imposing colonial stone structure troops sprayed the insurgents with machine-gun fire, killing several of them. The revolutionaries regrouped and attacked again. More machine-gun fire and more fighters fell dead. Again the Ejercito Rojo regrouped. After the third failed attempt, at 3:30 in the morning, they retreated and joined the other group of rebels, who had assaulted the municipal building and headed north out of town. The insurgents had counted on the support of soldiers, but the regime, days before the insurrection, had wisely discharged all suspicious soldiers and one officer, Vicente Hidalgo, commander of the artillery. According to one account, Hidalgo joined the Ejercito Rojo and fought in Tacuba.[39]

The revolutionary forces marched toward the town of Tacuba, where the column from Ahuachapán joined forces with the Tacubeños to attack the municipal building. They easily overpowered the handful of soldiers who were on guard and then proceeded to burn the archive and furniture, destroying most of the building. The insurgents overran and destroyed the barracks, which were guarded by twenty Guardia, killing their commanding officer. They captured some arms, including mausers and one machine gun. The revolutionaries executed two or three landowners in the region, including the retired general Rafael Rivas. Armed with a pistol, Rivas fought until his death. According to one source, the insurgents cut off his head and paraded it around town on a stake, calling on the townsfolk to "salute the general!"[40]

Ladinos and Indians joined the local revolutionary ranks in roughly equal proportion, reflecting the ethnic composition of the town (60 percent indigenous). The Cuenca brothers, ladino university students and sons of local merchants, led the insurgents in Tacuba. The most compelling tasks of the revolutionaries were to establish and legitimate their authority, to prepare their military defense, and to organize new assaults on the barracks in Ahuachapán. In Tacuba, as throughout the west, the insurgent leaders placed the former Communist candidates in positions of power. Abel Cuenca, denied a mayoral victory at the ballot box, was placed in charge of the revolutionary government.

Over the next two days it appears that the revolutionary troops attempted to move on the offensive, as did their comrades in Nahuizalco, Juayúa, and Izalco. Some insurgents marched along trails over the cordillera to Ataco in the direction of Juayúa. Others marched back north toward Ahuachapán. Heavily armed government troops blocked their advance in both directions. In one somewhat romanticized account of Tacuba under insurgent control, apparently based on interviews with survivors, Rodrigo Buezo wrote in 1944, "During the three following days, the working people had managed to impose their will on the landowners of the region, who, filled with an indescribable panic . . . had to accept the exigencies and necessities of revolutionary action." Buezo did not portray the "soviet" as a truly delibera- tive body akin to the revolutionary workers' councils in Russia during the February and October Revolutions, in large part because their tasks were eminently defensive. He wrote: "Once the insurrection took control of the government arms and offices and the working people had organized their own services—administration, food, etc.—then all the work was reduced to the coordination of the town's defense."[41]

The Defeat of the Insurrection

The army and National Guard could not immediately set out to put down the insurrection. In addition to the limited damage to the railroad line to the west, the insurgents posed a threat to the capital. On the 23rd and 24th, insurgents, including Indians from the Panchimalco area, staged nighttime guerrilla-like attacks that were successfully repelled by government troops. To the east they had to defeat mobilized campesinos from the leftist base around Lake Ilopango.[42]

Young middle- and upper-class volunteers responded to the call for formation of a Guardia Cívica while their parents footed the bill for arma- ments and additional troops from the eastern (unaffected) departments. The five hundred armed Civic Guards who patrolled the capital and Santa Tecla, along with the arrival of reinforcements from eastern Salvador, al- lowed the government forces to deal with the insurgency in the west.[43] At dawn on 24 January the armed forces under the command of General José Tomás Calderón set off by train to put down the insurrection. Upon arrival in Armenia, the main commercial center of an important plantation district, the army provided weapons to a civilian force of one hundred to supplement the fifty soldiers Calderón left behind in the city. Their objective was to pursue insurgent bands operating in the coffee region on the border between Sonsonate and La Libertad. Another regiment under the command of Major Francisco Marroquín marched out of Santa Tecla to pursue the informal guerrilla bands in La Libertad. After securing the geographically key town of Colón, most of the regiment marched westward from Colón toward Izalco.

After their arrival in Sonsonate troops under the command of General Jesús Bran set off from the west to occupy Sónzacate and Izalco. Expecting strong resistance in Sónzacate, they found only a few smoldering oil storage tanks. At 10:00, as they approached Izalco, they heard gunshots from the east, where the column from Colón had begun the attack. More troops at the nearby Caluco train station rapidly marched up the hill to Izalco. Attacking from three sides, the heavily armed troops overwhelmed the insurgents, who held out for an hour before fleeing into the countryside. Commander V. G. Brodeur of the Canadian destroyer the Skeena, who visited the area a few days later, estimated that the troops had killed over one thousand people in and around Izalco during this initial assault.[44]

A large force under the command of Lieutenant Colonel Francisco Salinas returned to Sonsonate and then moved up the steep, rocky road toward Nahuizalco and Juayúa. At the intersection between the main road and the side road to Nahuizalco, Salinas and his troops met several cars filled with armed rebels heading down to attack Sonsonate, presumably operating with the assumption that most of the government troops were fighting in Izalco. Salinas's troops rapidly dominated the insurgents, who retreated to the town. The expeditionary force then marched on Nahuizalco, which they retook by late afternoon on the 24th. After repelling sporadic attacks by indigenous insurgents throughout the night, on the following morning most of Salinas's troops joined those under the command of Bran as they marched on Juayúa.[45]

The revolutionary leaders had ordered their troops to cut down trees to block the road into the town and slow the government troops' advance. MacNaught recalled the scene on Monday 25 January: "About 2:00 p.m., I learned that the troops were on their way, somewhere between Nahuizalco and Juayúa. All of the reds went to the edge of town to await their coming. Everyone closed their doors and retired inside . . . The silence was intense. The town seemed devoid of all life. At about 3:00 p.m. the firing commenced. The communists armed with their machetes could make no resistance to the soldiers. At the first volley, they fled. In a few minutes, Juayúa was in the hands of the government forces."[46]

The revolutionaries staged their last stand in Tacuba. On 24 January, at the same time that the Nahuizalqueño rebels were on their way to attack Sonsonate, a large group of insurgents set out from Tacuba to attack the city of Ahuachapán. According to the testimony of Timoteo Flores, then sub-teniente in the National Guard, the revolutionaries encountered a military column moving toward Tacuba. A few soldiers were killed and some were injured, "But the Communist losses were greater and seeing this disaster, they fled to the fincas and ravines." The following day, a contingent of 150 Guardias set out from Ahuachapán to retake Tacuba. Flores described the military encounter succinctly: "It was a bloody battle. It was a huge blood bath. As the machine guns sprayed bullets intermittently, the bandit hordes, shouting savagely, attacked in wave after wave, wiped out without pity by the blazing guns."[47] Rodrigo Buezo reconstructed the events some years later, telling a similar tale with a different choice of modifiers:

> Over a thousand rebel troops armed with 100 mausers, one captured machine gun, and machetes awaited the attack at different points surrounding the town. Three o'clock in the afternoon found these [insurgents] in such visibly disadvantageous conditions. At that moment, one heard on the south side of town the unmistakable rattling of machine gun fire. The 80 revolutionaries who guarded the Depósito de Agua were the first to encounter the pelting of metal. Immediately, all of the insurgent forces were redeployed and hurled themselves with incredible enthusiasm against the enemy forces. The struggle was intense with numerous examples of heroism by the laborers. It was also very unequal. The government forces, although numerically inferior to those of the Ejercito Rojo, were far superior technically. The combat lasted two and a half hours . . . The [insurgent forces] were broken up and the government troops seized their positions with no obstacles . . . More than 800 bodies of communists—injured and dead—were incinerated. The peasant houses were burned and it was something to see how the women and children ran out of the burning huts only to face death at the hands of the enraged soldiers.[48]

The bloodbath at Tacuba effectively ended the insurrection. Guatemalan troops blocked the escape of many insurgents, who then fell to the machine-gun fire of the pursuing Salvadoran army. Government reports did claim that rebels staged numerous attacks in La Libertad and Soyapango (near San Salvador) during the following week. D. J. Rogers, the British consul and coffee planter, reported the situation on 30 January: "For the present, the situation may be summed up by saying that there are frequent smaller gatherings and attacks by Communists around the capital and in the country districts; there is no fighting on such a scale as at the outset . . . it may be said now, that the indications point to the end of this Communist rising as an organized movement, although there will probably be sporadic banditry for some time to come."[49]

Rogers's report, like others, must be taken *cum grano salis*, since he had been extremely frightened by the insurrection. Although there is no doubt that some insurgents continued to resist during the next week, in general such reports of fighting are hard to verify, as the attacks and the ensuing battles may at times have been massacres camouflaged as military skirmishes.[50] Very quickly the military proved quite adept at altering its own reports and manipulating a hysterical media.

Insurgent Power, Executions, and Collective Hysteria

Esto no fue comunismo, sino bandolerismo—Raúl Sigüenza, Juayúa, 2001

In addition to recounting the military actions of the rebels and the government troops, it is worthwhile to examine the different forms and objects of revolutionary violence, and the fears they engendered. Beyond the military engagements, whose outcomes were determined by the technological superiority of machine guns and submachine guns, insurgents also engaged in political assassinations, executing between fifteen and twenty civilians. Newspapers publicized several executions with lurid detail in late January and February, and these immediately became enshrined as symbols of communist barbarity in both official discourse and popular memories. The victims fell into two analytically separate but overlapping categories: political and class targets. Insurgents killed the recently elected mayor in Izalco and targeted the new mayors in Nahuizalco and Colón; they executed the former mayor of Juayúa and the political boss of Tacuba. These political executions were in direct response to the electoral fraud in early January. Though cold-blooded, they seemed to form part of a calculus less guided by vengeance than by political design, with the aim of deligitimating the former regime and legitimating the revolutionary one.

Three of the political targets were also class antagonists of a particular type: former patrons. In addition to being general manager of one of the largest coffee beneficios in the west, Emilio Redaelli was a major landowner, former mayor, and important dispenser of credit to smallholders. An Italian journalist who spent some days with Redaelli in 1928 wrote, "Don Emilio knew every piece of land and every man in the region . . . he knew who was whose kid, how much they earned, how much they spent, what they ate, how many times a day he fought with his wife, and how many times a week he got drunk. The brain of don Emilio was a library in which every Indian, every mestizo, every family, every plantation, every hut had its file card."[51] The journalist recalled that don Emilio was greeted in Nahuizalco "with great enthusiasm, [and was] extremely popular in the village because he advanced money on the tiny coffee harvests."[52]

Given his extensive patronage network, it is likely that Redaelli and other major landholders during the previous years of crisis had precipitated some of the numerous property foreclosures that affected smallholders in the area. In turn, there is little doubt that the economic crisis and political radicalization ruptured conditions for reproducing traditional forms of clientelism. Recall Ama's conversation with Diaz Barrientos: "We have been and will always be friends but you are capitalisto and we are proletarians." To cite another example of ruptured clientelism, Tacubeños accused General Rivas of usurious interest rates on his loans, with land as collateral. Local folks accused him of using his political connections to get away with the outrageous practice of hiding out just at the moment when a campesino came to pay a debt and then claiming that the borrower had defaulted on the loan.[53]

The breakdown of patronage networks, combined with the campesinos' perception of a violated moral economy that mediated their relations with landlords, made both the political and the economic élite extremely vulnerable to popular rage. Insurgents executed some landowners who were not political figures, yet as with the political assassinations there is doubt about the circumstances. The planters responded in some cases with gunfire against overwhelming odds. In others, rebels may have executed them in cold blood. In still others, the planters managed to escape. One wealthy ladino in Izalco recalled, "A group of campesinos, almost all mozos from the hacienda showed up led by Lalo's mayordomo who exclaimed 'today the patrón has his day.'[54] They ransacked his house but could not find him. In frustration, they killed the boss's horse and mule."

Without minimizing the importance of these attempted or successful executions, it is worth noting that insurgent forces controlled the large cities of Sonsonate and Ahuachapán for at least one night and controlled Izalco, Juayúa, Nahuizalco, and Tacuba for two days. In the two large cities there were no executions, and in the other four towns there were seven civilian deaths or executions during the period, despite the many "class enemies" to be found. In Izalco, for example, fourteen imprisoned "class enemies" survived the two days of occupation unharmed. In short, it seems extremely unlikely that the Comandantes Rojos in the west ordered their troops to indiscriminately execute the local landed élite. Whether following their commanders' orders of restraint or their own conscience, the great majority of the thousands of armed rebels did not plan to execute their class enemies.

Why weren't more civilians killed? In view of the high levels of class hatred and the opportunity to kill, what caused the restraint? Local leadership does seem to have played a key role in containing popular rage against the wealthy. Although the local and national leadership did not encourage indiscriminate killing, they probably did target some individuals and groups. In addition to the political targeting, one manifesto called on government troops and insurgents to execute military officers as part of efforts to seize the military garrisons. One government soldier recalled being told by the insurgents that they had spared his life and the lives of his wounded comrades in Tacuba because they had no officer stripes.[55] One explanation for the relatively small number of executions was the local leadership's ideological predisposition against personal violence as opposed to violence directed at symbols of illegitimate authority. Francisco Sánchez and Feliciano Ama, in particular, reportedly shared an aversion to executing individual members of the élite.[56]

Beyond the ideological aversion of local leaders to the use of terror, codes of masculinity, shared across class and political lines, probably placed limits on the number of arbitrary killings. We have already noted that masculine views of unacceptable behavior on the part of the repressive forces strongly influenced the nature of the mobilization. Campesinos refused to go to demonstrations if they were not permitted to retaliate against the violence of the authorities. We can thus conjecture that insurgents saw nothing masculine about killing a defenseless man, let alone a woman. The insurgents generally attacked people like Redaelli, who had probably been singled out for assassination, after they had brandished their weapons. Like Redaelli and Call, in the eyes of insurgents General Rivas represented political and economic exploitation; he was killed when he tried to join forces with the small group of National Guardsmen who resisted the insurrectionary assault.

The political executions should be understood in the context of a profound rupture in a patrimonial world in which residual and emergent cultural forms coexist. As Raymond Williams states, "The residual, by definition, has been effectively formed in the past, but it is still active in the cultural process, not only and often not at all as an element of the past, but as an effective element of the present. Thus certain experiences, meanings, and values which cannot be expressed in terms of the dominant culture, are nevertheless lived and practiced on the basis of residue— cultural and social—of some previous social and cultural institution or formation."[57] The rupture of those residual, vertical social bonds, and their exposure over the previous three years as illegitimate, had contributed to the popular rage against certain former patrons. The blatant destruction of moral-economy ties that once crossed class lines thus created the conditions for these executions, but at the same time limited them.

Notwithstanding the limits and form of political executions, national reports, fueled by fear and local hysteria, made the assassinations signify the brutality of "las hordas sedientas de sangre." Galindo Pohl recalls a particularly virulent form of collective hysteria: "Certain ladies were particularly seized by hysteria. When the noise from the entrance of the rebels had dissipated, you could hear terrified, penetrating cries that revealed the terror raised to the nth degree. 'My daughters . . . my daughters . . . my daughters!' The ladies could already see their daughters being raped, as it had been announced."[58] In every town that endured an insurgent attack, rumors circulated about a noche de bodas. In Juayúa the British consul reported, "On the last day of the occupation the communists, according to an eyewitness, made a choice of the best looking women in town, but the troops arrived the same afternoon."[59] The "choices" allegedly appeared on a list that matched women with the revolutionary leaders.[60] Another contemporary account stated that Sánchez "waited for the moment to unleash his hordes to rape our women."[61] The same report stated that in Izalco, "the Indians intended to spend the rest of that day [the 24th] completing the sack of the town and violating women."[62] According to one informant, the townsfolk of Izalco already knew, the day before the insurrection, of the communists' intention to rape single women.[63] Decades later, these images remained very much a part of the official story. Lieutenant Timoteo Flores, who participated in the military offensive against the rebels in Tacuba but had no direct knowledge of the events of Juayúa, wrote, "We now know that the destiny of the señoras and virgins [of Juayúa] was to satiate the morbosity of those stinking mobs of fanatical assassins. Then they also killed them."[64]

There is no evidence whatsoever that insurgents committed rapes. As we have seen, in El Salvador the social memory of sexual dominance and predation was of both recent and venerable stock. With the insurrection, the sexual fears and fantasies exploded. At the most fundamental level, the powerlessness of élite and middle-class urban males and the demonization of the insurgents facilitated these fantasies. One resident commented to a journalist a month after the events: "We felt humiliated by the Indians . . . it was preferable to die than to keep on living a life of vexations not knowing when it would end."[65] Moreover, in Juayúa, Izalco, and Nahuizalco the revolutionary leaders obliged middle-class women to make tortillas for the troops. This symbolic inversion of roles, a constant in mobilizations throughout modern history ranging from strikes, riots, and rebellions to revolutions, undoubtedly fueled the widespread hysterical notion among townspeople in San Salvador and the west that the "Indians" were going to rape their women.

But it was revolutionary action that stimulated the rape fantasies. Charles R. Hale has analyzed what he calls "the ladino political imaginary" in contemporary Chimaltenango, Guatemala, which "refers to ideas that [ladino] people feel deeply, that at times influence how they think and act, but do not necessarily guide their daily interactions with Mayas."[66] Hale found that rape fantasies connected to an image of the "insurgent Indian" lay at the core of the ladino political imaginary: "Ladinos rarely express fears of Indian ascendancy without reference to the sexualized violence and sexual conquest that would result."[67] In the Guatemalan case the rebellion of Patzcía in 1944 and the insurgent movement of 1980–81 nurtured these fantasies, which surfaced again with the growing strength of the Mayan movement. Hale further argues, referring to long-standing ladino sexual abuse of Indians, that "it seems reasonable to assume a cumulative historical understanding, a social memory of sorts that reinforces this basic association of anti-Indian racism with sexual dominance and predation. With the rising contestation and self-critique of this racism of times past, one can only expect that fears of in-kind retribution would be rife."[68]

In El Salvador fears of mass rape and coupling did not occur only in response to the dramatic, even traumatic, shift in power relations associated with the rebellion. We have posited a relationship between the uprising and hostile gender relations between Indians and ladinos. We noted that the growing contact between indigenous female coffee and domestic workers and ladino foremen and patronos led to numerous liaisons and illegitimate offspring that subalterns understood as sexual abuse of their women. Somewhat mythologized, but with some historical basis, the patrón's *derecho de pernada* (his "right" to his mozo's novia) synthesized the impunity and depravity of the landlord class. To ladinos the sexual practices of Indians often seemed barbaric; many believed that Indians engaged in incestuous relations. As in Guatemala, guilt about the élite's abuse of subaltern women may well have played a role in stimulating the rape fantasies. The cumulative ideological baggage of gender weighed heavily on the psyches of ladinos, suddenly made vulnerable by their loss of power. That women were revolutionary leaders in Sónzacate, Izalco, and Colón surely intensified their humiliation. In addition to the threats and reality of executions, the collective rape fantasies had great ideological salience in rallying middle-class and upper-class participation in the Guardia Cívica and as a justification for extraordinarily brutal repression.

Memories of Insurrection and *El Robo*

Despite their prominence in public accounts of the insurrection, political executions and rape do not figure significantly in subaltern memories. This is but one among many examples of glaring discrepancies between the documentary record of mobilization, repression, insurrection, and massacre and the recreation of those events in the memories of the survivors. Within those memories, indigenous agency in the insurrection tends to be suppressed, and at times the subsequent massacre is categorized as the work of "communists." The quasi-traumatic effects of witnessing the execution of loved ones and the fear caused by decades of military rule were the primary causes of this elision of indigenous agency. Similarly, the events that precipitated the insurrection, especially the electoral fraud and the violent repression of the prior grassroots mobilizations, were also erased from memory.

Yet some of the insurgent actions not only remained but stood out in testimonies, contributing to the creation of this memory framework. Compared to the military repression, the insurgency created a minimal amount of violence: very little in combat, fewer than twenty executions, some looting, and numerous acts of more symbolic violence, or its threat. In survivors' testimonies those acts of violence, coercion, and looting are given symbolic weight at times equal to, and even confused with, the military massacres.

Relatively insignificant in the broad sweep of events, the use of symbolic forms of coercion, such as obliging townsfolk to wear red ribbons, contributed to the creation of the dominant narrative, in which the Indians were innocent victims with no agency. In this account the insurrection is portrayed as little more than *el robo*, induced by ladino communist outsiders. We mention this not because these actions were particularly important in their historical context, but rather to underscore how survivors used them as markers to stand for the generic political innocence of Indians. Looting in particular, and the destruction of the municipal buildings, have loomed large in the counterrevolutionary reconstruction of events. They figure most prominently in the collective memories of survivors. It is difficult to determine the degree of intentionality and spontaneity of those actions. In every occupied town the Comandantes Rojos ordered the taking of telegraph offices and the destruction of the municipal archives (except the Juayúa municipal archive). A standard target in nineteenth- and early-twentieth-century agrarian rebellions and revolutions, the municipal archive typically housed land records, the destruction of which laid the groundwork for "free land" or "land without owners." Such an action was fully congruent with the goal of revolutionary agrarian reform and with the de facto transformation of landholding that had occurred over the month preceding the insurrection. Nevertheless, none of the survivors' testimonies in any way connect land distribution and the destruction of the archives. Most likely that suppression has been due to the overwhelming power of the trope of *el robo*, which dozens of survivors equated with *el Comunismo* as a way of explaining how "the just died for the sinners." Even among elderly informants on the left such as Raúl Sigüenza, the statement "This was not communism, it was *bandolerismo*"[69] is typical, in that it posits no legitimate political or social motive for the looting and destruction.

The notion of free land in some testimonies related in turn to property without ownership, *bienes sin dueño*.[70] At the risk of oversimplification, within the compass of Central American subaltern morality, it can be said that any claim to the sanctity of private property is tempered by its abandonment: if one abandons a possession it is morally acceptable for another to make use of it. What constitutes abandonment is highly subjective. Certainly the assertion of abandonment may form part of a justification for theft, and there is some evidence that the abandonment of property—primarily because the residents were hiding—provided some of the justification for looting during the Salvadoran uprising. Regardless of whether this particular justification was employed, the looting was not entirely random. According to the Canadian commander V. G. Brodeur, who during the latter days of January received a special military tour of the department of Sonsonate, "It was noticed that at each place visited the City Hall had been destroyed, and no other damage caused except in residences of rich plantation owners who had already fled . . . the residence of a rich planter . . . was left intact though properties on either side were completely destroyed, specially all articles of family value such as priceless old furniture and paintings, this was accounted for by the fact that the above named treated his hands in a far more generous way."[71] Francisco Sánchez, an indigenous communist leader from Juayúa, also offered an instrumental view of the looting, declaring upon capture, weeks after the insurrection, "Here, there are only rich people present so I can say nothing. We have robbed nothing, only some clothes to distribute to the poor who were going around naked."[72]

Several informants insist that the revolutionary leaders broke the locks on the stores to provoke looting by people who would then out of necessity join the insurrection. MacNaught, hiding out in his house in Juayúa, shared this perspective: "In fact they wanted all those, who were not otherwise lined up with them, to share in their ill-gotten gains, in order that they might be thus identified with their cause."[73] This instrumentalist interpretation is reasonable but incomplete, for in the cities of Ahuachapán and Sonsonate there was very little looting despite ample opportunity for it.[74] Rather, insurgents and others looted mainly where the insurrection had triumphed completely.

Beyond its instrumental uses, there was also an emancipatory, millenarian dimension to the looting. Numerous testimonies suggest that many of the insurgents shared a belief that the rich would cease to exist because their goods would become collective property. Although such a view lay within the broad sweep of socialist discourse, a millenarian component also infused the insurgency. This can be glimpsed in a remark uttered by an indigenous rural worker to an indigenous employer: "You folks are going to disappear because whoever doesn't want to join is going to disappear and whoever wants to join is going to appear."[75] Millenarian movements possess the collective belief in a sudden transformation of the world from evil to perfection, wrought by divine intervention. Patricia Pessar's recent study of Brazilian millenarianism argues that it should be understood as a cultural formation and as symbolic capital, contested by subaltern groups and élites over centuries.[76] Her study sharply criticizes Eric Hobsbawm's classic work on Andalusian anarchism and the Sicilian *fasci* for his teleological reasoning, that is, for linking millenarianism to a specific historical moment that ended with the flowering of modernity. For Pessar Brazilian millenarianism functioned as an alternative modernity.[77] Certainly this concept is congruent with our own view that the Salvadoran left and the peasantry engaged in the forging of such an alternative to authoritarian capitalistic modernity.

Notwithstanding the thrust of Pessar's criticism, Hobsbawm's studies are still highly instructive. First, he reveals the connection between millenarianism and utopianism, which he regards as a necessary ingredient of virtually any revolutionary movement. For Hobsbawm the "profound and total rejection of the present, evil world and the passionate longing for another better one"[78] is the key characteristic of millenarianism. Revolutionary movements often absorb that millenarian dimenision. His description of Andalusian village anarchism in the early twentieth century is apposite: "They saw a bad world which would initiate the good world, where those who had been at the bottom would be at the top, and the good of this earth would be shared among all."[79] Hobsbawm further argues that a belief in the sudden and total overturning of the social order need not be "a temporary phenomenon, but can, under favourable conditions, be the foundation of a permanent and exceedingly tough and resistant form of movement."[80]

In El Salvador there was undoubtedly a generalized belief among rebels that the world would be rapidly turned upside down. The phrase "whoever doesn't join will disappear" is echoed in other testimonies in the west that often include the biblical refrain "The last shall be first."[81] Such beliefs were not exclusive to indigenous or ladino campesinos. Even among urban, working-class PCS supporters, there is some anecdotal evidence to suggest chiliastic beliefs. For example, one woman recalls a workman telling her that pay was not necessary, since "tomorrow all of this will be ours."[82] An eyewitness to the repression, Commander Brodeur, reported the following: "Another interesting and illuminating fact observed was the very peaceful look on the faces of those dead, this fact is specially noticeable in the case of the Indian Chief . . . In fact it was proved that all the Indians executed were apparently glad to sacrifice their lives in the hope that this martyrdom might bring a brighter future for the next generation . . . the case of a young pregnant married woman who was informed her husband had just been executed by troops, her only answer being that she did not care as she was carrying his avenger and future rebel against society."[83]

As Hobsbawm wrote, "utopianism is probably a necessary social device for generating the superhuman efforts without which no major revolution is achieved."[84] Equating utopianism with a form of millenarianism, he goes on to show just how the movement itself, producing new social relations, often creates the conditions for propagating the utopian or millenarian current that creates the willingness to sacrifice one's life for the cause of social transformation. Hobsbawm's studies make no concerted effort to examine the mutual, if somewhat submerged, relations between religious and political millenarianism. Indeed, if the minimal definition of mille-narianism includes a notion of "divine intervention," and if the Andalusian anarchists rejected divine intervention, then is the term "millenarian" even appropriate? Pessar's notions of a cultural formation or cultural capital may be particularly useful. In El Salvador, for insurgents religious beliefs and narratives framed the dominant political imaginary. This seems to have been explicitly so in Ahuachapán, where the cult of the Virgin of Adelanto was strong. Yet in other areas without any allegiance to religious cults or icons, militants inhabited a social world thick with traditional religious practices. The millenarian dimension of the movement in those areas also had clear religious inspiration.

Although the millenarian nature of the movement was contagious, mili-tants nonetheless felt the need to commit wavering people to the struggle through coercion. Thus, for example, the revolutionaries obliged people in the occupied towns to wear red badges or ribbons. A typical testimony from Nahuizalco, Izalco, or Juayúa underscores the demands on the townsfolk: "They told us we had to put on these red things or they would kill us."[85] The report of the British consul substantiates these testimonies: "When they occupied the town [Juayúa] they compelled the inhabitants, under pain of death, to put on red badges." Similarly, there is some evidence that the official bando read by Arturo Carvajal in Juayúa obliged town residents to address each other as *camarada*.[86]

The tension between goals of emancipation and methods of coercion is a constant of twentieth-century social movements in Latin America. In far less violent and dramatic circumstances, such as during the peasant movements in mid-century Nicaragua, there was also a tension between the emancipatory and democratic goals of the movements and the forms of coercion, however mild, employed by them. The use of aggressive pickets in the first cotton pickers' strike in Nicaraguan history was analyzed in these terms: "In the Tonalá strike and in other forms of protest there was a curious relation at once authoritarian and democratic between the leadership and the rank and file. In one sense, their leaders also felt compelled to push the rank and file into action. In this way, workers abdicated full responsibility for action."[87] Throughout the nineteenth and twentieth centuries, most strikes and other forms of social protest employed some sort of coercion to push wavering supporters into the insurgent camp and, at the same time, to present a united front against their antagonists. Tactics of this sort have often been successful, indeed a key ingredient of many strikes.

Most popular rebellions, riots, or social revolutionary triumphs (however brief) unleashed symbolic coercion or forms of theater communicating to a multi-class audience that the world has turned upside down. In El Salvador we noted that insurgent leaders compelled middle- and upper-class women to grind corn and make tortillas. A "lavish" funeral for a campesino insurgent in Juayúa contrasted dramatically with the pauper's funeral for Redaelli. These symbolic actions crossed pre-modern and modern boundaries, as Indians had often cursed and humiliated officials in rebellions in Mexico during the colonial period.[88] Matagalpan Indians in a rebellion in 1881 compelled ladino landowners to perform menial labor for them.[89] The Russian and Spanish Revolutions exhibited numerous instances of symbolic inversions of power. For example, the Spanish revolutionaries' exhumation and display of the corpses of nuns revealed their spiritual triumph over the demonized church, a key ally of the counter-revolution.[90] These subversive acts are a particularly creative and at times less destructive way of expressing generations of subaltern ressentiment (see chapter 5).[91]

Despite their ubiquity, the meanings of these symbolic acts have been stripped from most testimonies of failed revolutions, and only the coercive elements remain etched in the officially framed memories inspired by the state and the counterrevolution. The Salvadoran insurrection of 1932 is no exception. The emancipatory aspects of the insurrection—free land and an end to élite domination over subaltern lives—have been buried in mass graves, covered with the toxic sediment of fear and propaganda.

Insurgent Narratives

The successful burial of alternative memories of the insurrection accounts in part for the survival of very few coherent subaltern testimonies about the events. This dearth of testimonies also derives from the age of informants and the climate of fear that pervaded the zone for decades. Most informants were too young to have participated in the revolt. Even so, Segundo Montes's study in the mid-1970s and other less comprehensive ethnographic works from the same period failed to encounter any informant who admitted participating in the insurrection. After the uprising was put down, the military and its allies executed the great majority of the insurgents, along with thousands of people who had nothing to do with the insurrection. Military rule during the next sixty years, which included leadership by some of the same officers who had led or participated in the massacres, also contributed to a culture of silence. Because of their anomalous level of coherence and their ethnographic and political detail, we will reproduce significant parts of some testimonies that refer to the insurrection, with a degree of coherence and detail.

As we have argued elsewhere, there has been a general tendency to deny subaltern agency in the movement.[92] In the accepted version, Indians were not participants in the revolutionary movement, much less leaders of it, but rather innocent victims. In indigenous villages where the repression was most intense, this denial surely started out as a form of defense, but over time it acquired the aura of truth. The effect can be seen in the frequent protestations that the revolutionaries came from elsewhere. The testimony of Andrés Pérez, son of the secretary of the local SRI in Nahuizalco, illustrates this.

Andrés Pérez

Pérez's narrative about his father's militancy (introduced in chapter 4) remains plausible, although chronologically confused, until January 1932: "The armed forces joined forces with the Ladinos—Cheles [whites], the

Andrés Pérez, Pushtan. Courtesy of the Museo de la Palabra y la Imagen.

indígenas didn't want anything to do with them. In December, the Ladinos looted the biggest stores in Nahuizalco—you can still see the machetazos— they said the Indians and Communists had done the robberies. On 2 January there was a meeting under the Ceiba—(that's where the market was what they called the plaza). There they were when the armed forces came from Sonsonate. My dad said, 'I'm going to get some water.' He left and thought to himself that he better not go back, so he went home. When he reached the canton he heard the roar of the trucks and headed for the bush. Near the river, he heard the shots. He told his mom, 'They killed my compañeros.' 'You escaped!' Later, he heard that they had killed all of his compañeros."[93]

Pérez's suppression of the role of his father and other indigenous activists in the insurrection renders his account incoherent. Many other testimonies from Nahuizalco present similar narratives of the events of 23 January. All agree that "Turinecos"—phenotypically and culturally non-Indian— were the main group involved in the takeover of the town. Many shared Andrés Pérez's view that "ladinos" did the looting. Many also blamed local ladinos (as well as Turinecos) for cutting the locks of stores owned by members of the same small community. The story of ladino looting remained compelling to rural Indians for several reasons. First, their hatred for the ladinos, at the time and subsequently, blinded them into wishing for a discursive vindication of indigenous innocence and a condemnation of ladino guilt. Second, there certainly was outside ladino involvement in a movement that in retrospect went terribly wrong. Finally, there is some evidence that local ladinos, confident of the eventual triumph of the revolution, supported the movement during the brief occupation. That the repression spared the ladinos helped to spur the creation of a memory according to which they themselves were culpable at the expense of the slaughtered Indians.

Of the over two hundred interviews with people who in one form or another experienced the insurrection and its macabre aftermath we encountered only two who admitted to directly participating in the insurrection and very few who admitted the participation of close relatives.[94]

Salomé Torres

In chapter 4 we recounted fragments from Salomé Torres's brutalized childhood on a coffee plantation in La Libertad during the 1920s. After the death of his parents, he recalls, "With my brothers and sisters we moved in with my grandmother, *una arrimada* [an invited squatter] in the coffee hacienda of Angel García. This *patrón* liked to beat up his workers just because he felt like it." One day, Salomé recalls, the patrón saw his little brother in a mango tree eating a ripe fruit. He shouted at the little boy to come down and then beat the boy so hard that he died. Salomé, then fifteen, flew into an impotent rage and left the hacienda. A couple of years later he was picking coffee when a fellow worker invited him to a union meeting. For over a year he attended meetings on various plantations where people discussed taking over land and the need to first storm the *cuarteles*. On 22 January the local leaders of the movement informed Salomé that the moment had come to "seize the barracks and then seize the land." Word reached his finca that the campesinos of the Cumbre de Jayaque were going to attack the barracks at Santa Tecla and then join others in an assault on the capital. He walked off his job and joined the "caravan" of revolutionaries as they descended down the mountain road that passed Comasagua. The only road that connected the towns of the Cumbre de Jayaque—Teotepeque, Talnique, and Jayaque— with Santa Tecla passed by the cantón "Los Amates." There the revolutionary march halted and spent the night. "Right around 5:30 in the morning a little red plane flew overhead . . . ordering us to rise and advance. I was pretty far in the rear and when we got to the turn where one way goes to Santa Ana and the other for la Cumbre they began to machine gun. I hid by the side of the road. Then came the order to retreat. I started running up to the slopes. From the ridge, I could see all of the people running."[95]

Although Salomé's narrative does not exhibit a great deal of ethnographic or political detail, its meaning is inscribed in the context that

Salomé Torres.
Courtesy of the
Museo de la Palabra
y la Imagen.

allowed him to recount it, however dryly, and to assume responsibility for his actions. As he was the only survivor we met who accepted his personal responsibility as a member of the insurgent forces, it is worth pondering why he remembered and how he understood his participation.

Salomé was lucky to survive. He hid out for days or weeks until Emilio Chicas, a *finquero* and retired military officer, decided to help him and others obtain a safe-conduct pass in Santa Tecla. They all walked to Santa Tecla under the protection of a white flag. Salomé went to the church, where he "confessed" (without admitting "guilt"), perceiving correctly that to admit participation was to invite a death sentence. Shortly thereafter he left La Libertad and traveled to a coastal area of Sonsonate where he was unknown. There he worked for years on a cattle hacienda in an area that had little involvement in the events of 1932. He was therefore not subjected to the communal reconstruction of events, often heavily influenced by the military regime, which either suppressed local subaltern agency or laid all the blame for the tragedy on "the communists." Though illiterate, Salomé managed to keep up with the news through circumspect conversations and, in the 1950s, radio. For whatever reasons, he remained immune to the barrages of anticommunist propaganda emanating from virtually every pore of the Salvadoran state and society.

Immediately after the triumph of the Cuban Revolution, Salomé's wife told him, "You know, you should meet Miguel Landaverde. He talks just like you." After twenty-seven years Salomé emerged from his leftist shell. During all that time he had heard or seen nothing to shake his early belief in the righteousness of the struggle for land and social justice or the perfidy of the landed élite, epitomized by the killing of his younger brother. Landaverde and his friends, for Salomé, were a select audience to whom he could recount his tale of January 1932.

The message of Salomé's testimony was simple and direct: his participation in the insurrection was a logical outcome of his brutalized life as a jornalero on coffee plantations and of the opportunity to resist. His primary goal was an agrarian revolution, and to achieve that he participated in the assault on the military barracks. Neither boastful nor ashamed, Torres today recounts his participation with a straightforward matter-of-factness, tinged with the bitterness of defeat and a life of privation.

Doroteo López

Doroteo López, an eighteen-year-old in 1932, also remembers that scene in Los Amates. His father, Victor López, was the general foreman on a coffee finca in San José occupying fifty manzanas, and a bitter enemy of the revolutionary movement. Nicknamed *el polaco*, he was despised by the local workers for his friendship with the Guardia officers and for his fierce loyalty to the patrones.[96] Late on the afternoon of 22 January, Abrahám López, an SRI leader and subordinate of Victor's on the finca, approached his house.

> Abraham told him, "Don Victor today is the day of the insurrection. Go hide. Ocúltese. Today they are going to liquidate all the reactionaries. As a Communist, I shouldn't tell you. But you are my jefe and are good to me." . . . But my dad was emboldened by his ties to the Guardia and responded: "I'm not hiding, no hijueputa is going to do anything to me! Let them come!" Saddened and worried, Abraham walked off. At around seven he returned: "Don Victor I already told you to hide. They already killed the son of the commissioner. Go look at the plaza!" I lived about a block from my dad, near the plaza. Since I had to work real early I was exhausted. The shuffling of so many feet worried me, so many people arriving in the plaza. A bit later, my dad appeared. "Look son, get up, we have to hide. Now it is serious. The plaza is filled with Communists. They killed Chavelo's son." We went to the ravine in a nearby big coffee grove. There had been volcanic eruptions in Guatemala and the ash covered everything. The moon was full and there was semi clarity. All the trees and bushes were covered with ash and then a light rain turned everything to mud. And so it rained. Everything was spectral. There was no wind and the air felt stale. It was a horrible sensation. Then they came to the house. Only my father's wife was there with their baby. They broke down the door and shouted "Where is el polaco?"

"They called him over to 'la Sirena' to get his work orders. He'll be back tommorrow."

"Let's look for them!"

We saw the lamps of the people searching for us . . . it seemed like a herd . . . we moved even deeper into the ravine, deep into the jungle of coffee. After a long time, the lamps receded. We suffered in the cold, covered with mud.

And then we heard the conch shell whistles. All of their force—that enormous number of people—moved to attack Santa Tecla.[97]

A remarkable personal history framed Doroteo's vivid recollection of 22 January. When he was fourteen Doroteo had learned how to read and write from a Jamaican bookkeeper while working on a coffee plantation. By the time he moved to Los Amates, his ability to read and his position as an *apuntador* probably translated into at least a sense of separateness from the *jornaleros* and reinforced his desire to identify with his father, who had abandoned the family during Doroteo's childhood. Four years after the insurrection, he was working at a coffee beneficio in Santa Ana when he engaged in lunchtime conversations with clandestine communist union activists. Despite his brush with death, he had been appalled at the indiscriminate repression. He recoiled when he heard a priest in Santa Tecla state that "evil has been eradicated at its roots," at the same time that executions of suspected communists were a daily occurrence. Moreover, Doroteo had broken off ties with his father, which to a certain extent freed his mind from the one-sided relation that had previously dominated him.

The relatively educated union militants sparked his intellectual curiosity. When the subject of 1932 came up, Doroteo recounted his story. He recalls that Virgilio Guerra explained to him, "it was class warfare and we had to give it to all of our enemies."[98] Although Doroteo did not immediately accept that rationale, he did eventually come to accept the broad outlines of the Marxist view of history and society, and for a decade he was a member of the clandestine PCS.

Doroteo's testimony provides a clue to how the revolutionary upsurge played out among the subaltern sectors of society. Although his father was a foreman on the plantation, he could not be considered middle-class in either cultural or economic terms. Typically, a foreman earned 50 percent more than field hands, but that would barely have provided for the subsistence needs of his family. It was an ambiguous class position that did not automatically lead to a counterrevolutionary posture. Indeed, two lower-

Doroteo López,
San Isidro. Courtesy
of the Museo de la
Palabra y la Imagen.

level *caporales* in Los Amates were local SRI leaders. Yet Victor López had demonstrated his political antipathy to the movement, and through his friendship with the Guardia he had probably singled out some militants for repression. Therefore at this local level he was a "reactionary enemy," and along with the local comandante of the *patrulla cantonal* was targeted for execution. That the insurgents ended up killing the son of the comandante was anomalous. This targeting of the son of the comandante and (perhaps) of Doroteo were exceptions to the general pattern of insurgency: elsewhere, insurgents executed only mature adults.

Doroteo's testimony again points to the logic of revolutionary violence. However mitigated by countervailing tendencies, it allowed for political executions of subalterns who did not occupy significant positions within the political, military, or economic hierarchy. That logic of terror derived from the perceived necessity and the overwhelming collective desire to enforce solidarity. Enforcement of solidarity, the need for unanimity, gave way to a desire to harm or execute those local subalterns who visibly opposed the movement.

Doroteo López's testimony also confirms other aspects of the cultural tumult that we have identified as part of the revolutionary process. In particular, the friendship between his father and Abrahám López again reveals the residual cultural forms that stretched across a bitter ideological divide. As a subordinate caporal on the finca, Abrahám López appreciated the way he had been treated at work by his superior, Victor López. Despite the universal application of the term *camarada*, at this moment of revolutionary rupture he still used the respectful term *don*, also indicating deference.[99] Based on that workplace relationship, he twice warned López, regardless of the risk that Abrahám ran by betraying the cause. Finally, the theme of machismo again cuts across class, ethnic, and political lines. "No me voy a esconder no me hacen nada ningún hijueputa. Que vengan!" The testimony of Sotero Linares, a jornalero, reveals similar themes of subaltern violence and machismo.

Sotero Linares

Linares was also a young man at the time of the insurrection. He was picking coffee in Cúntan, an ethnically mixed but divided canton a few miles east of Izalco.

> The three of us were picking coffee on the finca—three cousins, one a kid and the other two of us grown up. A picket halted us on Arnoldo Vega's finca. I showed my corvo and asked them what they wanted. There were a lot of them so they were able to grab me from behind and yank away my corvo.
>
> These were the same people who had gone off the night before to Izalco and Sonsonate to rob. I asked them what they wanted with us. Francisco Ishio answered, "we've been working in this so long and you haven't sought us out."
>
> So I told them, "you never invited us." They always had their comités at night. We didn't know anything. That's because this work was entirely done by naturales, by the most Indian of them (de los más inditos). Those of us who were mixed blood had nothing to do with it. So they took us to Anastasio Ishio, to his father's coffee finca. There were hundreds of men and women in the patio, almost all Indians. They were having this huge fiesta. They were shouting all these "vivas al Socorro Rojo Internacional" and they thought they had won. So Francisco Ishio comes back over to us where we are tied up to a tree, and starts talking to us about why we should have joined. So I argued back again about not inviting us. He responded, "We owe nothing to you. We are worth something—you aren't!"
>
> Then his buddy Feliciano Munto came over with a new lasso and shouted, "We're going to hang you. What are we waiting for? Let's hang this hijo de puta!"
>
> "Kill me then, you won't be killing a woman, but a man!" But they didn't.
>
> Then, at around 5:00 pm two of their scouts came into the patio running. "The troops are coming! Everyone has to hide!" So Ishio comes over to us, looks at us and says you aren't on our side, and I say we'll join you. But he drags us along as prisoners. When we get to a cafetal he lets us go and I say to him, "I need my corvo to fight on your side." So he gives it to me and we escape. I told my cousin, "If they follow us we'll give it to them with our corvos."[100]

Sotero Linares.
Courtesy of the
Museo de la Palabra y
la Imagen.

The reality and threat of captivity and death make both narratives compelling. The survival of Doroteo and Sotero permitted a certain de-traumatization of the memory of these events and allowed for a sharpened focus on ethnographic details. For Linares, the sharp contours of his narrative of capture made comprehensible and justifiable his subsequent role as part of the repressive apparatus: he searched for communists in hiding and when he found them he turned them over to the military authorities, most likely for execution.

In Los Amates revolutionary violence against subalterns had a strictly political basis. In the cantons of Izalco a peculiarly local ethnic conflict overdetermined this violence. As was underscored above, Indians of the cantons had little problem organizing ladinos on coffee plantations, yet in their own communities ethnic relations were strained. Class had little to do with the problem, as most ladinos were like Sotero Linares, jornaleros with tiny plots of land. Anastasio Ishio, by contrast, was a smallholder, with a coffee finca of five manzanas. (Ishio had also been comisionado del cantón until he was arrested for subversive activities in 1930.) Most Indian families, like Linares's, had relatively small plots supplemented by seasonal labor. Nor were there extreme cultural differences between Indians and ladinos. The indigenous people of the cantons were generally monolingual Spanish speakers who donned ladino dress when traveling to Izalco. Many did not participate in the civil or religious hierarchy of Barrio Abajo in Izalco. Rather, the conflict principally derived from the status of the ladinos as outsiders who had moved into the cantons over the previous generation and undoubtedly shared certain prejudices about Indians.

Linares thus gives us a portrait of what appeared to him to be a caste war within one village. But his description, taken at face value, would block out some of the meanings of the testimony. First, after the capture there was dialogue, not an execution. Linares lived to tell the tale precisely because Ishio released him. The dialogue is worth analyzing. Francisco Ishio simultaneously expressed anger and curiosity as to why Sotero had not gone to any meetings or joined the movement. To Ishio, despite the ethnic division and perhaps because of the universalistic message of the movement, Linares should have gone to the meetings. Linares, in turn, considered the movement "Indian" and therefore antagonistic to his own individual and group interests. The march up the slope to Cuyagualo interrupted the conversation. At the fiesta attended by hundreds of men and women celebrating victory, Ishio reiterated what was both an indictment and a query. To the response, "You didn't invite me," Ishio's exclamation, "We owe nothing to you. We are worth something—you aren't!" seems curious, as it did not directly respond to Linares's comment. But here it seems that Ishio's discourse operated within a code of respect, and that he understood Linares's comment that he should have been invited to have been a demand for respect. Ishio's shifting of the discussion suggested the generalization of the issue of respect and dignity to the entire revolutionary movement. At the same time, and in a manner not unrelated to the discourse of respect, it may well have been Linares's reassertion of the common code of masculinity that spared his life. The killing of a defenseless man who had not killed or raped was simply not a manly act.

Linares's testimony also reveals the moment of rupture of a residual code of mutual respect and deference. Put differently, the Indians of the cantons had long shown deference to ladinos and received insufficient respect in return, if any. This moment of rupture between residual and emergent cultural forms is at once similar to and different from those we have previously observed. What was different in Cuyagualo was that the tension led to an explosive confrontation between the meaning and uses of respect. In other words, the traditional cultural norms could no longer function as they had before; they needed a revolutionary cultural transformation, symbolized in changing the appellative from *don* to *camarada*.

This desire to reconstitute social relations along new lines of absolute respect relates to the symbolic actions and demands for enforced solidarity throughout the occupied zones. The insurgents had tactical reasons to compel solidarity for the revolution, but the testimony of Linares and others points to a moral imperative at this moment of rupture. Posing the question "Which side are you on?" in such violent and dramatic fashion, leaving no room for neutrality, would have unintended political consequences, facilitating the ideological work of the triumphant reaction. Given the large number of nonrevolutionary campesinos, workers, and Indians, the moral imperative of solidarity ran up against the kind of resistance that would lead to severe antagonism.

As the events of January gave way to February, the conflict in the western Salvadoran countryside began to resemble a civil war. Yet this one was different: one side was hesitant about killing individuals and the other rarely hesitated before firing at those who shared the class or ethnic markers of rebels—at point-blank range.

Chapter Seven

"They Killed the Just for the Sinners": The Counterrevolutionary Massacres

Ofrecieron una contraseña y la contraseña fue balas.
—Raimundo Aguilar, Cusamuluco, Nahuizalco

Latin American historiography has long recognized the massacre of thousands of rural people in western El Salvador as one of the most lethal acts of repression in the modern history of the region. Despite its prominent place in the continental hall of infamy, the extant descriptions of the repression are somewhat fragmentary, with the result that some key questions remain unresolved. Why did the military resort to mass killing once it had quelled the insurrection? Given that estimates of the number of fatalities range from a low of several thousand to an oft-repeated high of thirty thousand, can we arrive at a more accurate approximation? What was the role of specifically anti-indigenous racism in the killings? In recent years activists have used the terms "genocide" and "ethnocide" to describe the events of 1932.[1] Was this repression genocidal? How were the massacres portrayed and understood by different sectors of society? Through a detailed account of the events, we will offer tentative responses to these questions. In an attempt to grasp how survivors came to conceptualize

210

"They
Killed
the
Just
for the
Sinners"

the repression, we will examine the emergence of the phrase *mataron justos por pecadores*, an evocative and multivocal expression repeated by dozens of informants.

A counterrevolutionary coalition involving landed élite groups, coffee planters from mid-sized plantations, cattle ranchers, the church, and the military emerged before the insurrection. The words of one mid-size farmer probably were representative of his class: "We agricultores do not tolerate anyone putting their hands on our interests . . . it is unacceptable that our interests be touched; that is something we will not endure for any reason or circumstance or under any pretext whatsoever. Here I am, getting ready to defend myself, defend my property, and defend my woman."[2] In addition to this visceral reaction against any challenge to their property, the élite components of the counterrevolution shared an aristocratic ethos which held Indians and rural workers in contempt as semi-barbarians: "the lower class lives and thinks the way the Roman slaves lived and thought. They compose an infinitely low and remote stratum that does not feel the slightest need to educate or cure itself."[3]

Under the threat of agrarian revolution, this defense of material interests and the racist disdain for the rural poor would be a lethal combination. There was also an ideological byproduct of the repression that worked to the advantage of Martínez's regime. After the defeat of the insurrection, Gabino Mata, a technologically advanced cattle rancher and coffee planter, sketched this position in the following terms: "The honest agricultores, the true workers, we do not want impure politics; we want unity, fraternity, peace and work. In the future, politicians should be treated as communists."[4] The emphasis on employers as "producers," with the appeal to cleansing society of "politicians," were typical rhetorical gestures of fascism.[5] Although it would be a mistake to equate these relatively inchoate ideological expressions and the loose alliances with a mature counterrevolutionary movement and ideology, it is hard to imagine that Martínez's regime charted its sanguinary course without those ideological and tactical moorings.[6]

Although the shift from a relatively neutral role in the December strikes to violence and provocation in January was dramatic enough, it did not prove that a large-scale massacre was imminent. The military regime's strategy of provocation suggests that it did plan to crush the left into submission. With the discovery of the insurrectionary plans of the PCS, the regime surely upped the ante and prepared to execute its identifiable antagonists. Still, there would have been no particular logic (and no evidence) underpinning a plan to massacre unarmed Indians, peasants, and workers and using the insurrection as a pretext.

On 24 January the military began its lethal campaign, which lasted for over a month. To better approximate the various causes and methods of the massacres, a separation between different stages of repression is analytically useful, even if the historical reality was far more nuanced. Stage I refers to the immediate aftermath of the defeat of the insurgency, the period during which military hot pursuit coincided with the execution of thousands of people. Stage II refers to the weeks between the military defeat of the insurgency on 25 January and 13 February, during which time two large-scale massacres took place within the municipal borders of Nahuizalco. Stage III coincided with stage II but encompassed a much wider geographical area. From 25 January until the end of March the military and Civil Guards singled out many of their victims through lists of Communist voters or membership lists of the SRI.

Stage I: Military Defeat and Massacres

The first phase was extremely violent, accounting for thousands of deaths. Although it is hard to estimate the number of fatalities in these days of battle and the immediate aftermath, General Tomás Calderón's claim that his troops had liquidated 4,800 "Bolsheviks" seems fairly accurate, as it coincides with other partial estimates.[7] As we saw in chapter 6, this stage of repression involved mainly National Guardsmen who made ample use of machine guns to defeat the insurrectionary forces. The regular army, relying on recruits from eastern Salvador (primarily ladino), joined forces with the Guard.[8] In all the battles government forces defeated the insurgents in three hours or less of combat. After defeating them, the National Guard pursued the retreating rebels into the countryside. During the hot pursuit the troops often engaged in indiscriminate killing of males over twelve years old. In Tacuba they killed women and children as well. The killing fields were in the areas surrounding the major sites of rebellion: the countryside around Ahuachapán (mainly nonindigenous), Tacuba (largely indigenous), Juayúa (largely indigenous), Nahuizalco (indigenous), Izalco (bi-ethnic), and the Cumbre de Jayaque (some indigenous, mainly self-identified as non-Indian).

"They
Killed
the
Just
for the
Sinners"

Feliciano Ama
before hanging,
Izalco, January 1932,
from *Revolución
Comunista*, by Jorge
Schlesinger.

The rural areas around Ahuachapán, Juayúa, Tacuba, Izalco, and Nahuizalco suffered the greatest number of deaths, probably several thousand
during these critical first days. As one military officer wrote years later,
"The machine guns began to sow panic and death in the regions of Juayúa,
Izalco, Nahuizalco, Colón, Santa Tecla, the Volcano of Santa Ana, and
in all of the towns by the shore from Jiquilisco to Acajutla. Some towns
were razed to the ground and the workers in the capital were savagely decimated."[9] In the countryside surrounding Nahuizalco and Juayúa, in words
repeated by dozens of informants, "they killed all males from twelve on
up." One ladino artisan, a Nahuizalqueño, reported, "Well, in that moment when the government forces came in, they weren't going around
asking any questions when they found someone, right? No, it was a matter of killing them"[10] During the days following the military takeover
of the occupied towns, troops perpetrated massacres of groups of unarmed indigenous people. In Nahuizalco the military probably executed
over two thousand people. Cayetana Flores, an indigenous woman of Anal
Arriba, recalled, "They began to take out the people house by house and
they marched them further up. Once they had gotten everyone from Anal
Arriba they marched them to Nahuizalco. They shot all of them."[11] Ramón

Corpses in a common grave, January 1932. Courtesy of the Museo de la Palabra y la Imagen.

Esquina, who was nine at the time, remembered vivid scenes and incorporated knowledge from conversations with survivors: "Around here the dead were scattered all over—well now they have all turned to earth—the corpses were everywhere in San Juan, Tajcuilulah, Pushtan, Cusamuluco. In Nahuizalco, well there you can't imagine how it was: they opened ditches in the cemeteries along the sides and at the entrance where you walk in; everywhere they made big holes. They dropped the bodies, after they shot them and heaved them as if they were bales of sugar cane."[12] As Ramón Esquina exclaimed these words, he made arm gestures as if he were heaving bales of cane, suggesting an industrial technology of death. Less than human in life, in death Indians remained merely the objects and instruments of labor.

In Sónzacate, the site of a fierce battle between the insurgents and the military, Fabián Mojica, in prison in Cojutepeque at the time, recounted the following based on conversations with survivors. "When this guy met the officers, he said that 'Here in Sonzacate from the first to the last house was Communist. In the first house lived Sr. Figueroa. They yanked him up and shot him. And in the second house the same thing and so on.'"[13]

The city of Sonsonate witnessed indiscriminate as well as targeted killings.[14] Victims of documented executions included two of Mojica's brothers who were in jail. The commanding officer reports that these executions were in response to an escape attempt, but oral testimonies point to a firing squad that executed those prisoners who had been captured after the events of 17 May 1931. Twenty-five death certificates follow this pattern: "Partida No. 70. Alcaldía municipal sonsonate, on the twenty-seventh of January of nineteen thirty two. Felipe Mendoza died in the public prisons at one hour and thirty minutes today, of a gun wound without medical assistance. Par-

"They
Killed
the
Just
for the
Sinners"

tida No 76. Alcaldía municipal sonsonate on the twenty-seventh of january of nineteen thirty two. Jorge Purito died in the public prisons at one hour and ten minutes today, of a gun wound without medical assistance." Several of those executed had been important leaders in the SRI: "Partida No 65. Alcaldía municipal, on the twenty-seventh of january of nineteen thirty two. Gregorio Cruz Zaldaña, a carpenter, died in the public prisons today at one hour, of a gun wound without medical assistence." Julian Ortiz, the Nahuizalqueño Indian leader, and Manuel Mojica, the SRI leader and brother of Fabian and Julia "La Roja,"were among the others who died within half an hour of each other, "trying to escape."

Sotero Linares, a ladino campesino from a canton of Izalco who had been captured by the insurgents, recalled how he accompanied patrols who combed the cafetales searching for insurgents who would then be sent to Izalco, where they most likely were shot. Informants and written sources state that in Izalco for several days troops executed groups of fifty prisoners, mostly Indians. The Canadian commander of the Skeena, Brodeur, based on close contact with the military in the west, reported that twelve hundred "Indians" were killed in Izalco.[15]

In the area around Juayúa, the Reverend Roy MacNaught related a conversation with a coffee finca owner: "A few days later a finca owner came to me and told me about the death of another believer. This man, Don Guadalupe Delarosa, was out in a coffee plantation with a group of workers. The soldiers came along. Among the group were some who were real communists and these accused the others. The soldiers, without further word, lined up the whole group, twenty-two in all, and shot them then and there."[16] This report was atypical in its focus on Protestant "believers" and in its admission that "innocent" campesinos were shot. Yet it also represents one point of origin of the notion that the true "communists" betrayed innocent campesinos. This myth of communist treachery, the notion that the communist leaders either abandoned or betrayed their followers, had no basis in fact. Not surprisingly, when the military had defeated insurgent forces, leaders and rank-and-filers ran for their lives. Francisco Sánchez, for example, managed to escape from Juayúa as far as San Pedro Puxtla, on the border of the departments of Ahuachapán and Sonsonate. Most insurgents who survived the initial exchanges of fire at a certain moment also attempted to escape from the slaughter. The military caught and executed numerous other local leaders, in Ahuachapán and elsewhere. There is a counter memory that evokes the tragic stoicism of one local leader. María

Méndez recalls how Augusto Sarmiento, an Ahuachapaneco leftist leader, cried out to bystanders as he was carried off in an open vehicle to a firing squad, "Goodbye my comrades!"[17] Yet such memories of leaders (significantly, in this case, from a ladina) were largely absent in indigenous areas, replaced by a perspective enshrined in the phrases *pagaron justos por pecadores* (the just paid for the sinners) and *mataron justos por pecadores*. In other words, those who were "guilty" escaped and those who were "innocent" died. The military regime, as we shall see, actively promoted this view of communist perfidy and indigenous innocence.

The orgy of bloodletting was equally intense in the department of Ahuachapán, in ladino as well as Indian areas. Miguel Mármol recounted the following testimony from highland regions of Ahauchapán (a primarily nonindigenous coffee area): "A driver who years later joined the Party . . . told us a story about how he was working on a coffee plantation . . . on the 26th or 27th of January he was forced by an Army detachment to drive a truck that had a machine gun mounted in the cab. In the back was a squad of soldiers with automatic arms. They went out on patrol . . . and any group of peasants that they encountered on their way, whether they were just talking or walking, without any prior warning, from a distance of thirty meters or more, they'd unload their machine guns and smaller arms on them. Afterwards, the captain who was in command, with a .45 in his hand, forced our peasant comrade to continue driving the truck, running over them, including the dying who were writhing in pain on the ground, screaming."[18] According to several informants, the military took many captured prisoners to Los Ausoles, site of thermal hot springs outside the city of Ahuachapán, where they shot them.[19]

In Tacuba a woman recalls: "Look, even the houses over there were left as cemeteries, horrible!" Various witnesses state that the troops just opened fire on *ranchitos*, killing women and children, as they did nowhere else. Although we can only speculate, the length of leftist rule and the sharpness of the insurgent resistance probably provoked the excess of barbarity. During the days immediately following the military defeat of the insurgency, troops also indiscriminately killed ladino campesinos in Tacubeño cantons identified as leftist, such as Los Arcos. In general, though, the killing at this stage had nothing directly to do with political identification. That point was driven home by Alvaro Cortez, an indigenous Nahuizalqueño: "My father was a *patrullero* [member of a civil patrol organized by the government]; they didn't ask for a declaration, they just shot him."[20]

"They
Killed
the
Just
for the
Sinners"

General Tomás Calderón. Photo by Commander Victor Brodeur, National Archives of Canada, negative no. C115332.

Salvadoran soldiers. Photo by Commander Victor Brodeur, National Archives of Canada, negative no. PA125135.

The documentary and testimonial record indicate that although the military executed many ladinos during stage I, the majority of their victims
were Indians. The indiscriminate killing of Indians compels a discussion of
genocide. The anachronistic use of concepts is often problematic. As for the
term "genocide," however, developed during the Second World War, few
would dispute its applicability to the mass killings in Armenia. Yet in other
cases, such as the Indian massacres in the western United States, the use of
the term is complicated by the fact that mass repression and conquest
formed components of long-term practices that wavered between forced
assimilation and annihilation. Similarly, in the case of African American
slavery, the use of "genocide" has become politicized. Given the precedent
of German payment of reparations to Holocaust victims and their families,
an admission of genocide often raises the question of reparations. This is
also true with La Matanza: since the 1992 Peace Accords, use of "genocide"
to describe the killings of 1932 has become more widely accepted, and a demand for reparations recently has been propounded by indigenous groups.

The definition adopted by the United Nations Convention on the Preven-
tion and Punishment of the Crime of Genocide emphasized intentionality:
"the intention to destroy in 'whole or in part' a race, nationality, religion or
ethnicity."[21] The Comisión de Esclarecimiento Histórico (CEH), the Guatemalan truth commission, made their argument that the military committed
genocide in the early 1980s by underscoring the difference between intent
and motive in the UN Convention. Intention depends on knowledge that
certain actions will result in the partial or complete destruction of an ethnic
group. For Greg Grandin, who participated in and has written about the
CEH, the Guatemalan military committed genocide, regardless of its motive
(presumably, to destroy the base of the insurgency), because it intended to
kill all Indians in those areas considered to be potential areas of support.[22]
When the report was issued in 1999, the political élite and the military
rejected the CEH charge of genocide, arguing that the military did not
harbor any desire to exterminate an ethnic group (e.g., it had no motivation
to do so, and Indians outside the conflict zones were spared), and that it had
acted primarily out of concern for national security. What Grandin and the
CEH found, on the contrary, was that "racism came to be deeply embedded
in state structures and discourses . . . The imperatives of war, both civil and

217

"They
Killed
the
Just
for the
Sinners"

218

"They
Killed
the
Just
for the
Sinners"

General Hernández Martínez.
Courtesy of the Museo de
la Palabra y la Imagen.

Farabundo Martí.
Courtesy of the Museo de
la Palabra y la Imagen.

Miguel Mármol.
Courtesy of the Museo de
la Palabra y la Imagen.

class, accelerated nationalism, anticommunism, and racism into a murderous fusion: as a 'contextual ideological element,' Memoria del Silencio writes, racism allowed the army to equate Indians with the insurgents and generated the belief that they were "distinct, inferior, a little less than human and removed from the moral universe of the perpetrators, making their elimination less problematic."[23]

There are important parallels as well as significant differences between the two cases. The duration, scope, and ethnic specificity of the Guatemalan repression distinguish it from the repression in El Salvador. The Guatemalan campaign lasted two years and devastated nearly 600 indigenous communities out of a total of 626 affected, killing probably over 100,000 Indians, including many women and children. This difference is fundamental, and it would have been much more difficult for the CEH to make its convincing argument for genocide if the killings, as in El Salvador, had been compressed into a month and had affected numerous non-Indians as well. Moreover, the Guatemalan military was fully aware of the precedents and world condemnation of genocide, and of the powerful emergence of a discourse of human rights. Indeed, the administration of President Jimmy Carter cut off military aid to Guatemala in 1977 because of human rights abuses. The Salvadoran regime in 1932, at a time when the concept of genocide was unknown and human rights were absent from any list of western diplomatic priorities, could act out of ignorance or at least with little fear of international reprisals.

Notwithstanding the differences, there is evidence that the Salvadoran massacres amounted to a form of genocide. There is no question that the military regime of Martínez fostered the mass killings through direct orders, or that racism conditioned those orders and their execution. One officer recalls that Martínez gave "extremely drastic orders, without any restriction, to the military heads of the expeditionary force."[24] According to an official military history, "Indians were put through blood and fire. Martínez's implacable order was 'don't take [no dar cuenta de] . . . prisoners.' "[25] Another version of Martínez's order was: "Fire first and find out later."[26] There is also little doubt that in those insurgent regions where Indians made up a significant part of the population, they were singled out for execution. With the notable exception of those in the region of Ahuachapán and Atiquizaya and to some extent in the Cumbre de Jayaque, most of the victims of the first wave of executions were Indians, even though ladinos probably composed half of the insurrectionary forces.

220

"They
Killed
the
Just
for the
Sinners"

For our analytical purposes, the distinction between intent and motive, raised by Grandin and the CEH, is of fundamental importance. Although there is no evidence to suggest that the Martínez regime specifically planned to kill Indians qua Indians, we argue that the cumulative effect of the massacres amounted to a form of genocide, precisely because the military was cognizant that the indigenous communities would be devastated by the military actions. That said, it is important to contextualize the regime's actions, since in its historical consequences this particular form of genocide was quite distinct from the kind that Guatemala experienced and from what El Salvador would have suffered if the regime had set out to annihilate the entire Indian population. On one level, the massive killing of Indians immediately after the military defeat of the insurrection had much to do with their geographic proximity to the battles and to the order attributed to Martínez, "Don't take prisoners!" There was a geopolitical dimension to the repression, as there was to the insurrection. Indigenous people were more likely to be able to seize towns such as Tacuba, Nahuizalco, Izalco, and Juayúa, in no small part because of the successful organizing drive among the jornaleros in the surrounding cantons. The indigenous people were thus militarily positioned and politically motivated to surround and seize the municipal cabeceras. The majority of those who attacked the barracks in Santa Tecla, Ahuachapán, and Sonsonate were however ladinos, and many of those insurgents were able to retreat without immediate pursuit.[27]

Thus the first phase of repression involved the large-scale killing of both Indians and ladinos. Although there was a much higher proportion of indigenous than ladino people among the dead, this is less than a clear-cut case of genocide precisely because the liquidation was an equal-opportunity one. The charge of genocide, although justifiable and useful with regard to specifically indigenous communities, is complicated not only by the number of ladino dead in Ahuachapán but by the indeterminate identities of so many of the victims from the cantons of Izalco and Juayúa and in Sónzacate, where probably thousands of people lost their lives. Many had adopted non-indigenous identities, or at least had lost their traditional ethnic markers. From the point of view of their executioners, however, all the dark-skinned campesinos in these cantons and in Ahuachapán and La Libertad were indios, a term replete with highly charged and negative, if ambiguous, meanings. Although the ladinos' use of the term indio was unequivocally negative, it was contextually aspecific, attributing a fixed identity to what was in flux. The commander of the Skeena, for example, identified rural poor people as Indians, virtually without exception. Since his contacts were exclusively with military officers or representatives of the local and foreign élite, it is quite probable that they shaped his subjective understanding of race, based on phenotype and skin color. Although Commander Brodeur displayed none of the racism of his acquaintances, he probably shared with them a view of the rural poor in the west as indios, backward, ignorant, lazy, and dangerous. If we limit ourselves to the élite understanding of their own racial superiority and their subjective understanding of race as determined by phenotype and skin color rather than history or culture, we can state that one ethnic group led by generally lighter-skinned ladino officers ordered the execution of people whom they saw as darker and believed to be "racially" inferior, even if many of the victims would have considered themselves ladinos or non-Indians. In this broader definition of race and racism, the regime's primary motive—to crush the insurrection and strike fear and terror into the hearts and minds of the rural poor—fused with an intent framed by racism and overdetermined by class hatred—with a result that killed thousands of people in a form of genocide.

Stage II: Indian Massacres in Nahuizalco

The second phase of violent repression was unequivocally genocidal, in that it focused exclusively on self-identified Indians. There is no evidence to suggest, however, that Martínez's regime ordered or encouraged the two principal massacres that marked this phase. The first took place in El Canelo, a canton in the coffee region of Nahuizalco, bordering the municipality of Juayúa. There is ample testimony about the massacre but no documentary evidence which would allow us to determine the exact date or the number killed. The testimonies suggest that the killing occurred within a week after the military defeat of the insurrectionary forces in Nahuizalco.

The massacre occurred at "El Canelo," the hacienda of the proto-fascist ideologue Gabino Mata, who had suffered a major scare during the insurrection. One account published nearly a decade later stated that the hacienda had been occupied by a large group of insurgents.[28] Whether it was or not, there is no doubt that Mata believed he was threatened by the rebellion and that after its military defeat he decided to seek vengeance. He gathered together his colonos and other indigenous peasants under the

222

"They
Killed
the
Just
for the
Sinners"

Gabino Mata.
Courtesy of the
Museo de la Palabra
y la Imagen.

pretext of protecting them from the National Guard. Raimundo Aguilar
recalls that Mata's *mandador* played a key role in the tragedy: "He took all the
people, all the workers . . . he sent word that he was going to give them a
safe-conduct pass to save their lives. They didn't know any better and they
believed it; they thought they were going to save their lives but once they
were there the people from the armed forces began to tie them up . . .
like crabs, right, all of them, and when it was time, he sent the captain to
kill them."[29]

Raimundo's older sister screamed, "If they kill our father, let them kill
me too!" and threw herself among the prisoners. She and her father joined
the hundreds of indigenous peasants who fell under a hail of machine-gun
fire as they were ordered by Colonel Ortiz to make a run for it. Pedro Lue,
then a twelve-year-old in the neighboring canton of Sábana San Juan Arriba,
recalled, "Don Gabino Mata gathered all his people and all his laborers and
told them 'come here, because there is a brigade of national guardsmen
coming to kill you.' He wanted to cage them, the poor innocent people.
There were about five hundred of them. He kept them inside and then sent
one of the people to find rope to tie them up. When the troops arrived they

asked, 'Don Gabinito, are you ready?' He replied, 'Yes, I am ready . . . let's go make justice.' They walked off to make a cemetery . . . they killed them all . . . Gabino Mata turned over a lot of people."[30]

Another surviving eyewitness was Jesús Velásquez, a twelve-year-old ladino boy from Los Arenales:

> My grandfather belonged to the commander's patrol that got together at the *Puesto de Aguila*. He came home for lunch. Look, he said to my mother, there are about 800 Indians being held prisoner in el Canelo, around Gabino Mata's ranch. I wanted to follow him to see what was going to happen even though they forbade me to go out. Once I got there I figured out that in order to have a good look I had to go onto the straight road and that's how they saw me. I thought my grandfather or the others would hit me for being there. But in a little while a lot of people arrived tied together in the front and in the back. And suddenly Colonel Ortiz came with another platoon. The troops were drunk. All the patrols had to tear down the fences. The officials yelled, "You can go!" They took off running. Pe pe pe . . . sounded the machine gun. The officials ordered the soldiers to break into a shed to look for tools for digging. It was around five in the afternoon and already by 6 they had finished.[31]

Velásquez's testimony is the only one that offers a justification for the massacre. He repeated the words that his grandfather had said to him: "If we didn't kill them, they would have killed us."[32]

It is remarkable that these testimonies, which cross a locally sharp ethnic divide, coincide so closely in the details of the killings. Although there is no direct documentary evidence of the massacre, the narratives strongly suggest that Mata and Colonel Ortiz conspired to entrap and execute the Indians. Martínez's regime did nothing to punish the perpetrators, but that afternoon of killing was the result of local conditions and locally based actors.

Local forces also produced the other massacre. According to informants, the mayor of Nahuizalco, Francisco Brito, wanted his revenge after suffering the fear and indignity of having a crowd of Indians call for his head.[33] Following national governmental directives, Brito sent word by official bando that he would issue safe-conduct passes on 13 February. Each safe-conduct pass stated that the bearer was not a communist. One published account, substantiated by numerous testimonies, relates that the municipal building remained closed as the crowd of Indian males waited

"They
Killed
the
Just
for the
Sinners"

Pedro Lue,
Sábana San Juan
Arriba. Courtesy
of the Museo de la
Palabra y la Imagen.

Ramón Esquina,
Tajcuilulaj. Courtesy
of the Museo de la
Palabra y la Imagen.

for their *carnets*. Some apparently became suspicious and tried to leave, but the National Guard had blocked off the streets. "Suddenly they started shooting from the houses and the buildings surrounding the plaza. Those familiar bursts made its repetitive noise heard. Entire rows of those gathered there fell under the bullets."[34] Survivors recall the panic of people trying to escape the machine-gun fire.[35]

The regime and its supporters had another version of events. According to the strongly pro-government British consul, a coffee planter: "About a thousand people drifted into town and gathered in the town square, ostensibly with the object of procuring from the Mayor the new boleto de identidad. The mayor became alarmed when he saw how many were coming and then telegraphed urgently, twice, for help. Troops were sent from Sonsonate, Juayúa, and Izalco. They surrounded the town, lined up the Indians and searched them. Then it was found that many of them had concealed knives and a notice calling them to Nahuizalco for the 'day of atonement' 388 Indians were killed."[36]

The consul's suggestion that the Indians were planning to stage an attack echoed the statement of the minister of war that was reported in the officialist *Diario de El Salvador*: "Some three hundred indians from Nahuizalco rose up against the stationed troops, who left the towns to wait for the help of a brigade from Sonsonate. With the speed that is required in those circumstances, they proceeded to pacify the insurgents, but because they resisted, it became necessary to use force."[37] This version of events appears to have been a complete fabrication, although it is possible that the local authorities experienced fear when they saw a large number of Indians gathered in the town square. The immediate response of the regime to the events of 13 February suggests that the minister of war's story was meant to offer cover for the murderous actions of local élites and military officers in the region. On 15 February the government announced that the distributions of *boletos de identidad* had been suspended for "very powerful reasons."[38] In light of the timing of the decision (on the 14th), the "very powerful reasons" no doubt referred to the massacre, which the regime had not foreseen but was willing to cover up. What had been intended as a measure to bring the killings, or at least the indiscriminate ones, to a halt had the opposite effect. The regime recognized that further distribution of passes might result in more such occurrences or might be pointless because of the fear that would be induced throughout the region by the killings. Although there are some reports that the authorities carried out similar tactics in Juayúa and Izalco, there is no hard evidence to substantiate the claim. Rather, it seems that witnesses incorrectly placed the events of 13 February in Juayúa instead of Nahuizalco. For example, the *Historia Militar*, written by an officer, offers a description of an incident that is an exact replica of the events in Nahuizalco: "In Juayúa it was ordered that all honest men who were not communists present themselves to the Cabildo Municipal, in order to distribute safe-conduct passes, and when the public plaza was packed with men, children, and women, they closed the streets leading out of the plaza, and they gunned down the innocent multitude, not sparing the lives of even the poor dogs who always follow their indigenous masters so faithfully. A few days later, the commander who had orchestrated the terrible massacre recounted that macabre incident in copious detail in the parks and promenades of San Salvador, boasting that he had been the hero of such an action."[39] There is no other evidence that a massacre so similar to the one in Nahuizalco also took place in Juayúa, and in all probability the

225

"They
Killed
the
Just
for the
Sinners"

226

"They
Killed
the
Just
for the
Sinners"

document confused the two places. The officer's reported gloating does suggest just how cold-blooded the Nahuizalco massacre was. Even three weeks after it had defeated the insurrection, the regime had no intention of bringing murderers to justice. These two massacres, one provoked by municipal authorities and the other by a prominent landlord and political figure, revealed to indigenous survivors the extent of ladino cunning and unambiguous evil: they remain unmitigated examples of genocide.

Racism increased dramatically among ladinos during this period and undoubtedly influenced the conscious decisions to perpetrate these atrocities. The Reverend Roy MacNaught, the Protestant missionary stationed in Juayúa and a staunch anticommunist, noted the transformation. On 14 February, writing from Santa Tecla before he gained knowledge of the atrocities of the preceding day, he stated: "The Indians are hated now as never before. In Nahuizalco, there is a defense league composed of the Ladino element. These Ladinos have rounded up male believers and had them shot."[40] On 3 March he wrote: "We have word that there have been executed in Nahuizalco alone, 2500 men. One day they lined up 400 boys and shot them. They have tortured the women to make them tell where their husbands and brothers are." MacNaught's own view of the repression had changed from an acceptance of firing squads in Juayúa to an expression of horror. In his initial report he had written: "All day long (and this lasted for several days) we could hear the shots in the plaza as the work of execution went on . . . We cannot say that the government was too severe."[41] What had changed was MacNaught's full recognition of the innocence of many of its victims—brought home by the killing of Protestant converts—and the role of blatant racism in the executions.

There is no doubt that the ethnic and class tensions in Juayúa, Nahuizalco, Tacuba, and Izalco were exacerbated to the point of hysteria after occupations by largely indigenous revolutionary forces. Those occupations, despite their relatively small incidence of violence, burst the dam holding back the accumulated hostility and hatred toward Indians on the part of the élite, which was to some extent shared by middle-class and proletarian people. Very quickly Indian, barbarian, and communist became interchangeable epithets. One survivor recalls townsfolk shouting, "Finish off the Indian communists!" Others recall the phrase "Kill the Indians!" As MacNaught underscored, many town residents mobilized into a "Guardia Cívica" (defense league) as soon as the troops had retaken the municipal centers. Although the precise role of the Guardia Cívica in the local massacres remains unclear, they undoubtedly inspired the troops to kill *indios comunistas*, if they were not already so inclined.

There is also some evidence of virulent racism in the officer corps. One of the National Guard commanders, a Colonel Ortiz, injured while breaking up a peasant demonstration the previous year, reportedly uttered the command: "When you capture a suspect, if he's an Indian, shoot him, and if he is ladino, bring him in for questioning."[42] As we have seen, informants single out Ortiz as responsible for the massacre in El Canelo.

The combination of military exigency and brutal excess, local racist hysteria and a desire for vengeance (and at least one racist military commander), conditioned the two Indian massacres. Stage III, which coincided with but lasted longer than stage II, involved more discriminate forms of killing.

Stage III: *Las Listas* and Other Forms of Discriminate Killing

"Las listas" are engraved in the memory of the survivors throughout the west. National and Civic Guards carried around long lists of voters who had signed petitions to register the Partido Comunista Salvadoreño (PCS) as a political party in the elections. In some locales such as Juayúa, they captured and used lists of Socorro Rojo supporters. Throughout February and March, Civic patrols and the National Guard searched for those PCS supporters, and when they found them they shot them either with or without the benefit of judicial trappings.[43] As late as 25 February the British consul reported, "Executions are still taking place almost daily."[44]

A Wall Street attorney, Milo Borges, was present in San Salvador during January 1932. In a report dated 30 January 1932 he wrote: "The Government has been arresting all those who were listed as communists. I understand that in San Salvador, alone, there were 9,000 men listed. They were being arrested as rapidly as they can be located and after one or two days in jail are taken out late at night and conducted to some isolated spot where they are told to disperse and machine gun fire opened on them. They are usually buried where killed. I understand about 600 have been so disposed of in this city alone during the past week."[45] Borges was close enough to the Salvadoran élite to join a "Vigilance Committee" (along with the "young men of the best families"). Although his access may lend some credence to the

228

"They
Killed
the
Just
for the
Sinners"

Prisoners before execution, Sonsonate barracks, January 1932. Photo by Commander Victor Brodeur, National Archives of Canada, negative no. PA125136.

Executed Prisoners, Sonsonate barracks, January 1932. Photo by Commander Victor Brodeur, National Archives of Canada, negative no. C115331.

numbers that he reports, they are hard to corroborate. They do coincide with other accounts of mass executions of suspected communists in the capital area.

Outside the capital region the numbers become even more speculative, but there is no doubt that the lists loom heavily in memories of 1932. People recall the shape and size of the lists: in some cases they were foot-long books, the size of municipal *libros de actas*. The lists formed part of the theater of terror employed by the military, along with the rarer cases of kangaroo trials. In both cases the use of the list offered a rationale for killing, however flawed. Vicente Flores of Jayaque recalled the following episode: "We were carrying corn from a field when we saw that they brought out a lot of people from a finca. The Guardia stopped us. They were carrying some notebooks. My father never got involved in anything and they didn't find his name. But they gave him a good beating; they were whipping him in front of me. I was left traumatized. Since then I have hated the Guardia; I couldn't even look at them."[46] Flores recalls that the Guardia lined up those who did appear on the list and shot them in groups of four. Others in Jayaque recall that soldiers walked around with lists and executed anyone whose name appeared on them.

Although there is no documentary evidence supporting the vast amount of testimony that soldiers used the lists to single out victims for execution, there is documentary evidence that they did at least possess the lists. An order issued on 11 February 1932 from the minister of war to the departmental governor of Sonsonate reads: "As it is indispensible to make a selection of individuals who served in your ranks in the forthcoming recruitments, I request that you submit to this ministry a list of the communists in the various places of that department who presented themselves at the last elections to vote for the candidates of their party."[47] The request is somewhat elliptical. Since Sonsonate was the one department where most of the killings had been indiscriminate up to that point, it seems that now the military was ready to avail itself of the lists so as to pursue matters more rationally, as it were, in the department. Alternatively, and far less likely, it is possible that the military had finished its killing spree in Sonsonate, was seriously thinking of reconstituting its army, and thus wanted to make sure that it did not recruit "communists." In either case the document does establish the military's cognizance and use of voter lists.

Although the use of electoral lists was widespread, the military also employed other means to find its victims. Commander Brodeur reported that on Wednesday 27 January "the Government commenced its campaign of routing out Indians suspected of being or known to be Communists, and shooting them, after a short interrogation which consisted mainly of the question 'Are you a Communist?'; and if guilty, the prisoner almost invariably admitted it at once. If there was any doubt, the suspect was placed in a

230

"They
Killed
the
Just
for the
Sinners"

special prison, where he was kept until sufficient evidence of his guilt was forthcoming. It is rumored that on one or two occasions, some of these unfortunate prisoners were allowed to 'escape' after nightfall, and were immediately shot down for being at large after curfew."[48] Brodeur was referring to Sonsonate, and apparently the PCS voter list for that department had not yet materialized. We can deduce from this that the military and its Civic Guard supporters had other means of singling out suspected communists. Based on oral testimony, we may assume that after the first wave of terror the military would capture primarily the rural poor for "questioning." Manuel Linares, a ladino campesino from El Cacao, Sonsonate, related the following based on the accounts of family members who escaped from the area near Atiquizaya, Ahuachapán: "The repression was that they would take your name . . . the priests would take the names of the groups and they would say, 'You are a Communist,' and the person would say, 'No, Father, I am not, I haven't been involved.' 'You can leave.' The priests would then ask another one, 'You worked with the Communists?' and the guy would say 'No, well, they invited me,' so the priests would put him with another group. And they would be tied up and shot."[49] The testimony supports a key sentence in Brodeur's account, namely that the insurgents were often willing to admit association with the revolutionary cause. The notion of "invitation" to a meeting, as the reader will recall, referred to a cultural code that made attendance something of an obligation. The military and the Guardia Civil were of course profoundly uninterested in such cultural conventions. Linares's testimony also supports other testimonies about the role of the church in the repression.

Doroteo López, an eighteen-year-old in Los Amates at the time, recalled that in Santa Tecla, Padre Ravelo fully supported the repression, and in his sermon thanked God "that the evil has been yanked out at the root. God willing, it will never have life again."[50] Salomé Torres also had experience with the church in Santa Tecla, shortly after the insurrection: "They took us to Santa Tecla—we all were carrying white flags. We all went to church. It was a Monday and they told us to come back on Wednesday. So we got to the church and we all went to confession. The Father would ask us if we were involved in communism. I said no. But the others who admitted it, he put a little cross next to their name. They were shot."[51]

As we have seen, whether or not it was directly involved, the church benefited from the repression through the elimination of the tiny but growing Protestant presence in the west. As MacNaught recognized, the Guardia Cívica lumped Protestants together with communists, and a large proportion of the tiny minority of Protestant converts were singled out for execution. According to some testimony, a priest saved two jailed Protestants from their scheduled executions in return for their conversion back to the Catholic church. Considering the high level of paranoia about Protestant penetration evident in the writings of Conte (see chapter 4), the uprising and repression seem to have provided an expedient conjuncture for striking back.[52] The singling out of Protestants for retribution in a moment of counterrevolution fits the pattern established in revolutionary France and Russia. As Arno Mayer wrote, "Protestants and Jews were the perfect scapegoats on whom to discharge a broad range of anxieties and resentments activated or intensified by revolutionary turbulence. In particular, the last-ditchers of the old order portrayed these most prominent and vulnerable out-groups as incarnating a treacherous plot to desacralize, modernize, and level civil and political society."[53]

231

"They
Killed
the
Just
for the
Sinners"

The Spared

To recapitulate: there is little doubt that the military slaughtered over 2,500 Indians in Nahuizalco and Izalco. In their rage the officers and élite regarded all indigenous males as "communists." One *terrateniente* stated unequivocally: "There are no Indians who aren't Communists." Similarly, in Juayúa and Tacuba the military executed over two thousand rural people, many of whom were indigenous. A large number of ladinos and people without indigenous identities fell to the military in those locales, as in Ahuachapán and La Libertad.[54]

Notwithstanding the genocidal effect of the killings in these indigenous municipalities, other Indian areas in central and western Salvador were untouched by the massacre. A striking example of an area which was spared genocidal repression was the heavily indigenous municipality of Panchimalco. Indians from the rugged area south of San Salvador had participated in both the mobilization and the insurrection and yet suffered only light reprisals. One grassroots militant who had been active in the agrarian movement and participated in the skirmishes on the southern edge of San Salvador recalls that immediately after the insurrection, troops captured him; the authorities released him after two days. His uncle, a recognized

232

"They
Killed
the
Just
for the
Sinners"

revolutionary leader, was captured at the same time and spent two or three years in prison.[55] This mild repression took place against the wishes of some townsfolk. On 2 February the Junta de Orden Pública of Panchimalco protested against the release of revolutionary suspects in the nearby villages.[56] There is no evidence that would help to explain why the military authorities acted so differently toward the indigenous rebels and their homes in the Panchimalco region. It is entirely possible that Colonel Emilio Renderos, in charge of the expedition against the retreating rebels, simply had no stomach for massacres and that his superiors, recognizing that their victory was complete, had no interest in further bloodshed. If that explanation were valid, then it would place the onus of guilt for the latter phases of the massacres in the west largely on local military and civilian forces. Still, the regime never brought any of the executioners to justice.

Santo Domingo de Guzmán was an almost exclusively indigenous municipality in Sonsonate. With an altitude of only 190 meters, the town lay outside the coffee belt (600–1,500 meters). Only ten miles west of Sonsonate, it remained quite isolated during the early 1930s, and did not serve as a base for union or SRI activity. As a consequence, the Nahuate-speaking Indians of Santo Domingo suffered no repression. Residents of Santa Catarina Masahuat, another indigenous municipality that bordered Santo Domingo and Nahuizalco, did participate in the leftist movement, but only a handful of leaders were clearly identified as part of the insurrection. The military hanged those leaders but apparently spared the rest of the population despite its proximity to the seats of rebellion. It is likely that Santa Catarina was spared because insurgents did not take over the municipal building (controlled by Indians) or assault any of the few ladino properties in the area.

While many indigenous people from Cuisnahuat took part in the mass mobilization, and over one hundred probably took part in the assault on the barracks of Sonsonate, the military did not carry out violent retribution there. Some elders of Cuisnahuat, another Nahuate-speaking village, recall that San Lucas, its patron saint, saved the village and a local communist leader by appearing just as he was being hauled off to be shot in Sonsonate. We have heard of no other explanation for why the military struck violently in so many towns and cantons in the neighboring highlands of Jayaque but not in Cuisnahuat, even though it was known for having a large concentration of Indians who militated in the ranks of the left. As in Santo Domingo and Santa Catarina, the insurgent Indians seem to have neither occupied the town nor physically assaulted the ladino residents, despite a simmering history of resentment.

The existence of indigenous communities that were spared violence in no way mitigates the genocide committed against those who had supported the mobilization and insurrection, just as the decision by the Guatemalan military to spare Indians in non-conflict zones did not weaken the charges of genocide against it. Yet in reconstructions of the massacres, both immediately and over the next decades, the existence of the "spared" helped to allow the military to exonerate itself by equating insurgency, communism, and Indians.

The Prose of Massacre

On 29 January General Calderón announced that his troops had "liquidated 4,800" communists. Within days he modified his statement, stating that the communists had been neutralized, not necessarily killed. (Ten years later he explained that he had been compelled to backtrack by the horrified international reaction to what he had presumed to be a reassuring statement, coupled with massive demonstrations in Mexico City.) From that moment no official statements referred to the total number of deaths at the hands of counterrevolutionary forces. On 25 February Rogers, the British chargé d'affaires, ratified the impossibility of exact knowledge: "It will never be known how many have been killed, but the total cannot be less than 5,000 and it has even been put as high as 12,000. Executions are still taking place daily."[57] An official with the U.S. embassy in 1937 reported wide discrepancies in estimates of the number of dead (presumably from those close to the seats of power), from three thousand to seventeen thousand.[58] The left, with far less access to military sources, has referred to 25,000 or 30,000 deaths. General Calderón's initial assessment of 4,800 killed in the first phase corresponds with local estimates in Izalco, Nahuizalco, and Tacuba and is possibly low for the entire region. There is no way of estimating the number of those killed during the subsequent phases outside Nahuizalco (where five hundred to one thousand perished during the massacres in town and at El Canelo).[59] We would suggest that given the impossibility of arriving at anything approximating a scientific estimate, we are left to rely upon the figures offered by the British and American embassy

"They
Killed
the
Just
for the
Sinners"

officials and Calderón. Taking those estimates into account, the figure of ten thousand fatalities is reasonable.[60]

Regardless of the exact number, the massacre of thousands of unarmed people is a historical fact. How did official Salvadoran discourse portray this atrocity? The official and semi-official prose offers us clues about how the military and the élite were able to present their version of the events as a reality so powerful that it reshaped the very fabric of memory of the survivors. At the most general level, officialist discourse elided, distorted, or falsified descriptions of the killings in such a way that either perpetrators and victims were transposed or at the very least the distinction between them was made ambiguous. Joaquín Méndez, a journalist, traveled throughout the west interviewing military officials and élite local people. His account, published in April 1932, became something akin to an official full-scale narrative of the insurrection and repression. He masterfully applies the art of omission, combined with implied justifications, to render unintelligible the most blatant massacres, those in El Canelo and Nahuizalco. He simply does not mention the killings on 13 February in the center of town. He does, however, refer to Gabino Mata and events on his hacienda. After a brief description of the capture of some of the insurgents from Juayúa effectuated by the troops, he inserted a short section, "En la hacienda de don Gabino Mata," in which he relates an interview with a soldier who had been sent to guard his hacienda on 27 January. The day before, "they had told don Gabino that on that very day they would hand him his head. We had been there for twenty minutes when we made out a group of twenty-seven armed individuals . . . Maybe it was because we caught them by surprise but they seemed to lose their cold-blooded resolve and it seemed to us like they were surrendering. Some of them, however, made an attempt to attack us, so we had to shoot and kill a lot of them. After that—he finishes—it was demonstrated that it was true that they wanted to kill don Gabino. And when he realized that we had saved his life, he sent for us, to reward us, and he received us very well and gave us money."[61] Because of the lack of chronological specificity about the massacre in Mata's hacienda and the imprecision of the term muchos, we cannot be certain whether the soldier's account euphemistically described the mass shootings of defenseless indigenous workers, reported by numerous informants. If it did not refer directly to the massacre, it certainly justified it.[62] Indeed, as if to deny and neutralize his complicity in the massacre on his hacienda, a local newspaper converted Mata into a hero. Reporting on his role in creating an organization that mobilized financial support for the National Guard, *El Heraldo de Sonsonate* lauded him: "The cultured and philanthropic Gabino Mata, hijo has fanned the flames of patriotism in the hearts of all good Salvadorans and we must stand behind him."[63] Mata became one of the leading spokesmen for his social class. A short time after the massacre in El Canelo, he angrily denounced the situation in the countryside, where the "danger [was] still latent . . . Communism has deep roots."[64] Mata uttered this declaration on 12 February, the day before the massacre in the town of Nahuizalco, and it seems reasonable that in addition to espousing his anti-democratic, populistic ideology, he was also justifying in advance yet another massacre.

That Mata became a local counterrevolutionary leader is not surprising. Yet the ennobling of the man responsible for the cold-blooded execution of hundreds of his workers is a particularly salient case of the inversion of victims and executioners that characterized counterinsurgent discourse in the months following the insurrection and massacre.[65] The regime often asserted that the brunt of the violence was perpetrated by the insurgents and borne by soldiers and the wealthy. Consider the following official report, issued nearly a year after the events: "In these towns there were robberies and many agents of the government and numerous residents, who, because of their culture and economic and social position, never could have covered themselves with the tragic red flag, were assassinated pitilessly. The country lived through hours of pain, of anguish, and panic, during those terrible days, bathed in blood; so terrible and bloody that the Government, understanding that pain, that anguish, and that panic joined its energies and its firm patriotic will in a single effort . . . was able unhesitatingly to punish those who, in an evil hour, had forgotten their noble condition of human beings, and had thrown themselves unbridled into criminal attacks and punishable despoliation, in various forms and manifestations."[66] Shorn of the most venomous, hysterical prose that characterized the declarations of January and February 1932, the report nevertheless employs the same tropes to synthesize the dominant interpretation of the events. By referring only to an unspecified quantity of military and élite deaths ("many"), and not to those thousands of deaths at the hands of the military, the text suggests that the insurgents were responsible for most of the killing. That suggestion is amplified in the second sentence: "during those terrible days, bathed in

"They
Killed
the
Just
for the
Sinners"

blood; so terrible and bloody that the Government . . . joined its energies and its firm patriotic will in a single effort." The strong implication is that the government responded to the bloodbath (and thus did not create it), and then only did so to mete out just punishment. Finally, the text refers to the dominant trope of counterinsurgent discourse: the savage condition of the insurgents.

During the days of killing, newspapers and government proclamations dehumanized the massacred civilians and insurgents, portraying them as savages and their ideas and movement as a deadly disease.[67] They described the revolutionary insurgents as "bloodthirsty hordes," "hordes of vandals," or "a horde of raging savages,"[68] whose actions were characterized by saña fiera.[69] They described "communism," the ideology and the movement, as a disease attacking the body politic: "el comunismo, cáncer social." Certain places were "infested" by communists, and campesinos suffered from a "virus." The dehumanization of insurgents worked to legitimize their execution. It would be a mistake, however, to understand such statements as a univocal expression of anti-Indian racism. Dominant groups had long employed images of savagery to describe not only indigenous people but also those from the "dangerous" classes in Europe. Enzo Traverso writes of the massacre of Communards in Paris in 1871: "Political repression seen as the disenfection of the social body presupposed the dehumanization of the enemy, who was demoted to the level of an animal or an inferior biological species."[70] Adolphe Thiers, the architect of the massacre of between ten and thirty thousand Parisian Communards, wrote: "One day it happens that a careless jailer leaves his keys in the doors of this menagerie, and the wild beasts rampage with savage roars through the horrified town. Out of the open cages leap the hyenas of '93 and the gorillas of the Commune."[71] The reader will note the similarity in the depictions of French Communards and Salvadoran insurgents.

The repetitive description of insurgents as vandalic hordes by itself did not justify the indiscriminate slaughter of civilians, but one newspaper editorial came close to such a justification: "The violent and unjustified aggression has been met with the energy and harshness that the circumstances demanded; the red terror that tried to impose the enemies of the law has been met with the terror that must always be instilled in bandits through a just and severe punishment."[72] Here the equivalence of "terror" and "a just and severe punishment" suggests that the military limited its use of terror to those who deserved it. The term "terror" in reference to state actions never reappeared in officialist statements. The notion that "just and severe" punishment referred to the execution of "communists" was widespread inside and outside the country.

The military repression "of great severity"—namely the mass execution of "communists"—fell within the international boundaries of acceptable action on the part of a government faced with lower-class rebellion. The fear and hatred of the lower classes, combined with a transformation of mentalities wrought by the First World War, conditioned an "inurement to violent death and an indifference to human life."[73] Commenting on the markedly limited protests against the Armenian massacre, Traverso argues that "Europe had become accustomed to massacre."[74] Hysteria against Bolshevism only increased tolerance for slaughter. Thus Martínez's regime suffered no condemnation from European or American governments.[75] Undoubtedly the foreign coffee growers and merchants in El Salvador who enthusiastically backed the regime's repression influenced the United States and Great Britain. D. Rogers, the British chargé d'affaires in El Salvador, was in fact a coffee planter. According to a report by the U.S. government in March 1932, "The British move to recognize President Martínez was seriously considered after his speedy suppression of the January revolution . . . [he] suppressed the revolt within two or three days and the British were impressed by the way he handled the situation."[76] According to a report in the New York Times based in part on a conversation with the U.S. ambassador in El Salvador, Rogers had publicly suggested the need to recognize the regime "because of admiration for the way the Martínez regime suppressed the recent Communist outbreak . . . Other diplomats there and the foreign colony generally share that view and officials here [in Washington] have great sympathy with it."[77] There were no governmental denunciations of human rights violations apart from the USSR. Moreover, the Communist International, outside Mexico, made little effort to protest the killings in El Salvador.[78] To the extent that its organs devoted space to El Salvador, the Comintern-allied press lambasted the decimated PCS for its sectarian, putschist, and ultra-leftist failings.[79]

With the international community supportive, the left annihilated, and the Salvadoran élite and middle-class sectors "owing a debt of immeasurable gratitude" to General Martínez, the regime was able to build upon the counterrevolutionary narrative in a way that effectively shaped the memories

238

"They
Killed
the
Just
for the
Sinners"

of the traumatized survivors of the massacres in western Salvador. The most striking transformation in the officialist narrative referred to the "innocents" who died. Positing an *indio engañado* as the blind and ignorant subject of the insurrection laid the discursive groundwork on which the notion of "innocent" Indians and their demise developed. "Indigenous innocence" allowed the regime to attempt to forge political links with the survivors despite the atrocities it had committed. Within weeks Martínez dispatched his propagandists to the region and circulated pamphlets such as "La Verdad Sobre el Comunismo" (twenty thousand copies) and "Hermano Campesino No Seas Comunista" (three thousand copies).[80]

The government's story emerged along the following lines. First, the previous regimes had failed to meet the needs of the people, setting the stage for communist infiltration. The military immediately developed an explanation of the revolt that blamed previous governments and absolved the military itself from a decisive role in the massacre: "The history would have been very different if those in power had been inclined to listen to the just demands."[81] Second, the communists fooled the poor and ignorant Indians into fighting for something hopeless. Once the regime cast appropriate blame on past politicians and on the communists, and remade the Indians as innocents, the next dimension of the discourse could emerge, one that resonated and probably shaped emerging local memories whose condensation was expressed in the refrain: *murieron justos por pecadores*. Not only did this statement absolve many of the dead Indians from guilt, it also formed the organizing principle of the narrative that suppressed any notion of indigenous agency in the insurrection. The terrifying experience of witnessing the execution of loved ones and the fear caused by decades of military rule were the primary causes of the suppression of indigenous agency. Equally important was the power of military discourse that also managed, by turning assassinated Indians into innocents, to neutralize its own guilt.

There was of course no way to entirely stamp out the survivors' subversive memories of the bloody *engaño* perpetrated by the military and condensed by many with a variation of the phrase: *ofrecieron una contraseña y la contraseña fue balas* (they offered a password and the password was bullets). Yet within a few years, pro-regime politicians had at the very least added flesh to the image of the *indio engañado*, which may have mitigated the effect of the memory of the massacres in Nahuizalco and in El Canelo. The new version built on the innocence of Indians with a pithy aphorism that echoed the subversive one: "they offered them money, land, and even houses . . . the house was the cemetery."[82] This comment passed into survivors' memories. Ramón Esquina, a nine-year-old in 1932, synthesized the causal relationship between the mobilization and the massacres in the following terms: "They promised them nice little white houses; the white wall was the tombstone."[83]

239

"They
Killed
the
Just
for the
Sinners"

Regime discourse continued to play on the idea of Indian innocence. In 1935 the regime, facing a putative communist threat, issued a proclamation admitting that innocents had died in 1932 yet still exonerating the military: "Still fresh in the minds of Salvadorans is the vision of the sad tragedy to which the crowds were dragged not long ago, instigated by those who infected their hearts with the grim sentiments of hate and impiety. And it is enough to ask, how many were the innocent and how many the guilty? . . . The leaders, with the arrival of the hour of responsibility, hide the hand that threw the stone and abandon them to their own fates."[84]

The popular, condensed explanation of the massacre, "the just died for the sinners," echoed this official rhetorical question, "How many were innocent and how many were guilty?" Under military rule such phrases became the common sense of survivors, and with their repeated utterance, the events of January 1932—the elections, the strikes, the insurrection, and the killing fields—disappeared beneath the scars of memory.

Chapter Eight

Memories of La Matanza: The Political and Cultural Consequences of 1932

My father was having breakfast when the armed forces came and, just like that, they took him. They didn't even want to see a dog come out alive . . . There were 30 dead by the river. I was so afraid that my body swelled up.—María Antonia Perez, El Canelo

Everyone was running and hiding. The soldiers just opened fire on the huts.
—José Arnulfo Lima, El Tortuguero, Ahuachapán

I was coming back with my father from the fields and a group of National Guard stopped us. They couldn't find his name on their lists, but they beat him anyway, right in front of my eyes.
—Vicente Flores, Jayaque

I was fourteen years old and I had to flee too. They didn't ask for any declarations from anyone. Whoever they saw, they shot.—Antonio Valiente, Turín

A poor old señor was working when they decapitated him alive, and his body still stood upright about ten minutes or a little longer, until it collapsed . . . They looked for people the way you hunt an animal.—Alejandro Pérez Ortiz, El Carrizal

The massacres of 1932 had devastating long-term political and social consequences for the entire country. Until the peace accords of 1992, Miguel Mármol's comment in the mid-1960s that "El Salvador is . . . the creation of that barbarism"[1] accurately reflected the political legacy of 1932: an enormous concentration of wealth and power in the hands of the agrarian élite, who evinced a mixture of scorn and fear of the rural poor, and depended upon a brutally repressive regime to remain in power.

The political and cultural effects of 1932 on the survivors and subsequent generations are far less obvious. For decades there was a consensus among scholars and activists about the consequences of La Matanza: the killings directly produced the annihilation of indigenous culture by repressing the Nahuatl-Pipil language and indigenous dress. Moreover, a culture of fear and dependence emerged in the western communities, whose principal effect was political passivity. Although there is ample evidence to support these propositions, this chapter seeks to significantly modify and contextualize them. We argue that the transformation of indigenous culture, especially the loss of ethnic emblems, was a complex, often endogenous process, which began decades before 1932 and continued well into the 1970s. We will also argue that the generation of the 1970s, the first with access to secondary education, directly contributed to the disintegration of indigenous cultural forms, especially language and dress. This generational challenge arose even as there was greater horizontal contact with ladinos, contributing to a new wave of cross-ethnic mobilization. In 1980 the state, as in 1932, responded with brutality. Until recently the memories of the 1980 massacres have also been silenced.

General Martínez's Regime

After La Matanza General Martínez's regime took several bold steps that alleviated the most drastic effects of the economic crisis and allowed him to consolidate some popular support outside his base in the urban middle class and the élite. First, on 29 February 1932 the regime suspended payment on its foreign debt. This measure allowed it to suspend the coffee export tax, which contributed to the coffee economy's ability to maintain or reinitiate productive activities and thereby generate employment. On 12 March the regime declared a retroactive moratorium on debts, which rescued thousands of small and medium producers from foreclosure and loss of their lands.

In 1933 the regime created the Junta Nacional de Defensa Social, which made very modest efforts toward redistributing land and constructing housing for the poor. In ten years the regime constructed only 253 houses and distributed lots amounting to 29,000 manzanas.[2] Despite the limited thrust of these measures and a tax reform, Martínez earned the enmity of some sectors of the oligarchy as a result of his concessions to the poor.[3] Yet Martínez prevailed despite oligarchic dissent, primarily because he carried out all these initiatives while basking in a nationalist glow, as his stance against the United States policy of nonrecognition attracted the admiration of even progressive intellectuals in Central America. Martínez thus rapidly consolidated support among most sectors of society. Perhaps most remarkably, he began to forge a base among the indigenous communities. In the months following La Matanza the military regime provided food for the survivors and protected them against the vengeance of local ladinos. In Izalco an incipient military-Indian political alliance developed shortly after the massacres.[4] Pro-Indian policies included special schools for orphans of the massacre, support for Indians in land and water disputes, and official recognition of the civil and religious hierarchy that local ladinos attempted to abolish.[5] Lieutenant Alfonso Muñoz, who became the head of one of the schools for orphans, attempted to intervene on the side of the Indians, denouncing how much they were charged for electricity when they had no access to it, and in fact were "charged with more insistence than were the ladinos." In his own words, he strove to "reach a state of harmony between the naturales and the ladinos of these regions."[6]

It is within the framework of this military-Indian alliance that we must attempt to understand the cultural consequences of 1932. It exerted a strong influence in survivors' memories, and many elderly indigenous people in Izalco and elsewhere have favorable recollections of Martínez's regime.[7] Some pro-military stories circulated even before the massacres, such as ones about Martínez's indigenous origins and his sympathies for the pre-insurrection labor struggles. A typical account suggested that Martínez wanted the rural poor to engage in nonviolent protests so that he could use their mobilization as a political weapon against the oligarchy.[8] Others suggested that he personally was not to blame for La Matanza. The pro-Indian actions following the massacres gave additional credence to such stories.

The fruits of this alliance became visible in 1944. In April a democratic movement emerged among students, junior officers, professionals, and urban workers. Although the military rebellion of April failed, a *huelga de brazos caídos* in May led to the ouster of Martínez. The next months were a period of relative freedom of expression and political activity, on which the remnants of the working-class left and the democratic reformist students capitalized. Under the leadership of Dr. Arturo Romero, this alliance seemed assured of winning the elections scheduled for January 1945. Yet just as the Guatemalan democratic revolution triumphed in October, the

Martinista wing of the military staged a successful coup d'état, immediately instituting a state of siege. The Romerista coalition then organized to overthrow the new military junta. Over five hundred of Romero's backers, mainly students, launched an invasion from Guatemala that was overwhelmingly defeated in Ahuachapán.[9]

Although the people of Izalco and Nahuizalco did not participate in military actions, allegiances divided sharply along ethnic lines.[10] The indigenous people sided with the officialist candidate and also promised to seek vengeance for 1932 against those who supported the progressive democrat Romero. Indians in both towns wielded arms and threatened ladinos. Angel Olivares, of Nahuizalco, recalls Indians reminding ladinos of 1932 and then warning, "Now we'll see!"[11] Indigenous support for a rightist military figure paralleled the situation in Guatemala at the same time, when many indigenous people supported Ponce against the democratic revolution. This seemingly anomalous support for right-wing authoritarians whose hands were soaked in indigenous blood can only be understood in the context of a deep divide in the political culture of the two countries, dramatically exacerbated in Salvador by the legacy of 1932. In Salvador indigenous support mobilized for the military regime against a ladino-dominated democratic coalition marked perhaps the only significant indigenous political mobilization until the 1970s, an anomaly amid a political culture of fear.

Experience of Terror and the Absence of Mourning

The epigraphs at the beginning of this chapter are among numerous testimonies of eyewitnesses who recalled the sensation of overwhelming fear in 1932. On a more prosaic level, there were other symptoms of fear and trauma. Lieutenant Muñoz commented that the women who came to see him from Nahuizalco in October 1932 had a "terrible fear of authority."[12] The granddaughter of a survivor recalled that her grandmother would shout every time children would pop the plastic bags used as liquid containers.[13] Other informants describe the affect-less relations between parents (especially males) and their children. In video interviews, survivors themselves exhibit little expression or affect in their voices and faces. Others related that they felt fear whenever they saw soldiers on patrol. An ethnographic study carried out during the 1970s found that people in Sónzacate were still afraid even to walk by the municipal building.[14] Another informant described how a female survivor died of "affliction."[15] Military power certainly forms part of the explanation for the widespread adoption of a narrative that suppressed indigenous agency. Yet this experience of terror also affected the way informants remembered or could not remember specific events related to the insurrection and massacre.

There was little chance for individual or collective mourning, a fundamental step in any healing process. On the most basic level this was because many people simply did not know where their loved ones lay—they could neither be buried nor mourned. On 5 February 1932 El Diario de El Salvador reported: "At the moment in the department of Sonsonate, and in many places in Ahuachapán and some in Santa Ana, pork meat has become so discredited that it has almost no value . . . All of this is the consequence of pigs eating in great quantities the flesh of corpses that have been left in the fields."[16] Further evidence of this macabre phenomenon comes from several informants who recall that it was a long time before local folks would eat pork again.[17]

In addition to the lack of knowledge about the whereabouts of the corpses some informants claim that fear of repression blocked the possibility of proper mourning. The granddaughter of a survivor stated: "The mourners were afraid to have a wake for fear of the authorities."[18] Only in extremely rare cases could mourners practice the *novena*, the most critical rite in the Catholic mourning process, held on the ninth day following a death. An account based on ethnographic research in the late 1920s related a practice from a previous generation: "The deceased stays in the tomb for nine days, without being covered with earth until the people have demonstrated their love by night and by day . . . Once this display of love has come to an end, then it is covered with earth."[19] During the 1950s Richard Adams found that in Indian and ladino villages of El Salvador the practice of the novena, still a fundamental mourning ritual, involved eight days of familial prayer and a public gathering of prayer and refreshment on the ninth.[20] In 1932 there was no possibility of performing novenas for the victims. At some mass grave sites, however, widows did place crosses and left flowers annually. In El Carrizal in particular they maintained three "clandestine" grave sites. One informant recalled, "When they had been dead for one year, the mourners would go to see them; they would adorn the tombs, they would fix them up and fill them with flowers. When the mourners started to die, all the enfloradas began to disappear. Now you can't even see the tombs that were right here."[21]

The informants' narratives suggest the tenuous nature of generational transmission of memory and mourning; the practice of veneration did not survive the widows of the victims. Rosario Lué of Nahuizalco observed, "When the children grew up we stopped leaving flowers."[22] It is unclear why that practice ceased and why the crosses were not maintained. Some informants suggest that they were dissuaded from continuing to leave flowers at the mass graves because of a lack of assurance that their loved ones were actually buried at the site.[23] Another suggested that the privatization of land prevented the preservation of the clandestine cemeteries. One informant offered an economic explanation for an inability to mourn: "We couldn't [venerate my father properly] because in order to pray properly you have to buy coffee, bread, candles and prepare everything for the *rezadoras* . . . in the case of my father there was nothing, but in some other homes they mentioned him [in their prayers] but in my own home he was forgotten."[24]

Even those who could mourn their loved ones privately had no social framework in which to mitigate grief. The inability to mourn deaths of loved ones was probably akin to that experienced in the USSR during the great purges of the late 1930s. As the historian Catherine Merridale writes, "Personal grief had no wider framework, no mirror in which to observe itself gradually diminishing. In this sense, the official denial of loss compounded initial acts of state violence . . . The social recognition of violent death is a crucial stage in the process by which the bereaved come to terms with loss individually and as members of society as a whole."[25]

There was no form of social recognition in El Salvador, much less the development of a coherent narrative of events that would allow for recovery, that is, "the conversion of traumatic into narrative memory." As Elizabeth Snyder Hook writes, summarizing a generation of trauma scholarship, "Research of the last several decades reveals that the negative repercussions of trauma are compounded by the fact that, often, the survivor is rendered incapable of communicating his or her experience to others. The atrocities suffered are so painful, so overwhelming, that the victim's only means of psychic survival is to banish all memories of the event from the realm of discourse, in effect to equate silence with an absence of suffering. . . . Yet it is this very dismissal of trauma, and the resulting absence of any testimony to one's experience that blocks the victims' path to recovery."[26]

We have neither the empirical evidence nor the methodological tools to posit traumatized memories as a key causal explanation of the long term social and cultural transformations wrought by the massacres of 1932.[27] Nevertheless it behooves us intellectually and morally to recognize the probability that the survivors' witness of atrocity and experience of fear did scar them, and that their inability to mourn publicly impeded their ability to heal themselves. To alleviate the continuing pain inflicted by trauma, survivors living under military rule had little alternative but to silence the memories and avoid any effort to give meaning to the deaths of their loved ones.

The immediate impact of military power and discourse after 1932 strongly conditioned the suppression of indigenous agency among the terrorized population. As we have argued, there are glaring discrepancies between the documentary evidence of mobilization, repression, and insurrection and survivors' memories, which completely suppress indigenous agency in the insurrection. At times informants categorized the massacres as the work of "communists," or more frequently of el comunismo. Ramón Esquina, an indigenous campesino from a canton of Nahuizalco, offered one of numerous examples of this suppression of indigenous agency in memories of the insurrection: "A señor from Juayúa arrived with a mule. He was in contact with some people from Turín, who appeared at around five in the afternoon. You would see truckloads of guardias in the surrounding areas and the movements of these groups before the looting. The town of Nahuizalco was unjustly labeled communist by the authorities, on account of these people who came from Turín."[28] An informant from the canton of El Carrizal offered a similar testimony:

> And those people from Turín decided to come to steal here in Nahuizalco; they committed the robbery and they burned down the Alcaldía, and they took all the loot from Nahuizalco and the hacienda. Then they didn't say it was the people from Turín anymore, but they blamed the people from Carrizal instead.[29]

These informants emphasize the agency of non-Indians from Turín in the revolutionary takeover of Nahuizalco. Similarly, indigenous survivors from Izalco and Nahuizalco consistently blamed ladinos for insurrectionary action and exculpated Indians from any participation.

Charles R. Hale's recent work on Guatemala is instructive in its examination of radical changes in military strategy and the development of a military-inflected discourse about the repression. After depicting the genocidal thrust of the army's initial campaign in Chimaltenango, he writes: "By mid-1982, it had begun to follow a different logic. The army sought not to eliminate but to control the indigenous population, not even to eliminate the material bases of indigenous culture, but rather, to reshape it, with the utmost violence if necessary . . . affirming a space to be Indian within the constraints imposed by a fiercely militarized disciplinary state . . . repression provided a terrifying incentive to live within these constraints, while also advancing the perverse conclusion that dissenters were to blame for their own demise."[30] Military victory in Guatemala, as in El Salvador in 1932, conditioned the emergence of a narrative framework for understanding the repression. In Guatemala the *dos demonios* narrative emerged that posited a largely innocent indigenous population caught between two ladino military forces, "equally self-interested and brutal, both victimizers of civilians caught haplessly between." Although there is no direct analogue in El Salvador, the military-inflected narrative also emphasized the notion of innocence, extending it to include the Indian dead and survivors and even, in a sense, the troops. We earlier stressed how the phrase "they killed the just for the sinners" condensed fundamental understandings of the consequences of the massacre.[31] On the one hand it suggested the innocence of the indigenous victims, and on the other it created confusion about agents and victims. According to indigenous informants, the revolutionaries were always "others," for example mulattoes from Turín and Atiquizaya. The death of innocents clouds the salient questions of who did what to whom and why. At the very least, with the fatal construction indio = comunista radically broken, the onus of the guilt could be placed on communist trickery. In this version the military were trapped into killing the wrong people. The discursive creation of indigenous innocence in the insurrection, playing on a traditional theme, was largely successful at the cost of suppressing indigenous agency from the narratives of mobilization and insurrection. The suppression rendered the narrative of the insurrection incoherent, allowing for the military version to infiltrate local memories.

Brandt Peterson, drawing upon the work of Suárez-Orozco, discusses a three-part psychocultural response to terror: "denial, rationalization, and internalization-elaboration." Although power and propaganda often promote a denial that an event has taken place, denial can have varied political motivations and effects. More significantly, the response of "rationalization" was widespread among survivors, in particular the contradictory idea that those involved in an activity would be executed and yet that the executions were arbitrary. Peterson draws a fascinating conclusion about rationalization in the context of El Salvador post-1932 from his reading of Suárez-Orozco: "The point in these rationalizations is the contradiction between knowing that the killing itself is or was irrational and that one could never assure her safety on the one hand, and the insistence that any behavior that might appear political must be avoided on the other. In spite of the acknowledgement that people who were not involved in political activities, people who were 'innocent' by any measure, were none the less killed, a kind of irrational rationalization is formed that insists that there is a way to insure one's safety despite the clear evidence that no one is safe in the end. Thus niña Menche says that they killed everyone even though 'there were lots who were not involved.' That is why, she explains, she always told her children to stay away from politics and organizations."[32] This kind of "convoluted rationalization" formed an integral component of the ubiquitous trope of "mataron los justos por los pecadores." For Peterson this kind of rationalization resides in "an ultimately impossible effort to attribute linear reason to the traumatic experience.[33]

In view of the power of the military narrative, the suppression of indigenous agency, and the "rationalization effect," it is remarkable that there is so much clarity and unanimity in the memories of the El Canelo and Nahuizalco killings. Tentatively we could argue that the collective nature of this memory derives from the unambiguous moral position of the murdered Nahuizalqueños and the evil of the perpetrators. Both those killed in the canton of El Canelo and those executed while awaiting their *boleto de identidad* were innocent victims who had not been implicated in *el robo* and were divorced from *el comunismo*. Indeed the three weeks that separated the uprising from the last round of killing may have removed not only the victims but also the military and élite perpetrators from the more ambiguous categories of actors involved in the mobilization and the immediate repression. In other words, rather than communists, looters, and ladinos, the relevant categories became deceitful landlords, the military, and innocent indigenous workers.[34] In Nahuizalco the suppression of indigenous agency therefore did not impede survivors from identifying local sources of evil, thus subverting the official discourse.

Magic and Miracles

Religion, magic, and martyrdom formed another realm that was immune from official discourse. Rural people lived in worlds imbued with religiosity and magic and often cast the narratives of repression and survival in religious frames. To cite a common example, many survivors remembered that the killing lasted for forty days and nights, recalling the biblical period of penance.

Indians practiced an intimate form of saint worship. An ethnographer in the mid-1970s reported that "regarding the devotion for the saints . . . among the 'naturales' they are considered representatives of the divine, but they attribute to them very human needs and passions. The saints eat, sleep, get dressed, get angry, pray, suffer, etc. Altars dedicated to a particular saint are to be found in every house."[35] Indians and others mobilized the support of their saints in defense against the repression in 1932. As we saw earlier, saintly apparitions saved entire villages from harm. In Santo Domingo de Guzmán, an informant related the kernel of the village's social memory of 1932. As a large group of armed men approached Santo Domingo,

> A man with long white hair appeared. "Where are you going?" They couldn't shoot him. "We are going into that town. We are going to finish off that pueblo there." They couldn't shoot him.
>
> "You must go," said the man with the long white hair. He defended the pueblo.[36]

Saints saved collectivities, in Santo Domingo and elsewhere, from the revolutionary insurgents. In Tepecoyo the patron saint, San Esteban, appeared on an unusually large white horse and halted the advancing insurrectionary forces. A man on a large white horse also appeared in Nahuilingo (near Sonsonate) to halt the revolutionary advance on Sonsonate. In March 1932 the archbishop of San Salvador offered up the apocalyptic image of a *caballo rojo* as a key symbol in its anti-insurgent discourse.[37] Although we cannot with assurance ascribe the white horse to an apocalyptic imaginary rooted in the Bible, its function as a defender against communism does suggest its compatibility with the emerging military discourse.

Unlike stories of collective salvation, divine intervention saved individuals from the military and not from the insurgents. Consider the case of an indigenous artisan of El Carrizal: "It was the custom of Lázaro Patricio to appear in the performances during the fiestas of San Juan every year. It was around that time, he says, when he was coming back home from rehearsing, that around the Finca Las Flores they caught him and took him back to the cemetery. Then they gathered together a lot of people and the soldiers made a long grave. At the end they made them line up and they killed them.

And then it was that señor Lázaro, because he had great faith in the patron San Juan Bautista, the patron here in Nahuizalco, he begged San Juan. Lázaro was already on the edge of the grave, but in that instant that he prayed to San Juan, he was suddenly removed from the grave. Before he knew it, he was coming back from there and he says that when he passed the Finca las Flores, he could hear the sound of bullets that killed all the others."[38] Saints sometimes did intervene on the side of revolutionary leftists (Lázaro apparently was an SRI sympathizer). In another case Manuel Murillo, the union and SRI organizer in Jayaque, used the Niño de Atocha to protect himself from the repression. Murillo held an image of the Niño de Atocha, the patron saint of prisoners and pilgrims, for ninety days. When he emerged from his state of hiding, the authorities did not arrest him.[39] Every year subsequently he would celebrate a mass in honor of the Niño de Atocha.

Cuisnahuat had been a center of radical activity, and at least one hundred of its inhabitants participated in the attack on the barracks at Sonsonate. At some point shortly after the insurrection, authorities arrested the local leader Martín Bermúdez and locked him up in the Sonsonate jail. His wife prayed for three days in church to the patron saint of Cuisnahuat, San Lucas. Bermúdez then appeared back in town explaining that he had escaped from prison.[40]

Non-Christian forms of magic also played a pivotal role in narratives. Informants today remember how magic permeated rural life. Miguel Urbina of Ceiba del Charco, Izalco, said there was an *espíritu de brujos*.[41] An indigenous informant from Pushtan, Nahuizalco, commented that those who survived had to learn "the bad things to defend themselves from the military."[42] Andrés Pérez of Pushtan counterposes magic today with earlier forms: "My father had an uncle named José María Hernández. He practiced witchcraft; he was a 'brujo.' But he wasn't just a brujo; today a lot of people call themselves brujo."[43]

The magical and religious dimension of life was important to most sectors in society, before and after the Matanza, and there was no clear bifurcation between modern and traditional sectors. SRI members studied omens as others might study revolutionary texts.[44] Years after the defeat Doroteo Lopez recalled that an Izalqueño indigenous comrade at a PCS meeting in the mid-1930s offered to demonstrate to his fellow cell members that magic did not involve a "pact with the devil," saying that "it is a natural thing that has nothing to do with the satanic."[45] That magic is still a potent force in an otherwise thoroughly modern society challenges any facile relegation of this realm to the tradition-bound past. Then as now, brujos and brujas generally exercised their powers for good or evil in personal matters of love, envy, and revenge and rarely in matters of social consequence.

Yet in moments of severe crisis, people not surprisingly employed magical powers to try to elude death. Various accounts relate that insurgents about to be executed transformed themselves into animals.[46] An informant in El Carrizal recalled: "The grandfather of my wife, Candelaria Reyes, told us that the troops arrived at the home of a señor whose name I don't remember. But when the troops arrived, that person was not there: he had turned into a bunch of bananas."[47] Others survived by turning into monkeys; except when there was a crisis, such a conversion was a sign of evil.

Andrés Pérez's father recounted what happened when he went to visit his uncle, the tío mago mentioned above: "I went to ask my uncle three days before the killing—what's going to happen? He said to me yes, and the spirit let out a laugh. Three days later they killed him."[48] For the narrator, Pérez's father, the spirit's mocking laughter and the subsequent demise of his uncle proved the weakness of his magical powers and the irrelevance of magic. Yet for many others, the overwhelming power and the terror inflicted on a defenseless population strongly influenced understandings of how people had survived. People hid out for weeks in holes in the ground, breathing through reeds. Others hid for weeks in the rocky, cave-like region of Los Teshcales near San Isidro. Many hid in trees. From any perspective their survival was miraculous.

Magical survival at times related to Christian themes. In one striking account, troops fired three volleys against an insurgent. After each volley the rebel arose again. Similar miracles were recounted in Izalco, Colón, and Sacacoyo. In Sacacoyo informants recall that when troops tried to execute a local insurgent, Lucio Linares, in front of the church, "they shot him and then he got up again. They shot him again, and he arose again. Then they took him to Armenia, where they shot him again and again he arose. Finally they burned him and buried him alive."[49] In addition to the resurrection theme, rising from death three times resonates with Christ's three statements on the cross. Informants in three sites related very similar versions of this resurrection, suggesting an important motif, a submerged and subversive attribution of saintly qualities to the revolutionaries. These tales of religious faith, magic, and heroism are all about individuals; divine intervention in favor of collectivities was always against the insurrectionary forces. The interventions served to ennoble the victims of the massacre but did little to restore any form of agency to indigenous participants in the movement.

The magico-religious dimension of rural western Salvadoran life is an important area of research for historians and anthropologists. One of the major thrusts of the *iglesia popular* was to counter "magical consciousness." Progressive priests defined this as consciousness that "fatalistically appeals to magical explanations and finds in a distorted vision of God explanations for the irreversibility of such situations . . . As the difference between the socio-cultural world and the natural world becomes obscured, the individual forgets that this world has been and is co-produced by himself, by his work, and by his passivity, allowing for the development of fatalistic attitudes."[50]

Although the liberation theology conception of magical consciousness is not entirely congruent with the pattern of supernatural belief that characterized much of the Salvadoran countryside, it does point to an interesting problem. As other scholars have argued, the iglesia popular grew out of Catholic Action, one of whose primary goals was to extirpate popular religiosity from the practices and ideas of its parishioners and converts. As the above descriptions of magical consciousness suggest, for progressive priests that goal remained essentially unchanged, since they viewed the magical elements as inextricably tied to those of passivity and resignation. Some of the testimony reproduced here offers, to the contrary, an alternative view: magical or alternative religious perspectives do not necessarily directly shape understandings of the social world.

Violence and the Subordination of Indigenous Culture

There is no doubt that the events of 1932 had an important impact on the decline of Nahuatl-Pipil in western Salvador, although not through the prohibition suggested by contemporary indigenous and leftist militants.[51] The demise of the language has meant the loss of at least some aspects of a worldview, namely those areas of experience and communal lore that the Spanish language could not express. Both Indians and non-Indians had long regarded the language as the sine qua non of indigenous identity. Thus language loss accompanied a severe questioning of the legitimacy of indigenous identity by internal and external actors. In short, the demise of Pipil as a dominant idiom in western Salvador was not merely an aspect of cultural change, inevitable or not, but rather a catalyst of it, both because of its intrinsic value as a vehicle of cultural knowledge and expression and because of its salience as an emblem of authenticity.

In chapter 4 we argued that Pipil usage was in rapid decline in many areas of western Salvador before 1932; there is no doubt that the massacres accelerated the pace. Oral and documentary sources, however, contradict the leftist and Indian activist view that governmental policies after La Matanza directly caused the accelerated process of mestizaje in the 1930s and 1940s, suggesting that the loss of ethnic signs had primarily endogenous causes. The possibility exists that bilingual speakers in particular associated the indigenous language with the killings and thus avoided speaking it. There is some anecdotal evidence that people in Izalco were afraid to speak the language immediately after the massacre. However, not only did the Martínez regime refrain from prohibiting use of the Nahuatl-Pipil language, but at least one National Guard officer actively tried to revivify it. Lieutenant Muñoz, the first director of the Rafael Campo School for orphaned Indian children on the outskirts of Izalco, stated in his inaugural address in August 1932: "The taciturn heart disappears with familiar conversations . . . you enter into his true soul when you speak his language. We have to revive it if we want the labors of the Escuela de Indígenas to be effective."[52] Muñoz then called for language training for the teachers of "Rafael Campo," where all instruction was to be offered in the indigenous language. He even called for Nahuatl instruction in all western Salvadoran schools. There was not, in Salvador of the early 1930s, an educational infrastructure that would have permitted his plan to be realized. Yet Muñoz's position within the National Guard and his appointment as school director do suggest that only a few months after the massacres the regime did not have the ethnocidal intentions often imputed to it by militants.

The misunderstanding of the historical record is of course understandable given what seems to have been a concerted effort by the regime to cover up all traces of the events of 1932 and the fear that the regime instilled in those who might have written about the consequences of the massacres. In addition to the disappearance from national archives of newspapers and other documents related to those events, there are striking examples of scholars and writers who published books and articles in the years, even decades, following 1932 that dealt with contemporary western indigenous communities and yet made no mention of the massacres.[53]

Another significant source of historical misunderstanding was a lack of recognition that well before 1932 language loss had advanced significantly. By that year the number of native speakers, including bilinguals, probably did not surpass 25,000 out of a total national indigenous population of perhaps 300,000. As we noted in chapter 4, there was a correlation between language loss and the spread of primary education. During the Martínez regime many schools were built in indigenous cantons, and without doubt, the education of orphans and other children contributed to the declining use of Nahuate.[54] Moreover, after La Matanza, with many adult males gone, there were even fewer opportunities or incentives to speak or listen to the indigenous language. As one informant stated, "At this time, most of the elderly folks spoke Nahuate. But since they killed the men, the women didn't teach it, since as women they didn't hang out with us young folks. No one in our canton has been interested in teaching us Nahuate."[55] Although this statement is hard to decipher, it does suggest that dominant gender norms, especially regarding adult female and adolescent males, impeded the recreation of a bilingual linguistic community.

Bilingual speakers predominated in several cantons of Nahuizalco and in Barrio Asunción of Izalco during the 1920s. Nahuate was the dominant language in the contiguous Nahuizalco cantons of Anal, Pushtan, Tajcuilulaj, and Sábana San Juan. Although village residents worked seasonally on coffee plantations they were not colonos: their household economy was largely based on subsistence economic activities (milpas and petate weaving). In these cantons the events of 1932 accelerated language loss, as people were thrust into greater contact with ladinos as the spaces of subsistence economic activities closed down. When coffee plantation owners or foremen came upon people speaking Nahuate, they scolded them: "hable bien . . . no hable chapeado" (speak well, don't speak all chopped up).[56] Another informant recalled the admonition: "Deje de hablar esas babosadas!" (Stop speaking that foolishness!).[57] Rosario Lué, of Anal Abajo, stated: "No we didn't speak Nahuate because it was impolite to speak it in front of outsiders. They could be offended."[58]

The "outsiders" were by no means exclusively ladinos, as more and more town-based Indians could not understand the language. Various elements

María Antonia Pérez,
El Canelo. Courtesy
of the Museo de la
Palabra y la Imagen.

seem to intermingle in the collective memory of language loss. At the most elemental level, in those cantons most affected by La Matanza, Nahuate had become a language of familial intimacy, and after 1932 that particular linguistic community had become drastically reduced. The fear of offending people cut both ways. Ladinos and non-Nahuate-speaking Indians could have taken offense at conversations they could not understand, and outsiders scorned Nahuate speakers.[59]

Finally, bilingualism was not easy to maintain either individually or collectively in a drastically reduced linguistic community, and people may have seen little point in expending more energy in an exhausting life when the payoffs seemed so paltry. There are numerous testimonies suggesting that the generation of children who survived the massacres had little interest in learning or speaking the language. María Antonia Pérez, of El Canelo, recalls: "My grandparents spoke to me in Nahuate . . . and so I learned it but when I had to go to work I forgot it."[60]

Writing in 1935, Adolfo Herrera Vega, a local ladino educator who had taught in Izalco for ten years, wrote (without any reference to the events of 1932), "Over the last few years, Nahuat has suffered a sharp decline."[61] Herrera Vega remarked on this phenomenon: "The most striking detail of this desire to forget the language is that most of the young Indians do not speak it and those who do are ashamed to speak it."[62] It is difficult to assess Herrera Vega's account of linguistic "shame" in relationship to 1932, since it was present as a linguistic factor before that year. Yet his account does unintentionally reveal how the *symbolic violence* of an educational institution, designed to help Indian children, provoked a strong sense of shame about language.[63] He writes, "The child arrives at school conditioned by the environment in which he grew up; he speaks very little; answers all questions with monosyllables, if at all. Almost always refuses to give his name . . . He is habitually sad and taciturn."[64]

The school examined the students to determine their intellectual age. One can only imagine the administration of the Binet-Simon tests to these children, who scored extremely low. Despite Herrera Vega's promotion of Pipil, symbolic violence riddled his own program for language instruction as he detailed the need to eliminate the children's dialectal form of Spanish, for example "piegra, magre, pagre" (instead of piedra, madre, padre).[65] The irony of imposing one language while wanting to save another is missed, but the message is no less poignant as the educator explains the risk of this method: "The teacher has to avoid this danger: when the Indian begins to learn Castellano, he becomes repulsed by his Pipil and considers it inferior. . . . We should understand that the disappearance of this dialect would be a shame."[66]

The perceived need to teach standard Spanish by denigrating the indigenous Spanish dialect could only have created more shame about other Indian linguistic and cultural forms. Elsewhere, Gould has touched on different aspects of the notion of vergüenza as a form of symbolic violence.[67] In western Salvador, shame about Nahuate (or about how one spoke Spanish) had a powerful impact well past the Matanza years. In Cuisnahuat and Santo Domingo de Guzmán, two municipalities outside the coffee zone, Nahuate was the main language of intimate communication for all generations until the 1970s. The Army and National Guard had spared both places in 1932. Linguistic change developed along lines quite different from those in the massacre-ravaged areas in and around Nahuizalco and Izalco. The first stage replicated the experience of the rest of the region: a younger generation began to distance itself from the language as a result of increasing interaction with ladinos. Consider the testimony of a Santo Domingo resident: "Well, I spoke Nahuate and later I learned to speak [in Spanish]. The patronos told me 'speak well' and so I had to learn how to speak like they did, to speak Spanish rapidly. At that time, I did speak some Spanish since all of the young kids spoke it; when I went to work in Sonsonate I couldn't speak to people in Nahuate, only in Spanish. In the work environment, I hung out with kids and you couldn't speak Nahuate . . . All of them spoke Spanish and had no interest in the other language."[68] Despite the radically different historical circumstances, this villager experienced linguistic change very similarly to other former Nahuate speakers, albeit at a different rhythm. More intense levels of contact with Ladinos and in particular patrones pushed him toward increasing reliance on Spanish.

In the 1970s Nahuate continued as an underground idiom among some families in the Nahuizalqueño cantons, and especially in Cuisnahuat and Santo Domingo. Linguists and anthropologists were convinced that many families throughout the region spoke the indigenous language at home but denied knowledge to outsiders. The second stage of language change, the shame and scorn of the younger generation, dealt a staggering blow to Nahuate. It is difficult to estimate the number of speakers in the cantons of Nahuizalco, but the linguist Lyle Campbell estimated that most adults in Santo Domingo as well as some forty in Cuisnahuat spoke the language. Yet those speakers were on the defensive. An ethnographer reported that in Cuisnahuat during the 1970s many indigenous youths rejected and even mocked the language of their parents: "The young people no longer speak Nahuate and they do not appreciate that their elders speak it. They think of it as a 'bayuncada' [silly] and they laugh at the Nahuat-speakers. They try to erase everything that stigmatizes them as Indians."[69]

There are similar stories about el refajo, the other salient ethnic marker of the Salvadoran Indians. As with the indigenous language, scholars and leftists have explained the disappearance of this female garment (really its decline) as a direct consequence of La Matanza. According to that version, racist repression drove women to wear ladino clothes. A few testimonies from Izalco and from the coffee zone of Nahuizalco offer some evidence to support that contention.[70] Nevertheless, there is abundant documentary and testimonial evidence that the most significant decline in the use of el refajo came at least two decades later. An article in National Geographic in 1944 offers visual and textual evidence that indigenous dress still predominated in the region: "Women dress in a wrap-around sarong type of skirt and loose blouse . . . Women of even the more modernized villages cling stubbornly to their sarong skirts. 'I will not put on a round skirt,' they say, speaking of the conventional women's dress."[71]

Indigenous women and men in El Salvador, as in the Nicaraguan highlands, offer several different explanations for the demise of indigenous garb. Most emphasize that the best fabric, imported from Guatemala at least since the 1940s, eventually became more expensive than ladino clothes. Others suggest that el refajo is not suitable for field or factory labor. One refajada claimed that her daughters did not want to wear it because it was "too hot."[72] These arguments are contradicted by those who underscore how much longer the garment lasts than ladino dress and note that indigenous women dressed in el refajo have always performed all manner of field and market labor. Regardless of the validity of the arguments, children subtly and not-so-subtly pressured their mothers to plegarse (change to ladino clothing).[73] Women compelled their children to wear it, but by adolescence they gave up the losing battle with their daughters: "I grew up that way, all of us refajadas. But my daughters didn't want to wear el refajo."[74]

Interviews and documentary sources point to the effect of formal primary and secondary education in leading children to pressure their mothers to abandon their refajos; there is little doubt that the pressure derived from a sense of shame about their mothers' dress.[75] An informant in El Carrizal relates, "Around the 1950s and 60s, all the women were refajadas. Refajo use declined with more civilization and intellectual development. When a son or daughter went to school or in meetings they were ashamed that their mothers wore refajos; there are still some around here who went through that: they wore el refajo and then changed to dresses."[76] Beyond rejecting a symbol of inferiority, it is likely that to a limited extent they had acquired some of the ladino prejudices about the "filthy" and "evil" nature of el refajo. Ladinos considered the garment "filthy" in both the ordinary and sexual senses of the word. Women supposedly did not wear what others thought of as undergarments with el refajo, thus offending ladino sensibilities. Others believed that the garment itself was a source of evil witchcraft.[77]

The cultural changes that took place in western El Salvador from 1940 to 1980 are unremarkable in the Latin American context. As has been shown in analyses by Joanne Rappaport in Colombia, Marisol de la Cadena in Peru, and Gould in Nicaragua, cultural mestizaje often occurs as a largely endogenous process with a minimum degree of coercion.[78] What is unique about the Salvadoran experience is that the decisive cultural changes took place against the backdrop of the massacres of 1932. This violence at once conditioned the emergence of sharply unequal power relations but at the same time provided a powerful trope that *explained* the cultural transformation as a coercive process.

The new cultural power of ladinos in turn conditioned what social psychologists call chains of shame and anger.[79] Indigenous people felt shame, for example, at speaking Nahuate in front of ladinos and at the same time despised those ladinos for making them feel that way. Ironically, where indigenous people refused to submit to the scornful gaze of ladinos, their sons and daughters absorbed the embarrassment. Consequently, the pace of losing ethnic markers accelerated in the 1960s and 1970s, primarily as they were rejected by a new generation that saw them as emblems of submission.

Gender, Generation, and Mestizaje

Generational shame about language and el refajo by the 1970s had political consequences, further dividing the surviving communities and eroding loyalty to emblems of indigenous ethnicity. As we noted in chapter 4, indigenous patriarchy in its different manifestations played a critical role in the development of ethnic tensions before 1930. In particular, greater economic contact with ladinos threatened indigenous male control over indigenous women, and the illegitimate and unrecognized offspring of ladino-indigenous unions deeply resented their fathers. After the events of 1932 the sexuality of Salvadoran indigenous women continued to be an extremely charged issue. First, *hacendados*, here as elsewhere, exerted their power sexually. Salarrué, a ladino of Sonsonate and a leading figure of Salvadoran letters, wrote the following in his novelistic rendition of La Matanza, written in 1933: "Indian women still turn their heads when they see automobiles pass them by . . . where according to them, go the enemies, the whites, the ladinos, the damned, the ugly. But like before the battle, the Indian woman, (impelled by a magnetic force of pure necessity, now even greater) will return to being the petatillo in the black market of slavery; she will once again allow herself to be possessed by the white and the mestizo."[80] This contemporaneous view of a sympathetic ladino blames the "whites and mestizos" for what the author suggests was a very widespread phenomenon. Yet he also echoes a common ladino and indigenous perception that the economic power of *los ricos* turned the impoverished Indians into *petatillos* (literally, small grass sleeping mats). Herrera Vega, the Izalqueño educator, also argued that there was widespread prostitution among indigenous women, particularly in Nahuizalco.[81] Finally, an observer at the U.S. embassy, commenting in 1933 upon a labor shortage in the coffee industry, wrote of rural-to-urban migrants: "The men prefer to become town 'sheiks' with a gaudy colored shirt in the evening and a casual job at a pittance less than farm labor," while the women prefer to become "ladies of easy virtue or become the unlawful wives of the sheiks."[82] In short, sympathetic observers (like informants today) insinuated that misery compelled many Indian women to prostitute themselves.

The view from the cantons was different. Although there are some discrepancies in the memories of informants about the role of the military and the hacendados, several informants directly blame the hacendados for coerced sex and for illegitimate births. María Antonia Perez, whose father was shot in El Canelo, argued that Gabino Mata abused widows: "Gabino Mata was fat and red-faced—very bad-tempered. He left many children of poor women. Any girl he happened to like, he just took. In Tajcuilullaj he left many daughters. He brought about the matanza in order to keep for himself the young women and the land."[83] There is not enough evidence to verify that landlords abused their female workers or servants in any significant numbers after the massacres. There is even less testimonial evidence of rape on the part of the military or political authorities at the time of the massacres. But birth records show that in the years following 1932 the rate of illegitimate births increased significantly.[84]

The products of these unions, which Salarrué called *descolorida* (although their color might have been pleasing to the mothers), carried a heavy emotional load. Consider the following testimony of a child born in Nahuizalco in 1932: "My grandmother was a servant for Gabino Mata. My mother used to visit her at the hacienda. So then I was born. Three years later, my mother died. Then my grandmother started to take me to the hacienda so Don Gabino could get to know me. He embraced me and told me that I was his child and he gave me his name. When I was ten years old, my grandmother died and I was left alone. Then I was sent to Don Gabino's hacienda to work cutting trees. My father remembered me, you know. He embraced me, 'My son, my son!' But I came there barefoot and I left barefoot."[85] It does not stretch the imagination to assume that those numerous children of hacendado-indigenous sexual relations have been tormented by similar memories (even without the intrusive probing of academics) and that anguish over origins and identity has caused much shame and resentment, as well as provided additional "physical" evidence of the eclipse of the indigenous population.

The coming of age of those people born around 1932, regardless of parentage, coincided with the decline in the more rigid forms of indigenous patriarchy. As in the highlands of Nicaragua, the decline of indigenous patriarchy in Salvador is treated as a crucial moment in the loss of indigenous identity. Some thirty or forty years ago, arranged marriages, a key institution of patriarchy and endogamy, began to die out. Not coincidentally, the new generation of the 1960s and 1970s pushed away the last vestiges of arranged marriage practices at the same time as young women rejected el refajo.

The questioning of traditional indigenous cultural forms became particularly intense during the 1960s and 1970s. Beyond language and dress, the youths contested their elders' religious beliefs, as well as their deep suspicion of everything ladino. That questioning coincided with an awakening to the possibilities of political and social change. An ethnographer in the municipality of Cuisnahuat, with a population of 6,800 in 1971, identified the major political fault line in the community as being not between the small ladino population and Indians but between generations: "The most important relational problems are evident between the more conservative groups of 'naturales,' who want to retain their customs, and those groups who, on the contrary, accept foreign influences and wish to break with the past."[86] When the generational conflict erupted on the local political scene in Cuisnahuat, the actors were not clearly identified with national political forces, but a short time later some of the youths did gravitate to the left.[87]

1980: The Return of Violent Repression

The cultural transformation within indigenous communities coincided with the renewal of social and political mobilization in the west. A leftist message of social and political change again came to the western towns and villages, this time carried by a peasant organization sponsored by the United States, radical priests, high school students, and young urban workers. Although this wave of mobilization during the late 1970s and 1980s never approximated the levels attained in other regions of the country, to recognize it is nonetheless to challenge the generally accepted view of widespread political passivity in the west, the legacy of 1932.

The generational struggle within the indigenous communities and the concomitant intensification of cultural mestizaje did not directly translate into radicalization. Many indigenous youths participated neither in the cultural change nor in the new movements. Others participated in the cultural shift with no political or social engagement. At the same time, the mobilization affected nonindigenous areas (by the 1970s the large majority of the western population), where such cultural issues were irrelevant. Among the non-Indians of Ahuachapán and La Libertad memories of the events of 1932 had a much less pacifying influence on even the older generations. The events were at times posited more as an example of a tradition of struggle and hatred of the military than as the imperative voiced in the cantones of Nahuizalco and elsewhere to "never belong to an organization."[88]

Throughout the 1970s student activists and unionized workers in the western cities of Santa Ana, Ahuachapán, and Sonsonate experienced processes of social and political protest like those experienced in San Salvador and other cities, followed by repression and further radicalization. To cite an important example, in January 1978 between six hundred and a thousand workers went on strike at the Central Izalco, a major sugar mill between Izalco and Sonsonate. The army intervened, crushed the strike, and imprisoned twenty-two union activists, some of whom were executed after their release.[89]

In Nahuizalco, Cuisnahuat, and Santo Domingo the cultural change did allow for the circulation of progressive ideas that previously would have been silenced. Generational conflict also created the conditions in which youths rejected their parents' "Indianness"—specifically, the surviving ethnic emblems—while still recognizing their own indigenous heritage. Like the process that we uncovered in Nicaragua in the 1960s and in Jayaque in the early 1930s, this form of mestizaje was in some cases a precondition for an alliance with the left.[90]

Yet we must not overstate the impact of mestizaje in the west. Although many youths rejected any form of indigenous identity, during the 1980s an indigenous organization, the Asociación Nacional Indígena Salvadoreña, which promoted an agrarian reform and a culturalist agenda, appealed to different sectors of the population, including youth. ANIS (whose history remains to be written) seems to have emerged from the Unión Comunal Salvadoreño, an organization backed by USAID and AIFLD and the Christian Democratic Party. During the mid-1970s its primary function was to obtain bank credits for smallholders and colonos. This peasant organization established important bases of support in the cantons of Nahuizalco, in Santo Domingo de Guzmán, and in the department of Ahuachapán, primarily among basic-grains producers. Despite its mild reformist inclinations, the UCS was significant precisely because it represented one of the first alternatives to the Partido de Conciliación Nacional (the official party) in the western countryside.[91] By 1979 the military regime was targeting UCS activists for repression. Informants cite the lack of political or ideological response by the group to repression as a key factor in explaining the rapid transition from reformism to revolution among a relatively small group of activists in western Salvador.[92] Margarito Vásquez, of Santo Domingo de Guzmán, offered an account of this transformation: "Well, we began to understand all of this when we organized through the Unión Comunal Salvadoreño. From there we started to get to know people from other places. . . . So here we established a nucleus for communicating with other groups . . . But later it withdrew [from the UCS] and it wasn't referred to under any name; I think they took it as a clandestine group. All the youth would get together in hiding, clandestinely. This began in '79. Many people came, and various groups began to be organized. Some worked with one group, others with the other one. There were at least three groups. Later we put things into practice."[93] The principal difference between the radicalization process in places like Santo Domingo and Nahuizalco and in the northern and eastern parts of the country was the complete absence of a radical peasant organization engaged in wage or land struggles.[94] Although the history of the UCS has yet to be examined, apparently its limited agenda, focused primarily on obtaining credits for cooperatives, attracted fewer followers than did the more radical organizations in the other parts of the country, which developed mass followings before succumbing to state-sponsored terrorist repression by 1980. Throughout the country, however, the net result was the same for activists: the transition from legal, pacific forms of activity to support of a violent revolutionary movement as a viable route to withstanding the repression.[95]

There was less active support for the leftist alternative in the west than in other parts of the country. In 1980 in Santo Domingo de Guzmán (population under ten thousand), between fifty and a hundred people participated in revolutionary organizations to some degree. In El Carrizal and El Canelo, cantons of Nahuizalco with a combined population of less than three thousand, some fifty to sixty youths joined communal organizations affiliated with revolutionary groups. In Santa Ana, La Libertad, and Ahuachapán, where unions made significant inroads in the coffee industry, more people joined leftist organizations.

On 15 October 1979 reformist elements in the military overthrew the rightist military regime, the most repressive since Martínez. The civilian-military regime that took over the reins of government had a forceful reformist and democratizing agenda that offered tremendous hope to most Salvadorans, including those identified with the left. But the regime proved unable to contain the paramilitary and military forces on the right, and some of the guerrilla groups responded with violent resistance. On 22 January 1980 an estimated 250,000 backers of the revolutionary left took to the streets of San Salvador in probably the largest demonstration in the country's history. Soldiers opened fire on the demonstrators, killing twenty and wounding two hundred. These killings of unarmed protesters marked the beginning of a period of unbridled violent repression that would claim over eight thousand civilian lives over the next year.

At the moment of the October coup, the leftist organizations in the west were in the earliest stages of development. Despite the far greater popular impact of mobilization in the early 1930s compared to that of the late 1970s and early 1980s, there is one key similarity: both were extremely compressed in time. Whereas the earlier transition from union to revolutionary activity took place over a two-year period (December 1929 to January 1932), for most of the rural activists in the department of Sonsonate in 1980, a similar transition of political styles and loyalties was telescoped into a period of months. In the cantons of Nahuizalco, the first political experience that some of the youths had was with the Fuerzas Populares de Liberación, a semi-clandestine political and military organization that by 1981 would form part of the guerrilla front Frente Farabundo Martí de Liberación Nacional (FMLN). In both the early 1930s and 1980 state violence was the radicalizing factor that hastened the events. That said, it is not entirely clear why the process started later in the west than in the rest of the country.

Beyond suggesting that 1932 traumatized the population, scholars have advanced structural arguments to explain the relative absence of radical activity. The boom in the coffee economy in the latter part of the 1970s translated into significant wage increases in the sector without the pressure of notable union activity. Whereas between 1971 and 1980 real minimum wages declined in the sugar sector by 4 percent and increased in cotton by only 3 percent, in coffee there was a 59 percent increase.[96] With compelling comparative evidence, Wickham-Crowley argues that the lowest levels of radicalization would take place in those areas that have already experienced proletarianization. A high proportion of farmers to landless proletarians would indicate an area in the process of proletarianization and a likely candidate for radical protest. The author thus explains the lack of radicalism in the western coffee-growing departments as a function of their high proportion of agricultural workers to owners.[97] Although these arguments are compelling, they essentially explain why there were not many strikes on the coffee plantations. Yet they do not tell us to what degree full-time employment was available in the west, or to what degree coffee harvesters could supplement their labor by farming or obtain other sources of income. Coffee pickers became militants, as we will see, but it was their lives off the plantation that were equally salient in the process. The problem of finding sufficient work to do outside of harvest times became all the more compelling in areas of extremely unequal land tenure arrangements, such as Sonsonate, where in 1964 just over two hundred properties occupied 60 percent of the total land.[98]

Although the structural explanation helps to explain the social struggle in the west, it is impossible to avoid some reference to 1932. In the first place, the legacy of the informal military-indigenous alliance and an intense network of surveillance led to greater levels of local collaboration with the military regime during the 1970s. Most significantly, this reality confirmed the perception that the western population had been traumatized into passivity by 1932, in turn influencing leftist organizations, consciously or unconsciously; they avoided trying to organize the region until its local militants besieged them with requests to do so. Regardless of the reasons for the delayed mobilization, western Salvadorans, both Indians and ladinos, suffered the same fate as their compatriots in the rest of the country. But because of the myth of the trauma of 1932—the notion that there was no political or military activity in the west—the very real violent repression that took place has been largely overlooked or forgotten.

The first killings took place in Santo Domingo de Guzmán on 26 February 1980. The local militants, affiliated with two revolutionary groups, were up at dawn, expecting a military action. Soldiers surrounded the village. During the confusion some militants managed to escape, but soldiers killed eleven others. A few days later they executed three others identified with the left.[99] The military and its paramilitary allies then placed the village under martial law: "the other young men who could escape fled to Santa Ana, but the rest of us stayed here. The armed forces were coming, along with the death squads, who are from this very place, but they would cover their faces so that no one could recognize them. That is how we were left without any connections, and the people suffered for being 'stained.' "[100] In Santo Domingo the incipient organization connected to the Ligas Populares 28 de Febrero barely managed to survive the intense repression by hiding out at night and bringing almost all political activity to a halt.

El Carrizal was another center of incipient leftist activity in 1980. Although it was only ten miles from Santo Domingo, there was virtually no contact with their organization. Several union members were among the founders of the local organization, secretly affiliated with the Fuerzas Populares de Liberación (FPL). The two leaders of the group had participated in the violently repressed Central Azucarera strike in Izalco in 1978, and one had received some military instruction in Cuba. A few others had participated in construction unions and strikes in the city of Sonsonate. Most of the twenty to thirty male youths affiliated with the group worked on coffee plantations during the planting and harvest periods. According to informants, the tight relation between the finca owners and the military, exemplified by the arrival of the military in response to the slightest expression of discontent (usually about working and living conditions or cheating at the scales), drove home the connections between the struggle for economic survival and the need for revolutionary political change.[101] From January until July 1980 the newly minted FPL members traveled to San Salvador to participate in demonstrations, but otherwise maintained a low profile.

Yet the repressive forces, as in Santo Domingo, did not allow such consciousness and incipient organization to develop. The paramilitary peasant organization ORDEN (Organización Democrática Nacional) played a fundamental role in the repression throughout the country, and the west was no exception. In the Nahuizalco area, *finqueros* and their *capataces* formed the leadership of ORDEN and compelled their colonos and other workers to join it. Their most significant role was to call for military intervention in the canton and to finger militants once the military arrived. On 13 July 1980 two army battalions marched into El Carrizal from four directions. They entered each house, with a list of names. Masked men (presumably local ORDEN members) singled out suspected militants, who were immediately executed. Thirteen died that day. Some escaped and spent weeks hiding out in caves.[102] The military maintained a massive presence of troops over the next weeks, however, during which time death squads executed twenty-nine other male youths in the canton.

El Canelo, the site of the massacre on Mata's hacienda in 1932, became another zone of organization and repression in 1980. As in Santo Domingo and El Carrizal, the recently formed local radical group had engaged in no significant activities other than meetings. During the same year the death squads visited the canton. Twenty-one years later we interviewed María Eduwiges Pérez, daughter of María Antonia Pérez, whose husband had been shot by soldiers near the same house in 1932. María Eduwiges's facial expressions and voice betrayed the range of intense emotions that had afflicted her in the 1980s. She recalled how her *compañero* Miguel Hernández had joined the FPL. He had buried some arms for future use and the military had discovered the cache.

On a Thursday, July 3, my husband said to me, "I'm going to start making the milpa and I have to go buy the fertilizer." He finished work early, at around 11, and he said, "I'm leaving now to buy the fertilizer." He left that day, the third of July, and never returned after that date. Three days later they told me that they had taken him down in Sonzácate. When they told me I went to tell his parents and they told me they didn't know anything and they didn't want to get involved. Trucks full of soldiers were coming to set up a station here.

The death squad came on Friday. They came into my house—I was making breakfast for my children—they told me to come out and that if I didn't want to they would leave me dead. They pushed their shotgun against me. I had a base-ball cap with the letter 'f' on it—it belonged to my son. They tore it apart thinking it had something to do with the FMLN. They said to me that if I wanted I could continue to sleep there . . . 'In the night we have to come.' What I did was I went to stay with my brother in another cantón. They caught a lot of the muchachos—[they sliced] a cheek like this, or [cut off] an arm, and they would walk around with them like that, telling them to turn in whoever they knew. They had my husband. They had cut off one of his cheeks. He lasted a long time. They killed a lot of people, 32 persons.[103]

This remarkable testimony graphically synthesizes the brutality of the repression. The intervening decades have done little to lessen the horror for María Eduwiges or for the listener. The banality of one moment contrasts sharply with the brutality of the next (as in her mother's description of her husband's death at breakfast in 1932). Her compañero goes to buy some

Political Prisoners,
El Salvador, 1980.
Courtesy of the
Museo de la Palabra
y la Imagen.

María Eduwiges
Pérez, El Canelo.
Courtesy of the
Museo de la Palabra
y la Imagen.

fertilizer for the milpa. She is feeding her children. Her child has a cap with an "F" printed on it. A death squad bursts upon the quotidian scene. From that point on the story turns horrifying. The *escuadraneros* cut off cheeks, cut off ears, in order to get their victims to turn over others. Beyond the immediate horror of the scenes, the very public nature of the torture is striking. Far more typically, the military and the death squads tortured their victims out of public view and then left the corpses in relatively isolated locations.[104] These acts of torture surpass any similar violent acts in 1932. If mass execution was the modus operandi of the earlier repression, in 1980 the military added torture to accompany massacre. The terroristic violence of the early 1980s found its justification in 1932. As Greg Grandin has pointed out, the administration of President Ronald Reagan avoided blame for its own complicity with the death squads by citing their deep roots in Salvadoran history.[105] Its other rhetorical move was to separate the death squads' activity from the purview of the military allies of the United States.

Testimonies from these villages offer a different perspective on death squads. Unlike in much of the rest of the country, the death squads and the military in these areas were interchangeable: the testimonies make no distinction between soldiers and *escuadraneros de la muerte*. Rather, *escuadraneros* referred to the most brutal of the soldiers or to those masked people (presumably neighbors belonging to ORDEN) who signaled out "subversives." This is an important point, as much of the rationale for sending aid to the Salvadoran regime from Washington hinged on the distinction between the death squads and the military. According to the Reagan administration, either aid from the United States would help to sever the military from the death squads, or the two had nothing to do with each other in the first place.

Lacking documentary sources on these killings, we are compelled to rely exclusively on testimonies by victims and witnesses; some potentially key events and themes that emerge from them remain imprecise. Although it is impossible to cite figures with any real accuracy, ample testimony suggests that there were from 350 to 1,500 troops in El Carrizal and Santo Domingo. Why did the army deploy so many troops for so long in villages where no armed actions had taken place? We have no answers to these questions, but the testimonies suggest that the military may have employed unique tactics in the west, based on different strategic considerations. At the very least, the military probably recognized the generational divide rooted in the experience of 1932 and the corresponding weakness of the left's new bases of support. Perhaps it also realized that a massive and public display of execution and torture would have a devastating effect on the population as a whole, inoculating the region against any further development of the radical movement. Although as many scholars have pointed out, torture is a form of theater meant to traumatize or at least intimidate spectators, rarely in the Latin American context was torture employed for truly "public" consumption, as in El Canelo. It is one thing to stumble upon a mutilated corpse and quite another to see a neighbor with his arm and cheek cut off before his execution.

Regardless of the military's intention, there is no question that the effect of the killings was profound. The elder generations experienced the killings as the return of a repressed trauma, intensifying the fear, anxiety, and loss that witnesses of repression elsewhere in the country experienced. In El Carrizal informants linked the events of 1980 with 1932. Manuel Ascencio Pérez, whose son was executed in 1980, compared the two massacres, concluding simply, "Nuestra comunidad sí ha sufrido, verdad?"[106]

Manuel Ascencio,
El Carrizal. Courtesy
of the Museo de la
Palabra y la Imagen.

Another informant echoed this sentiment: "And then they came and committed the massacre here in El Carrizal; this community has always suffered the most, suffering terribly, victims in 1930 and '80."[107] Another comparison stressed the arbitrariness of the killings and the innocence of the victims: "The same thing happened in '32 and '82. They took advantage with personal hatreds to involve and assassinate so many innocent people."[108] A testimony from Santo Domingo emphasizes how the terror imbued itself into the fabric of village life: "that's when the people with the 'long tongue' [informants, slanderers] took advantage. They would say, 'aaa! It's this guy!' and because during that time anyone who was accused didn't escape; they wouldn't investigate if he was or he wasn't. . . . The armed forces and the death squads got him at night; in the end, they decided who had to be killed. They raped women, they tortured, stole, killed. They did what they wanted."[109] As the last quotation indicates, the testimonies of 1980, like those of 1932, stress the innocence of the victims. Yet there are fundamental differences. First, in 1980 there is a clear recognition of the agency of local youths. All the informants state that youths were beginning to "organize" to "improve the community" and to "struggle for social justice." By affording agency to the actors, the narrative maintains a coherence and a degree of precision that are notably absent in the 1932 accounts.

Two factors influenced this fundamental difference between the 1980 testimonies, which acknowledge if not highlight local agency, and the narrative suppression of the 1932 testimonies. First, the 1980 interviews are biased toward people who were involved in the "organization." Many of those people still maintain involvement, allegiance, or sympathy with the left or the indigenous rights movement, and thus militancy in the 1980s offers a degree of heroism to the informants and martyrdom to the deceased—even if neither status is recognized outside the community. Second, the informants were in a better position than their parents or grandparents to remember and frame events. They were young adults, with some education; their ability to recall specifics from two decades earlier (as opposed to six) was more highly developed.

The absence of an ethnic dimension in the 1980 narratives marks another fundamental difference. In 1932 the Indian-ladino binary was fundamental in Indian areas and absent in the non-Indian areas of mobilization. In 1980 this lack of ethnic identification reflects several aspects of the political and cultural conjuncture. Youths mobilized not as Indians but as part of the oppressed masses chafing under military rule. Although to some extent this may have reflected the left's immersion in the discourse of mestizaje, the silencing of ethnicity also reflects their own generational rejection of their parents' political and cultural world.[110]

There is a dearth of documentation by scholars, human rights organizations, and political parties that relate to the three sites of mass execution. Even in the literature of denunciation, there are virtually no references to any of the massacres (except one) that took place in indigenous areas of western Salvador.[111] Why did the left and the human rights activists associated with the church fail to report on the four massacres? Part of the reason is that these cases only accounted for between 100 and 150 deaths during a year in which the military and its allies executed over eight thousand civilians. Yet there is perhaps a more significant reason, namely that the left came to believe its own myth of indigenous and western political passivity, a result of the trauma of 1932.

The myth of political passivity was based on a bedrock of reality. The vast majority of indigenous people who had experienced 1932 were consciously apolitical. A smaller number were active supporters of the regime and only a tiny minority supported the left. Yet as we have stated, there was most definitely a small but growing base of support for the left among indigenous youths and others, largely mobilized by ANIS.

ANIS and the Massacre at "Las Hojas"

The sole exception to the silence on massacres in the west occurred in "Las Hojas," several miles from El Carrizal. According to the report of the "Truth Commission": "On February 22, 1983, elements of the Jaguar Battalion, under the command of Captain Carlos Alfonso Figueroa Morales, participated in an operation in the Canton, 'Las Hojas' . . . The soldiers detained 16 campesinos and later shot them at point blank range. . . . With the help of the members of the 'Defensa Civil'—who covered their faces with bandanas to hide their identities . . . they signaled out those on the list. They pulled them out of their houses—striking them and tying them up—and then they took them from the cooperative along the road in the direction of the Cuyuapa River."[112] At 7:00 a.m. Adrián Esquina, the *cacique*, or leader, of ANIS, went to the military to denounce the captures of the members of the cooperative. The military commander replied that they had captured some "subversives." Later that morning ANIS members found sixteen corpses by the side of a river, with clear indications that they had had their fingers tied together behind their back. This massacre garnered attention from the national and even international community in part because ANIS was in a position to publicize the killings (usually referring to seventy victims), because it directly involved an agrarian reform cooperative, and because it occurred during a period of declining human rights violations.[113]

During the 1980s ANIS attracted what appears to have been a significant following in the cantons of Nahuizalco and Santo Domingo, among other sites in the west. It combined programs promoting indigenous culture and supporting human rights and agrarian reform. No study has examined the reception of the cultural agenda of ANIS during the 1980s. Their repertoire included an appeal to the Maya, Lenca, and Nahuat peoples and to their religious traditions rooted in "Nana Naturaleza y el Tata Sol," in addition to promoting the study of Nahuatl-Pipil. Regardless of its relevance at the time to those people in the west who accepted an indigenous identity, it was the social and human rights program that gained support and led to direct government intervention. In 1985 the organization split into a pro-government faction, ASID (Asociación Salvadoreña de Indígenas Democráticas), and ANIS, which remained nongovernmental. For twenty months the divided organization was mired in a legal battle that ended when the Supreme Court ruled in favor of ANIS as the legitimate owner of the headquarters and cooperative lands.[114] The division probably led to an increase in the power and international prestige of Esquina Lisco, which ultimately led to bitter enmities within the organization and numerous charges of corruption against the cacique.[115] Esquina Lisco's international prestige also kept intense focus on the case of "las Hojas." In 1992 the Comisión Interamericana de Derechos Humanos ruled that the guilty officers should be brought to justice and that the victims' families should be indemnified.[116]

Although the exact connections between ANIS and the FMLN are unclear, there is no doubt that ANIS's agenda, summarized by the slogan "Tierra, Indio, Unidad," was congruent with the evolving posture of the Frente. Notwithstanding the real and potential reservoirs of support as indicated by the relative strength of ANIS, strategically it was impossible for the revolutionary left to maintain bases of guerrilla insurgency in western Salvador. Notwithstanding this, throughout the 1980s a nucleus of activists, inspired by liberation theology and discourses of indigenous identity, began to organize again in the rural communities.

This group of activists who came to the fore especially in the Nahuizalco area in the 1990s embodied what Greg Grandin referred to as an alternative form of modernity, the mutually reinforcing link between self and community (see chapter 3). Remarkably, in the early twenty-first century some community activists, living on the margins of impoverished villages of western El Salvador, tirelessly organized to benefit their communities and sacrificed endless hours of "free time" to lobby government agencies and NGOs in support of communal development. Although their utopian visions are radically scaled down from those that circulated in the country in the late 1970s and early 1980s, their level of commitment to a better world reproduces the "insurgent individuality" that we found applicable to the mobilization of the early 1930s and that Grandin saw correctly as a major casualty of the counterrevolution of the 1980s.

The massacres of 1980 compelled the inhabitants of El Carrizal and El Canelo to relive the terror that the eldest generation had experienced in 1932, a shocking reminder that they still endured the long night of military rule and repression begun under the Martínez regime. But when a new dawn finally arrived in the west, the survivors of this latest round of massacres neither forgot the perpetrators nor accepted the oblivion surrounding the events of 1932 and 1980.

Epilogue

The support of a growing body of community activists contributed to FMLN victories in the municipal and congressional elections of 1997 and 2000 throughout western El Salvador, including in Nahuizalco, Tacuba, and Santo Domingo de Guzmán as well as in all the departmental cabeceras of Ahuachapán, La Libertad, Santa Ana, and Sonsonate. In light of the relative passivity of the region during the 1980s, these victories raise the question of how the FMLN had acquired such political strength.

During the 1970s, 1980s, and 1990s the rural areas of Sonsonate developed politically at a rhythm different from the rest of the country. Several historical and ethnographic characteristics marked the contours of this unique political development. Peasant and rural worker associations, as mentioned in chapter 8, got off the ground much later than they did elsewhere, yet faced the same rhythm of repression as elsewhere. Moreover, the iglesia popular also arrived later in Sonsonate (though it was more active in Santa Ana and La Libertad). For example, an activist priest arrived in Nahuizalco only in 1982. Yet the later presence of the iglesia popular allowed activists to mobilize during the war in ways not possible in other areas of the country.

When the left emerged in the 1990s, it did so simultaneously with a new wave of indigenous rights activity. Initially the movements involved many of the same people and reinforced one another. Most of the local activists had participated in the Pastoral Indigenista, organized in the late 1980s as an attempt by activists inspired by liberation theology to ally themselves with the aspirations of indigenous peoples. The Pastoral marked a departure from earlier forms of Catholic activism that were indifferent if not hostile to indigenous religious ideas and practices. The local rebirth of the left during the 1990s coincided with the reforging of indigenous identities, linked in turn to efforts by small groups of community activists. Thus activists from the Frente Farabundo Martí para la Liberación Nacional (FMLN) joined with others to engage in activities ranging from teaching Nahuate in schools to founding an Indian radio station.

Although the left's rejection of violence beginning in the 1990s marks a fundamental departure from its previous history, there are interesting parallels with the growth of the left in the early 1930s. In chapter 3 we argued that the SRI profited from its ability to project a populist discourse, *los pobres* against *los ricos*. The deep levels of resentment of the bulk of the population against the agrarian élite combined with sharp fissures within the dominant power block to inject the labor and radical organizing drives with populist fervor.

Before the massacres of 1932 the procommunist left was aware of the discursive breadth of its message and did not push its recently formed categories so hard as to displace the populist idiom of the indigenous and ladino campesinos who formed its base of support. The formulation of a leftist program could become concretized in a populist idiom: "quitarles las tierras a los ricos" (take the land from the rich). At the apex of the mobilization, the left leadership behaved more like the colonial Catholic church faced with the impurities of its Indian parishioners than like Stalinist apparatchiks. In short, it was the left's lack of will to disarticulate the socialist from the populist elements of its discourse that ensured its growth during the early 1930s.

During the 1990s the FMLN similarly grew in the west as a grassroots, populist movement resembling that of the early 1930s in its direct appeal to the people and the poor against the élite and the authoritarian state. Indeed, years of military and élite rule had done very little to dry up the reservoir of populist sentiment. If anything, the binary of pueblo versus rico was as strong in the 1990s as at anytime in the past, and the FMLN could make a convincing case that it was "the party of the poor."[1]

We argued in chapter 4 that the left appealed strongly in El Salvador in the early 1930s, as it did in Nicaragua in the 1960s, to generations whose indigenous forebears had suffered a wave of primary accumulation. The encounter of the left with western youth in the 1970s exhibited similar characteristics, in that many rejected the ethnic emblems and politics of their parents. Despite the devastating effects of the repression of 1980, a core of these militants remained active in the region. This core group experienced another cultural transformation during the 1980s. In the early 1930s the left at once stimulated and enjoyed the benefits of a shift away from a clientelistic political culture. During the 1980s and 1990s, with similar adaptability to cultural changes, the FMLN gained politically through the reemergence of a movement which claimed new forms of indigenous identity.

In 2003 the FMLN was swept from office in nearly all the municipalities it had won in 1997 and 2000. Objective and structural reasons account for much of the failure of the leftist municipal governments to maintain political support. With an extremely limited financial base and a national government in the hands of the rightist ARENA party, the municipal governments had limited means and space for an agenda of social change. Yet equally decisive in the local failures were FMLN national politics and policies that had decidedly negative effects on local activists. In particular, the sectarian split between the Ortodoxos (putatively leftist) and Renovadores (centrist) wreaked havoc locally. Moreover, the political alignments made no local political or ideological sense whatsoever: the "orthodox" mayor of Nahuizalco made little effort to modify the abysmal socioeconomic situation in the countryside, and those who most insistently demanded social change in the cantons were those who by default were aligned with the Renovadores. Regardless of their factional alignment, no municipality led by the FMLN offered any support for the minimum demands of rural labor or for the real, remaining need for land distribution. In 1999, 62 percent of the rural population of the country lived in poverty and the rural minimum wage was at most enough to supply rice, beans, and tortillas to a small family.[2] The acceptance of the social economic status quo in order presumably to gain national legitimacy and organizational stability led directly to the squandering of political capital.

Alexander Segovia, among others, has argued convincingly that El Salvador has undergone a structural shift, and that the agro-export model of accumulation is no longer relevant in an economy increasingly dependent on financial operations for the élite and *remesas* for the people.[3] The consequences of this structural shift for the rural poor of the *occidente* are far less obvious. The west, former heart of the agro-export model, also seems out of step with the structural shift. Surely because of the migratory circuits opened as a direct consequence of the war, Sonsonate has one of the lowest levels of family remesas in the country, and it is a rare campesino family that receives them. So there they remain, in a dysfunctional economy, with no jobs left in the coffee economy and no available land, struggling to feed and clothe their children. Although the lower-elevation coffee plantations have been abandoned, the left joins the right in viewing even the most moderate forms of land distribution as hopelessly passé.

The Frente's failure to capitalize on its victories was at least in part due to its inability to fully recognize and stimulate its own sources of strength. In particular, its failure to support its most abnegated militants in places like Santo Domingo and Nahuizalco certainly contributed to subsequent electoral defeats. As mentioned above, a group of campesino and indígena activists played a vital role in the FMLN victories at the polls in 1997 in the predominantly indigenous municipios of Nahuizalco and Santo Domingo Yet the leadership of the Frente refused to fully integrate and empower those self-identified indígenas, community activists who had provided the key to victory—and indeed they were marginalized from an active role in decision making.[4]

In Nahuizalco the socioeconomic and cultural subjugation of Indians, and their historic enmity with ladinos, conditioned a political struggle within the Frente during the six years of its municipal rule. That struggle reached its apotheosis when campesino groups rooted in the communal organizations of the cantones staged an occupation of the municipal building to protest the regime's abuses and disregard toward the rural poor. This violent rift in the left coalition, rooted in a profound distrust embedded in local histories, ensured the defeat of the FMLN in the election of 2003. Although this electoral defeat was qualitatively different from that of 1932, both defeats reflect the failure of the national leadership to fully acknowledge and engage with local memories and cultures. In 1932 the leftist leadership, despite its remarkable achievement of uniting ladino and indigenous peasants, failed to fully understand the distinct levels and qualities of local support. During the late 1990s the left again squandered a high level of political support in the west because of a failure to take into account the deeply conflictual history of local communities, a recognition that would have forced the leftist leadership to accept divisions within its own ranks and its own culpability in the political marginalization of those whose lives long had been marked by exclusion.

The rebirth of leftist and indigenous grassroots activism led to a remarkable historical reversal: the scorned and vilified left won elections and indigenous identity became a badge of pride and honor. Yet the failure of the left to deliver on its promise of democratic social change also reflected an inability to free itself from what Marx called the "nightmares of the past." The full encouragement of social, political, and cultural democracy within its ranks and a recalibration of the relationship of national leaders and intellectuals to local actors would allow the left and Salvadoran society as a whole to finally bid adieu to the toxic residue of the past. Together they might then confront the problems of a new society as unjust and unequal as the old one, but with none of the structural and ideological moorings that made it comprehensible and therefore susceptible to social transformation.

Scars of Memory: Notes On Documentary Film, Politics, and History

Jeffrey L. Gould

Shortly after beginning to interview massacre survivors in January 1998, I met Carlos Henríquez Consalvi ("Santiago"), former director of Radio Venceremos, the first clandestine radio station of the FMLN. In postwar El Salvador he had devoted himself to creating the Museo de la Palabra y la Imágen, which in its earliest stages focused primarily on presenting exhibitions of images of the war and reconciliation in towns and cities throughout the country. When I discussed the project with Santiago he suggested that we also make video recordings of the interviews. Without giving it much thought, I agreed to the suggestion, assuming that the interviews might be shown as part of one of the Museo's exhibitions.

From the beginning of this research project, as mentioned in the Preface, I relied a great deal on the help of Reynaldo Patriz. A native of El Carrizal with an eighth-grade education, Patriz, in addition to offering penetrating commentary on contemporary politics and culture, helped me to break down some levels of distrust and fear on the part of informants. As a community activist tied to the progressive wing of the church, he had a wide range of contacts in Nahuizalco. Further, this was a propitious moment throughout the west to carry out oral history research.

For Patriz the idea of creating a video archive of the interviews made little sense, and he prodded us toward developing a documentary film. Fundamentally, our decision to make the film derived from a recognition that the reading public was minimal in El Salvador, and that a documentary film would reach a much larger public than the Museo's exhibits could. In the fall of 2000 Santiago and I created a forty-five-minute rough cut, weaving together photos from the early 1930s and a narrative of the insurrection and massacre, based on preliminary research and on selections from interviews mostly from the municipalities of Nahuizalco and Izalco. We presented this preliminary version to different audiences ranging from a secondary school social studies class to various community groups.

These initial audience responses awakened us to the potential of the film. Most memorable were the reactions of aged informants in the Casa de Cultura of Nahuizalco. Tears of joy and amazement at seeing their images seemingly blended with tears of sorrow and rage at the narrated events. We did not have the temerity to interview the informants about their reactions to seeing their image on the screen or to the rest of the footage. Yet others in the audience did offer a torrent of commentary, ranging from political-style denunciations of contemporary oppression to suggestions on how to improve the film.[1]

A presentation of the film to a small audience of ladino FMLN supporters in Izalco elicited a remarkably different reaction. First, several viewers expressed dismay that their city did not play a central role in the film, a role that they assumed corresponded to historical reality. More significantly, one FMLN militant denounced the film as "the official story" because of its emphasis on the activities of Socorro Rojo and the PCS in the mobilization and insurrection. The militant exclaimed, "For years, every time we tried to do anything, any strike, any meeting, any protest at all and they'd accuse us of being Communists. In '32 it was a question of starving Indians; the left didn't have anything really to do with it. So what you are doing is providing grist for their mill [agua para su molino]." The same militant also objected that the documentary did not present any Indians, people with "conciencia indígena."

These criticisms were provocative. The lack of an adequate portrayal of

Reynaldo Patriz,
el Carrizal. Courtesy
Museo de la Palabra y
la Imagen.

the movement and repression in Izalco remains a fair one, yet the film does serve as a corrective to the notion that the city was the main center of the movement or the main focus for the repression.[2] The charge of supporting "an official story" was more challenging. The commentary highlighted the intensity of the politics of memory of 1932. The militant rejected a relatively benign portrayal of the left in favor of an alternative vision that absolved the left of real responsibility in the events. Historiographical currents that stress the weakness of the organized left and the "autonomy" of the campesinos and Indians fuel this political position in the struggle over memory. By stressing the divorce between the left and the rural subalterns, however, this perspective inadvertently reflected and in a sense justified the military version that the communists tricked and deceived the innocent Indians. After this encounter in Izalco, it became clear to us that there would be no way to present a film that would remain outside the decades-old struggle over control over the memories and narratives of 1932.

The commentary by the Izalqueño militant also spoke to the subterranean contemporary conflict between indígenas and ladinos. The implicit argument that Indians could not stage anything more than a spontaneous rebellion caused by hunger betrays assumptions about them that most social scientists would consider racist. The statement that "true Indians" have a specifically, discernible "indigenous consciousness" rooted in notions of nature and communal property suggests a radically essentialized view of Indians. This position is all the more striking given the large number of people in the militant's home town who consider themselves "indígenas." For this militant, his neighbors are not Indians because they do not exhibit certain forms of consciousness. Since these "non-authentic" indígenas were actual or potential allies for the FMLN, the consequences of this cultural misunderstanding are apparent.

The final version of the film benefited from these varied reactions, commentaries, and discussions; it ended up substantially different from the earlier version. Another six months of research allowed us to expand the geographic scope of the project, thus creating a film that was less focused on Nahuizalco, reflecting the expansion of my oral history research toward the departments of La Libertad and Ahuachapán. In response to the charge of feeding "the official story," we sharpened the argument about the role of the left in the mobilization and insurrection. Indeed, the film at times uses a style of scholarly exposition (thesis statement plus supporting evidence) that perhaps detracts from the quality of the documentary.[3] Yet in light of the "stakes" that had been revealed in the preliminary showing, we wished to make a strong case that this was not a rebellion of hungry Indians, nor an Indian movement "manipulated" by communists.[4]

In the film and the book, we respond to the historiographic and public discourse that posits two separate mobilizations and insurrections, one "Indian" and the other "communist." Rather, we show that the mobilization was in fact led by a relatively large cadre of revolutionaries, of different subaltern backgrounds, many of whom were informed by communist and socialist utopias, ideologies, and strategies. The movement as it gathered force over three years developed an extensive anticapitalist agenda that challenged the foundations of élite wealth and power. An important argument of the film and the book is that the dramatic power of the mobilization and insurrection derived from the active, mutually conditioning relationship between grassroots activists, with varied identities, and different levels of leftist leadership. The union and SRI activists were as "authentically" leftist as the PCS Central Committee and at least as important in shaping the development of the movement.

The visual imagery of the documentary supports this argument.[5] The late Pedro Lue, for example, easily and with demonstrative gestures talks about his neighbor, Saturnino Perez, as the "cabecilla comunista": "Too bad Pedro that you're still a kid or else I could give you this button to show that you are one of us." The viewer can recognize the intimacy of the relation between "communist and indigenous peasant" and the methods of person-to-person organization. Similarly, other witnesses offer memories of meetings at which activists discussed "tomas de tierra," and still others, mixing admiration with disapproval, comment, "querían quitarles tierras a los ricos." The videotaped interviews allow us to glimpse the outlines of the re-creation of a communist discourse. Ordinary people in ordinary settings appropriated leftist discourse and used it to create new understandings and strategies to transform their social world. It is in the gestures, facial expressions, and phrasing that we see the way "communism" operated as discourse in the villages in ways more visible and comprehensible than through the specific content of the testimonies, let alone our film makers' narrative.

If the filmic portrayal of the argument about communist and subaltern agency is successful, a reinterpretation of the ethnic dimension of the mobilization and the insurrection—another important contribution of our research—is definitely not adequately portrayed in the film. For six decades, from the 1930s until the 1990s, the left described the mobilization and rebellion of 1932 in solely class terms and the right described it as a communist manipulation of ignorant rural folk (with ethnic identity unimportant). During the 1990s scholars rediscovered the indigenous nature of the rebellion, now seen as a revolt against a ladino élite, and the racist nature of the repression. Our research as presented in this book reveals that although ethnic relations did play an important role in the mobilization, they did so in highly complex and contradictory ways. Any attempt to view the mobilization and revolt as ethnic conflict alone misses far more than it captures. Although ethnicity as an analytical tool is essential to understanding the movement, ethnic ideologies did not motivate a substantial proportion of the actors. Indeed, what was remarkable about the movement was how rural workers and peasants with very different forms of identity responded to and reinterpreted the class ideology promoted by the leftist activists. These class-based messages and activities appealed to a wide range of people: those who looked on Indians as a somewhat backward "other"; those who identified strongly with indigenous political authority, signs, and culture; and those who simply did not care.

Scars of Memory does not adequately portray these subtleties of ethnic difference and conflict, discussed in chapter 4. On one level this argument about mestizaje and class conflict is simply too complex to present in a documentary that purports to offer a comprehensive account of the causes and long-term consequences of 1932. On another level, even without the time limitations, visually it would be very difficult to capture ethnic differences between Indians and ladinos, especially as they may have been envisioned and lived at the time, in view of the dearth of photos and film footage from the early 1930s. Also, there are no clearly distinguishing characteristics of the informants. Some of the women wear *el refajo*, and the Central American or academic viewer assumes that person to be "indigenous." Most do not wear indigenous dress whether or not they possess an indigenous identity. Males who look the same may or may not be self-identified Indians or ladinos. To fully explore the cultural differences in the contemporary society of western Salvador would make an interesting project but would necessitate a different film.

Ironically, the weakest part of the documentary from a scholarly standpoint—namely the description and analysis of ethnic relations—has been precisely the part of the film that has become an empowerment tool used by indigenous activists. This appropriation of the film by community activists is an unintended consequence of our work. Although we foresaw that possibility when we got comments in response to the forty-five-minute rough cut that we showed to various audiences, we could not imagine that the film would some day be seen and ardently discussed in community centers throughout the area.[6] Moreover, in 2005 indigenous groups and NGOs used the film to substantiate their "Shadow Report" to the Commission to End Racial Discrimination in Geneva, critiquing a government report.[7]

The use of *Scars of Memory* as a tool in the politics of identity goes against several implicit interpretive positions within the documentary. Relying in part on the elders' testimonies, the documentary suggests that the loss of the key ethnic markers—Nahuatl and el refajo—was a largely endogenous process. Contrary to the position of the indigenous rights movement, as we saw in chapter 8, there was no prohibition of the Nahuatl language after the massacre. Indigenous activists during the late 1990s pointed to exclusively exogenous causes to exonerate, as it were, the indigenous people from any complicity in the process of their own cultural transformation. Nevertheless, it seems that the documentary has stimulated at least some reevaluation of the argument about cultural loss and cultural mestizaje.

There is yet another contradiction between the content of the documentary and its appropriation by activists as a representation of communal history and identity. The documentary (like the book) suggests extensive indigenous involvement in the mobilization and insurrection. The memories of the elders, as noted in chapters 7 and 8, deny this involvement and

Commemoration of
the seventy-third
anniversary of the
massacres, El Carrizal.
Courtesy of the
Museo de la Palabra
y la Imagen.

in fact, through a variety of narrative processes shaped by decades of political repression, the social memories of the indigenous survivors of the massacre suppressed the indigenous subject of the insurrection. In large part this suppression derived from the inherited, collective necessity to remove the indigenous dead and survivors from any agency in the narrative. The common phrase "mataron justos por pecadores" (they killed the just instead of the sinners) synthesizes this perspective. In other words, Indians did not participate in the rebellion but became the scapegoats in the bloody repression.

We had to grapple with this dilemma: to reproduce the suppression of indigenous agency as part of the documentary would have rendered it virtually incomprehensible. Although we experimented with the idea of offering multiple narrations to reproduce the fragmentary forms of memory, we eventually dropped the idea in favor of a conventional narration, and thus we sacrifice an accurate portrayal of the highly fragmentary social memories of the indigenous survivors.

We also made a conscious choice—one that has been criticized by some Central American scholars—to include a component about the mobilization and repression in western Salvador during the 1980s. In part the criticism reflected a common perception on both the left and the right that this region of the country was unimportant during the civil war, largely because its population was still traumatized by the events of 1932. The film—and we believe the historical record—suggest that although the civil war per se did not have much direct significance in the region, mobilization and brutal repression characterized the period directly preceding it. As pointed out in chapter 8, the commonsense understanding of the political effects of the trauma inflicted by the massacres of 1932 erased the smaller but locally

Fabian Mojica y Santiago and
Carlos Henriquez Consalvi
("Santiago"). Courtesy of the
Museo de la Palabra y la Imagen.

devastating massacres of 1980 from public recognition (including within
the human rights community), both at the time and subsequently.

The videotaped testimonies of the massacres of 1980, like the testimonies of the massacres of 1932, communicate a sense of immediacy to an
audience through their images. That immediacy in both cases derives from
the urgency of communicating a significant, arguably traumatized memory
that had never been verbalized (at least) publicly before. In the most dramatic testimony from 1980, María Eduwiges Pérez had mentioned in a
previous conversation, without providing the details, that her husband had
been murdered. She agreed to discuss the murder for the video (see chapter
8). After dozens of viewings, her expression of anguish, horror, and condemnation still tear me up. Her intense, vivid testimony is powerful because
of the arbitrariness of the horror inflicted in such an ordinary setting. At the
same time, her testimony offers a voice of protest against the neglect of the
thousands of people who lost family members to death squads throughout
the country and region. They have received neither recognition nor compen-
sation for their loss of loved ones, income, and emotional well-being.

For those viewers who have not suffered such repression, the documentary potentially is a form of what Alison Landsberg calls "prosthetic
memory."[8] Landsberg develops her argument through a discussion of new
technologies of memory that are vital not so much because they preserve
memory but because they create new subjective understandings of history

Presentation of the documentary Cicatriz de la Memoria in Tierra Blanca, Usulatán.
Courtesy of the Museo de la Palabra y la Imagen.

and the contemporary world. These form part of what she calls experiential knowledge. Viewers do not fully assimilate testimonies, but rather the viewer-listener constructs a (prosthetic) memory "triggered by the testimonial and yet intimately connected to one's own archive of experience."[9] For Landsberg, there are critical political consequences of using these technologies of memory: "Images become recognizable . . . events and issues need to be represented in order to become politics."

A question emerges from this discussion of prosthetic memory, experiential knowledge, imagery, and politics: from what ethical position can we intervene in the politics of memory of 1932 or 1980? This project is rooted in several propositions. As suggested above, it does have its origins to some extent within Salvadoran civil society. Secondly, the massacres of both 1932 and 1980 were gross violations of human rights that demand not only denunciation but the public testimony of survivors. Similarly, they require the fullest possible elucidation and analysis of empirical research. That said, we recognize that the record is notoriously incomplete because of the intentions of the perpetrators, the impact of their terror, and the passage of time. Therefore the book and film do not purport to record any definitive version of events. And as suggested above, the narrative form is not particularly well suited to the task of recording the more subtle cultural effects of the massacres, more visible perhaps in gestures and speech. The film and the book thus complement each other and offer the possibility of opening discussions among diverse audiences inside and outside El Salvador.

The response to the film underscores what many scholars and writers have observed, namely the interconnectedness between the past and the present. The bitter afterlife of 1932 and 1980 makes these connections all the more apparent. Walter Benjamin's comment is apposite: "For every image of the past that is not recognized by the present as one of its own threatens to disappear irretrievably." Perhaps the animated response in western Salvador reflects a collective "flash of recognition" of a dimly outlined recurring nightmare that when brought into focus becomes less disturbing.

In "Scars of Memory," over the back-and-forth sound of a saw, Manuel Ascencio commented about the massacres in El Carrizal in 1932 and in 1980, when his son was murdered: "This community has suffered, right?" This understatement can be grasped as a commentary about the endurance of a community that labors on despite the horrors of its past. Yet his facial expression and tone of voice, like those of María Eduwiges, do not accept this past as preordained or inevitable. Rather they denounce the murder of a loved one and ask that we neither forget the dead nor allow atrocities to occur for a third time.

Notes

Bibliographic Abbbreviations

AGA   Archivo de la Gobernación de Ahuachapan
AGN   Archivo General de la Nación, San Salvador
AGS   Archivo de la Gobernación de Sonsonate
Ah   Ahuachapan
AMJ   Archivo Municipal de Jayaque
AMS   Archivo Municipal de Sonsonate
CG   Coleción Gobernaciones
CM   Colección Ministerios
MG   Ministerio de Gobernación
MID   H. M. Gwynn, War Department Military Intelligence Division, "Correspondence and Record Cards of the Military Intelligence Division Relating to General, Political, Economic, and Military Conditions in Central America 1918–1941" (1926)
So   Sonsonate
USNA   United States National Archives, Washington

Preface

1   Interview with Reynaldo Patriz, El Carrizal, Nahuizalco, 1998. This account is based on many conversations with Patriz over the period 1998–2001.

2 A cantón is a geographical and political unit of a municipality. In size it corresponds to a village. The average population of the cantones of Nahuizalco is roughly a thousand inhabitants. When talking about rural people, a person will often refer to the "gente de los cantones."

3 This was a novel experience for Gould, since in his previous oral history research in Nicaragua he did not rely on assistants, except in the last stage of the project, which resulted in *To Die in This Way*, he worked with Holger Cisneros, a sociology student.

4 Daniel James, "Between Memory and History: Reflections of a Reluctant Oral Historian," paper presented at the Conferencia Sobre la Historia Oral, Buenos Aires, 2003. Encuentro Sobre la Historia Oral, Buenos Aires, 2003.

5 Grandin, *The Last Colonial Massacre*, 171.

6 State Dept report, 816.48n 1934/15, 15 June 1934, USNA.

7 This was a common refrain of numerous informants in the Nahuizalco area.

8 Interview with Dionisio Ramirez, el Carrizal, Nahuizalco, 1998.

9 See for example Catherine LeGrand, "Living in Macondo: Economy and Culture in a United Fruit Company Enclave in Colombia," *Close Encounters of Empire*, ed. Joseph, LeGrand, and Salvadore, 333–68; Eduardo Posada-Carbó, "Fiction as History: The *Bananeras* and Gabriel García Márquez's *One Hundred Years of Solitude*," *Journal of Latin American Studies* 30, no. 2 (May 1998), 395–414.

10 Michel-Rolf Trouillot, *Silencing the Past: Power and the Production of History* (Boston: Beacon, 1995), 24.

11 Daniel James, *Doña María's Story: Life History, Memory and Political Identity* (Durham: Duke University Press, 2000), 124.

12 See Gould, *To Lead as Equals*, 7–10.

13 Gould, "Proyectos del Estado-nación y la supresión de la pluralidad cultural."

14 Lauria-Santiago's work on the nineteenth-century development of coffee in El Salvador has provided a baseline to this study confirming Mario Samper's suggestion that El Salvador's coffee production was not premised on the most extreme model of land concentration and labor control and did not stand as a polar opposite to conditions in Costa Rica.

15 Samper K., "El Significado Social de la Caficultura Costaricense y Salvadoreña"; Roseberry, "Beyond the Agrarian Question in Latin America"; William Roseberry, "La Falta de Brazos"; Yarrington, A Coffee Frontier; Marco Palacios, *Coffee in Colombia, 1850–1970* (Cambridge: Cambridge University Press, 1980); Paige, "Coffee and Politics in Central America."

16 Wickham-Crowley's basic argument is a revised version of Scott's about peasant motivations for revolt: that peasants rebel when damaging economic transformation is tied to the decline of previously existing patron-client or patronage networks. Wickham-Crowley adds to this the need to consider the "physical dislocation from land itself" experienced by peasants as a motivation for revolt.

17 The notion of historical specificity is borrowed from Karl Korsch.

18 Carr, "Identity, Class and Nation."

19 Similarly, revolutionary rhetoric inspired minor insurrectionary movements in a coffee-growing region of Antioquía, Colombia, in 1929 and in urban Brazil in 1935. Sánchez, *Los Bolcheviques del Libano*.

20 Turits, *Foundations of Despotism*; Richard Turits, "A World Destroyed, a Nation Imposed"; Helg, *Our Rightful Share*.

21 The killings in Trujillo, Peru, in 1932 would provide another interesting comparative case. The similarity resided in the Peruvian military's efforts to inflict revenge killings on an entire region (not ethnically targeted) that supported an insurrection led by the APRA. See Villanueva and Crabtree, "The Petty-Bourgeois Ideology of the Peruvian Aprista Party."

22 Jorge Schlesinger, *Revolución Comunista*; Alfredo Schlesinger, *La Verdad Sobre el Comunismo*; Buezo, *Sangre de Hermanos*; Bustamante, *Historia militar de El Salvador*; J. Méndez, *Los sucesos comunistas en El Salvador*; José Tomás Calderón, "Breve reseña histórica del Comunismo en El Salvador," *Anhelos de un ciudadano*, ed. Calderón; Filio, *Tierras de centroamérica*. The exceptions to this rigid anticommunist bent are by Buezo and Bustamante (a military officer), who provided the first sympathetic attempts to understand the social origins of the movement and condemn the mass repression carried out by the state.

23 Candelario, "Representación de lo irrepresentable"; Candelario, "Patología de una Insurrección"; Cáceres, "Después del 32."

24 Public statements by the PCS about 1932 before the 1960s are rare, but a set of internal documents offer a sense of the party's perspective on the events. The documents blame the government for being consistently repressive and promoting "anarchy" by putting forward "many" presidential candidates. A strong alliance between the military and élites sought to provoke a popular revolt throughout 1931 with constant acts of "provocation," including the "anarchy" of the Araujo presidency. Popular hunger led to strikes, which when repressed led to revolt. An understandable but "mistaken" path was taken, prodded by the Caribbean Bureau's alleged line of "seizing power." Instituto Historico De Cuba, PCS documents.

25 Larín, "Historia del movimiento sindical de El Salvador," *Universidad* 96, no.4 (July–August 1971); Marroquín, "Estudio sobre la crisis de los años treinta en El Salvador"; Salazar Valiente, Luna, and Gómez, *El Proceso Político Centroamericano*; López Vallecillos, "Trayectoria y crisis del estado salvadoreño"; Luna, "Análisis de una dictadura fascista latinoamericana"; Torres, "More from This Land"; Luna, *Manual de historia económica de El Salvador*; Luna, "Un heroico y trágico suceso de nuestra historia"; López Alas Rosales and Escobar Cornejo, "La crisis de 1929 y sus consecuencias en los años posteriores"; López Vallecillos, *El periodismo en El Salvador*.

26 Arias Gómez, *Farabundo Marti*.

27 See Vázquez Olivera, " 'País mío no existes,' " and Harlow, "Testimonio and Survival."

28 Dalton, "Miguel Mármol: El Salvador 1930–32"; Dalton, *Miguel Mármol: Los sucesos de 1932 en El Salvador*; Pablo Benítez, "Miguel Mármol es una memoria política en formato testimonial (entrevista a Jaime Barba)," *Diario Co-Latino*, 29 July 2005, http://www.diariocolatino.com/tresmil/detalles.asp?NewsID=141.

29 Lara Martínez, "Indigenismo y encubrimiento testimonial El 32 según 'Miguel Mármol. Manuscrito. 37 páginas' de Roque Dalton."

30 A Harvard undergraduate, Andrew Ogilvie, traveled to El Salvador to conduct research for his undergraduate honors thesis, which remains unpublished. Ogilvie, "The Communist Revolt of El Salvador."

31 Anderson, *Matanza*.

32 Browning's book is the first major attempt to understand the longue durée in El Salvador's agrarian history. Strongly motivated by the need for agrarian reform apparent by the late 1960s, the book sought to posit the contradictions between land ownership and land use.

33 Wilson, "The Crisis of National Integration in El Salvador"; Anderson, *Matanza*; White, *El Salvador*; Ogilvie, "The Communist Revolt of El Salvador"; Browning, *El Salvador*; Elam, "Appeal to Arms."

34 Luna, *Manual de historia económica de El Salvador*; Bulmer-Thomas, *The Political Economy of Central America since 1920*; Dunkerley, *Power in the Isthmus*; Edelberto Torres Rivas, *Interpretación del desarrollo social centroamericano: Procesos y estructuras de una sociedad dependiente* (San José: Editorial Universitaria Centroamericana, 1981); López Alas Rosales and Escobar Cornejo, "La crisis de 1929 y sus consecuencias en los años posteriores"; Zamosc, "Class Conflict in an Export Economy"; Zamosc, "The Definition of a Socio-economic Formation"; Burns, "The Modernization of Underdevelopment."

35 For discussions of the revolt that emphasize peasant participation, see López Vallecillos, "La insurrección popular campesina de 1932"; Segundo Montes, "Levantamientos campesinos en El Salvador" (although Montes, *El compadrazgo*, emphasizes ethnic relations); Montes, "El campesinado salvadoreño"; Mario Lungo, *La lucha de las masas en El Salvador* (San Salvador: UCA, 1987); Flores Macal, *Origen, desarrollo y crisis de las formas de dominación en El Salvador*; Kincaid, "Peasants into Rebels." Most recently, Jeffery M. Paige, in *Coffee and Power*, emphasizes the mobilization of what he terms the "pobretariado."

36 Montes, *El Compadrazgo*. Important works by exiles include Menjivar, *Acumulación originaria y desarollo del capitalismo en El Salvador*; Menjivar, *Formación y lucha del proletariado industrial salvadoreño*; Guidos Vejar, *El Ascenso del Militarismo en El Salvador*; Flores Macal, *Origen, Desarrollo y crisis de las formas de dominación en El Salvador*; Mario Flores Macal, "El movimiento sindical Salvadoreño: características principales," *Anuario de Estudios Centroamericanos* 6 (1980), 17–24; Richter, *Proceso de Acumulación y Dominación en la Formación Socio-Política Salvadoreña*.

37 Federación de Trabajadores del Campo, "Perspectiva Histórica del Movimiento Campesino Revolucionario en El Salvador" (San Salvador: Ediciones Enero 32, 1979), 14–15.

38   Ferman Cienfuegos, "El Salvador: La Revolución Inevitable," 1982, NACLA archives, roll 14, file 89, 15.

39   Ibid.

40   The first scholar to emphasize the ethnic origins of the movement was Luna in his essay "Un heroico y trágico suceso de nuestra historia" (1964). Anderson also sought to establish correctly the role of Indigenous leaders and ethnic conflict in the emergence of the revolt. Recently Ching and Tilley have discussed ethnicity, politics, and the state during the 1920s and 1930s, arguing that Indian ethnicity was not as decimated after the repression as thought by some observers: "Indians, the Military, and the Rebellion of 1932"; Ching, "From Clientelism to Militarism." Also see Alvarenga, *Cultura y ética de la violencia*, and Pérez-Brignoli, "Indians, Communists, and Peasants." William Krehm in 1949 characterized the insurrection as "a cross between an old fashioned Indian uprising and a jacquerie of starving peasants, doubled here and there with a sophisticated veneer of communism." Krehm, *Democracies and Tyrannies of the Caribbean*, 8.

41   See "La Insurrección Indígena," El Periodico Nuevo Enfoque, 24 January 2005. This article refers to the role of the PCS as one of trying to "take advantage of the situation so that the PCS could lead" the "indigenous insurrection."

Chapter One: Garden of Despair

1   Wallace Thompson, *Rainbow Countries of Central America* (New York: E. P. Dutton, 1924), 94–95.

2   Ruhl, *The Central Americans*, 201.

3   Thompson, *Rainbow Countries of Central America*, 102.

4   Rothery, *Central America and the Spanish Main*, 78.

5   Ranajit Guha. *Dominance without Hegemony: History and Power in Colonial India* (Cambridge: Harvard University Press, 1997), vii.

6   William Roseberry, "Hegemony, Power, and the Language of Contention," *The Politics of Difference: Ethnic Premises in a World of Power*, ed. Wilmsen and McAllister (Chicago: University of Chicago Press, 1996).

7   Roseberry, "Hegemony, Power, and the Language of Contention," 80.

8   Gould, *To Lead as Equals*, 68–69.

9   See Gould, *To Die in This Way*.

10   McCreery, *Rural Guatemala*, 333–34.

11   Martin, *Salvador of the Twentieth Century*.

12   Koebel, *Central America*, 275.

13   This loan resulted in the controversial customs receivership. An agent appointed by banks in the United States controlled customs revenues and used a large share of these to pay the purchasers of the bonds issued in 1922.

14   Wilson, "The Crisis of National Integration in El Salvador," 3–42.

15   Hill, "Raising Coffee in El Salvador."

16 Dirección General de Estadística, *Anuario Estadístico* (San Salvador, 1911–40).

17 Lopez Harrison, *Patria*, 10 August 1931; *Revista de Agricultura Tropical* 1930, cited in Wilson, "The Crisis of National Integration in El Salvador," 40.

18 Lauria-Santiago. *An Agrarian Republic*; Geraldina Portillo, "Cafetaleros del Departamento de Santa Ana 1882–1898," paper presented at the VII Congreso Centroamericano de Historia, Tegucigalpa, Honduras, 28 April 2004; Geraldina Portillo, "Clases y sectores sociales participantes en la agroindustria cafetalera en el Departamento de La Libertad 1897–1901" (unpublished manuscript); Geraldina Portillo, "La tenencia de la tierra en el Departamento de La Libertad, 1897–1901" (unpublished manuscript). Their involvement in railroad and bank ownership also gave them a great advantage in developing their agricultural holdings.

19 *Anuario de la America Latina* (Barcelona: Bailly-Bailliere y Riera, 1914); Nomina de las Haciendas y Fincas mas importantes del depto. de La Libertad, 1929, AGN-MG–La Libertad.

20 S. L. Wilkinson, 25 April 1929, U.S. Foreign Agricultural Service, USNA.

21 Higher prices still were paid for plots adjacent to large plantations, with some paying from $1,500 to $2,500 for small tracts. S. L. Wilkinson to secretary of state, 25 April 1929, U.S. Foreign Agricultural Service, USNA.

22 The region attracted both permanent and seasonal wage workers from other parts of the country and even Honduras and Guatemala during periods of peak demand. The massive migration of Guatemalan workers dated back to the 1870s: Lauria-Santiago, *An Agrarian Republic*, chapter 6. The importance of these seasonal workers even in 1931 is acknowledged in Larín J. Lisandro, Gobernador de Sonsonate, Carta al Alcalde de Sonsonate, 23 December 1931, AGN-CG-So.

23 *Diario Oficial*, 14 April 1920, "Memoria de Hacienda: Problema del crédito, falta de liquido circulante, ¿quien se beneficia mas de escasez liquida? . . . ," 631. In 1921–22 nine exporters purchased insurance for one-third of the country's total coffee exports. Wilson, "The Crisis," 44, 60, 130–32.

24 The market was controlled by four investors: Suc. Dorila de Letona, Atilio G. Prieto, Peccorini Hmnos, and Samuel Quiroz. Government of El Salvador, Dirección General de Estadística, *La Republica de El Salvador* (San Salvador: Imprenta Nacional, 1924).

25 Mccafferty to secretary of state, 22 April 1925, United States Foreign Agricultural Service, USNA. Panela, crude unrefined sugar, was produced throughout the country in small animal-driven mills and used in food and candy production—items of popular consumption. See Geraldina Portillo, "Persistencia de lo tradicional en la producción agrícola y artesanal de la caña de azúcar en el Departamento de San Vicente," paper presented at the Sexto Congreso Centroamericano De Historia, Ciudad de Panamá, Panamá, 22–26 July 2002.

26 Rothery, *Central America and the Spanish Main*, 79–80.

27 Bulmer-Thomas, *The Political Economy of Central America since 1920*, 2.

28 Jimenez, "At the Banquet of Civilization," 284.

29 "Los Alvarez: Recuerdos de una Familia" (San Salvador: Mauricio Alvarez Geoffroy, 1995) [incl. "Memorias de la Familia Alvarez," written in 1951 by Carlos Alvarez Angel], 37.

30 Ibid., 109.

31 Ibid., 138.

32 Ruhl, *The Central Americans*, 203.

33 See Fink, *Workingmen's Democracy*, and Montgomery, *The Struggle for Worker's Control in America*.

34 "El Café de El Salvador" (San Salvador: Asociación Cafetalera de El Salvador, July 1932), 42.

35 Ruhl, *The Central Americans*, 200.

36 A. R. Harris, Degree of Economic Development, Report no. 14, San José, 22 December 1931, Department of State, USNA. The report also revealed how the élite used land concentration to reduce the cost of labor.

37 Cardenal, *El Poder Eclesiástico en El Salvador*, 369.

38 Francisco Osegueda, "La vida del campesino salvadoreño de otros tiempos y la del campesino actual," *Revista del Ateneo de El Salvador* 20 (1932), 12.

39 In 1926 Ambassador Caffery noted that the *Asociación Agrícola* ignored "the needs of small growers in debt." Caffery to Department of State, 30 August 1926, State Department, USNA.

40 W. W. Schott to Department of State, 20 January 1930, State Department, USNA; Paige, *Coffee and Power*; Rodolfo Castro. "Un proceso de modernización estatal 'autoritario' (1931–1939)" (unpublished manuscript, San Salvador, n.d.), 10–12; Asociación Cafetalera de El Salvador Gerente, "Carta al Sub-Secretario de Agricultura," 28 January 1931, AGN-CM-MG.

41 Wilson's characterization of this élite remains the most compelling because it stresses the inconsistency between the structural formation of this class and its weak political mechanisms. Wilson, "The Crisis," 60–63.

42 Ibid., 86.

43 Thompson, *Rainbow Countries of Central America*, 96.

44 Frederick Palmer, *Central America and Its Problems: An Account of a Journey from the Rio Grande to Panama* (New York: Moffat, Yard, 1910), 110.

45 Lauria-Santiago, *An Agrarian Republic*, chapters 6–7.

46 From 612,000 in 1880 to 1,437,000 in 1930.

47 For the northern and eastern regions of El Salvador, Honduras served as release valve for agrarian pressures. By the mid-1920s there were thousands of Salvadorans working in Honduras, although western El Salvador continued to receive significant seasonal migrant workers from eastern Guatemala to pick coffee. Thompson, *Rainbow Countries of Central America*, 183. Wilson claims that there were between twelve and sixty thousand Salvadorans in Honduras, with some Honduran towns composed of 50–100 percent Salvadoran im-

migrants. Wilson, "The Crisis," 118. Durham, *Scarcity and Survival in Central America*.

48 "There is a large percentage of small landowners, although at the present there is a tendency among the large plantation owners to purchase all the small farms which can be bought. This tendency today is more pronounced than it has been for some time, owing to the surplus of money these plantation owners have available through high prices for their coffee crops." MID, USNA. Another report by observers from the United States noted the tendency of smaller growers to lose their properties because of debt. Caffery to Department of State, 30 August 1926, Department of State, USNA.

49 Marroquín, "Estudio sobre la crisis de los años treinta en El Salvador," 120; Bradford Burns, "The Modernization of Underdevelopment: El Salvador, 1858–1931," *Journal of Developing Areas* 18, no. 3 (April 1984), 308.

50 Galindo Pohl, *Recuerdos de Sonsonate*.

51 The "Documentos Privados" kept by municipalities provide an important window into the many small transactions and obligations that tied hundreds of peasants to a handful of landowning families who also lent money and financed crops.

52 The 1930 census was published in 1942. Government of El Salvador, Dirección General de Estadística, *Población de la república de El Salvador* (San Salvador: Taller nacional de grabados, 1942).

53 Because of an increased demand for seasonal work and relatively high wages, thousands of Guatemalan and Honduran workers continued to supplement Salvadoran hands at harvest time.

54 Gobernación de Sonsonate, "Registro de los Individuos sin Trabajo" (1929), Archivo de la Gobernacion de Sonsonate. In mid-1931, at the time of lowest demand for labor in coffee and sugar production, shoemakers who had earned three colones a day in the boom times now earned two. Common-laborer wages were 50 cents for half a day's work. Coffee pickers received one-half cent a pound, which meant that the most effective pickers could earn one colon a day, while 60–70 cents a day was more likely for most workers. A. E. Carleton to Foreign Agricultural Service, Commerce and Industries Report, 15 August 1931, United States Foreign Agricultural Service, USNA.

55 The overwhelming majority were *colonos*, although the figure includes a handful of artisans and administrators.

56 There is no evidence of significant changes in the number or proportion of *colonos* during the 1930s. These data are based on preliminary calculations based on the printed version of the 1938 census and a more detailed manuscript version of the same data held in the Biblioteca del Banco Hipotecario. Asociación cafetalera de El Salvador, *Primer Censo Nacional del Café* (San Salvador: Talleres gráficos Cisneros, 1940). See also Galindo Pohl, *Recuerdos de Sonsonate*, 274, 280.

57 Outside the coffee sector, and especially in central and eastern El Salvador,

colonato involved more traditional practices in which colonos rented land for a fixed rent paid in corn or other agricultural products. Benjamin Muse, Foreign Service Report, American legation, 19 September 1924, Department of State, USNA; S. L. Wilkerson to Foreign Agricultural Service, 25 April 1929, United States Foreign Agricultural Service, USNA.

58 This made *colonato* not much different from *aparceria*. Benjamin Muse, Narrative Reports, El Salvador, 19 September 1924, United States Foreign Agricultural Service, USNA.

59 S. L. Wilkinson to secretary of state, 25 April 1929, United States Foreign Agricultural Service, USNA.

60 Ruhl, *The Central Americans*, 192.

61 One of the effects of the crisis was that banks withheld loans to farmers in 1931, forcing them to minimize their outlay of cash funds. A. E. Carleton, U.S. consul, excerpt, Commerce and Industries Review, 27 January 1931, United States Foreign Agricultural Service, USNA.

62 Wilson, "The Crisis," 118

63 Galindo Pohl, *Recuerdos de Sonsonate*, 274.

64 See Wickham-Crowley, *Guerrillas and Revolution in Latin America*, 117–18, 243.

65 One notable from the region recalls an agreement among employers to lower wages during 1931. Galindo Pohl, *Recuerdos de Sonsonate*, 297. Between 1929 and 1931 rural and urban unemployment also increased. Government officials were ordered to keep lists of the unemployed workers in the major cities and encourage employers to hire workers and rent unused lands. Ministerio del Trabajo al Gobernador de Sonsonate, Legajo de Cartas al Gobernador de Sonsonate, 8 April 1931, AGN-CG-So. In the relatively small town of Juayua four hundred unemployed workers petitioned President Araujo for relief. Ogilvie, "The Communist Revolt of El Salvador, 1932," 53. When Araujo offered plots for rent on government-owned haciendas the requests came at the rate of one hundred for each available plot. Galindo Pohl, *Recuerdos de Sonsonate*, 273. See also Solicitudes de Lotes, 1931, AGN-CM-MG.

66 A. E. Carleton, Commerce and Industries Quarterly Report, 15 August 1931, United States Foreign Agricultural Service, USNA. Even lower wages were reported in more heavily Indian localities. Llanes, "A History of Protestantism in El Salvador," 127.

67 Tesis sobre la situación internacional, nacional y de la federación regional de trabajadores de El Salvador, Comintern 495.119.10, pp. 27–28.

68 Ogilvie, "The Communist Revolt of El Salvador, 1932," 53; "Conatos Subversivos Promovidos por Varios Individuos Sindicalistas en la Hacienda 'La Preza' Propiedad de Doña Claudia de Borbon, Coatepeque," 1930, AGN-CM-MG.

69 Similar claims are also found in other contexts. The tax filings of Concha v. de Regalado show that in 1937–38 profits from her stores were 9,000 colones, while profits from her company's principal hacienda (San Isidro) were 63,000 pesos. AGN–Tax Records.

70 Ironically this group of small-scale peddlers, many of whom were Eastern European or Russian Jewish immigrants, was decimated during the repression of 1932 with the excuse that some labor organizers had presented themselves as such. *La Tribuna* (Costa Rica), January–February 1932.

71 "Informe Sobre las Condiciones de Vida de los Jornaleros del Departamento," 1932, AGN-CM-MG.

72 Alcalde de Nueva San Salvador, "Informe Rendido por el Alcalde Municipal y Jefe del Distrito de Nueva San Salvador al Sr. Gobernador," 28 April 1932, AGN-CM-MG.

73 Gobernación de Sonsonate, "Registro de los Individuos sin Trabajo," April 1929, AGS.

74 Ogilvie, "The Communist Revolt of El Salvador, 1932"; Ministerio de Hacienda Jose E. Suay, Crédito Público, "Carta al Ministro de Gobernación," 1928, AGN-CM-MG.

75 Ogilvie, "The Communist Revolt of El Salvador, 1932," 52.

76 Ministro de Gobernación J. Novoa, "Telegrama al Gobernador de Sonsonate," 1931, AGN-CM-MG; Gobernador de Sonsonate Aristides Castillo, "Carta al Alcalde de Sonsonate," 16 May 1931, AGN-CM-MG; P. Diaz, "Carta al Ministro de Gobernación," 20 August 1931, AGN-CM-MG.

77 Galindo Pohl, *Recuerdos de Sonsonate*, 296–97.

78 Wickham-Crowley, *Guerrillas and Revolution*; Alan Knight, *The Mexican Revolution*; Gould, *To Lead as Equals*; Paige, *Coffee and Power*; Lauria-Santiago, *An Agrarian Republic*, chapter 8.

79 López, "Tradiciones inventadas y discursos nacionalistas," chapter 3.

80 Dana Munro, *The Five Republics of Central America* (New York: Oxford University Press, 1918), 106–7.

81 Morley Roberts, *On the Earthquake Line: Minor Adventures in Central America* (London: Arrowsmith, 1924), 114.

82 Thompson, *Rainbow Countries of Central America*, 178.

83 Ruhl, *The Central Americans*, 204.

84 Interview with Margarita Turcios, El Guayabo, Armenia, 2001.

85 Wilson, "The Crisis."

86 Approximately 25 percent of the country's adult labor force had to participate in the harvesting of coffee in 1929. This is a projection based on the country's demographics, the size of the crop, and the productivity and labor indices provided in CEPAL et al., *Tenencia de la tierra y desarollo rural en centroamérica* (San José: EDUCA, 1980), 172.

87 Alfredo Schlesinger quoted in Castro Moran, *Función política del ejercito Salvadoreño en el presente siglo*, 125–26.

88 Interview with Alberto Shul, Nahuizalco, 1999.

89 Mintz, "The Rural Proletariat and the Problem of Rural Proletarian Consciousness," 191.

90 Lauria-Santiago, " 'That a Poor Man Be Industrious.' "

91 White, *El Salvador*, 101.

92 It wasn't just peasants who held this memory. The editor of *Patria*, Masferrer, wrote in 1928, "About forty-five years ago the land in the country was distributed among the majority of the Salvadorans, but now it is falling into the hands of a few owners." *Patria*, 29 December 1928, 1.

93 This was so in Usulutan's coffee regions, for example, where most workers came from other regions of the country. See Lauria-Santiago, "La historia regional del café en El Salvador."

94 Galindo Pohl, *Recuerdos de Sonsonate*, 280–81.

95 Carl Vilhelm Hartman, "Estudios etnográficos sobre los indios de raza azteca existentes en El Salvador," *Boletín de la Dirección General de Estadística de la República de El Salvador*, nos. 7–8 (July–August 1902), 124–26, 146–48, trans. Andres Bang.

96 Scott, *The Moral Economy of the Peasant*.

97 Karl Marx, *Capital*, vol. 1 (London: Penguin, 1976), 875. On memories of primitive accumulation see Gould, *To Die in This Way*, 231–32.

Chapter Two: A Bittersweet Transition

1 Wilson, "The Crisis"; *Censo de Población 1930*; Menjivar, *Formación y lucha del proletariado industrial salvadoreño*.

2 Wilson, "The Crisis," 50; Bulmer-Thomas, *The Political Economy of Central America since 1920*, chapter 2.

3 This was considered the best-equipped and most independent of Central American militaries at the time.

4 See Uriarte, *La esfinge de Cuscatlan*, *El Presidente Quiñonez*, and Arias Gómez, *Farabundo Martí*. In Nahuilingo, for example, one hundred men were the founders of the local "liga de amigos sinta roja" in 1918. See Alvarenga, *Cultura y ética de la violencia*, for a well-documented discussion and reinterpretation of the role of the Ligas Rojas. Erik Ching challenges the classic perception of the Ligas as a populist institution, finding instead—at least in some localities— wealthy landowners in control of local chapters; Ching, "From Clientelism to Militarism."

5 Wilson, "The Crisis," 95.

6 One Guatemalan observer in 1932 noted how during the 1920s the "masses" had been mobilized for reform since the Quiñónez campaign against Palomo in 1918, which saw great unrest and violence in the countryside. See "En El Salvador: Origen del comunismo," *El Liberal Progresista*, 9 February 1932. One author traces attempts by President Carlos Meléndez to incorporate mass support to 1915: Castro Morán, *Función política del ejercito Salvadoreño en el presente siglo*, 38–43.

7 Uriarte, *La esfinge de Cuscatlan*; Ching, "From Clientelism to Militarism," chapters 5–6.

8 Dalton, *Miguel Mármol: Los sucesos de 1932 en El Salvador*, 96. According to Gómez, several hundred demonstrators attacked a police station. Arias Gómez, *Farabundo Martí*, 42.

9 Its commercial employees organized self-protection associations and gained significant reforms from the government, including recognition of their associations and work rules by the late 1920s.

10 Morley Roberts, *On the Earthquake Line: Minor Adventures in Central America* (London: Arrowsmith, 1924), 121.

11 In effect the U.S. embassy worried about this potential after 1918, but government efforts to keep the Ligas in check offered reassurance. Bedford, "Setting the Tone," 183–84.

12 Franklin Dallas Parker, *The Central American Republics* (London: Oxford University Press, 1964), 151.

13 G-2 report no. 1383, 12 May 1925, MID, USNA.

14 Quijano Hernández, *Dejados de la Mano de Dios*, 37. Other estimates place the number of demonstrators as high as fifteen thousand. See Arias Gómez, *Farabundo Martí*, 46.

15 Quijano Hernández, *Dejados de la Mano de Dios*, 40.

16 Ibid., 43–44.

17 Ruhl, *The Central Americans*, 199.

18 Dalton, *Miguel Mármol: Los sucesos de 1932 en El Salvador*, 85

19 Ibid., 88.

20 Gould, *To Lead as Equals*, 188–93.

21 James, *Resistance and Integration*.

22 See for example Molina, "The Polarization of Politics," 163–69.

23 Ruhl, *The Central Americans*, 198–99.

24 *New York Times*, 5 October 1930, 3.

25 In some ways Romero Bosque's presidency maintained continuity with the practices of Melendez and Quiñónez. Romero Bosque's own son was a broker for payoffs to the national assembly for concessions and contracts. See Jefferson Cafferey to secretary of state, 30 April 1928, no. 1102, Department of State, USNA; Krehm, *Democracies and Tyrannies*, 3.

26 "Legajo de Cartas al Gobernador de Sonsonate," 1931, AGN-CM-MG. Nonetheless, as the president's brother-in-law, Romero Bosque at this point seemed to be a safe potential candidate for the PND.

27 *La Voz de la Nación*, November 1926 thorugh September 1927.

28 Romero Bosque and Gómez Zarate were approved as their their candidates. *La Voz de la Nación*, 15 September 1927. Erik Ching points out the extent of continuity between local officials who often changed their loyalties to retain power. Ching, "From Clientelism to Militarism," 277–78.

29 Marcial Pereira, Marcial Vela, and Gonzalo Hernández to Novoa, MG, San Vicente, 7 November 1927.

30 *¡Alerta!! ¡Obreros Trabajadores!*, imprint, San Vicente, October 1927; a similar

insurgent campaign was run by members of the San Vicente élite, who emphasized the abuses and cronyism of the populist Liga Roja, which for years had controlled local elections. Vicentinos, imprint, San Vicente, 19 November 1927.

31 Manuel de Mendoza, Ministerio de Gobernación, "Memorandum a los Gobernadores," 22 November 1927, AGN-CM-MG.

32 On Romero's intervention in Atiquizaya see Pío Romero Bosque, telegram to Minister of Gobernacion, 5 December 1927, AGN-CM-MG.

33 Ramón al Gobernador del Departamento, 3 November 1927, AGN-CM-MG.

34 Bustamante, Historia militar de El Salvador; Castro Moran, Función política del ejercito Salvadoreño en el presente siglo. For the trial proceedings see Government of El Salvador, Procesos Relativos a la Rebelión del 6 de Diciembre de 1927.

35 Pío Romero Bosque to Gobernadores, telegram, 6 December 1927, AGN-CM-MG. Even after the consolidation of Romero Bosque's government conspiracies against him continued; in 1929 a murder plot was discovered, but this did not stall his reforms. Diario Latino; New York Times, 17 April 1929, 24.

36 La Voz de la Nación.

37 Magdaleno Alvarez, "Carta al Presidente de la República, Pío Romero Bosque," 20 November 1927, AGN-CG-So.

38 Samuel M. Rodríguez, "Carta al Ministro de Gobernación," 28 January 1930, AGN-CM-MG.

39 In December 1930 Romero Bosque changed the long-standing electoral law and allowed the formation of mixed electoral committees with representatives of all the major parties. Ministerio de Gobernación, "Telegrama Circular a los Gobernadores," 31 December 1930, AGN-CM-MG.

40 Ching, "From Clientelism to Militarism," 422.

41 Borghi B. Daglio was the Italian consul to El Salvador. In 1910 he owned one of Sonsonate's largest coffee processing plants in Juayúa and others in Santa Ana, Ahuchapan, and San Pedro Nonualco. He was one of the country's largest coffee exporters, controlling five million pounds in 1916. By 1930 he had purchased a second beneficio in Juayúa (Buena Vista). Ward, ed. and comp., Libro azul de El Salvador, 246.

42 Erik Ching describes this clan as a network of landowners connected through business relations and marriage, dating to around the turn of the century. Ching, "From Clientelism to Militarism,"422.

43 Alcalde de Juayúa Francisco Rivera Cortez, "Telegrama al Gobernador de Sonsonate," 1931, AGN-CG-So.

44 For the dissolution of the community of Dolores Izalco and the Ladinization of the neighborhood see Lauria-Santiago, "Land, Community, and Revolt in Indian Izalco, El Salvador."

45 Roughly half of Izalco's population was identified as Indian in official statistics.

46 Gobernador de Sonsonate, "Informe de la Visita Oficial a los Pueblos del Departamento," 20 September 1913, AGN-CG-So.

47 Annually the indigenous organization would formally notify the national government of the election of authorities. In 1924 two hundred males voted. Alcalde Indio de Izalco Sotero Pasín, "Carta al Gobernador del Departamento de Sonsonate," 29 March 1924, AGN-CG-So.

48 For a conflict over water rights in 1927 see "Diligencias de Varios Vecinos de Izalco: Eduardo Salaverria le Pone Obstaculos para Regar Sus Terrenos," 1928, AGN-CM-MG; for a conflict over water rights in 1929 see Izalco Francisco Tespan, "Carta al Gobernador del Departamento," 17 April 1929, AGN-CG-So.

49 "Lista de las Personas Que Cultivan Café en la Jurisdicción de Izalco," 12 July 1926, AGN-CG-So.

50 "Informativo Instruido a Efecto de Averiguar Varios Abusos del Secretario Municipal de Izalco, Denunciado por la Señora Francisca Roque de Minco," 1928, AGN-CM-MG.

51 "Informativo Instruido a Efecto de Averiguar Varios Abusos del Secretario Municipal de Izalco, Denunciado por la Señora Francisca Roque de Minco"; "Diligencias Seguidas a Efecto de Averiguar Varios Abusos Cometidos por el Secretario Municipal de Izalco Don Tomas Sicilia," 1927, AGN-CG-So.

52 Heraldo de Sonsonate, 14 January 1930, 2.

53 Gobernador Departamental de Sonsonate Lisandro Larin Z., "Carta al Ministro de Gobernación," 6 December 1929, AGS.

54 The Directorio was formed by "gente consciente" and "obreros de la ciudad." "Sobre Nulificación de Elecciones en Izalco," 1929, AGN-CG-So. The governor also claimed, as a sign of the illegitimacy of the protest, that some of the complaints were from the cantones San Isidro and El Sunza, hinting that they were mostly indigena hacienda workers and colonos aligned with Arturo Araujo, already known as a reformer.

55 "Sobre Nulificación de Elecciones en Izalco," 1929, AGN-CG-So.

56 El Heraldo de Sonsonate, 10 December 1929.

57 Ibid.

58 Ministerio de Gobernación, "Vecinos de Nahuizalco Piden Se Apoye la Candidatura de Gregorio Gutiérrez . . . ," 27 September 1923, AGN-CM-MG.

59 "Telegramas Sobre Politica y Elecciones," 10 December 1927, AGS.

60 Telegram from M. Mora Castro to Ministry of War, 30 December 1929, AGN-CM-MG.

61 Ching, "From Clientelism to Militarism," 152. Brito was under indictment for arson.

62 See Gould, To Die in This Way.

63 Espino, Prosas Escogidas, 20.

64 Rochac in Patria, 9 October 1929, 3.

65 See Wilson, "The Crisis." This stance is in marked contrast to that of other Central American intellectuals who welcomed the decline of the indigenous population, for example Salvador Mendieta.

66 See for example New York Times, 9 July 1914, 1.

67 Some of this was because until the early 1920s El Salvador's main sources of foreign investment and trade were in Europe, especially Germany, which bought most of the country's coffee.

68 This was still felt a few years later when Ruhl visited the country. For a detailed discussion of the customs receivership see Buell, *The Central Americans*.

69 *La Epoca*, 17 June 1931.

70 *New York Times*, 3 March 1928, 3; *New York Times*, 20 February 1928, 1.

71 Galindo Pohl, *Recuerdos de Sonsonate*, 329; *Diario de Ahuachapan*, 10 July 1928; Arias Gómez, *Farabundo Marti*.

72 U.S. Department of State, "American Legation: General Correspondence."

73 *Diario de Ahuachapan*, 10 July 1928, 5.

74 Richard Salisbury, "The Middle American Exile of Victor Raul Haya de la Torre," *Americas* 40, no. 1 (July 1983), 1–17; Jussi Pakkasvirta: "Víctor Raúl Haya de la Torre en Centroamérica: ¿La primera y última fase del aprismo internacional?," *Revista de Historia* 44 (2002), 9–31. The U.S. and Peruvian embassies protested and called for the suppression of his activities. Ministerio de Relaciones Exteriores N. Martínez Duarte, "Carta al Ministro de Gobernación," 1928, AGN-CM-MG.

75 Galindo Pohl, *Recuerdos de Sonsonate*, 329.

76 López, "Tradiciones inventadas y discursos nacionalistas," chapter 3.

77 Ibid.

78 *Diario de Ahauchapán*, 5 July 1928, 1. Pavletich was Central American organizer for APRA, based in Peru. In 1928 he and the APRA founder Haya de la Torre toured El Salvador. N. Martinez Duarte, "Carta al Ministro de Gobernación," AGN-CM-MG. He was allowed to give public speeches but Romero Bosque managed to keep him from giving a more radical anti-imperialist speech while there. J. Caffery to secretary of state, no. 1292, 4 February 1928, Department of State, USNA.

79 Dalton, *Miguel Mármol: Los sucesos de 1932 en El Salvador*, 116.

80 State Department records between 1926 and 1930 show constant attempts by Washington to force the Salvadoran government to crack down on supposed Mexican agents and propaganda directed against the United States.

81 *New York Times*, 3 December 1930.

82 *El Heraldo de Sonsonate*, 17 February 1930.

83 Ibid., 9 January 1931 (signed "Sandokao").

84 Choussy cited in Wilson, "The Crisis," 120–21.

85 See Karen Racine, "Alberto Masferrer and the Vital Minimum: The Life and Thought of a Salvadoran Journalist, 1868–1932," *Americas* 54, no. 2 (1997), 225. Vitalismo "captured the imagination of reform-minded humanitarians across the isthmus" (225). Masferrer also linked the social reformism of these years with its anti-imperialism. Alberto Masferrer. "En la hora de crujir de dientes," *La Prensa*, 3 February 1927, 1, cited in Jaime Barba, "Masferrer, vitalismo y luchas sociales en los años veinte," *Región: Centro de Investigaciones* (1997). For

discussions of Masferrer and *Patria* and their relationship to broader reformist movements see Barba, "Masferrer"; García Giráldez, "El Unionismo y el Anti-imperialismo en la década de 1920"; Casaus, "Las Influencias de las redes intelectuales teosóficas en la opinión pública centroamericana"; López, "Tradiciones inventadas y discursos nacionalistas."

86 For a discussion of the student movement during this period see Ricardo Antonio Argueta Hernández, "Los estudiantes universitarios y las luchas sociales en El Salvador (1920–1931)," Sexto Congreso Centroamericano de Historia (Panama, 2002).

87 See for example Mayorga Rivas, "Los indios de Izalco, terruño salvadoreño." One reformist governor noted the "movimiento a favor del Indio" throughout "nuestra America" and complained that "Centroamérica, que en parte tienen un sedimento indigena considerable ha olvidado, ha descuidado totalmente la situación de sus indios." He thought that "el indio de ciertas zonas de nuestro país no es un problema, antes mejor significa una avanzada a la civilización." Rochac in *Patria*. See also López, "Tradiciones inventadas y discursos nacionalistas," for a discussion of Maria de Baratta's ethnographic work and other evidence of this revaluation of indigenous culture.

88 Bedford, "Setting the Tone," 208.

89 "Informe del VI Congreso Regional Obrero y Campesino, 1930," Comintern 18, p. 125.

90 Dalton, *Miguel Mármol: Los sucesos de 1932 en El Salvador*, 104.

91 Thompson, *The Making of the English Working Class*, 831.

92 Gould, *To Lead as Equals*, 69.

93 Laclau, *Politics and Ideology in Marxist Theory*, 107.

94 See Marx, *Capital*, vol. 1 (London: Penguin, 1976), 457–515.

95 "Informe de la Industria Textil en C.H." Comintern 495.119.1, 1930.

96 "Libro Copiador de Telegramas," 1929, AGN-CM-MG. In February a rare strike of colonos broke out on the hacienda El Paisnal, near Izalco.

97 Arias Gómez, *Farabundo Martí*, 93.

98 "Libro Copiador de Telegramas," 1929, AGN-CM-MG; WDR to secretary of state, 27 July 1929, Diplomatic Correspondence no. 100, USNA. It appears that the port agency instituted the eight-hour day.

99 "Le travail et la situation des jeunesses communistes," Comintern 495.119.1, 1930.

100 Araujo's father disputed lands bordering between his hacienda and Izalco's Dolores community when this community surveyed its lands as part of the partition process of the 1890s. Most of his properties came from colonial-era haciendas and lots purchased around the turn of the century. See Lauria-Santiago, "Land, Community, and Revolt in Indian Izalco, El Salvador."

101 El Sunza produced thirty thousand quintals in 1926. In 1932 it was estimated to produce sixteen to eighteen thousand quintals of sugar cane from three hundred manzanas. In Armenia he owned a large coffee farm, a cattle ranch

(San Eugenia), and the El Carmen sugar mill. His hacienda El Triunfo in San Julian consisted of ten *caballerías* with cattle, coffee, and balsam trees. He shared control of the Salvador Railways with other investors.

102 Most accounts of Araujo emphasize his connections to Britain, what Erik Ching described as his Anglophilia, and his admiration for the British Labour Party. Ching, "From Clientelism to Militarism,"249.

103 Wilson, "The Crisis," 50.

104 For a discussion of Melendez-Quiñónez's manipulation of these elections and their exclusion see Ching, "From Clientelism to Militarism," 249–53.

105 Bedford, "Setting the Tone," chapter 4.

106 "Boletín del Ministerio de Guerra," 833; *Diario oficial*, 14 May 1920; *New York Times*, 16 May 1920, 4.

107 "Informe Anual de la Guardia Nacional," 31 December 1922, AGN-CM-MG.

108 Gobernador Departamental de Sonsonate Lisandro Larin Z., "Carta al Ministro de Gobernación," 1929, AGN-CG-So.

109 Galindo Pohl, *Recuerdos de Sonsonate*, 149.

110 The Partido del Proletariado Salvadoreño played a critical role in linking Araujo to labor. The PPS was formed by reformist leaders of the FRTS who were expelled when the left gained control of the organization.

111 Sectors supportive of *Araujismo* initially, like the Partido del Proletariado Salvadoreño, sought land reform. In the weeks right after Araujo's electoral victory, according to one account, peasants reportedly occupied lands in haciendas in western El Salvador. Ogilvie, "The Communist Revolt of El Salvador, 1932," 44; Alvarenga, *Cultura y ética de la violencia*, 305; Casaus, "Las Influencias de las redes intelectuales teosóficas en la opinión pública centroamericana"; García Giráldez, "El Unionismo y el Antiimperialismo en la década de 1920."

112 "Mi primer mensaje al pueblo salvadoreño," *Diario del Salvador*, 6 November 1930, repr. in enclosure 1, despatch no. 388, 6 November 1930, MID, USNA.

113 *Diario Latino*; Gobernador de Sonsonate, "Carta al Ministro de Gobernación," 28 November 1930, AGN-CG-So.

114 Schlesinger, *La Verdad Sobre el Comunismo*.

115 Ibid.; Proceso Contra el Alcalde de Tacuba por Quejas de los Partidos Araujistas," 1930, AGN-CG-So.

116 "Informativo Seguido Contra Don Perfecto Eleuterio Chafoya Acusado por Comunista ó Bolcheviquista, Atiquisaya," 21 November 1930, AGN-CG-Ah.

117 "Lista de Electores, Inscritos y Votantes para Todo el País, Elecciones Enero 1931," 1931, AGN-CM-MG.

118 U.S. Department of War, MID, "Correspondence and Record Cards of the Military Intelligence Division Relating to General, Political, Economic, and Military Conditions in Central America, 1918–1941," USNA.

119 Gobernador de Sonsonate Lisandro Larín J., "Carta al Alcalde de Sonsonate," 1931, AGN-CG-So; Fred Cruse, San José, 30 April 1931, no. 3110, MID, USNA.

120 *New York Times*, 6 January 1930, 4.

121 In November the *New York Times* reported an agreement reached by Romero Bosque with all candidates that only two candidates would run, one a civilian and the other a military man. Clearly this pact did not hold. *New York Times*, 2 November 1930, E, 6.

122 Warren D. Robbins to assistant secretary of state, 16 January 1931, no. 424, Department of State, USNA.

123 AGN-Tax Records.

124 Warren D. Robbins to secretary of state, 31 October 1930, no. 386, Department of State, USNA.

125 Bedford, "Setting the Tone."

126 Meardi wrote to the minister of interior about "el comunismo que nos ha invadido guiado por grupos de extranjeros." Detalle sobre los sucesos ocurridos en aquella ciudad los días 22 y 23 del mes de Oct. ppdo., 1930, AGN-CM-MG.

127 Warren D. Robbins to secretary of state, 31 October 1930, no. 386, Department of State, USNA.

Chapter Three: Fiestas of the Oppressed

1 Interview with Fabián Mojica, Sonzacate, 1999.

2 Carlos Figueroa Ibarra, "El 'Bolchevique Mexicano' de la Centroamérica de los veinte" (interview with Hernández Anaya), *Memoria* 4, no. 31 (September–October 1990), 218.

3 Figueroa Ibarra, "El Bochevique Mexicano," 217–18. In an interview with Mojica (2000) he stated that the same campesinos from the cantons of Izalco went to organize the plantation workers in the San Julián area. Many of the village residents worked on the plantations and returned home every fortnight, especially during the coffee harvest.

4 Lauria-Santiago, *An Agrarian Republic*, chapter 5; Mahoney, *The Legacies of Liberalism*.

5 Report sent to the Sección Latino Americano of the ISR, 25 March 1930, San Pedro Sula, Comintern 495.119.11.

6 Schlesinger, *Revolución Comunista*, 230.

7 Dalton, *Miguel Mármol: Los sucesos de 1932 en El Salvador*, 130–31.

8 "La Situación del El Salvador," 10 June 1930, Comintern 495.119.3. Interview with Fabian Mojica (Sonzacate, 1999, 2000), a carpenter from Sonzacate, who was a rural union organizer in 1929 and 1930.

9 J. Díaz del Moral, *Historia de las agitaciones campesinas andaluzas* (Madrid, 1929), cited in Hobsbawm, *Primitive Rebels*, 87–88.

10 Dalton, *Miguel Mármol: Los sucesos de 1932 en El Salvador*, 118.

11 On the social and geographical roots of the sugar proletariat see González, *La Fiesta de los Tiburones*. On the 1933 movement see de la Fuente, *A Nation for All*, 139–212; Barry Carr, "Mill Occupation and Soviets: the Mobilization of

Sugar Workers in Cuba, 1917–1933," *Journal of Latin American Studies* 28 (1996), 129–58.

12 "Organizing was greatly facilitated by the fact that many union activists lived in the same neighborhoods as the field laborers." Gould, *To Lead as Equals*, 77.

13 "Conatos Subversivos Promovidos por Varios Individuos Sindicalistas en la Hacienda 'La Preza' Propiedad de Doña Claudia de Borbon, Coatepeque," 1930, AGN-CM-MG.

14 Ibid.

15 Ibid.

16 Ibid.

17 Various reports in the Comintern documents purport to list all strike activity. Several reports and references from the FRTS congress of May 1930 discuss two urban strikes, one in a textile mill and one at a water company. Comintern 495.119.10, p. 60. In 1931 there were two strikes in San Salvador, one involving bus workers and the other shoe workers. There were no reported rural strikes that got off the ground or lasted more than a day until late in 1931. See report during the latter part of 1932 to the Comintern by "Comrade Hernández," 495.119.4, p. 27. Through an analysis of all available documentation we have determined that "Hernández" could only have been Max Cuenca. "Hernández" / Cuenca formed part of the three-person "comité militar" appointed by the Central Committee once the insurrection was decided upon. The other two members were Mármol (in hiding) and Martí (executed). In addition to this argument there are numerous points of coincidence between the account by "Hernández" of his own positions (for example at the decisive meeting of the Central Committee on 20 January) and those attributed to "the intellectual" Cuenca by Mármol.

18 "Actividad Comunista desarrollase ahora en San Isidro, Izalco," *Diario Latino*, 23 January 1931.

19 Lauria-Santiago, *An Agrarian Republic*, chapter 5.

20 Interviews with Doroteo López, San Isidro, 1999 and 2001.

21 Ibid. Most of the information on the organization in Los Amates derives from extensive interviews with Doroteo Lopez in 1999 and 2001. Lopez (born in 1914) lived in Los Amates during the early 1930s, where his father was a foreman on a coffee finca.

22 Onofre Durán, a successful commercial farmer and large landowner, had been governor of Ahuachapán and member of the national assembly.

23 The farms of Jayaque hired approximately 3,500 coffee pickers during the high season (1938 Coffee Census, manuscript, Biblioteca del Banco Hipotecario). A core of about twenty-five highly capitalized commercial farms (most equipped with their own powered mills) hired most of the workers (Directorio 1924).

24 All informants in the general area remember him. In the town of Armenia, among other activities he helped to organize a soccer team.

25 Benjamin Arrieta Rossi, Gobernador del Departamento de La Libertad, "Carta

al Ministro de Gobernación, Dr. Manuel V. Mendoza," 13 March 1930, AGN-CM-MG.

26 Acta de la Quinta Sesión, Congreso FRTS, 7 May 1930, 10(12) Comintern 495.119.10.

27 Interviews with Vicente Flores, Jayaque, 2001; Jacinto Mendez, Jayaque, 2001.

28 Interviews with Ramón Vargas, Turin, 1999; Salomé Torres, El Cacao, Sonsonate, 2001; Manuel Linares, El Cacao, 2001; Miguel Lino, El Tortuguero, Atiquizaya, 2001.

29 Interview with Ramón Vargas, Atiquizaya, 1998.

30 The relationship between celebrating and political organizing extended to the indigenous cofradías of Izalco, where local élites noted the connection between celebration, organizing, and the strengthening of a culture of solidarity. One of the first measures taken by the imposed mayor of Izalco after the defeat of the insurrection justified his request for removing religious images from the control of the cofradía by explaining how "Siendo muchas las cofradias de imagenes entre la clase indígena que acuerpado por ello mismo hacen sus grandes reuniones en donde no solamente se trataba de sus fiestas, sino que se fraguaban actos que están reñidos con nuestras leyes." Alcalde municipal de Izalco, "certificación de acta municipal," 3 February 1932, AGN-CG-So; Telegramas al Gobernador de Sonsonete, 1932, AGN-CG-So.

31 Maurice Agulhon's pioneering concept of sociability referred mainly to sites inhabited by urban middle sectors (including workers) and specifically those settings removed from both the family and political institutions.

32 Victor Turner, *Dramas, Fields and Metaphors: Symbolic Action in Human Society* (Ithaca: Cornell University Press, 1974), 52.

33 Ibid., 248.

34 Ibid., 274.

35 Cited in Erhard Doubrawa, "Martin Buber, Anarchist," *Gestalt Journal*, spring 2001.

36 Interview with Sotero Linares, Las Higueras, Izalco, 2001.

37 "Sobre la Situación internacional, nacional y de la FRTS, Las Tareas Fundamentales, Nuestro Programa," Jorge Fernández Anaya, May 1930, 19(126) Comintern 495.119.10.

38 Ibid., 12(119) Comintern 495.119.10.

39 Ibid., 21(128) Comintern 495.119.10.

40 Although in Cuba there are no references to his ideological deviations, Mella was suspected of being a Trotskyite. He edited a journal in Mexico called *El Tren Blindado*, in direct reference to Trotsky's military leadership against the counter-revolution that followed the rise of the Bolshevik party in Russia. See Pino Cacucci, "Los Motivos Porque Asesinaron a Julio Antonio Mella," *La Jornada* (Mexico City), 19 June 2005.

41 "Informe," 12 August 1930, Comintern 495.119.12.

42 Martí years earlier seemed aware of the cultural dimension of campesino

organizing. See Taracena's discussion a memo by Martí to the Central American Communist Party in Guatemala in Taracena, "El Primer Partido Comunista de Guatemala."

43 Laclau, *Politics and Ideology in Marxist Theory*, 107.

44 Ibid., 172–73.

45 Ibid., 174.

46 Ibid., 175.

47 Cardenal, *Historia de Una Esperanza*, 452.

48 Ibid.

49 "Informe del VI Congreso Regional Obrero y Campesino Constituyente de la Federación Regional de Trabajadores de El Salvador," 4 May 1930, Comintern 495.119.10, p. 106, laments the lack of membership statistics. "La situación actual de El Salvador," an internal document of the PCS dated 10 June 1930, gives a partial account of rural labor organizing: Santiago de Texacuango 400; Armenia 2,500; Ahuachapán over 1,000; Nahuizalco 1,703 (including 544 women); Juayúa 600. Comintern 495.119.3.

50 These often combined coffee with sugar production.

51 Salvador Manuel Mendoza, "Carta al Director General de Policía," 5 February 1931, AGN-CM-MG.

52 *Diario Latino*, 6 February 1931.

53 Schlesinger, *Revolución comunista*, 211.

54 Comintern 495.119.10, p. 29 (31).

55 "Informe del Gobernador," 1930, AGN-CM-MG.

56 "Cartas y Telegramas al Gobernador de Sonsonate," 1931, AGS; "Cartas y Telegramas al Gobernador de Sonsonate," 1931, AGN-CG-So.

57 He wrote: "No ha habido gobernador hijo de puta que no haya enviado sus chingaderas de telegramas acusando de subversivas nuestras organizaciones, y pidiendo castigos ejemplares." Jorge Fernández Anaya, "Informe," Guatemala, 12 August 1930, Comintern 495.119.12.

58 Telegrama from Comandante de Puesto, Timoteo Flores to Alcalde de Jayaque, 19 August 1930, AMJ, located in Municipalidad de Jayaque. The Comandante de Puesto of Jayaque reported also on the 19th on the capture of "Cabecillas Andres Solís and Tomas Barrera, los que intentaban anteanoche asaltar esta ciudad."

59 Alcalde de Jayaque, Telegrama al Ministro de Guerra, 21 August 1930, AMJ; Ministro de Gobernación Manuel Mendoza, "Carta al Gobernador de Sonsonate," 1930, AGN-CG-So.

60 See a report by Jorge Fernández Anaya, 12 August 1930, Comintern 495.119.12, p. 6. Also see arrest lists for Nahuizalco and Izalco in August 1930 in Eladio Campos, Director de Policia, "Informes al Gobernador de Sonsonate," August 1930, Archivo de la Gobernación de Sonsonate (AGA).

61 Ministro de Gobernación Manuel Mendoza, "Carta al Gobernador de Sonsonate," 1930, AGN-CM-MG; Alcalde de Nahuizalco, "Telegrama al Gobernador de Sonsonate," 21 September 1930, AGS.

62 Alcalde de Nahuizalco, "Telegrama al Gobernador de Sonsonate," 21 September 1930, AGS; Interviews with Alberto Shul, Nahuizalco, 1999–2001; Angel Olivares, Nahuizalco, 1998.

63 See for example Acta 9 del Comité Central de PCS, 21 November 1930, Comintern 95.119.3, referring to discussions of insurrection among militants in Sonsonate; "La situación actual de El Salvador," Partido Comunista Salvadoreo, dated 10 June 1930, mentions the campesinos' "deseo de ir a las manifestaciones machete en manos."

64 "Informe Sobre el Salvador," Jorge Fernández Anaya to Alberto Moreau, secretary general of Colonial Department, CPUSA, 8 September 1930, Comintern 495.119, p. 9.

65 Ibid., p. 10.

66 Comintern, Informe rendido por los camaradas de El Salvador, Santa Ana, 1936, 495.119.7, p. 1 (23).

67 Legajo de Cartas al Gobernador de Sonsonate, 1931, AGS. It is quite likely that the color red also harkened back to the state-supported Ligas Rojas (1918–22), which had empowered indigenous people in local politics and legitimized the use of force in defense of corporate political interests

68 William D. Robbins to secretary of state, 3 December 1930, no 401, U.S. Department of State, USNA.

69 New York Times, 24 December 1930. The Times reported two dead and eleven wounded. SRI reported eight dead.

70 Informe de la sección de le El Salvador rendido pro el camarada Hernandez en la Junta del Secretariado del Caribe del SRI, 12 July 1932, Comintern 495.119.12, p. 1 (32). Hernández appears to be Max Ricardo Cuenca.

71 Cuenca report, 11 (18), Comintern.

72 Ibid., 12 (19), Comintern.

73 José Tomás Calderón General de División, "Contestación al Cuestionario . . . ," 1931, AGN-CM-MG; "Informativo Sobre Averiguar los Hechos Motivados por un Numeroso Grupo de Comunistas," May 1931, AGN-CG-So.

74 Informe del VI Congreso FRTS, Comintern 495.119.10, pp. 88–95. The thesis and platform were drawn up by Fernández Anaya.

75 The relationship between the electoral campaign and the labor organizing was noted by a periodical in Santa Ana, Idea Libre, which accused the "aristocratic" landowners of Santa Ana of not selling water to workers and Volcaneños as revenge for their vote in the last elections "so that they will obey next time." "Informativo Seguido por la Gobernación Politica Departamental de Santa Ana, para Averiguar Quien Sea el Autor de un Comentario Publico en Idea Libre del 12 de los Corrientes," 17 April 1931, AGN-CM-MG.

76 The following informants either stated "querían quitarles las fincas a los ricos" or used a very similar phrase: José Antonio Chachagua, Achapuco, Ahuachapán, 2001; Isabel Miranda, Sacacoyo, 2001; Margarita Turcios, el Guayabo, Armenia, 2001; Cecilio Martínez, Ateos, 2001; Salomé Torres, El Cacao, 2001;

Manuel Linares, El Cacao, 2001; Manuel Ascencio, Carrizal, 1998; María Hortensia García, Ahuachapán, 2001.

77 José Antonio Chachagua, Achupaco, Ahuachapán, 2001.

78 Legajo de Cartas al Gobernador de Sonsoante, 1931, AGN-CG-So.

79 R. C. Valdez, telegrama al Gobernador de Sonsonate, 20 March 1931, 7 April 1931, AGN-CG-So.

80 However the FRTS did have a presence in the area. In January 1931 more than a hundred men led by Gregorio Cortéz, union organizer from Armenia, met in Izalco's Barranca las Victorias on 19 January 1931. Armenia Emeterio Torres, "Telegrama al Gobernador de Sonsonate," 19 January 1931, AGN-CG-So.

81 "Cartas Sobre la Revuelta Comunista y Listas de los Adheridos al Gobierno," 1932, AMS.

82 Also arrested were Sergio De Leon and Agripino Guevara, who were known to use their salaries for "propaganda" purposes. Both had been arrested previously and were seen as organizers of previous protests in Sonsonate. The governor requested that they be found jobs in San Salvador to keep them away from Sonsonate! Gobernador to MG, 14 March 1931, AGN-CM-MG; Gobernador al Director General de policía, "Legajo de Cartas al Gobernador de Sonsonate." San Salvador, 17 March 1931; "Legajo de Cartas al Gobernador de Sonsonate," 1931, AGN-CM-MG.

83 Masen was reportedly the local "secretario" of the communist movement and named as such directly by Farabundo Marti. Alcalde de Izalco R. C. Valdez, "Telegrama al Gobernador de Sonsonate," 7 April 1931, AGN-CG-So.

84 Alcalde de Izalco R. C. Valdez, "Telegrama al Gobernador de Sonsonate," 30 April 1931, 1 May 1931, AGN-CG-So.

85 Municipal authorities in Izalco reported that large contingents of *Araujistas* mobilized in protest over alleged irregularities. The final results reported by telegram to the governor had Izalco voters divided between Araujo (940) and Gómez Zarate (1,367), but a later report (January 12) gave equal numbers of 434 for each. This discrepancy was confirmed in a complaint filed by Izalco's Araujista Laborist party, its members representing themselves as "ladino farmers and artisans" who complained that the Zaratistas party had committed fraud. Other reports described the local landlord and political boss Alfonso Diaz Barrientos paying people half a *colon* and drink to vote for Zarate. "Telegramas Sobre Politica," 1931, AGN-CM-MG; Alcalde de Izalco R. C. Valdez, "Telegrama al Gobernador de Sonsonate," 1931, AGN-CG-So; "Solicitud del Comité Araujo," 1931, AGS.

86 Gobernador del Departamento de Cabañas Francisco Baldovines, "Carta al Ministro de Gobernación," 8 August 1931, AGN-CM-MG.

87 SRI bulletin, no 2, 25 April 1931, 2.

88 Interviews with Fabian Mojica, Sonzacate, 1999 and 2001; SRI bulletin.

89 Interview with Doroteo López, San Isidro, 2001.

90 SRI bulletin, no 2, 25 April 1931, p. 1. Martí himself managed to visit workers

in the jail of Sonsonate, a concession that got the warden in trouble with the governor. Arístides Castillo Gobernador Politico de Sonsonate, "Carta al Alcalde Municipal de sonsonete," 5 June 1931, AGN-CG-So.

91 SRI bulletin, 17 May 1931.

92 Gobernador de Sonsonate, "Carta a Arturo Araujo, Presidente de la Republica," 7 May 1931, AGN-CM-MG.

93 Gobernador de Sonsonate, "Carta al Comandante Departamental de Sonsonate," 13 May 1931, 20 May 1931, AGN-CM-MG.

94 Gobernador de Sonsonate, "Carta al Ministro de Gobernación," 6 May 1931, AGN-CM-MG The mobilization in this region was so extensive that even local police commissioners like Anastasio Ishio, from Canton Cuyagualo in Izalco, were arrested for their "communist" activities.

95 SRI bulletin, 23 May 1931.

96 Diario Latino, 18 May 1931, 19 May 1931, 1 June, 1931.

97 Galindo Pohl, Recuerdos de Sonsonate, 337–39.

98 Ibid., 339.

99 Diario Latino, 22 May 1931.

100 Ibid., 1 June 1931. Araujo also related reports from local people from Izalco who claimed that they thought the protest would be a "celebration, like when they supported Araujo," but one that would help improve their conditions. Indeed, this also points to the potential power of "communitas," the recreation of egalitarian social bonds through festive acts.

101 José Tomás Calderón General de División, "Contestación al Cuestionario . . . ," 21 May 1931, AGN-CM-MG.

102 Gobernador de Sonsonate, "Carta al Ministro de Gobernación," 25 May 1931, AGN-CG-So. Government officials confiscated the only photo negatives of Agripino Guevara in order to keep the left from using them to denounce the killing.

103 SRI, Comité Ejecutivo, Comintern 539.3.1060, p. 6.

104 Gobernador de Sonsonate, "Carta al Ministro de Gobernación," 27 May 1931, AGN-CG-So.

Chapter Four: "Ese Trabajo Era Enteramente de los Naturales"

1 Gobernador de Sonsonate, "Carta al Ministro de Gobernación," 27 May 1931, AGN-CG-So.

2 SRI bulletin, May 1931.

3 El Indio, 17 May 1931.

4 Jules-Humbert Droz, "Tesis sobre la unidad nacional y continental," Congres de Fondation de la Cofederation Syndicale Latin Americaines (May 1929), 468.

5 Jules-Humbert Droz, "Tesis sobre la unidad nacional y continental," Congres de Fondation de la Cofederation Syndicale Latin Americaines (May 1929), 469.

6 "Manifiesto a las Masas Obreras y Campesinas del Salvador, Hoy 1 de Mayo Día de los Trabajadores . . .," Comintern 495.119.8, 21, 1934.

7 *El Movimiento Revolucionario Latinoamericano*, 303.

8 Jeffrey L. Gould, "Proyectos del Estado-nación y la supresión de la pluralidad cultural: perspectivas históricas."

9 Lillian Elwyn Elliott, *Central America: New Paths in Ancient Lands* (London: Methuen, 1924), 118.

10 Gould, *To Die in This Way*, 32–39.

11 Antono Conte, *Treinta Años en Tierras Salvadoreñas* (San Miguel: Tipografía el Progreso, 1934), vol. 2, 98.

12 Ibid., vol. 3, 122.

13 Conte shared with anthropologists certain teleological notions that Indians would inevitably be transformed by modernization. Yet stripped of its teleological and essentialist framework, Conte's positing of a process of "ladinización," wrought by highly negative material processes, was prescient. We will employ his term in Spanish to denote a process by which people rejected or withdrew loyalty to the ethnic emblems of language and dress in particular. The recognition that this change at the same time related to a perception of indigenous authenticity, or the lack of it, we will call cultural mestizaje. See *To Die in This Way*, 10–11, 134–39.

14 Conte, *Treinta Años en Tierras Salvadoreñas*, vol. 2, 93. This is a very early use of the term "ladinización."

15 Ibid., 95

16 Ibid.

17 Ibid., vol. 3, 87. Indeed one of the more significant revelations of Conte's book remains implicit in the text. With a generally acute ethnographic eye he describes numerous indigenous communities in eastern Salvador during his earlier missions (1906–15), but in his later missions these communities are either not described as Indian or not referred to at all.

18 Kenneth Grubb in *Religion in Central America* (London: World Dominion, 1937), offers a higher estimate. He claimed that 45,000 "still talk and understand Pipil" and that 30,000 speak more Pipil than Spanish. According to Grubb, virtually all Indians understood Spanish and therefore "the Indian language will disappear within a generation." Grubb offers no explanation for how he arrived at his estimates.

19 Interviews with Pedro Lue, Sábana San Juan, 1998; Ramón Esquina, Tajcuillulah, 1998; Rosario Lue, Nahuizalco, 1999; Benito Sarco, Nahuizalco, 2001; Celestino Lue, El Canelo, 1999.

20 Conte, *Treinta años en Tierras Salvadoreñas*, vol. 3, 195.

21 Interviews with Francisco Pérez, Buenavista, Sacacoyo, 2001; Isabel Saldaña, Sacacoyo, 2001; Jésus Vargas, Tepecoyo, 2001; José Gonzalez, Tepecoyo, 2001; Cecilio Martínez, Ateos, 2001; Vicente Flores, Jayaque, 2001; Jesús Monterrosa, Jayaque, 2001; Doroteo López, San Isidro, 1999, 2001; Jacinto Méndez, Jayaque, 2001.

22 Civil Records, Archivo Municipal Tepecoyo.

23 Gould, *To Die in This Way*, 228–45.

24   Jeffrey L. Gould, "Vana Ilusion: The Highlands Indians and the Myth of Nicaragua Mestiza," *Hispanic American Historical Review*, 1993, 393–429.

25   Wilson claims that there were between twelve and sixty thousand Salvadorans in Honduras, with some Honduran towns composed of 50–100 percent Salvadoran immigrants. Wilson, "The Crisis of National Integration in El Salvador," 118

26   "Informe de la Visita Oficial a los pueblos del Departamento," Gobernador de Sonsonate to Minister of Gobernación, 20 September 1913, AGN-CG-So.

27   Roy MacNaught. "The Gospel in Nahuizalco. Salvador." *Bulletin*, no. 168 (January 1930), 7, cited in Llanes, "A History of Protestantism in El Salvador."

28   "Informe de la Visita Oficial a los pueblos del Departamento," gobernador de Sonsonate to minister of Gobernación, 20 September 1913, AGN-CG-So.

29   Conte, *Treinta años en Tierras Salvadoreñas*, vol. 3, 127.

30   The Guatemalan case is quite distinct. See Taracena, "Guatemala." However, there were definite signs of ethnic and religious revitalization during this same period in Guatemala, for example in Momostenango in 1931.

31   See Gould, *To Die in This Way*, 26–68, and Gould, "Proyectos del Estado-nación y la supresión de la pluralidad cultural: perspectivas históricas."

32   Conte, *Treinta Años en Tierras Salvadoreñas*, vol. 2, 97.

33   Ibid., vol. 2, 99.

34   Ibid., vol. 2, 100.

35   Ibid., vol. 2, 173.

36   "Informe de la Visita Oficial a los pueblos del Departamento," gobernador de Sonsonate to minister of Gobernación, 20 September 1913, AGN-CG-So.

37   Cardenal, *El Poder Eclesiástico en El Salvador*, 230.

38   Ibid., 233.

39   Conte, *Treinta Años en Tierras Salvadoreñas*, vol. 2, 185.

40   *El Heraldo de Sonsonate*, 18 January 1930.

41   *El Heraldo de Sonsonate*, 22 April 1931.

42   Alvarenga, "Los indígenas y el Estado."

43   Gould, *To Die in This Way*, 182–83.

44   Gaspar, *Historia Bautista en el Salvador*, 37.

45   Llanes, "A History of Protestantism in El Salvador." Juayúa and Nahuizalco each had roughly twenty adults in their congregations.

46   Roy MacNaught, "Horrors of Communism in Central America," 26.

47   Conte, *Treinta Años en Tierras Salvadoreñas*, vol. 3, 171.

48   Ibid., vol. 3, 169.

49   Ibid.

50   Interview with Andrés Pérez, Pushtan, 2001.

51   Gobernador de Sonsonate, "Informe de la Visita Oficial a los Pueblos del Departamento," 20 September 1913, AGN-CG-So.

52   F. Machón Vilanova, *Ola Roja* (Mexico City, 1948), 30–31.

53   *El Heraldo de Sonsonate*, 24 February 1930, reported the opening of schools in Talcomunco and las Higueras (Izalco).

54 Interview with Marcos Bran, Cusamuluco, Nahuizalco, 2001.

55 Gould, *To Die in This Way*, 195.

56 Conte, *Treinta Años en Tierras Salvadoreñas*, vol. 3, 195.

57 Interview with Cecilia Perez Lue, El Canelo 2001; on the use of the expression "speak well" see Schultze Jena, *Indiana*.

58 Conte, *Treinta Años en Tierras Salvadoreñas*, vol. 2, 109. During the twentieth century this practice may have been unique to Cuisnahuat.

59 Hartman, "Reconocimiento Etnográfica de los Aztecas de El Salvador."

60 "Informe de la Visita Oficial a los pueblos del Departamento," gobernador de Sonsonete to minister of Gobernación, 20 September 1913, AGN-CG-So.

61 See Tábora, "Género y Percepciones Etnico-raciales en el Imaginario de la Clase Política."

62 Hartman, "Reconocimiento Etnográfica de los Aztecas de El Salvador."

63 Wallace Thompson, *Rainbow Countries of Central America* (New York: E. P. Dutton, 1924), 100–101.

64 Nulidad de Elecciones en Cuisnahuat, 5 May 1901, AGN-CS.

65 *El Día*, 2 October 1931.

66 Gould, *To Die in This Way*, 73.

67 There is strong evidence to the contrary. As the Swedish ethnographer Hartman wrote: "Las mujeres se bañan casi todos los días su ropa se encuentra siempre impecable aún durante la época seca del año, cuando el polvo vuela por los caminos." Of course "filth" also referred to the idea that "refajadas" wore no undergarments. Although it is not clear exactly what was worn in lieu of the ladino undergarment, this notion also appears to have been false.

68 *El Heraldo de Sonsonate*, 18 November 1931.

69 See Gould, *To Die in This Way*, 47–50.

70 *El Heraldo de Sonsonate*, 8 December 1931.

71 *El Heraldo de Sonsonate*, 21 May 1931.

72 Gould, *To Die in This Way*, 47–50, 73–74.

73 Interview with Andrés Pérez, Pushtan, Nahuizalco, 2001.

74 For a strikingly similar process in Guatemala during the 1940s and 1950s see Grandin, *The Last Colonial Massacre*.

75 Cardenal, *El Poder Eclesiástico en El Salvador*, 225.

76 Alvarenga, *Cultura y ética de la violencia*; Alvarenga, "Los indígenas"; Ching, "From Clientelism to Militarism."

77 Alvarenga, "Los indígenas y el Estado."

78 Interview with Paulino Galicia, Cara Sucia, 1999.

79 *El Heraldo de Sonsonate*, 17 May 1931, reports that people allied with the cura took away the image of the Beatísima during the middle of a religious procession.

80 Informe sobre las Elecciones en Izalco, 14 December 1914, AGN-CG-So.

81 Ministerio de Gobernación, Sonsonate, 11 August 1931, AGN-CG-So, reported that in Izalco Antonio Calzadillo, 34, a tailor, Candelario Gonzalez, 50, a carpenter, and Camilo Muscio, 20, a carpenter, were arrested for possessing communist propaganda and that Leonardo Palma was arrested for using his

house as the meeting place. Muscio, Calzadillo, Palma, and possibly Gonzalez were indigenous.

82 "Report on Communist Activities in El Salvador," British Consul, D. Rogers to Grant Wilson, 16 February 1932, Foreign Office 813/23 no. 24 238/13a. Several weeks after the nullification of the elections, when the rebellion broke out, the mainly Indian rebels proclaimed Chávez mayor.

83 Some of the complexities of ethnic conflict and the decline of Indian identities in Izalco during an earlier period are discussed in Lauria-Santiago, "Land, Community, and Revolt."

84 Interviews with Eulalio Chile, Cuyagualo, Izalco, 2001; Sotero Linares, Las Higueras, Izalco, 2001; Francisco Ishio, Cuntan, 2001.

85 Conte, *Treinta Años en Tierras Salvadoreñas*, vol. 3, 125.

86 Interview with Miguel Urbina, Ceiba del Charco, 2001.

87 Interview with Sotero Linares, Las Higueras, Izalco, 2001.

88 Interview with Jesús Velasquez, San Luis, Izalco, 2001.

89 Interview with Fabián Mojica, Sonzacate, 1999.

90 Interviews with Felipe Gomez, San Julián, 2001; Luis Ramos Linares, Los Gramales, Sonsonate, 2001.

91 Conte, *Treinta Años en Tierras Salvadoreñas*, vol. 2, 171; Buezo, *Sangre de Hermanos*,

92 Conte, *Treinta Años en Tierras Salvadoreñas*, vol. 2, 171.

93 Mendez, *Los Sucesos Comunistas en El Salvador*, 187.

94 Commander Brodeur, for example, who spent a week in El Salvador in late January 1932, referred to all poor rural Salvadorans as "Indians." See "Secret Report of Situation as It Developed at Acajutla," V. G. Brodeur to Naval Secretary, Ottawa, 7 April 1932, FO 371/15814. Similarly, D. J. Rogers, coffee grower and British consul, also employed the term "Indians" in the same indiscriminate fashion; see "Communist Rising in Salvador, January 1932," Report of the British consul, FO 371 15813, 12 February 1932.

95 Gobernador de Ahuachapán al ministro de Gobernación, 1892, AGN-CM-MG.

96 The report indicates no indigenous births in the municipalities of Atiquizaya, Turín, El Refugio, and San Lorenzo. Gobernador de Ahuachapán al ministro de Gobernación, 1892, AGN-CM-MG.

97 Conte, *Treinta Años en Tierras Salvadoreñas*, vol. 2, 190.

98 Interviews with Miguel Lino, El Tortuguero, Atiquizaya, 2002; Miguel Jimenez, Santa Rita, Ahuachapán, 2001; and Leonora Escalante, Santa Rita, Ahuachapán. The Guatemalan government arrested Corado twice and sent her to an asylum, the second time at the peak of the mobilizations of January 1932; "Una virgen roja hacia milagros," *Excelsior* (Mexico) 1, no. 3 (15 February 1932), 1; "Ingreso al asilo de alienados el Santo Angel," *El Imparcial* (Guatemala), 6 February 1932, 1; telegram from Jorge Ubico to Jefe Político de Jutiapa, 5 February 1932, Jefaturas Departamentales, AGCA.

99 R. C. Valdez, alcalde de Izalco, telegramas al gobernador de Sonsonate, 13 December 1931, AGN-CG-So; alcalde de Cuisnahuat, telegrama al gobernador de Sonsonate, 22 March 1931, AGN-CG-So; Partes de policía, Departamento de

Sonsonate, July–September 1931, AGS; telegramas sobre elecciones y precios, 1930, AGN-CG-So; Alberto Engelhard, alcalde de San Julián, telegramas al gobernador de Sonsonate, 13 December 1931, AGN-CG-So.

100 We are making the distinction between communities or municipalities with traditional forms of indigenous authorities, such as Nahuizalco, Izalco, Cuisnahuat, and Santo Domingo (all in Sonsonate), and other communities made up of people with varying identities but who were not subject to specifically indigenous forms of government.

101 Gould, *To Die in This Way*, 164.

102 Jena Schultze, *Indiana*. To cite one unusual practice that probably continued into the twentieth century: an indigenous bride would be assigned to a community elder with whom she would engage in sexual relations over a period of one month before joining her spouse.

103 María de Baratta and Jeremías Mendoza, *Cuzcatlán típico: Ensayo sobre etnofonía de El Salvador, folklore, folkwisa y folkway* (San Salvador: Ministerio de Cultura, 1951).

104 Carol A. Smith has argued persuasively that there are significantly different values attached to female sexuality within and outside Guatemalan indigenous communities. Carol A. Smith, "Race-Class-Gender Ideologies."

105 Ward, ed. and comp., *Libro Azul de El Salvador*.

106 Conte, *Treinta Años en Tierras Salvadoreñas*, vol. 2, 110.

107 See Appelius, *Le terre che tremano*, 109–10. For a further discussion of the codification of indigenous marriage see Lauria-Santiago and Gould, " 'They Call Us Thieves and Steal our Wage.' "

108 Alejandro Dagoberto Marroquín, *Panchimalco* (San Salvador: Ministerio de Educación, 1959), 194–95. A similar practice existed in a western Honduran indigenous community. See Rocío Tábora, "Género y Percepciones Etnico-raciales en el Imaginario de la Clase Política 'Mestiza' y del Movimiento Indígena-Negro en Honduras."

109 Ruhl, *The Central Americans*, 203; Hill's comments refer to both indigenous and ladina women.

110 Although we do not have evidence for a causal connection, there is also no doubt that rates of illegitimacy were quite high.

111 Conte, *Treinta años en Tierras Salvadoreñas*, vol. 3, 126.

112 Informe del Sexto Congreso Regional Obrero y Campesino Constituyente de la Federación Regional de Trabajadores, May 1930, Comintern 495.119.10, p. 92.

113 Interviews with Alberto Shul (Nahuizalco), Ernesto Shul (Nahuizalco), Ramón Esquina (Tajcuillah, Nahuizalco), and Ramón Aguilar (Cusamuluco, Nahuizalco). All provide anecdotal evidence of the connection between illegitimate origin and participation in the movement.

114 Conte, *Treinta Años en Tierras Salvadoreñas*, vol. 2, 101.

115 We do not have the expertise to point to a definitive connection between disciplinary practices that today would be considered "abusive" or worse and a predisposition toward violent responses to authority or aggression.

116 Hartman, "Reconocimiento Etnográfica de los Aztecas de El Salvador."

117 Interview with Salomé Torres, El Cacao, 2001.

118 Patricia Alvarenga, in *Cultura y ética de la violencia* and "Auxiliary Forces in the Shaping of the Repressive System," examines the multiple levels of state coercion in peasant society.

119 "General Resumé of Proceedings of H.M.C. Ships whilst at Acajutla, Republic of Salvador, January 23–31st, 1932," FO 371/15814. For further discussion of violence in rural Salavador see Lauria-Santiago and Gould, " 'They Call us Thieves and Steal Our Wage,' " 223–24.

Chapter Five: "To the Face of the Entire World"

1 *Diario Latino*, 9 June 1931.

2 National Guard and local police focused on arresting leaders like Salvador and Tomas Mujica, arrested on 12 July during a meeting in Sonzacate. Partes de Policia, Departamento de Sonsonate, 1931, AGS; Records of the Foreign Service Post, San Salvador, El Salvador, Department of State, RG84, USNA.

3 U.S. Department of State, Records of the Foreign Service Post, San Salvador, El Salvador, Ministerio de Gobernación, 1931, USNA.

4 Comintern 495.119.4, doc 2.

5 For a discussion of the administrative near-collapse of the state during this period see Guidos Vejar, *El Ascenso del Militarismo en El Salvador*, and Wilson, "The Crisis of National Integration in El Salvador."

6 MID, USNA.

7 Harold Finley to secretary of state, 8 July 1931, no. 537, Records of the Foreign Service Post, San Salvador, El Salvador, Department of State, RG84, USNA. The demand for change led to the removal of three ministers. See Iraheta Rosales, Lopez Alas, and Escobar Cornejo, "La crisis de 1929 y sus consecuencias en los años posteriores."

8 Presidente Araujo, telegrama al gobernador de Sonsonate," 14 September 1931, AGN-CG-So.

9 Ogilvie, "The Communist Revolt of El Salvador, 1932," 53.

10 Letter of Ismael Hernández (Comité Ejecutivo SRI del Salvador) al secretariado del Caribe SRI, 29 November 1931, Comintern 539/3/1060, p. 8.

11 Ibid.

12 "La Situación Política," PCS document, 8 October 1931, Comintern 495.119.7, p. 11.

13 Although it has long been assumed that Ama was the mayordomo of the Cofradía de Santa Ana, recent ethnohistorical work casts some doubt on that assertion, as his name is not listed among the cofrradía leadership during the early 1930s. Carlos Benjamín, Lara Martínez, and América Rodríguez Herrera, "Identidad etnica y globalizacion: Las identidades indigenas de izalco y cacaopera," *Memorias de Mestizaje*, ed. Euraque, Gould, and Hale.

14 Montes, *El Compadrazgo*, 266.

15 Williams, *Marxism and Literature*, 123.

16 Ibid., 122.

17 Grandin, *The Last Colonial Massacre*, 181.

18 Ibid., 184.

19 "General Resumé of Proceedings of H.M.C. Ships whilst at Acajutla, Republic of Salvador, January 23–31st, 1932," FO 371/15814, p. 6.

20 Letter of Ismael Hernández to the secretariado del Caribe SRI, 29 November 1931, Comintern 539.3.11060, p. 8.

21 Dalton, *Miguel Mármol: Los sucesos de 1932 en El Salvador*, 229.

22 Ibid., 230.

23 Urban and suburban nucleation was the result of mid-nineteenth-century state policies as well as the forms of settlement encouraged by the collective owner- ship and administration of land. See Lauria-Santiago, *An Agrarian Republic*, chapter 4.

24 *Diario Latino*, 26 June 1931.

25 A. R. Harris, 8 December 1931, MID, USNA. It should not go unnoticed that in the past, a president's minister of war had been considered the likely suc- cessor to the presidency.

26 The *New York Times* placed the number between fifty and sixty. *New York Times*, 20 December 1931, E, 6; the Comintern documents cite "dozens killed" at the presidential palace alone. Ismael Hernández, Secretario General, Informe 236, San Salvador, 8 December 1931, Comintern 495.119.12.

27 *New York Times*, 7 December 1931.

28 Reprinted in *El Diario de Hoy*, 19 January 1967.

29 Report by Comrade "Hernández," Comintern 495.119.4, p. 36. This leader somewhat feebly also claimed that the PCS had no funds to publish mani- festoes explaining its position with respect to the regime (p. 29).

30 Report by Cuenca, Comintern 495.119.4, p. 36.

31 José D. Solís, Armenia, telegrama al gobernador de Sonsonate, 13 December 1931, AGN-CG-So; two accounts suggest that as late as 20 December the regime publicly tolerated the PCS, provided that it would limit its activities to the electoral arena. *Patria*, 21 December 1931; *Diario Latino*, 22 December 1931.

32 Report by Cuenca, Comintern 495.119.4, p. 32.

33 Dalton, *Miguel Mármol: Los sucesos de 1932 en El Salvador*, 233. Schlesinger sup- ports Mármol's recollection by citing his own report from the period, "en todo su jira pudo converncerse de que las nuevas ideas toman cuerpo, porque a su paso por todos los poblados donde hay una organización aunque sea celular, el entusiasmo cunde y acuden presurosos a escuchar sus conferencias." *Revo- lución Comunista*, 140.

34 Comintern 495.119.4, p. 31.

35 According to the Cuenca report (38), Martínez sent invitations to "to all those he considered to be the leaders of the CP in the Occident."

36 Comintern 495.119.4, p. 32.

37 Montes, El *compadrazgo*, 288.

38 Report by Cuenca, Comintern 495.119.4, p. 39.

39 Comintern 495.119; The De Sola coffee farms, not unlike other large units, typically combined coffee with cattle, basic grains, or sugar, thus bringing to the fore issues of interest to colonos. *Terraje* had different meanings at different times and in different locales. Evidence suggests that landlords, in response to the crisis, were forcing their tenants to pay in cash for their land plots and that this practice, in turn, pushed the tenants toward the labor movement.

40 Cuenca Report, Comintern 495.119.4, p. 39.

41 Galindo Pohl, *Recuerdos de Sonsonate*, 319–20.

42 *Diario de El Salvador*, 24 December 1931.

43 J. L. Arévalo to gobernador político, 6 January 1932. The subsecretary of gobernación reproduces the letter from the Asociación de Cafetaleros, which met in Ahuachapán on 24 November and drafted a letter to to the Ministro de Gobernación, 8 December 1931.

44 A letter from Farabundo Marti to activists in Honduras on 16 December 1931 expected the lack of recognition by the United States to weaken Martínez's government. The actions of the U.S. ambassador and special emissary Cafferey should not be underestimated. On the one hand, Ambassador Curtiss pushed to turn over the presidency to Martínez so as to provide a semblance of constitutionality. On the other, the conversations of Curtiss and Cafferey with military officials and members of the oligarchy during December sought allies that would either push Martínez out of power or join him. That tentative intervention elicited a nationalist response even from former supporters of Araujista like the *Diario Latino* that began to call for mass protests against the "international policeman." Dur, "U.S. Diplomacy and the Salvadorean Revolution of 1931"; Kenneth J. Grieb, "The United States and the Rise of General Maximiliano Hernandez Martinez," *Journal of Latin American Studies* 3, no.2 (1971), 151–72; Quino Caso, "Response to Salvador Peña Trejo's Narración Histórica de la Insurrección Militar," press clipping section, Bibliôteca Gallardo.

45 Dur, "U.S. Diplomacy and the Salvadorean Revolution of 1931."

46 Gertrudis Germán al Gobernador Político, 29 December 1931, AGA.

47 Benjamín Cárcamo to Gobernador Político, 29 December 1931, AGA.

48 *El Diario de El Salvador*, 31 December 1931.

49 Cuenca report, Comintern, p. 35.

50 Cuenca report, Comintern 46/53.

51 Cuenca report, Comintern, p. 50. There were at least three other parties contesting the municipal elections (and then the congressional election on 10 January).

52 Several hostile commentators concurred that the PCS would have won. Schlesinger, *Revolución Comunista*, 149; see *Diario de Hoy*, 12 February 1967; and Galindo Pohl, *Recuerdos de Sonsonate*, 346.

53 Cuenca report, Comintern 46/53.

54 Dalton, *Miguel Mármol: Los sucesos de 1932 en El Salvador*, 228.

55 Marcial Contreras to the Gobernador Político of Ahuachapán, 1 January 1931, AGA. Although dated 1931, the context of the letter makes abundantly clear that it was written on New Year's Day, 1932.

56 Sheila Fitzpatrick, "Vengeance and Ressentiment in the Russian Revolution," *French Historical Studies* 24, no. 4 (fall 2001), cites a dictionary definition of "ressentiment": "a state of hostility maintained by the memory of an offense which it aspires to avenge." Fitzpatrick adds: "ressentiment (like vengeance) must always be present in the mix of emotions that lead people to support revolutions and commit acts of revolutionary violence" (580).

57 Interviews with Miguel Urbina Ceiba del Charco, Izalco, 2001; Rosario Lue, Nahuizalco, 2001.

58 Cuenca implied that the PCS relied very little on written propaganda, primarily because of their limited resources.

59 Circulares del Partido Comunista, 6 November 1931, AGN-CG-So.

60 J. A. Mendoza, alcalde de Nahuizalco, to Gobernador Departamental, 2 January 1931, AGN-CG-So; J. Antonio Mendoza, alcalde de Nahuizalco, to Gobernador Departamental, 3 January 1931, AGN-CG-So.

61 Schlesinger, *Revolución Comunista*, 139.

62 Letter from D. J. Rogers, 1/7/32, Foreign Office Documents.

63 Interview with Lieutenant Timoeteo Flores, *Diario de Hoy*, 12 February 1967.

64 Local officials, on the contrary, registered their own slate of candidates on 2 January in Sonsonate.

65 J. Antonio Mendoza, alcalde de Nahuizalco, to Ministerio de Gobernación, 3 January 1932, AGN-CM-MG; "Telegramas Sobre Política," 1932, AGN-CG-So.

66 Interviews with Esteban Tepas, Pushtan, Nahuizalco 1998, 2001; Paulino Galicia, Cara Sucia, 1999.

67 Galindo Pohl, *Recuerdos de Sonsonate*, 346–47. Galindo Pohl did note a certain degree of apathy about the election.

68 Dalton, *Miguel Mármol: Los sucesos de 1932 en El Salvador*, 234.

69 D. J. Rogers to John Simon, San Salvador, 13 January 1932, Foreign Office A8651918. Ironically the consul, in a subsequent letter, cited a newspaper report that affirmed the same point about the discipline of the large group of communist voters as evidence of "receipt of considerable payments from Communist sources."

70 FO 19/13 D. J. Rogers to John Simon, 7 January 1932, Foreign Office. According to the British consul, the candidate of General Claramount, moderately opposed to the regime, won with 1,109 votes, followed by the candidate of Córdoba with 1,102 votes and the PCS candidate with 1,046.

71 Cuenca report, Comintern 38/45.

72 *Cicatriz de la Memoria: El Salvador, 1932* (Jeffrey L. Gould and Carlos Henriquez Consalvi, Icarus Films, 2003).

73 Petition to Alcalde Municipal of Ahuachapán signed by Mariano Gonzalez Medrano et al., 27 November 1932, AGA.

74 Schlesinger, *Revolución Comunista*, 157.

75 Cuenca Report, Comintern 39/46. Miguel Mármol also claimed that the strikers had killed fourteen Guardia. Newspaper accounts suggest that the initial confrontation resulted in two dead or missing Guardia, two wounded Guardia, one missing Guardia, and one dead striker. Also see *El Diario de El Salvador*, 6 January 1932 and 7 January 1932.

76 Interviews with Antolín López, la Montañita, Ahuahapán; Leonora Escalante, Santa Rita, Ahuachapán; Miguel Jimenez, Santa Rita, Ahuachapán, 2001.

77 Jefe Político of Jutiapa to Secretaria de Relaciones Exteriores de Guatemala, 16 June 1932, AGCA. The letter includes a note from the consul.

78 *El Diario de El Salvador*, 7 January 1932.

79 Interview with María Hortensia García, Ahuachapán 2001.

80 This calculation is based on coffee production and labor requirements. The May 1930 census lists 63,000 *jornaleros* in the three departments and another 33,000 in Santa Ana. The census categories are not broken down, but there is an overwhelming preponderance of jornaleros to agricultures: 17:1 in Sonsonate, 8:1 in Ahuachapán, and 15:1 in La Libertad. It is likely that microfinca owners (e.g. semi-proletarians) were listed as jornaleros.

81 Tomás Calderón, minister of war, estimated some eighty thousand affiliates, but that figure is uncorroborated by other sources.

82 19/13, Rogers to Simon, 7 January 1932, Foreign Office.

83 Based on analysis of two slates of candidates for municipal office. Compare petition to Alcalde Municipal of Ahuachapán signed by Mariano Gonzalez Medrano et al., 27 November 1932 (including at most one artisan—an albañil constructor—and members of the local professional and planter élite), and petition to Alcalde Municipal of Ahuachapán signed by Presentación Rodriguez et al., 25 November 1932 (including four artisans out of eight regidor candidates).

84 Even the archbishop (Alfonso Belloso y Sánchez) sent a public letter asking capitalists to give a "solucion cristiana a problemas de los salarios de los trabajadores del campo," because "sus presentes condiciones de vida son inhumanas." *Diario de El Salvador*, 17 January 1932.

85 Letter from Rogers, 1/13/32, Foreign Office.

86 *Diario Latino*, 9 January 1932.

87 *El Diario de El Salvador*, 31 December 1931.

88 Cuenca Report, Comintern.

89 Rogers to Sir John Simon, A 865/9/8, 13 January 1932, Foreign Office.

90 *La Epoca*, 20 January 1931.

91 Buezo, *Sangre de Hermanos*, 60. Buezo makes the argument for Zapata's authorship of most of the book, although this seems impossible to corroborate.

92 Ibid., 62.

93　Excelsior (Mexico), 25 January 1932. The paper reported an encounter in which Juan Uriarte, the ministro plenipetenciario de El Salvador, remarked on the involvement of Araujo's followers in the movement without blaming Araujo himself. The Mexican consul directly blamed Araujistas.

94　El Diario de El Salvador, 31 December 1931.

95　Lisandro Larín J, gobernador de Sonsonate, "Carta al Alcalde de Sonsonate," 23 December 1931, AGN-CG-So; "Cartas al Gobernador de Ahuachapan," 1931, AGN-CG-Ah.

96　Diario de Centro America (Guatemala), 5 January 1932. The official paper reported that Salvadoran finqueros in the West needed thousands of workers because Salvadorans demanded higher wages. As noted above, there were in fact "co-mapas" (natives of neighboring Comapa, Guatemala) in Ahuachapán

97　For example, one denunciation of the Ahuahcapenco left referred to "los de la ciudad de Ahuachapán y los de la ciudad de Atiquizaya." Also, Dalton, Miguel Mármol: Los sucesos de 1932 en El Salvador (228), describes the "townspeople of Ahuachapán" as ready to seize power if the elections were stolen from them.

98　Interview with María Delvina Méndez, Ahuachapán, 2001.

99　Cuenca, Comintern 39/46.

100　Schlesinger, Revolución Comunista, 157.

101　Ibid., 152.

102　Ibid.

103　Ibid., 153.

104　El Diario Latino, 9 January 1932. This Araujista paper echoed the charge that the PCS lacked control over the western militants and called on the Ahuachapa-neco Communists to behave more like those of San Salvador.

105　El Día (Sonsonate), 6 January 1932.

106　Cuenca cites 10 January as the date for the plenum (Cuenca Report, Comintern 39/46). Mármol cites 8 January, after the meeting with General Valdéz. Schle-singer cites a document dated 9 January, in which the Central Committee formed Comités Militares Revolucionarios (Revolución Comunista, 157–58). It seems plausible that the Plenum met continuously during those days, but only on the day of the congressional elections, the 10th, arrived at the fateful decision.

107　On Zapata and Hernández see Buezo, Sangre de Hermanos, 63; on Cuenca see Dalton, Miguel Mármol: Los sucesos de 1932 en El Salvador, 240–44.

108　Legajo de Correspondencia a Julio Sánchez la noche del 20 de agosto 1934, 320, archive, Museo de la Palabra y la Imagen, San Salvador.

109　Letter from Jorge Fernández Anaya to Alberto Moreau, 8 September 1930, Guatemala City, Comintern 495.119.12, p. 9.

110　Dalton, Miguel Mármol: Los sucesos de 1932 en El Salvador, 240.

111　There is no doubt that some Araujistas were willing to join the revolutionary left in military action. In any event, there is some evidence that they were also organizing a revolt and supplied weapons, although most national Araujista leaders had left for Guatemala, where they were arrested. On 2 January notable Araujistas who were also conspiring were arrested in Guatemala at the request of Salvadoran authorities: Colonel Lopez Rochac, Dr. Blas Cantizano, Salvador Godoy, and Luis Felipe Recines.

112 Comintern 495.119.1, p. 5/30.

113 *Diario Latino*, 15 January 1932. This paper reported seven hundred workers on strike and also mentioned strikes in Acajutla and by railroad workers in Sonsonate. "Communist Rising in Salvador," 1.

114 Similarly, the left had little presence in Santo Domingo de Guzmán or Santa Catarina Masahuat, two of the more traditional indigenous communities.

115 Wood, *Insurgent Collective Action and Civil War*, 157. The FMLN in the 1980s had active support from perhaps one-third of the peasantry in an important base area. Wood reminds the reader that the great strike movements of Great Britain (1926), the United States (end of the Second World War), and South Africa (1987), involved under 20 percent of the workforce.

116 Carta al Gobernador de Sonsonete, 11 April 1931, AGN-CG-So: "dedicanse a propaganda comunista e inculcar ideas entre soldados cuartel ocatavo regimiento entre sus familiares campesinos."

117 Schlesinger, *Revolución Comunista*, 160.

118 "Communist Rising in Salvador," 10.

119 Ibid., 11, describes officers disarming their soldiers in the Sixth Infantry barracks on 19 January. Schlesinger depicts a similar event on the 16th.

120 Ibid., 1.

121 Schlesinger, *Revolución Comunista*, 179.

122 Cuenca, Comintern 52/59.

123 Mayor Otto Romero Orellano, "Génesis de la Amenaza Comunista en El Salvador," appendix: "Manifiesto del Comité Central del Partido Comunista a Las Clases Trabajadoras de la República, 20 January 1932" (San Salvador: Centro de Estudios Estratégicos de las Fuerzas Armadas, 1994), 97.

124 Dalton, *Miguel Mármol: Los sucesos de 1932 en El Salvador*, 296–300.

125 The PCS leader Max Cuenca and a Comintern official both refer to this document as authentic, but the articles are slightly off. They assert that article 19 calls for the establishment of Soviets, but in the document circulated by the government article 18 does so.

126 Dalton, *Miguel Mármol: Los sucesos de 1932 en El Salvador*, 247.

Chapter Six: Red Ribbons and Machetes

1 We employ the term "insurgent" here, relying on a dictionary definition of someone in revolt against established authority without receiving international recognition as a belligerent force. In this sense we resist the tendency of the news media and the current administration to conflate insurgency and terrorism. "Revolutionary" implies a uniform program for change, a problem-

atic notion. We offer a very approximate breakdown based on documentary sources: La Libertad, 900; Sonsonate, 800; Izalco, 600; Juayúa, 600; Nahuizalco, 500–800; Ahuachapán and Tacuba, 1,000–2,000. In addition, hundreds participated in armed actions in the areas south and east of the capital.

2 This broad description of the insurrection is based on several written sources: Méndez, *Los Sucesos comunistas en El Salvador*; Montes, *El Compadrazgo*; "Communist Rising in Salvador," Report of the British Consul, FO 371 15813; Galindo Pohl, *Recuerdos de Sonsonate*. It is also based on numerous interviews, many of which are listed in other notes to this chapter.

3 "Communist Rising in Salvador," 4. Notably, a woman named Micaella, from the canton of Barrancas, emerged as a leader of the insurgent forces.

4 Méndez, *Los Sucesos comunistas en El Salvador*, 158, also refers to the seventy-eight-year-old former candidate, but as Isabel Zaldaña from Sacacoyo.

5 Interview with Doroteo López, San Isidro, 2001.

6 "Communist Rising in Salvador," 4. Similarly, rebels in the area around Jayaque threatened to take the town but were driven off by the army contingent which had pursued them since the attack on Santa Tecla. *Diario de El Salvador*, 27 January 1932.

7 Interviews with Luis Ramos Linares (Los Gramales); Teofilo Lopez (Los Gramales).

8 Interviews with Margarita Turcios, El Guayabo, 2001. It is difficult to evaluate Turcios's claim, given that it follows a pattern of denials of involvement in the insurrection throughout the region.

9 "Communist Rising in Salvador," 6.

10 Naval Intelligence officer Major Harris noted four hundred dead insurgents.

11 A woman named Micaella in the attack on Colón and another woman in Izalco also achieved prominence among the revolutionary fighters.

12 Montes, *El Compadrazgo*, 280.

13 According to *La Tribuna*, one thousand people took Juayúa, armed with mausers.

14 Méndez, *Los sucesos comunistas en El Salvador*, 52.

15 Montes, *El Compadrazgo*, 295.

16 Schlesinger, *Revolución Comunista*, 192–93; Méndez, *Los sucesos comunistas en El Salvador*, 82–83; Anderson, *Matanza*, 136; interview with Raúl Sigüenza, Juayúa, 2001.

17 Galindo Pohl, *Recuerdos de Sonsonate*, 383.

18 Montes, *El Compadrazgo*, 295.

19 Ibid., 354.

20 A. Roy MacNaught, "Horrors of Communism in Central America," 8.

21 Interview with Raúl Sigüenza, Juayúa, 1999.

22 Cuenca report, Comintern, p. 63.

23 Interview with Raúl Sigüenza, Juayúa, 1999.

24 Galindo Pohl, *Recuerdos de Sonsonate*, 385.

25 El *Heraldo de Sonsonate*, 19 March 1932; interview with Cisneros; "Communist Rising in Salvador," 8.

26 El *Heraldo de Sonsonate*, 19 March 1932.

27 "Communist Rising in Salvador," 8.

28 Interview with Raúl Sigüenza, Jauyúa, 1999, 2001.

29 MacNaught, "Horrors of Communism in Central America."

30 "Communist Rising in Salvador," 9.

31 Quoted in Méndez, *Los sucesos comunistas en El Salvador*, 102. A version of this same testimony was reported in the British consul's report, "Communist Rising in Salvador," 8.

32 Montes, El *Compadrazgo*.

33 Quoted in Méndez, *Los sucesos comunistas en El Salvador*, 46.

34 Interview with Alberto Shul, Nahuizalco, 1999, 2001.

35 Interview with Ramón Esquina, Tajcuilulaj, 1998.

36 It is possible that outsiders did instigate the looting. See the testimony in Méndez, *Los sucesos comunistas en El Salvador*, 37: "Eso de las siete y cincuenta minutos de la noche, llegaron a Nahuizalco, procedentes de Juayúa, tres camiones cargados de comunistas. En cuanto se pusieron de acuerdo con los ocupantes de la población procedieron a saquear las tiendas."

37 Interview with Bertha Calderón, Nahuizalco, 2001 (Brito was Calderón's grandfather).

38 Interviews with Luis Alberto Castillo, Atiquizaya, 2001; María Delvina Méndez, Ahuachapán, 2001; Miguel Angel Cepeda, Ahuachapán; José Antonio Chachagua, Achapuco, Ahuachapán, 2001; Schlesinger, *Revolución Comunista*; Piñeda, "Tragedia Comunista," *Diario de Hoy*, 9 February 1967.

39 Gustavo Piñeda, "La Tragedia Comunista," *Diario de Hoy*, 9 February 1967; Calderón, *Anhelos de un Ciudadano*.

40 Gustavo Piñeda, "La Tragedia Comunista," *Diario de Hoy*, 9 February 1967.

41 Buezo, *Sangre de Hermanos*, 92–93.

42 "Communist Rising in Salvador," 11–12.

43 Ibid, 12. The consul reported two thousand volunteers, but other reports indicate that the Guardia Cívica recruited five hundred volunteers in San Salvador.

44 Méndez, *Los sucesos comunistas en El Salvador*; V. G. Brodeur to naval secretary, Ottawa, 7 April 1932, FO 371/15814.

45 Schlesinger, *La Revolución Comunista*, 195; Méndez, *Los sucesos comunistas en El Salvador*.

46 MacNaught, "Horrors of Communism," 10.

47 El *Diario de Hoy*, 10 February 1967.

48 Buezo, *Sangre de Hermanos*, 94.

49 Rogers to Simon, San Salvador, 30 January 1932, in FO A 1055/9/8.

50 Among the evidence of this continued, uncoordinated resistance: On the 30th, after all rebel held areas had been lost and the massacres were well under way, an attempt to attack the Alvarez beneficio was reported in Santa Ana. In the

volcan region of Santa Ana 150 troops were sent to capture people hiding in the farms of San Jose de Concha v. de Regalado, Julia de Alvarez Bros, cantones Potrero Grande Arriba, Calzontes Arriba, and Palo de Campana. A group of twenty-five men also attacked the Beneficio las tres puertas in the Volcan area (owned by James Hill).

51 Appelius, *Le terre che tremano*, 105.

52 Ibid., 105.

53 Montes, *El Compadrazgo*, 311.

54 Ibid., 271.

55 Méndez, *Los sucesos comunistas en El Salvador*, 126.

56 Sánchez reportedly warned landlords to hide in anticipation of the insurrection. Galindo Pohl, *Recuerdos de Sonsonate*, 382–83.

57 Williams, *Marxism and Literature*, 122.

58 Galindo Pohl, *Recuerdos de Sonsonate*, 356.

59 "Communist Rising in Salvador," 9.

60 Méndez, *Los sucesos comunistas en El Salvador*, 67.

61 *El Heraldo de Sonsonate*, 19 March 1932.

62 Ibid.

63 Interview with Lola de Olamede, Izalco, 1998.

64 *Diario de Hoy*, 9 February 1967.

65 Méndez, *Los sucesos comunistas en El Salvador*, 66.

66 Charles R. Hale, *Más que un Indio = More Than an Indian: Racial Ambivalence and Neoliberal Multiculturalism in Guatemala* (Santa Fe: School of American Research Press, 2006), 156

67 Ibid., 159.

68 Ibid., 161.

69 Interview with Raúl Sigüenza, Juayua, 1999.

70 Interview with Silvestre Panche, Nahuizalco, 1999. Panche refers to his father's remark that the insurgents "recogieron bienes sin dueños."

71 V. G. Brodeur to naval secretary, Ottawa, 7 April 1932, FO 371/15814.

72 *Diario Latino*, 2 February 1932. Millenarian beliefs also motivated some of the revolutionary forces. In Ahuachapán peasants rendered to the cult of the Virgin of Adelanto, originally venerated in El Adelanto, Guatemala, near the border. Although some claimed that the Virgin was a leftist hoax, grassroots militants took the cult very seriously. The cult did not extend beyond Ahuachapán and the border region of Guatemala, yet in other parts of western Salvador revolutionary beliefs were also tinged with millenarian aspirations. It is thus quite possible that the millenarian promise, the "last shall be first," may have contributed to the looting.

73 MacNaught, "Horrors of Communism," 9.

74 Galindo Pohl, *Recuerdos de Sonsonate*, 358, notes the very limited scale of looting in Sonsonate. The "montepío" and one store were the targets, despite the ample opportunity to loot on a massive scale.

75 Interview with Paulino Galicia, Cara Sucia, Ahauchapán, 1999.

76 Pessar, *From Fanatics to Folk*, 225–26.

77 Ibid., 6–7.

78 Hobsbawm, *Primitive Rebels*, 57–59.

79 Ibid., 90.

80 Ibid., 105.

81 Interview with Paulino Galicia, Cara Sucia, Sonsonate, 1–99. Galicia was twelve years old in 1932.

82 Interview with Manuela Chicas, San Salvador, 2001.

83 Commander V. G. Brodeur, "Secret Report of Situation, as It Developed at Acajutla," 7 April 1932, Foreign Office Archives, FO 371/15814.

84 Hobsbawm, *Primitive Rebels*, 60–61.

85 Interview with Gregorio Shul, Nahuizalco, 1998.

86 *Diario Latino*, 30 January 1932, also cited in Alfredo Schlesinger, *La Verdad Sobre El Comunismo*, 95.

87 Gould, *To Lead as Equals*, 197.

88 Taylor, *Drinking, Homicide and Rebellion in Colonial Mexican Villages*.

89 Gould, *To Die in This Way*.

90 Fraser, *Blood of Spain*, 150–52.

91 Sheila Fitzpatrick, "Vengeance and Ressentiment in the Russian Revolution," *French Historical Studies* 24, no. 4 (fall 2001).

92 Gould, "Revolutionary Nationalism and Local Memories in El Salvador."

93 Interview with Andrés Pérez, Pushtan, Nahuizalco, 2001.

94 We also encountered another informant, Ricardo Carillos of the municipality of Panchimalco, whose group planned to participate in an assault on San Salvador which never materialized. Interview with Ricardo Carrillos, Panchimalco, 2001.

95 Interview with Salomé Torres, El Cacao, Sonsonate, 2001.

96 Interview with Doroteo López, January 1999. The use of the term "el polaco" is curiously early with respect to the rest of the region. In other parts of Central America, particularly after the Second World War, "polaco" was a term that conflated "Jew" with door-to-door salesman. Not surprisingly "judio" or "polaco" also meant traitor.

97 Interview with Doroteo López, San Isidro, 1999.

98 Interview with Doroteo López, San Isidro, April 2001.

99 For an analagous process of cultural change in Chinandega, Nicaragua, in a nonrevolutionary situation see Gould, *To Lead as Equals*, 133–46.

100 Interview with Sotero Linares, Las Higueras, Izalco, April 2001.

Chapter Seven: "They Killed the Just for the Sinners"

1 See "La Insurrección Indígena," *El Periodico Nuevo Enfoque*, 24 January 2005. This article refers to the massacre of thirty thousand Indians. Speeches by indigenous activists frequently have used the term "genocidio." There is cur-

rently a movement to demand reparations for the "genocide" of 1932; the Ama Foundation held an "International Forum on Genocide and Truth" in Izalco in January 2007.

2 Galindo Pohl, *Recuerdos de Sonsonate*, 318.

3 "El Café de El Salvador," Asociación Cafetalera de El Salvador, San Salvador, July 1932, 42.

4 *Diario Latino*, 3 February 1932.

5 Michael Mann, in *Fascists*, 13, defines fascism as "the pursuit of a transcendent and cleansing nation-statism through paramilitarism." Mata clearly appealed to the need for cleansing and implied the suppression of democracy. Without referring to paramilitary groups, the Guardia Cívica was playing an important paramilitary role throughout the region. Finally, fascist rhetoric typically considered its subject to be the "productive classes" (Mann, *Fascists*, 7).

6 Moreover, there is no question that the regime developed marked corporatist policies tilted heavily toward Franquismo and Fascist Italy, until the United States imposed its geopolitical will in the early 1940s.

7 *New York Times*, 30 January 1932. Commander Brodeur reported that on 29 January General Calderón had reported the 4,800 communists "liquidated." "The Commanding Officer [Brodeur] immediately went ashore to verify this statement in a general way, and to pay his respects to General Calderón. He was enthusiastically embraced by the General and invited to lunch the following day in Sonsonate, and to 'witness a few executions.' " "General Resumé of Proceedings of H.M.C. Ships whilst at Acajutla, Republic of Salvador, January 23–31st, 1932," FO 371/15814, p. 14.

8 Only in Sónzacate did the rebels under the leadership of Julia Mojica register a victory, a successful defense against a vastly outnumbered unit of the National Guard, which attacked them on the morning of 23 January after a failed assault on the Sonsonate barracks, two miles away.

9 Bustamante, *Historia militar de El Salvador*, 106.

10 Montes, *El Compadrazgo*, 254.

11 Interview with Cayetana Flores, Anal Arriba, Nahuizalco, 1998.

12 Interview with Ramón Esquina, Tajcuilulaj, Nahuizalco, 1998.

13 Interview with Fabián Mojica, Sónzacate, 1999.

14 Interview with Salvador Deras, Nahuizalco, 1999. Deras, a native of Sonsonate, recalls that troops machine-gunned unarmed people who looked like campesinos on the city streets.

15 "General Resumé of Proceedings of H.M.C. Ships whilst at Acajutla, Republic of Salvador, January 23–31st, 1932," FO 371/15814, p. 12.

16 MacNaught, "Horrors of Communism," 26.

17 Interview with María Méndez, Ahuachapán, 2001.

18 Dalton, *Miguel Mármol: Los sucesos de 1932 en El Salvador*, 308. One might consider the bias of one who became a communist if it were not for so many other examples of sadism and brutality.

19 Interviews with María Hortensia García, Ahuachapán; Manuel Ramos Rivas,

Ahuachapán; María Méndez, Ahuachapán. Rivas states that he saw "caminadas de gente" taken by the troops to be shot in "Los Ausoles." García claimed that live prisoners were tossed into the boiling springs.

20 Interview with Alvaro Cortez, El Canelo, Nahuizalco, 1999.

21 Weitz, A Century of Genocide.

22 Grandin, "History, Motive, Law, Intent."

23 Grandin, "The Instruction of Great Catastrophe," 62–63.

24 Bustamante, Historia Militar de El Salvador, 106.

25 "Síntesis de la Penetración de Comunismo en el Salvador" (San Salvador: Dirección Nacional de Inteligencia, 1990), 113.

26 Galindo Pohl, Recuerdos de Sonsonate, 427. Galindo Pohl wrote that this was one of the "consignas que se escuchó en círculos biene informados," and that it was circulated primarily to scare people.

27 The Sonsonate attackers retreated to nearby Sónzacate, where on the morning of 23 January they defeated a mixed unit of the national guard and army that had attacked them. Then they dispersed, some going to reinforce the insurrectionary forces in Nahuizalco and Izalco while others remained in the countryside. Some of these were ladino hacienda workers (interview with Margarita Turcios, El Guayabo, 2001). In Ahuachapán it is still somewhat unclear where the rebels went after the attack, but it seems likely that many went into hiding. National guard units did pursue the Cumbre de Jayaque rebels who attacked Santa Tecla, but it is not clear how many died and from which causes. Interviews with Doroteo López, San Isidro, 1999, 2000; Salomé Miranda, Sacacoyo, 2001; Juan Miranda, Sacacoyo, 2001; Jesús Monterrosa, Jayaque, 2001.

28 Calderón, Anhelos de un Ciudadano, 228.

29 Interview with Raimundo Aguilar, Cusamuluco, 1999.

30 Interview with Pedro Lue, Sabana San Juan Arriba, 1998.

31 Interview with Jesús Velásquez, San Luis, Izalco, 2001.

32 Ibid.

33 Interview with Alberto Shul, Nahuizalco, 2001.

34 Galindo Pohl, Recuerdos de Sonsonate, 433.

35 Interviews with Alberto Shul, Nahuizalco, 1999, 2001; Angel Olivares, Nahuizalco, 1998.

36 D. J. Rogers to Grant Wilson, 16 February 1932, FO 813/23 no. 24 238/13a.

37 Diario de El Salvador, 17 February 1932.

38 Diario Latino, 15 February 1932.

39 Bustamante, Historia Militar de El Salvador, 107.

40 MacNaught, "Horrors of Communism in Central America."

41 Ibid., 25.

42 Galindo Pohl, Recuerdos de Sonsonate, 428.

43 Several dozen suspected rebels were imprisoned in Sonsonate and Ahuachapán. Some were still in prison two years later.

44 D. J. Rogers to Sir John Simon, San Salvador, 25 February 1932, British FO docs A 1643/9/8 123.

45 Milo Borges to Severo Mallet-Prevost, 19 February 1932, 816.00 Revolutions/ 134, Department of State, USNA.

46 Interview with Vicente Flores, Jayaque, 2001.

47 Letter to the departmental governor of Sonsonate from Colonel J. Antonio Beltrán, 11 February 1932, AGS, Jefe de Estado Mayor Presidencial. Beltrán issued a similar note the day before.

48 "General Resumé of Proceedings of H.M.C. Ships whilst at Acajutla, Republic of Salvador, January 23–31st, 1932," FO 371/15814, p. 13.

49 Interview with Manuel Linares, El Cacao, 2001.

50 Interview with Doroteo López, San Isidro, 2000.

51 Interview with Salomé Torres, El Cacao, 2001. That Torres and Linares live in the same area suggests that Linares may have been merely repeating Torres's story. However, Linares did have an uncle involved in the leftist movement on La Labor (between Atiquizaya and Ahuachapán) who he claims told him this tale.

52 On official Catholic reaction to the Protestant "threat" and its relation to "Bolshevism" see Cardenal, El Poder Eclesiástico, 280–82.

53 Arno Mayer, The Furies: Violence and Terror in the French and Russian Revolutions (Princeton: Princeton University Press, 2000), 485.

54 Although in all these cases a certain degree of racism based on phenotype might have played a role. The civilian and military forces might have falsely assumed that they were killing Indians had they bothered to think about it at all. Rarely did they bother to talk with their victims and thus potentially discern their accent.

55 Interviews with Alberto Ventura and Ricardo Carillos, Quezalapa, Panchimalco, 2001.

56 Diario Latino, 11 February 1932.

57 Rogers to Sir John Simon, FO A1643/9/8, 123.

58 Memorandum by William Cochran, no 281, 10 February 1937, Department of State, USNA.

59 In Nahuizalco we can estimate based on the British report and on ample oral testimony that the military executed between five hundred and one thousand people, almost all indigenous males twelve or older in the weeks following the defeat of the uprising.

60 A calculation based on an examination of birth records which suggests a fatality number well below ten thousand is nevertheless skewed by the unknowable number of coercive or noncoercive relations between indigenous women and others during the period following January 1932.

61 Méndez, Los sucesos comunistas en El Salvador, 76.

62 In another short section, without mentioning Mata by name, Méndez alludes to a hacendado in El Canelo who escaped on horseback from a mob of two

hundred Indians about to take over local haciendas when they had to return to Nahuizalco to confront the troops. Méndez, 104.

63 *El Heraldo de Sonsonate*, 7 March 1932.

64 *Diario Latino*, 13 February 1932.

65 See Ranajit Guha, "The Prose of Counterinsurgency," *Subaltern Studies*, vol. 2, ed. Ranajit Guha (New Delhi: Oxford University Press, 1983).

66 Annual Report of War, Navy, and Aviation, 1932, trans. in Confidential US Diplomatic Post Records, Central America, El Salvador, 1930–45, 2 March 1933.

67 Candelario, "Representación de lo irrepresentable" and "Patología."

68 Méndez, *Los sucesos comunistas en El Salvador*, 101; *Memoria de Guerra, Marina y Aviación, 1932* (San Salvador: Imprenta Nacional, 1933).

69 *El Diario de El Salvador*, 27 January 1932.

70 Traverso, *The Origins of Nazi Violence*, 111.

71 Ibid., 111–12.

72 *El Diario de El Salvador*, 28 January 1932.

73 Traverso, *The Origins of Nazi Violence*, 90.

74 Ibid., 91.

75 Although apparently there was some protest when Calderón announced 4,800 liquidated communists, a search of the *Times* (London), *La Epoca* (Madrid), *Vossiche Zeitung* (Berlin), *Le Populaire de Paris* newspapers in western Europe and others in Latin America uncovered no diplomatic protests about the massacres.

76 *New York Times*, 12 March 1932.

77 Ibid., 13 March 1932. That Washington sympathized with the Martínez regime's energetic repression did not stop it from taking a principled stand against diplomatic recognition.

78 Other than Calderón's statement of a siege of the Salvadoran embassy in Mexico City, we have found no corroboration. The Mexican left was clearly incensed at the killings of communists in Salvador and passed out leaflets. The consul of El Salvador in Mexico had the audacity to speak at an anti-imperialist rally, where the left challenged his rationalization of the revolt and the repression. According to *Excelsior* on 28 January 1932, "un tumulto entre partidarios de los dos grupos" erupted.

79 See Cerdas Cruz, *La Hoz y El Machete*, 298–305, for the reaction of the Comintern and the SRI to the insurrection and massacres.

80 15 March 1932, AGS.

81 *Memoria del Ministerio de Fomento, Gobernación . . .* (San Salvador: Imprenta Nacional, 1933), 8.

82 Interview with Alejandro Pérez Ortiz, Carrizal, 2002. The politician who uttered these words was a Dr. Morales.

83 Interview with Ramón Esquina, Tajcuilulaj, 1998.

84 "Statement of the Government regarding Present Communist Activities," repr. and trans. 800.B, 22 June 1935, Department of State, USNA.

Chapter Eight: Memories of the Massacre

1 Dalton, *Miguel Mármol: Los sucesos de 1932 en El Salvador*, 305.
2 Cáceres, "Después del 32," 111.
3 Ibid., 112.
4 Alvarenga, "Los indígenas y el Estado: alianzas y estrategias políticas en la construcción del poder local en El Salvador; Ching and Tilley, "Indians, the Military, and the Rebellion of 1932 in El Salvador."
5 See Adams, *Cultural Surveys of Panama, Nicaragua, Guatemala, El Salvador, Honduras*, 494, on the hierarchy in the 1950s, especially the independent role of the cacique. In Izalco the civil religious hierarchy before 1932 formed a structure largely independent of the municipality and the state. In Nahuizalco, on the contrary, until 1932 the indigenous people, over 80 percent of the population, often won control over the municipal government. This political control tied to the national state probably weakened the religious dimension of the civil and religious hierarchy. In any event, the hierarchy did not survive the *matanza*.
6 Alfonso Muñoz to General Felipe Ibarra, 14 October 1932, #368, AMS.
7 The evidence for these assertions is still fragmentary, although recent work by Erik Ching and Virginia Tilley substantiates the argument that the military often supported the Indians against wealthy ladinos during the 1930s. Memory studies such as Daniel James, *Doña María's Story: Life History, Memory, and Political Identity* (Durham: Duke University Press, 2003), Luisa Passerini, *Fascism in Popular Memory* (Cambridge: Cambridge University Press, 1987), and Portelli, *The Death of Luigi Trastulli and Other Stories*, have analyzed the impact of élite domination on subaltern memory in other historical contexts.
8 Interviews with Paulino Galicia, Cara Sucia, 1999; Prudencio Hernández, La Sabana, Nahuizalco, 1998; Carlos Alarcón, Salcoatitán, 1998.
9 See Castellanos, *El Salvador*, 149–67. Also see Mariano Castro Moran, *Relámpagos de Libertad: Abril, Mayo y Diciembre 1944* (San Salvador: LIS, 2001), 109–254, for an extremely detailed account of the period, with an emphasis on the participation of anti-Martinista officers.
10 Nevertheless two Izalqueños, General Alfonso Marroqín and Colonel Tito Calvo, both key military players in the massacre in Izalco, joined the conspiracy against Martínez. According to Castellanos their distrust of civilians (for fear of communist infiltration) led to the failure of the April rebellion. Castellanos, "El Salvador," 151.
11 Interview with Angel Olivares, Nahuizalco, 1998. See Alvarenga, "Los indígenas y el Estado: alianzas y y estrategias políticas en la construcción del poder local en El Salvador."
12 Lt. Alfonso Muñoz to General Felipe Ibarra, 4 October 1932, AMS.
13 Interview with Angelica Lué, Tajcuilulah, 1998
14 Clará de Guevara, *Exploración etnográfica, Departamento de Sonsonate*, 171.
15 Interview with Arsenio Pérez, El Carrizal, 2001.

16 El Diario de El Salvador, 5 February 1932.

17 Similarly, one informant recalls stumbling across human bones and his elders telling him: "there are your brothers." Interview with Esteban Tepas, Pushtan, Nahuizalco, 1998.

18 Interview with Angelica Lué, Tajcuilulah, 1998.

19 Leonhard Schultze Jena, Mitos y Leyendas de los Pipiles de Izalco, trans. Gloria Menjívar and Armida Parada Fortín (San Salvador: Ediciciones Cuscatlán, 1977), 142 [orig. pubd Berlin, 1934].

20 Adams, Cultural Surveys of Panama, Nicaragua, Guatemala, El Salvador, Honduras.

21 Interview with Arsenio Perez, El Carrizal, 2001.

22 Interview with Rosario Lué, Nahuizalco, 2001.

23 An informant from the cantón, Carrizal, stated that the survivors converted one of these sites into a cemetery where people left flowers (interviews with Manuel Acensio Perez, El Carrizal, 1998; Ramón Aguilar, Cusumaluco, 1999).

24 Interview with Ramón García, Cusumaluco, 1998.

25 Catherine Merridale, "War, Death and Remembrance in Soviet Russia," 73.

26 Snyder Hook, "Awakening from War."

27 Peterson, "Uncertain Remains." In his study, rooted in fieldwork in Tacuba, Peterson offers a highly sophisticated discussion of lay trauma theory, arguing against the version that posits an "instrumental response" by the afflicted. See chapters 3 and 8.

28 Interview with Ramón Esquina, Tajcuilulaj, 1998.

29 Interview with Arsenio Pérez, El Carrizal, 2001.

30 Hale, Más Que un Indio, 67.

31 Informants used variants of this expression around the verb "deber," for example "los que debían no murieron y los que no debían nada si murieron."

32 Peterson, "Uncertain Remains," chapters 3, 10.

33 Ibid.

34 For a thoughtful analysis of the temporal dimension of memories see Portelli, The Death of Luigi Trastulli and Other Stories.

35 Clará de Guevara, Exploración etnográfica, Departamento de Sonsonate, 209.

36 Margarito Vásquez, Santo Domingo, 2001. A version of this account is repeated by nearly all elderly informants in Santo Domingo.

37 "El Caballo Rojo" (Editorial Don Bosco, March 1932), quoted in "Después del 1932, Ernesto Cáceres," Boletín de Ciencias Económicas y Sociales 9, no. 2 (March–April 1986), 106.

38 Interview with Cruz Perez, El Carrizal, 2001. It is possible, as Peter Guardino has suggested (in a personal communication), that the name "Lázaro" was something of a nickname, awarded after the events, or that the character was in some way "constructed" among the survivors, though he certainly has a family lineage in El Carrizal.

39 Interviews with Vicente Flores, Jacinto Mendez, Jayaque, 2001.

40 Clará de Guevara, Exploración etnográfica, Departamento de Sonsonate, 324; interview with Jorge Pérez, Cuisnahuat, 1998 (with Patricia Alvarenga).

41 Interview with Miguel Urbina, Ceiba del Charco, 2001.

42 Interview with E. Zetino, Pushtan, 1999.

43 Interview with Andrés Pérez, Pushtan, 2001.

44 Interview with Alberto Shul, Nahuizalco, 1999, 2001. Shul recalls how the elders would use a device with water and weights and then exclaim, "Vamos a triunfar!"

45 Interview with Doroteo Lopez, San Isidro, 1999. His nervous comrades graciously declined the offer.

46 Interview with Jesús Velásquez, San Luis, 2001.

47 Interview with Alejandro Perez Ortiz, El Carrizal 2001.

48 Interview with Andrés Pérez, Pushtan, 2001.

49 Interview with Salomé Miranda, Sacacoyo, 2001.

50 Cardenal, *Historia de Una Esperanza*, 235–36.

51 On the view of indigenous and leftist militants on ethnocide see Gould, "Revolutionary Nationalism and Local Memories." Linguists employ the term "Nahuatl-Pipil" or Pipil to refer to a dialect quite distinct from the Mexican variants. Locals often call the indigenous language "Nahuate." We will use the local term interchangeably with Pipil in the text.

52 *El Heraldo de Sonsonate*, 13 August 1932.

53 de Baratta and Mendoza, *Cuzcatlán Típico: Ensayo Sobre Etnofonía de El Savator*; Herrera Vega, *El Indio occidental y su incorporación social por la escuela*. It is remarkable that in Herrera Vega's 110-page book, dealing directly with the condition of Izalqueño Indians, the author omits any mention of the massacre, despite his purported sympathy for their plight. One can only assume that he was afraid to potentially manifest any criticism of the regime by mentioning its role.

54 Interview with Patrocinio Hernandez, Cuisnahuat, 1998 (with Patricia Alvarenga). This informant claimed that the local schoolteacher during the 1930s prohibited the speaking of Nahuate in the school, arguing that books were not written in the language.

55 Interview with Alejandro Perez Ortiz, El Carrizal 2001.

56 Interviews with Rodrigo Malía, 1998; Pedro Lué, Sábana San Juan, 1998. Both informants recall the same phrase.

57 Interview with Benito Sarco, Nahuizalco, 2000.

58 Interview with Rosario Lué, Nahuizalco 1999.

59 There is also some evidence that authorities around the time of la Matanza, especially in Izalco, cast a threatening glance at anyone who spoke the language, which was regarded as a possible form of subversive activity.

60 Interview with María Antonia Pérez, El Canelo, 2001.

61 Herrera Vega, *El Indio occidental y su incorporación social por la escuela*, 27.

62 Ibid., 28.

63 Pierre Bourdieu and Loïc Wacquant, *An Invitation to Reflexive Sociology* (Chicago: University of Chicago Press, 1992), 167.

64 Herrera Vega, *El Indio Occidental y su Incorporación Social por la Escuela*, 78.

65 Ibid., 104.

66 Ibid.

67 Gould, *To Die in This Way*; Gould, "Revolutionary Nationalism and Local Memories in El Salvador," 161.

68 Anonymous informant, Santo Domingo de Guzmán, 1999.

69 See Clará de Guevara, *Exploración etnográfica, Departamento de Sonsonate*. Also see Pineda Ortiz and Ramírez Cruz, "Vision Socio-cultural de Nahuizalco," 95; Contreras, "Monografía de la población Indígena de Nahuizalco." He writes: "Durante la investigación todos negaron hablar el dialecto Nahuate . . . y que es una 'bayuncada' hablar en 'lengua' . . . La verdad es que todos hablan el Nahuate, sólo que no lo hablaban en público porque los mestizos se burlan de ellos" (45). Lyle Campbell states: "In Cuisnahuat there are about 40 [Nahuatel speakers] and in Santo Domingo de Guzmán the majority of indigenous adults still know how to speak it, although there are few youths who have learned it." "La Dialectología Pipil," 833.

70 Interview with Juan Cestino Lué, El Canelo, March 2000. This witness claimed that women who had relatively new refajos were afraid of being implicated as looters. Others suggest that one group of indigenous village patrolmen right after the first wave of repression ordered women in El Canelo and Sábana San Juan Arriba (neighboring cantones in Nahuizalco, bordering on Gabino Mata's plantation) to stop wearing indigenous garb.

71 Marden, "Coffee Is the King in El Salvador," 602. Interviews with virtually all informants suggest that the decline of "refajo" use came a generation later.

72 Interview with Rosario Lué, Nahuizalco, 1999. This argument should not be dismissed, as it is entirely possible that temperatures did increase in the area because of deforestation.

73 Interview, Nahuizalco, 1998. The name has been changed.

74 Interview with María Antonia Pérez, El Canelo, 2001.

75 One informant in particular, Carlos Shul (pseud.), claimed pride in his mother's indigenous identity, but when we spoke with his mother she reminded him with bitterness, "No te acordás? Me rogaste de quitarme el refajo!" Interviews with Carlos Shul and his mother, El Cerrito, Nahuizalco, 1999.

76 Interview with Arsenio Pérez, El Carrizal, 2001; also see Gould, "Revolutionary Nationalism and Local Memories in El Salvador."

77 Clará de Guevara, *Exploración etnográfica, Departamento de Sonsonate*.

78 Rappaport, *Cumbe Reborn*; de la Cadena, *Indigenous Mestizos*; Euraque, Gould, and Hale, eds., *Memorias del Mestizaje*.

79 Scheff, "Emotions and Identity." Also see Reddy, "Against Constructionism." Reddy's following remark is worthy of consideration in the Salvadoran context: "Shame, I would argue, also derives from thoughts about how one is seen by others . . . Thus, shame can lead to withdrawal coupled with action aimed at managing appearances; such action can, in turn, take the form of emotive utterances and behavior that drum up and intensify socially approved feelings and play down or deny deviant ones. Local varieties of shame are therefore, in

many cultural contexts, a principal instrument of social control and political power" (347).

80 Salarrué, *Cataleya Luna*, 172.

81 Herrera Vega, *El Indio occidental y su incorporación social por la escuela.*

82 A. J. Harris, Labor Conditions and Problems, 24 February 1933, 816.504/29, Department of State, USNA.

83 Interview with María Antonia Perez, El Canelo, 2001.

84 The civil registry in Nahuizalco shows that from 1932 to 1935, 67 percent of births were recorded as illegitimate. Since the pre-1932 records were destroyed in the insurrection there is no basis for comparison, but anecdotal evidence suggests that the rate of illegitimacy increased. In Izalco in 1930, 60 percent of births were illegitimate, and in 1933 the rate was 76 percent.

85 Interview with Ernesto Shul, Nahuizalco, 1999.

86 The generational conflict in Cuisnahuat, a municipality with a large indigenous population, had a specifically political expression. Modernizers and traditionalists without specific national affiliations battled for control of the municipality in the early 1970s. See Clará de Guevara, *Exploración etnográfica, Departamento de Sonsonate.*

87 Interview with anonymous informant, Cuisnahuat, 2000.

88 Interview with Reynaldo Patriz, El Carrizal, 1998. On nonindigenous transmission of memory see for example interviews with Carlos Castillo and his father Luis Alfonso Castillo, Atiquizaya, 2001; Miguel Lino, El Tortuguero, 2002; Vicente Flores, Jayaque, 2001.

89 Tula, *Hear My Testimony*, 33–52; Gordon, *Crisis Política y Guerra en El Salvador*, 247.

90 Interviews with Reynaldo Patriz and Manuel Ascencio Perez, El Carrizal, 1998–99; Margarito Vásquez and Manuel Vásquez, Santo Domingo, 1998; Carlos Lue, Nahuizalco, 1998, 1999, 2001.

91 The leftist-influenced Partido Acción Revolucionario had some support in the region during the 1960s.

92 The UCS seemed to gain more support in the wake of the agrarian reform of 1980.

93 Interview with Margarito Vásquez, Santo Domingo, 1998.

94 The impact of one such organization, FECCAS, is magnificently described and analyzed in Cabarrús, *Génesis de una Revolución*. Also see Wood, *Insurgent Collective Action and Civil War.*

95 For a state-centered analysis of this transformation in El Salvador and elsewhere see Goodwin: *No Other Way Out.*

96 Charles D. Brockett, *Political Movements and Violence in Central America* (Cambridge: Cambridge University Press, 2005), 53.

97 Wickham-Crowley, *Guerrillas and Revolution in Latin America*, 243–44. The ratio of workers to farmers in La Libertad (5.6:1), Ahuachapán (6.7:1), and Sonsonate (8.4:1) was far higher than in the insurgent areas, where the ratio ranged from 0.6:1 (Chaletenango) to 2.9:1 (Usulatán).

98   Gordon, *Crisis Política y Guerra en El Salvador*, 30.

99   Interviews with Margarito Vásquez, Manuel Vásquez, and Ambrosio Benitez, Santo Domingo, 1998, 2000.

100 Interview with Margarito Vásquez, 2001.

101 Interviews with Reynaldo Patriz, 1999, 2001; Juan Francisco Hernández, 1998; Alejandro Pérez Ortiz, 2001.

102 Based on testimony from interview with Ciro Cáceres with Patricia Alvarenga, Nahuizalco, 1998. The account is substantiated by Reynaldo Patriz, 1999, 2001; Juan Francisco Hernández, 1998; and Alejandro Pérez Ortiz, 2001.

103 Interview with María Eduwiges Pérez, El Canelo, Nahuizalco, 2001.

104 For example, on the outskirts of San Salvador they left the bodies in a place called "Los Playones"; also see *Voz Popular* (San Salvador), July 1979, NACLA Archive File no. 12.

105 Grandin, *Empire's Workshop*, 2006.

106 Interview with Manuel Ascencio Pérez, El Carrizal, 1998.

107 Interview with Arsenio Pérez, El Carrizal, 1980.

108 Inteview with Cruz Perez, El Carrizal, 2001.

109 Interview with Manuel Vásquez, Santo Domingo de Guzmán, 1998.

110 On the left's immersion in the discourse of mestizaje in Nicargaua see Gould, *To Die in This Way*, 228–82.

111 Remarkably, the only reference to the El Carrizal massacre was a highly distorted military report suggesting that the guerrillas had initiated a reign of terror in the canton. See *El Latino*, 18 July 1980, for the military report.

112 *De La Locura a la Esperanza: La Guerra de 12 años en El Salvador*, Informe de la Comisión de la Verdad Para El Salvador (New York: United Nations, 1993), 76.

113 On Las Hojas see Mac Chapin, *La Población de El Salvador* (San Salvador: Ministerio de Educación, 1990). On Los Gramales, interview with Pedro Sánchez, Tajcuilulaj, 1998. The military gunned down from fifteen to one hundred in these incidents.

114 "Carta Infmativa de ANIS," August 1987, ANIS archive, Sonsonate.

115 Interview with Consuelo Roque, Santo Domingo, 1998 (with Patricia Alvarenga); interview with Margarito Vásquez, Santo Domingo, 2001; interview with Manuel Vásquez, Santo Domingo, 2001.

116 *De La Locura a la Esperanza*, 81.

Epilogue

1   Populist sentiment was so deep that the rightist ARENA party, as it modernized, strove to maintain its own version of the populism that had helped it to power in the 1980s.

2   Segovia, *Transformación Estructural y Reforma Económica en El Salvador*, 182.

3   Segovia, *Transformación Estructural y Reforma Económica en El Salvador*.

4   See Gould, "Revolutionary Nationalism and Local Memories," 160–64, for a

brief discussion of the alienation of rural activists in Nahuizalco. The discussion of contemporary Nahuizalco politics is also based on observations made during a visit in 1999 and for six months in 2001.

Afterword

1 A few indigenous activists suggested that we give greater emphasis to "indigenous culture."

2 The principal factor accounting for this relative weakness of the documentary is, in turn, reflected to a lesser degree in the book. For a variety of reasons (including this screening) Reynaldo, Santiago, and I found it more difficult to develop a network of informants in Izalco. During an earlier stage of the research project, the Costa Rican historian Patricia Alvarenga did concentrate her efforts here and many of the informants were first approached by her.

3 On one level those limitations could be summarized by what I somewhat euphemistically describe as the "creative tension" with my collaborator, a journalist by training who had served as director of Radio Venceremos, the clandestine radio station of the Salvadoran guerrillas from 1981 to 1992. Our differences were not so much political as disciplinary. He sought synthesis and I pushed for explanation. To me he often responded, "Save it for your book." In an interview in a major Salvadoran paper, he commented that "if it were up to Gould, the documentary would have been six hours long." Although an exaggeration, the comment was not entirely off the mark.

4 See "La Insurrección Indígena," El Periodico Nuevo Enfoque, 24 January 2005.

5 "Scars of Memory: El Salvador, 1932," directed and produced by Jeffrey L. Gould and Carlos Henríquez Consalvi (New York: First Run/Icarus Films, 2003). The selection of the interviews was not consciously based on the visual imagery.

6 Georgina Hernandez, "El Ejerciicio de la Memoria Histórica en la Construcción de las Identidades" (unpublished manuscript, 2005). This report stated: "it was through the documentary forum that spectators exhibited certain social practices of identification."

7 "El Salvador Was Denounced before the UN Committee against Racism," Lutheran World Federation, 1 March 2006.

8 "Prosthetic memories are memories that circulate publicly, are not organically based, but are nevertheless experienced with one's own body—by means of a wide range of cultural technologies—and as such, become part of one's personal archive of experience, informing not only one's subjectivity but one's relationship to the present and future tenses . . . like an artificial limb they are actually worn by the body; these are sensuous memories produced by experience." Landsberg, "America, the Holocaust, and the Mass Culture of Memory," 66.

9 Ibid., 84.

Bibliography

Adams, Richard N. *Cultural Surveys of Panama, Nicaragua, Guatemala, El Salvador, Honduras.* Scientific Publications, no. 33. Washington: Pan American Sanitary Bureau, 1957.

Alvarenga, Patricia. *Cultura y ética de la violencia: El Salvador 1880–1932.* San José: EDUCA, 1996.

——. "Auxiliary Forces in the Shaping of the Repressive System: El Salvador, 1880–1930." *Identity and Struggle at the Margins of the Nation-State: The Laboring Peoples of Central America and the Hispanic Caribbean,* ed. Aviva Chomsky and Aldo Lauria-Santiago. Durham: Duke University Press, 1998.

——. "Los indígenas y el Estado: alianzas y estrategias políticas en la construcción del poder local en El Salvador, 1920–1944." *Memorias del mestizaje: cultura poaitica en Centroamérica de 1920 al presente,* ed. Dario A. Euraque, Jeffrey L. Gould, and Charles R. Hale, 363–94. Guatemala City: CIRMA, 2005.

Americas Watch and American Civil Liberties Union. *Report on Human Rights in El Salvador.* New York: Vintage, 1982.

Anderson, Thomas. *Matanza: The Communist Revolt of 1932.* Lincoln: University of Nebraska Press, 1971.

Appelius, Mario. *Le terre che tremano, Guatemala, Salvador, Honduras, Nicaragua, Costarica, Panama.* Verona: A. Mondadori, 1933.

Araujo, Arturo. *Mi programa de gobierno, 1931–1935.* San Salvador, 1931.

Arias Gomez, Jorge. *Farabundo Marti*. San José, 1972.

Asociación cafetalera de El Salvador. *Primer Censo Nacional del Café*. San Salvador: Talleres Gráficos Cisneros, 1940.

Baloyra, Enrique. *El Salvador in Transition*. Chapel Hill: University of North Carolina Press, 1982.

Baratta, María de, and Jeremías Mendoza. *Cuzcatlán Típico: Ensayo Sobre Etnofonía de El Salvador, Folklore, Folkwisa y Folkway*. San Salvador: Ministry of Culture, 1951.

Becker, Mark. "Una Revolución Comunista Indígena: Rural Protest Movements in Cayembe, Ecuador." *Rethinking Marxism* 10, no.4 (winter 1998), 34–51.

Bedford, Joseph Anthony. "Setting the Tone: US-Salvadoran Relations, 1900–1932." Diss., Rutgers University, 1991.

Bermudez, Alejandro. *El Salvador al vuelo*. San Salvador: Moisant Bank Note Co., 1917.

Binford, Leigh. *The El Mozote Massacre: Anthropology and Human Rights*. Tucson: University of Arizona Press, 1996.

Browning, David. *El Salvador: Landscape and Society*. Oxford: Clarendon, 1971.

Buell, Raymond Leslie. *The Central Americans*. New York: Foreign Policy Association, 1930.

Buezo, Rodrigo. *Sangre de Hermanos*. Havana: Universal, 1936.

Bulmer-Thomas, Victor. *The Political Economy of Central America since 1920*. Cambridge: Cambridge University Press, 1987.

Burns, Bradford. "The Modernization of Underdevelopment: El Salvador, 1858–1931." *Journal of Developing Areas* 18, no.3 (April 1984), 293–316.

——. "The Intellectual Infrastructure of Modernization in El Salvador, 1870–1900." *Americas* 41, no.3 (January 1985), 57–82.

Bustamante, Gregorio. *Historia militar de El Salvador*. San Salvador: Talleres Gráficos Cisneros, 1935.

Cabarrús, Carlos Rafael. *Génesis de una revolución: Analisis del surgimiento y desarollo de la organización campesina en El Salvador*. Mexico City: Casa Chata, 1983.

Cáceres, Ernesto. "Después del 32." *Boletín de Ciencias Económicas y Sociales* 9, no.2 (1986).

Calderón, José Tomás. *Anhelos de un ciudadano*. San Salvador, 1942.

——. "Breve reseña histórica del Comunismo en El Salvador." *Anhelos de un ciudadano*. San Salvador, 1942.

Campbell, Lyle. "La Dialectología Pipil." *América Indígena* 35, no. 4 (1975).

Candelario, Sheila. "Representación de lo irrepresentable: Violencia, muerte y la guerra en El Salvador." Diss., State University of New York, Stony Brook, 2001.

——. "Patología de una Insurrección: La prensa y la Matanza de 1932." *Istmo: Revista virtual de estudios literarios y culturales centroamericanos*, no. 3 (January–June 2002).

Cardenal, Rodolfo. *El poder eclesiástico en El Salvador, 1871–1931*. San Salvador: UCA, 1980.

——. *Historia de una Esperanza: Vida de Rutilio Grande*. Colección Teología Latinoamericana v. 4. San Salvador: UCA, 1985.

Carr, Barry. "The Mexican Communist Party and Agrarian Mobilization in the La-
guna, 1920–1940: A Worker-Peasant Alliance?" *Hispanic American Historical Review*
67, no.3 (1987), 371–404.

———. "Identity, Class and Nation: Black Immigrant Workers, Cuban Communism,
and the Sugar Insurgency, 1925–1934." *Hispanic American Historical Review* 78, no. 1
(1998), 83–116.

Casaus, Marta. "Las Influencias de las redes intelectuales teosóficas en la opinión
pública centroamericana (1870–1930)." Sexto Congreso Centroamericano de Historia (Panamá, 2002).

Castellanos, Juan Mario. *El Salvador, 1930–1960: Antecedentes Históricos de la Guerra Civil.*
San Salvador: Publicaciones e Impresos, 2001.

Castellanos, Sergio. *Informe de la corte de cuentas.* San Salvador: Imprenta Nacional,
1897.

Castro Moran, Mariano. *Función política del ejercito Salvadoreño en el presente siglo.* San
Salvador: UCA, 1984.

Cerdas Cruz, Rodolfo. *Farabundo Marti, la internacional comunista y la insurrección salvadoreña de 1932.* San José: Centro de Investigación y adiestramiento político
administrativo, 1982.

———. *La hoz y el machete: la Internacional Comunista: América Latina y la revolución en
Centroamérica.* San José: EUNED, 1986.

Ching, Erik. "La Historia de Centroamérica en los Archivos Rusos del COMINTERN:
Los Documentos Salvadoreños." *Revista de Historia* 32 (July–December 1995),
217–47.

———. "From Clientelism to Militarism: The State, Politics and Authoritarianism in El
Salvador, 1840–1940." Diss., University of California, Santa Barbara, 1997.

———. "In Search of the Party: The Communist Party, the Comintern, and the Peasant
Rebellion of 1932 in El Salvador." *Americas* 55, no.2 (October 1998), 204–39.

Ching, Erik, and Virginia Tilley. "Indians, the Military and the Rebellion of 1932 in
El Salvador." *Journal of Latin American Studies* 30 (1998), 121–56.

Clará de Guevara, Concepción de. *Exploración etnográfica, Departamento de Sonsonate.*
San Salvador: Ministerio de Educación, 1975.

Colindres, Eduardo. *Fundamentos económicos de la burguesía salvadoreña.* San Salvador:
UCA, 1977.

Comisión de la Verdad. *De la Locura a la Esperanza: La Guerra de 12 Años en El Salvador.*
San José: Departamento Ecuménico de Investigaciones, 1993.

Conte, Antono. *Treinta Años en Tierras Salvadoreñas.* San Miguel: Tipografía el Progreso, 1934.

Contreras, Juan José. "Monografía de la población Indígena de Nahuizalco." Diss.,
Faculty of Medicine, University of El Salvador, 1963.

Cuenca, Abel. *El Salvador: una democracia cafetalera.* Mexico City: AR-Centro, 1962.

Dalton, Roque. "Miguel Mármol: El Salvador 1930–32." *Pensamiento crítico* 48 (January 1971), 6–113.

——. *Miguel Mármol: Los sucesos de 1932 en El Salvador*. San José: Educa, 1972; repr. San José: Editorial Universitaria Centroamericana, 1982.

de Baratta, María, and Jeremías Mendoza. *Cuzcatlán Típico Ensayo Sobre Etnofonía de El Salvador: Folklore, Folkwisa y Folkway*. San Salvador: Ministerio de Cultura, 1951.

de la Cadena, Marisol. *Indigenous Mestizos*. Durham: Duke University Press, 2000.

de la Fuente, Alejandro. *A Nation for All: Race, Inequality, and Politics in Twentieth Century Cuba*. Chapel Hill: University of North Carolina Press, 2001.

Domville-Fife, Charles William. *Guatemala and the States of Central America*. London: Francis Griffiths, 1913.

Dunkerley, James. *The Long War: Dictatorship and Revolution in El Salvador*. London: Junction, 1982.

——. *Power in the Isthmus: A Political History of Modern Central America*. London: Verso, 1988.

Dur, Philip F. "U.S. Diplomacy and the Salvadorean Revolution of 1931." *Journal of Latin American Studies* 30, no.98 (February 1998), 95–119.

Durham, William. *Scarcity and Survival in Central America*. Stanford: Stanford University Press, 1979.

Elam, R. V. "Appeal to Arms: The Army and Politics in El Salvador, 1931–1964." Diss., University of New Mexico, 1970.

El Movimiento Revolucionario Latinoamericano. Buenos Aires: Correspondencia Sudamericana, 1929.

El Salvador, Dirección General de Estadística. *La Republica de El Salvador*. San Salvador: Imprenta Nacional, 1924.

El Salvador: Estudio físico y administrativo. San Salvador: La Republica, 1913.

El Salvador, Government of. *El Impuesto Sobre la Renta*. San Salvador: Imprenta Nacional, 1915.

——. *Ley de Impuesto Sobre la Renta*. San Salvador, 1915.

——. *Procesos Relativos a la Rebelión del 6 de Diciembre de 1927*. San Salvador: Imprenta Nacional, 1930.

El Salvador, Government of, Ministry of Finance. *Contribuyentes matriculados y presuntos del impuesto general sobre la renta*. San Salvador: Imprenta Nacional, 1923.

——. "Entre la Memoria y la Historia." *Encuentro Sobre la Historia Oral*. Buenos Aires, 2003.

Espino, Miguel Angel. *Prosas Escogidas*, 6th edn. San Salvador: UCA, 1995.

Euraque, Darío A., Jeffrey L. Gould, and Charles R. Hale, eds. *Memorias del Mestizaje: Cultura Política en Centroamérica de 1920 al Presente*. Guatemala City: CIRMA, 2005.

Filio, Carlos. *Tierras de Centroamérica*. Mexico City, 1946.

Fink, Leon. *Workingmen's Democracy: The Knights of Labor and American Politics*. Urbana: University of Illinois Press, 1985.

Flores Macal, Mario. *Origen, desarrollo y crisis de las formas de dominación en El Salvador*. San José: SECASA, 1983.

Fraser, Ronald. *Blood of Spain: An Oral History of the Spanish Civil War*. New York: Pantheon, 1979.

Galindo Pohl, Reynaldo. *Recuerdos de Sonsonate: Crónica del 32*. Sonsonate: Tecnograff, 2001.

García Giráldez, Teresa. "El Unionismo y el Antiimperialismo en la década de 1920." *Sexto Congreso Centroamericano de Historia* (Panamá, 2002).

Gaspar, Cirilo. *Historia Bautista en el Salvador*. San Salvador: Moreno, 1942.

Gómez, Jorge Arias. *Farabundo Martí*. San José, 1972.

González, Reynaldo. *La Fiesta de los Tiburones*. Havana: Ciencias Sociales, 1978.

Gonzalez, Vinicio. "La insurrección salvadoreña de 1932 y la Gran Huelga hondureña de 1954." *Revista Mexicana de Sociologia* 40, no.2 (April–June 1978).

Goodwin, Jeff. *No Other Way Out: States and Revolutionary Movements, 1945–2001*. Cambridge: Cambridge University Press, 2001.

Gordon, Sara. *Crisis Política y Guerra en El Salvador*. Mexico City: Siglo Veintiuno, 1989.

Gould, Jeffrey. *To Lead as Equals: Rural Protest and Political Consciousness in Chinandega, Nicaragua, 1912–1979*. Chapel Hill: University of North Carolina Press, 1990.

——. *To Die in This Way Nicaraguan Indians and the Myth of Mestizaje, 1880–1960*. Durham: Duke University Press, 1998.

——. "Revolutionary Nationalism and Local Memories in El Salvador." *Reclaiming "the Political" in Latin American History: The View from the North*, ed. Gilbert Joseph, 138–71. Durham: Duke University Press, 2001.

——. "Proyectos del Estado-nación y la supresión de la pluralidad cultural: perspectivas históricas." *Memorias del Mestizaje: Cultura Política en Centroamérica de 1920 al presente*, ed. Darío Euraque, Jeffrey L. Gould, and Charles R. Hale, 53–78. Guatemala: CIRMA, 2004.

Grandin, Greg. *The Blood of Guatemala: A History of Race and Nation*. Durham: Duke University Press, 2000.

——. "History, Motive, Law, Intent: Combining Historical and Legal Methods in Understanding Guatemala's 1981–83 Genocide." *The Specter of Genocide: Mass Murder in Historical Perspective*, ed. Ben Kiernan and Robert Gellately. Cambridge: Cambridge University Press, 2003.

——. *The Last Colonial Massacre: Latin America in the Cold War*. Chicago: University of Chicago Press, 2004.

——. "The Instruction of Great Catastrophe: Truth Commissions, National History, and State Formation in Argentina, Chile, and Guatemala." *American Historical Review* 110, no. 1 (February 2005).

——. *Empire's Workshop: Latin America, the United States, and the Rise of the New Imperialism*. New York: Metropolitan, 2006.

Guha, Ranajit, "The Prose of Counterinsurgency." *Subaltern Studies II*, ed. Ranajit Guha. New Delhi: Oxford University Press, 1983.

Guidos Vejar, Rafael. *El Ascenso del Militarismo en El Salvador*. San Salvador: UCA, 1980.

Guillen Chacón, José Antonio. "Historia y comentarios de la tributación cafetalera en El Salvador." Thesis, University of El Salvador, 1963.

Hale, Charles R. *Más Que un Indio = More Than an Indian: Racial Ambivalence and*

Neoliberal Multiculturalism in Guatemala. Santa Fe: School of American Research Press, 2006.

Harlow, Barbara. "Testimonio and Survival: Roque Dalton's *Miguel Mármol*." *Latin American Perspectives* 18, no. 4. (autumn 1991), 9–21.

Hartman, Carl. "Reconocimiento Etnográfica de los Aztecas de El Salvador." *Ymer* 3 (1901), 151; repr. in *Mesoamérica* 41 (June 2001).

Helg, Aline. *Our Rightful Share: The Afro-Cuban Struggle for Equality*. Chapel Hill: University of North Carolina Press, 1995.

Herrera Vega, Adolfo. *El indio occidental y su incorporación social por la escuela*. Santa Ana: Izalco, 1935.

Hill, James. "Raising Coffee in El Salvador." *Tea and Coffee Trade Journal*, 1936,424.

Hobsbawm, Eric. *Primitive Rebels: Studies in Archaic Forms of Social Movement in the 19th and 20th Centuries*. Manchester: Manchester University Press, 1959.

Iraheta Rosales, Gerardo, Vilma Dolores Lopez Alas, and Maria del Carmen Escobar Cornejo. "La crisis de 1929 y sus consecuencias en los años posteriores." *Universidad* 6, no. 755 (1971), 22–74.

Jackson, Harry Franklin. "The Techological Development of Central America, 1823–1913." University of Chicago, 1948.

James, Daniel. *Resistance and Integration*. Cambridge: Cambridge University Press, 1988.

Jimenez, Michael, "At the Banquet of Civilization: the Limits of Planter Hegemony in Early-Twentieth Century Colombia." *Coffee, Society, and Power in Latin America*, ed. William Roseberry, Lowell Gudmundson, and Mario Samper. Baltimore: Johns Hopkins University Press, 1995.

Juarez, Benedicto. "Debilidades del movimiento revolucionario de 1932 en El Salvador." *ABRA* 2, no.13 (1976).

Kincaid, Douglas A. "Peasants into Rebels: Community and Class in Rural El Salvador." *Comparative Studies in Society and History* 29, no.3 (July 1987),466–94.

Knight, Alan. *The Mexican Revolution*. Cambridge: Cambridge University Press, 1986.

Koebel, William Henry. *Central America*. New York: T. Fisher Unwin, 1925.

Krehm, William. *Democracies and Tyrannies of the Caribbean*. Westport, Conn.: Lawrence Hill, 1984.

Laclau, Ernesto. *Politics and Ideology in Marxist Theory*. London: Verso, 1977.

LaFeber, Walter. *Inevitable Revolutions: The United States in Central America*. New York: W. W. Norton, 1984.

Landsberg, Alison. "America, the Holocaust, and the Mass Culture of Memory: Toward a Radical Politics of Empathy." *New German Critique* 71 (spring–summer 1997), 63–86.

Lara Martínez, Rafael. "Indigenismo y encubrimiento testimonial El 32 según 'Miguel Mármol. Manuscrito. 37 páginas' de Roque Dalton." *Istmo: Revista virtual de estudios literarios y culturales centroamericanos* 11 (July–December 2005).

Lauria-Santiago, Aldo. "Una Contribución Biográfica a la Historia del Partido Comunista Salvadoreño." *Revista de Historia* 33 (January–June 1996), 157–83.

——. "La historia regional del café en El Salvador." *Revista de Historia (San José)* 38 (July–December 1998), 9–61.

——. "Land, Community, and Revolt in Indian Izalco, El Salvador, 1855–1905." *Hispanic American Historical Review* 79, no.3 (September 1998), 495–534.

——. " 'That a Poor Man Be Industrious': Coffee, Community, and Capitalism in the Transformation of El Salvador's Ladino Peasantry, 1850–1900." *Identity and Struggle at the Margins of the Nation-State: The Laboring Peoples of Central America and the Hispanic Caribbean*, ed. Aldo Lauria-Santiago and Aviva Chomsky. Durham: Duke University Press, 1998.

——. *An Agrarian Republic: Commercial Agriculture and the Politics of Peasant Communities in El Salvador, 1823–1914.* Pittsburgh: University of Pittsburgh Press, 1999.

Lauria-Santiago, Aldo, and Leigh Binford. *Landscapes of Struggle: Community, Politics, and the Nation-State in El Salvador.* Pittsburgh: University of Pittsburgh Press, 2003.

Lauria-Santiago, Aldo, and Jeffrey Gould. " 'They Call Us Thieves and Steal Our Wage': Towards a Reinterpretation of the Salvadoran Rural Mobilization, 1929–1931." *Hispanic American Historical Review* 84, no.3 (September 2003).

Lindo Fuentes, Héctor. *Weak Foundations: The Economy of El Salvador in the Nineteenth Century.* Berkeley: University of California Press, 1990.

Llanes, Hector B. "A History of Protestantism in El Salvador, 1896–1992." Diss., New Orleans Baptist Theological Seminary, 1995.

Long, W. Rodney. *Railways of Central America and the West Indies.* Trade Promotion Series, no. 5. Washington: U.S. Government Printing Office, 1925.

López, Carlos Gregorio. "Tradiciones inventadas y discursos nacionalistas: el imaginario nacional de la epoca liberal en El Salvador, 1876–1932." Unpublished manuscript.

López Vallecillos, Italo. *El periodismo en El Salvador.* San Salvador: UCA, 1974.

——. "La insurrección popular campesina de 1932." *ABRA* 2, no.13 (June 1976).

——. "Trayectoria y crisis del estado salvadoreño, 1918–1981." *Estudios Centroamericanos* 36, no. 392 (1981).

Luna, David. "Un heroico y trágico suceso de nuestra historia." *El Proceso Político Centroamericano.* San Salvador: Editorial Universitaria, 1964.

——. "Análisis de una dictadura fascista latinoamericana: Maximiliano Hernández Martínez, 1931–1944." *Universidad* 94, no. 5 (1969).

——. *Manual de historia económica de El Salvador.* San Salvador, 1971.

MacNaught, A. Roy. "Horrors of Communism in Central America." *Central American Bulletin* 15 (March 1932).

Mahoney, James. *The Legacies of Liberalism: Path Dependence and Political Regimes in Central America.* Baltimore: Johns Hopkins University Press, 2001.

Mann, Michael. *Fascists.* Cambridge: Cambridge University Press, 2004.

Marden, Luis. "Coffee Is the King in El Salvador." *National Geographic*, November 1944.

Marroquín, Alejandro. "Estudio sobre la crisis de los años treinta en El Salvador."

America Latina en los Años Treinta, ed. Pablo Gonzalez Casanova. Mexico City: Siglo Veintiuno, 1970.

Martin, Percy Falcke. *Salvador of the Twentieth Century*. London: E. Arnold, 1911.

Martínez Peñate, Oscar. *El Salvador Historia General*. San Salvador: Nuevo Enfoque, 2002.

Mayorga Rivas, Ramón. "Los indios de Izalco, terruño salvadoreño." *Revista del Ateneo del Salvador* 11 (1913), 372–74.

McClintock, Michael. *The American Connection: State Terror and Popular Resistance in El Salvador*. London: Verso, 1985.

McCreery, David. *Rural Guatemala, 1760–1940*. Stanford: Stanford University Press, 1994.

Méndez, J. *Los sucesos comunistas en El Salvador*. San Salvador: Funes y Ungo, 1932.

Menjivar, Rafael. *Acumulación originaria y desarollo del Capitalismo en El Salvador*. San José: Editorial Universitaria Centroamericana, 1976.

——. *Formación y lucha del proletariado industrial salvadoreño*. San José: Editorial Universitaria Centroamericana, 1982.

Merridale, Catherine. "War, Death, and Remembrance in Soviet Russia." *War and Remembrance in the Twentieth Century*, ed. Jay Winter and Emmanuel Sirvan, 61–83. Cambridge: Cambridge University Press, 1999.

Mintz, Sidney. "The Rural Proletariat and the Problem of Rural Proletarian Consciousness." *Peasants and Proletarians*, ed. Robin Cohen, Peter Gutkind, and Phyllis Brazier. New York: Monthly Review, 1979.

Molina, Iván. "The Polarization of Politics, 1932–48." *The Costa Rica Reader: History, Culture, Politics*, ed. Steven A. Palmer and Iván Molina. Durham: Duke University Press, 2004.

Montes, Segundo. *El compadrazgo: una estructura de poder en El Salvador*. San Salvador: UCA, 1979.

——. "El campesinado salvadoreño." *Revista Española de Antropologia Americana* 11 (1981).

——. *El agro salvadoreño (1973–1980)*. San Salvador: UCA, 1986.

——. "Levantamientos Campesinos en El Salvador." *Realidad Económico-Social* 1, no.1 (1988).

Montgomery, David. *The Struggle for Worker's Control in America: Studies in the History of Work, Technology and Labor Struggles*. Cambridge: Cambridge University Press, 1979.

Montgomery, Tommie Sue. *Revolution in El Salvador*. Washington: Westview, 1982.

Morrill, Gulian Lansing. *Rotten Republics: A Tropical Tramp in Central America*. Chicago: M. A. Donohue, 1916.

Ogilvie, Andrew Jones. "The Communist Revolt of El Salvador, 1932." Thesis, Harvard College, 1970.

Osegueda, Francisco R. "Observaciones sobre la vida del campesino salvadoreño de otros tiempos y la del campesino actual." *Revista del Ateneo de El Salvador* 20 (1932).

Paige, Jeffery M. *Agrarian Revolution Social Movements and Export Agriculture in the Underdeveloped World*. New York: Free Press, 1975.

——. "Coffee and Politics in Central America." *Crisis in the Caribbean Basin*, ed. Richard Tardanico, 141–90. Newbury Park, Calif.: Sage, 1987.

———. "The Social Origins of Dictatorship, Democracy and Socialist Revolution in Central America." Comparative Study of Social Transformations, vol. 35. University of Michigan, 1989.

———. Coffee and Power: Revolution and the Rise of Democracy in Central America. Cambridge: Harvard University Press, 1997.

Pakkasvirta, Jussi. "Víctor Raúl Haya de la Torre en Centroamérica: ¿La primera y última fase del aprismo internacional?" Revista de Historia 44 (2002), 9–31.

Pérez-Brignoli, Héctor. "Indians, Communists, and Peasants: The 1932 Rebellion in El Salvador." Coffee, Society, and Power in Latin America, ed. William Roseberry, Lowell Gudmundson, and Mario Samper Kutschbach. Baltimore: Johns Hopkins University Press, 1995.

Pessar, Patricia. From Fanatics to Folk: Brazilian Millenarianism and Popular Culture. Durham: Duke University Press, 2004.

Peterson, Brandt. "Uncertain Remains: Race, Trauma, and Nationalism in Millennial El Salavdor." Diss., University of Texas, 2005

Pineda Ortiz, Leyla, and Ana Lilliam Ramírez Cruz. "Vision Socio-cultural de Nahuizalco." Thesis, School of Social Work, University of El Salvador, 1975

Portelli, Alessandro. The Death of Luigi Trastulli and Other Stories: Form and Meaning in Oral History. Albany: State University of New York Press, 1991.

Quijano Hernández, Manuel. Dejados de la Mano de Dios (Una Tiranía Audaz y un Pueblo Inerte). San Salvador: Talleres Gráficos Cisneros, 1931.

Rappaport, Joanne. Cumbe Reborn: An Andean Ethnography of History. Chicago: University of Chicago Press, 1993.

Reddy, William. "Against Constructionism: The Historical Ethnography of Emotions." Current Anthropology 38, no. 3 (June 1997), 327–51.

Richter, Ernesto. Proceso de Acumulación y Dominación en la Formación Socio-Política Salvadoreña. San Pedro de Montes de Oca, Costa Rica: Programa Centroamericano de Ciencias Sociales–CSUCA, 1976.

Rodríguez G., Salvador. Política hacendaría del nuevo Gobierno. San Salvador: Imprenta Nacional, 1911.

Romero Orellano, Mayor Otto. Génesis de la Amenaza Comunista en El Salvador. San Salvador: Centro de Estudios Estratégicos de las Fuerzas Armadas, 1994.

Roseberry, William. Coffee and Capitalism in the Venezuelan Andes. Austin: University of Texas Press, 1983.

———. Anthropologies and Histories: Essays in Culture, History, and Political Economy. New Brunswick: Rutgers University Press, 1989.

———. "La Falta de Brazos: Land and Labor in the Coffee Economies of Nineteenth-Century Latin America." Theory and Society 20 (1991), 351–82.

———. "Beyond the Agrarian Question in Latin America." Confronting Historical Paradigms: Peasants, Labor, and the World System in Africa and Latin America, ed. Frederick Cooper et al., 318–68. Madison: University of Wisconsin Press, 1993.

Rosenberg, Tina. Children of Cain Violence and the Violent in Latin America. New York: William Morrow, 1991.

Rothery, Agnes. Central America and the Spanish Main. Boston: Houghton Mifflin, 1929.

Ruhl, Arthur Brown. *The Central Americans: Adventures and Impressions between Mexico and Panama*. New York: C. Scribner's Sons, 1928.

Salarrué. *Cataleya Luna*. San Salvador: Ministry of Education, 1974 [1933].

Salazar Valiente, Mario. "El Salvador: crisis, dictadura, lucha, 1920–1980." *America Latina: Historia de Medio Siglo*, ed. Pablo González Casanova. Mexico City: Siglo Veintiuno, 1981.

Salazar Valiente, Mario, David Alejandro Luna, and Jorge Arias Gómez. *El Proceso Político Centroamericano*. San Salvador: Editorial Universitaria, 1964.

Salisbury, Richard. "The Middle American Exile of Victor Raul Haya de la Torre." *Americas* 40, no. 1 (July 1983), 1–17.

——. *Anti-Imperialism and International Competition in Central America, 1920–1929*. Wilmington, Del.: SR Books, 1989.

Samper K., Mario. *Generations of Settlers Rural Households and Markets on the Costa Rican Frontier, 1850–1935*. Boulder: Westview, 1990.

——. "El Significado Social de la Caficultura Costaricense y Salvadoreña: Análisis. Histórico Comparado a Partir de los Censos Cafetaleros." *Tierra, Café y Sociedad: Ensayos Sobre la Historia Agraria Centroamericana*, ed. Héctor Pérez-Brignoli and Mario Samper Kutschbach, 117–225. San José: FLACSO, 1994.

Sánchez, Gonzalo. *Los Bolcheviques del Libano*. Bogotá: El Mohan, 1976.

Scheff, Thomas. "Emotions and Identity: A Theory of Ethnic Nationalism." *Social Theory and the Politics of Identity*, ed. Craig Calhoun, 277–303. Cambridge, Mass.: Blackwell, 1996.

Schlesinger, Alfredo. *La Verdad Sobre el Comunismo*. Guatemala City: Tipografia Nacional, 1932.

Schlesinger, Jorge. *Revolución Comunista*. Guatemala City, 1946.

Schultze Jena, Leonhard S. *Indiana*, vol. 2, *Mythen in der Muttersprache der Pipil von Izalco in El Salvador*. Jena: Gustav Fischer, 1935; repr. San Salvador: Cuzcutlan, 1977.

Scott, James C. *The Moral Economy of the Peasant: Rebellion and Subsistence in Southeast Asia*. New Haven: Yale University Press, 1976.

Segovia, Alexander. *Transformación Estructural y Reforma Económica en El Salvador*. Guatemala City: F&G, 2004.

Smith, Carol A. "Race-Class-Gender Ideologies: Modern and Anti-Modern Forms." *Comparative Studies in Society and History* 37, no. 4 (1995).

Smith, Lynn T. "Notes on Population and Rural Social Organization in El Salvador." *Rural Sociology* 10, no.4 (1945).

Snyder Hook, Elizabeth. "Awakening from War: History, Trauma, and Testimony in the Work of Heinrich Böll." *The Work of Memory: New Directions in the Study of German Society and Culture*, ed. Alon Confino and Peter Fritzsche. Urbana: University of Illinois Press, 2002.

Stanley, William. *The Protection Racket State: Elite Politics, Military Extortion, and Civil War in El Salvador*. Philadelphia: Temple University Press, 1997.

Suarez, Belarmino. *El Impuesto Sobre la Renta*. San Salvador: Imprenta Nacional, 1920.

Suter, Jan. " 'Pernicious Aliens' and the Mestizo Nation: Ethnicity and the Shaping of Collective Identities in El Salvador before the Second World War." *Immigrants and Minorities* 20, no.2 (July 2001): 26–57.

Tábora, Rocío. "Género y Percepciones Etnico-raciales en el Imaginario de la Clase Política 'Mestiza' y del Movimiento Indígena-Negro en Honduras." *Memorias del Mestizaje: Cultura Política en Centroamérica de 1920 al presente*, ed. Darío Euraque, Jeffrey L. Gould, and Charles R. Hale. Guatemala City: CIRMA, 2004.

Taracena, Arturo. "El Primer Partido Comunista de Guatemala (1922–1932): Diez Años de una Historia Olvidada." *Anuario de Estudios Centroamericanos* 15 (1985), 49–63.

———. "Guatemala: El Debate Histórico en Torno a Mestizaje." *Memorias del Mestizaje: Cultura Política en Centroamérica de 1920 al presente*, ed. Darío Euraque, Jeffrey L. Gould, and Charles R. Hale, 79–110. Guatemala City: CIRMA, 2004.

Taylor, William B. *Drinking, Homicide and Rebellion in Colonial Mexican Villages*. Stanford: Stanford University Press, 1979.

Thompson, E. P. *The Making of the English Working Class*. New York: Vintage, 1963.

Torres, Abelardo. "More from This Land." *Americas* 14, no. 8 (1962).

Traverso, Enzo. *The Origins of Nazi Violence*. New York: New Press, 2003.

Tula, María Teresa. *Hear My Testimony*, ed. and trans. Lynn Stephen. Boston: South End, 1994.

Turits, Richard. "A World Destroyed, a Nation Imposed: The 1937 Haitian Massacre in the Dominican Republic." *Hispanic American Historical Review* 82, no. 3 (August 2002), 589–635.

———. *Foundations of Despotism: Peasants, the Trujillo Regime, and Modernity in Dominican History*. Stanford: Stanford University Press, 2003.

Uriarte, Juan Ramón. *La esfinge de Cuscatlan, El Presidente Quiñónez*. Mexico City: Manuel Sánchez León, 1929.

Vázquez Olivera, Mario. " 'País mío no existes': Apuntes sobre Roque Dalton y la historiografía contemporánea de El Salvador." Unpublished manuscript.

Villanueva, Victor, and Peter Crabtree. "The Petty-Bourgeois Ideology of the Peruvian Aprista Party." *Latin American Perspectives* 4, no. 3 (summer 1977), 57–76.

Ward, L. A., ed. and comp. *Libro azul de El Salvador*. San Salvador: Bureau de Publicidad de la América Latina, 1916.

Weitz, Eric D. *A Century of Genocide: Utopias of Race and Nation*. Princeton: Princeton University Press, 2003.

White, Alastair. *El Salvador*. New York: Praeger, 1973.

Wickham-Crowley, Timothy P. *Guerrillas and Revolution in Latin America: A Comparative Study of Insurgents and Regimes Since 1956*. Princeton: Princeton University Press, 1991.

Williams, Raymond. *Marxism and Literature*. Oxford: Oxford University Press, 1977.

Wilson, Alan Everett. "The Crisis of National Integration in El Salvador, 1919–1935." Diss., Stanford University, 1969.

Wood, Elisabeth Jean. *Insurgent Collective Action and Civil War: Redrawing Boundaries of*

        Class and Citizenship in Rural El Salvador. Cambridge: Cambridge University Press, 2002.

Yarrington, Doug. *A Coffee Frontier: Land, Society, and Politics in Duaca, Venezuela, 1830–1936*. Pittsburgh: University of Pittsburgh Press, 1997.

Zamosc, Leon. "The Definition of a Socio-economic Formation: El Salvador on the Eve of the Great World Economic Depression." Thesis, University of Manchester, 1977.

——. "La intervención imperialista en America Latina: el desembarco de tropas canadienses en El Salvador." *Desarollo Indoamericano* 14, no.52 (1979).

——. "Class Conflict in an Export Economy: The Social Roots of the Salvadoran Insurrection of 1932." *Sociology of "Developing Societies": Central America*, ed. Edelberto Torres Rivas. New York: Monthly Review, 1988.

Zamosc, Leon, and Bernardo Sorj. "La Reproducción del Capitalismo Periférico Exportador: Estructuras y Contradicciones." *Cuadernos del Departamento de Ciencias Políticas* 4 (1977).

Ziegler, Sarah. "Wifely Duties: Marriage, Labor, and the Common Law in Nineteenth-Century America." *Social Science History* 20, no. 1 (spring 1996), 79–83.

Index

JEFFREY GOULD is a professor of history and director of the Center for Latin American Studies at Indiana University.

ALDO LAURIA-SANTIAGO is an associate professor in the department of history and chair of Latin and Hispanic Caribbean studies at Rutgers University.

Library of Congress Cataloging-in-Publication Data

Gould, Jeffrey L.
To rise in darkness : revolution, repression, and memory in El Salvador, 1920–1932 / Jeffrey L. Gould and Aldo A. Lauria-Santiago.
p. cm.
Includes bibliographical references and index.
ISBN 978-0-8223-4207-6 (cloth : alk. paper) — ISBN 978-0-8223-4228-1 (pbk. : alk. paper)
1. El Salvador—History—Revolution, 1932.
2. Massacres—El Salvador—History—20th century.
3. Collective memory—El Salvador—History—20th century.
I. Lauria-Santiago, Aldo. II. Title.
F1487.5.G68 2007
972.8405′2—dc22
2007042437